S0-BJK-030

MASTERPLOTS
FIFTEEN-VOLUME
COMBINED EDITION

Volume Eleven
Pers-Purp

MASTERPLOTS

15-Volume Combined Edition
FIFTEEN HUNDRED AND TEN
Plot-Stories and Essay-Reviews
from the
WORLD'S FINE LITERATURE

Edited by
FRANK N. MAGILL

Story Editor
DAYTON KOHLER

VOLUME ELEVEN — PERS-PURP

SALEM PRESS
INCORPORATED
NEW YORK

Copyright©, 1949, 1952, 1953, 1954, 1960, 1964,
by FRANK N. MAGILL
All rights in this book are reserved. No part of the
book may be used or reproduced in any manner
whatsoever without written permission from the
copyright owner except in the case of brief quotations embodied in critical articles and reviews. For
information address the publishers, Salem Press,
Inc., 475 Fifth Avenue, New York 17, N. Y.

This work also appears under the title of
MASTERPIECES OF WORLD LITERATURE IN DIGEST FORM

Sale of this book restricted to the
United States of America
PRINTED IN THE UNITED STATES OF AMERICA

PERSIAN LETTERS

Type of work: Satirical essays in letter form
Author: Charles de Montesquieu (1689-1755)
Time: 1711-1721
Locale: Paris, Smyrna, Venice, Ispahan
First published: 1721

Principal characters:
  USBEK, a Persian in Paris
  RICA, a young friend of Usbek
  IBBEN, a Persian in Smyrna
  RHEDI, a Persian in Venice
  ZEPHIS,
  ZACHI,
  ZELIS. and
  ROXANA, some of Usbek's wives in his seraglio in Ispahan
  SOLIM, one of Usbek's servants in Ispahan
  THE CHIEF BLACK EUNUCH, guardian of Usbek's seraglio

In these 161 letters written by various fictional correspondents, Montesquieu gives a sharp picture of many facets of Parisian society and the customs of the early eighteenth century. The correspondence also reveals much of the thinking of the time on comparative religions.

Although the writing is in a formal mode in keeping with the status of the correspondents, Montesquieu's tone and style never become stiff or artificial. The satire is by turns muted in the mellowness of friendly correspondence and proclaimed in the harshness of intentional criticism. Unlike many similar collections of letters, however, *Persian Letters* is entertaining, pleasant reading. The concise, clear sentences have a conversational tone. In spite of Montesquieu's title, the aim of the writing is not a sociological picture of life in a Persian harem. It is a subtle, accurate satire of French society, pointing up the decadent attitudes and loose morals, from 1712, in the last years of the reign of Louis XIV and the regime of Philip Duc de Orléans, during the minority of Louis XV. In *Persian Letters* there are numerous resemblances to Dufresney's *Amusements,* *The Spectator,* and the *Decameron,* writings known to have been among Montesquieu's favorite books.

Persian Letters, printed in Amsterdam and published anonymously in 1721, was an immediate success. As a friend of Montesquieu had predicted, copies of the work "sold like loaves."

Because of a thin thread of story, *Persian Letters* may be said to contain a sustained narrative. Usbek, from his youth a courtier, was given to sincerity in his resolution to remain uncorrupted by wordly concerns. Finally the ministers came to question his intentions because he was not given to flattery. Persecuted, he resolved to go to Europe and eventually to visit Paris. Rica, a young friend, went as his companion. Other Persians with whom these two exchanged letters were Ibben, in Smyrna, and Rhedi, in Venice.

Letters to Usbek from his wives, the eunuchs, and other servants reported unrest in the harem. These letters told of the jealousies and the temperamental behavior of the wives, the inadequacies of underlings with responsibility but without authority, and the efforts of those persons to maintain their status through Usbek's support.

The revolt continued; violence grew. The wives wrote, variously proclaiming their devotion to, or their hatred of, Usbek. The chief eunuch was killed while attempting to maintain order in the harem. Roxana, the most recent of Usbek's wives, had been the instigator of that unrest and violence. Hers is the last letter in the book; in it, she tells of having betrayed Usbek. Personifying liberated womanhood (a transition apparent in eighteenth-century France), Roxana wrote:

> Yes, I have deceived you; I have led away your eunuchs . . . and I have known how to turn your frightful seraglio into a place of pleasure and delight. . . . How could you think that I was such a weakling as to imagine there was nothing for me in the world but to worship your caprices; that while you indulged all your desires, you should have the right to thwart me in all mine? . . . I have remodelled your laws upon those of nature; and my mind has always maintained its independence. . . .

Rica, good-humored and sardonic, represents the lighter side of Montesquieu's nature. Rica jibed at groups and individuals, at religion and government, at customs and beliefs. Nothing escaped his cynical eye. It was his observation that the King of France was much wealthier than the King of Spain; even though the latter owned mines of gold and silver, the French king's wealth came from a more inexhaustible source, the vanity of his subjects. The gullibility of the French people, Rica wrote, was so great that should the king be short of money, he had only to suggest that a piece of paper was the coin of the realm, and the people were at once convinced of its value.

In Rica's estimation, the Christian religion consisted of an immense number of tedious duties. Among the tradespeople in Paris, he noted that a "good natured creature will offer you for a little money the secret of making gold"; another "promises you the love of the spirits of the air, if you will see no women for a small trifle of thirty years"; "an infinite number of professors of languages, of arts, and of sciences, teach what they do not know; and their talent is not by any means despicable; for much less wit is required to exhibit one's knowledge, than to teach what one knows nothing of."

Rica disdained the pseudo-intellectual and everyone's apparent desire to write a book on any topic of conversation fashionable in the salons. "I am exasperated," he wrote, "with a book which I have just laid down—a book so big that it seems to contain all science: but it has only split my head without putting anything into it."

Although Usbek was as brilliant and on occasion as satirical as the younger Rica, he was graver and given more to meditation and reflection. Throughout his many discussions of religion in the letters, Usbek showed respect for all faiths. The social and the theological are as one, according to Usbek, because God established religions for man's happiness; and he can most surely please God by obeying the laws of society and by loving his fellow man. That all religions had their foundations in God was expressed in Usbek's prayer: "Lord, I do not understand these discussions that are carried on without end regarding Thee: I would serve Thee according to Thy will; but each man whom I consult would have me serve Thee according to his." Usbek did not believe that it was necessary to hate and persecute those of other faiths in order to serve God; nor was it necessary to try to convert them.

Although the Persian is Montesquieu's mouthpiece for philosophical viewpoint and discussion, Usbek is quite capable of cryptic analysis. In one letter he asserted that "a poet [is] the grotesquest of humankind. These sort of people declare that they are born what they are; and, I may add, what they will be all their lives, namely almost always, the most ridiculous of men. . . ." On another occasion, having been cornered at a party by a dandy who boasted of his successful conquests with ladies, Usbek told him that "If you were in Persia, you would not enjoy all these advantages; you would be held fitter to guard our women than to please them."

In *Persian Letters* communication is direct and immediate, character is self-portrayed, and ideas reveal the working of a shrewd, incisive mind that is always reflective of the author, yet in keeping with the personalities of the principals who are allowed to speak for him.

THE PERSIANS

Type of work: Drama
Author: Aeschylus (525-456 B.C.)
Type of plot: Historical tragedy
Time of plot: 480 B.C.
Locale: Susa, capital of Persia
First presented: 472 B.C.

Principal characters:
XERXES, King of Persia
ATOSSA, his mother
PERSIAN ELDERS
THE GHOST OF DARIUS, Xerxes' father

Critique:

The Persians can hardly be called a tragedy in the classical Greek sense; rather, it is a glorification, by indirection, of the invincible Greeks. It might possibly be said that the tragic hero of this play is Persia itself, for its presumption in attacking indomitable Greece; certainly the individual catastrophe of Xerxes would have aroused neither pity nor terror in the Greek audience. Glorification of Greece is achieved obliquely in The Persians through a plot concerned wholly with the Persian reaction to Xerxes' defeat at Salamis. According to tradition, Aeschylus was a soldier at Salamis; if this tradition be true, then his magnificent description of this decisive engagement is invaluable for its authenticity.

The Story:

Xerxes, son of the late King Darius of Persia, was a man of overwhelming ambition, who, eager to add more countries to his tremendous empire, had led a great army against the Greek states. During his absence he had left only the Persian elders to maintain authority in Susa, his capital. The old men waited apprehensively for some word of the invasion forces, and their fears grew as time passed and no message came from Xerxes. They lamented that the land had been emptied of the young men who had marched valiantly to war, leaving their wives and mothers to wait anxiously for their return.

Atossa, widow of Darius and mother of Xerxes, was also filled with vague fears. One night she saw in a dream two women,

one in Persian dress, the other in Greek robes, and both tall and beautiful. When they began to quarrel, King Xerxes appeared and yoked them to his chariot. The woman in Asian costume submitted meekly enough, but the other broke the reins, overturned the chariot, and threw young Xerxes to the ground. Then in her dream Darius came and, seeing his son on the ground, tore his robes with grief. Later, awakening, Atossa went to pray for her son's safety. While she was sacrificing before the altar, she saw an eagle pursued and plucked by a hawk. To her these visions seemed to portend catastrophe for the Persians.

The elders, after hearing her story, advised her to pray to the gods and to beg great Darius, from the realm of the dead, to intercede to bring success to the Persian expedition. Atossa, her thoughts far across the sea with her son, asked the elders where Athens was. The elders told her that it was in Attica, in Greece, and that the citizens of Athens were a free people who derived great strength from their freedom. Their words did little to reassure the troubled mother.

A messenger arrived and announced that the Persian host had been defeated in a great battle fought at Salamis, but that Xerxes, to Atossa's relief, had been spared. His news threw the elders into sad confusion. Atossa told them that men must learn to bear the sorrows put upon them by the gods. Quieted, the elders listened while the messenger related the story of the defeat.

At Salamis more than twelve hundred Persian ships had been arrayed against three hundred and ten vessels of the Greeks. The defenders, however, proved themselves craftier than their enemies. Deceitfully, a Greek from the Athenian fleet informed Xerxes that at nightfall the far-outnumbered Greek ships would leave their battle stations and fly, under cover of darkness, to escape the impending sea fight. Xerxes immediately gave orders that his fleet was to close in about the bay of Salamis and to be on the alert that night to prevent the escape of the Athenian vessels. But the wily Greeks kept their places in the bay. When morning came, the light showed the Persian ships crowded so closely into the outlet of the bay that they were unable to maneuver. The Greeks thereupon moved against the Persians and destroyed them.

Meanwhile, the messenger continued, Xerxes had sent troops to the island of Salamis, where he planned to cut off all Greeks who sought refuge on land. But the Greeks, having destroyed the Persian fleet, put their own soldiers ashore. In the fierce fighting that followed, the Persians, unable to escape by water, were slain. Seeing his great army scattered and killed, Xerxes ordered the survivors to retreat. As the Persians, now without ships, marched overland through hostile Greek territory, many of them perished of hardships or were slain by enraged men of the lands through which they traveled.

The elders of Susa bewailed the terrible misfortune brought upon Persia by the king's desire to avenge his father, who had been defeated years before by the Greeks at Marathon.

Having heard the story of her son's defeat, Atossa retired to make offerings to the gods and to pray for the warriors who had lost their lives in the war with Athens. In mourning, she invoked the spirit of Darius, for whom she and the old men had great need at this most depressing time.

The shade of Darius appeared and asked what dire event had occurred in Persia to make necessary his summons from the lower regions. The elders were struck speechless with fear and respect by his august appearance, but Atossa bravely confronted the ghost of her dead husband and told him that Persia had met disaster, not by plague or by internal strife, but by defeat at the hands of the Athenians.

Darius was shocked to hear of the losses Xerxes had suffered and to learn the ambitious scope of his enterprise. He lamented his son's god-offending pride in bridging the sacred Hellespont and in gambling away all the manpower and wealth of Persia upon the success of his ill-fated expedition. Atossa tried to defend Xerxes by saying that he had been influenced by evil advisers. Darius reminded his listeners that he and his forebears had never jeopardized the welfare of the country to such an extent.

In despair, the old men asked Darius how Persia could redeem her great defeat. The dead king replied that the Persians must never again attack Greece, for the gods unquestionably favored those free people. He urged the elders to teach the Persian youths to restrain all god-provoking pride, and he advised Atossa to welcome Xerxes and to comfort him on his return. With these words the shade of Darius disappeared into his tomb.

Xerxes returned, sorrowing that he had not perished on the field of battle. Filled with remorse at the catastrophe he had brought upon his people, he blamed only himself for his defeat. The old men sang a dirge, asking what had befallen various great Persian warriors. Xerxes replied that some had drowned in the sea battle and that others had been slaughtered on the beach. Many, he said, were killed and buried without final rites.

Xerxes, in the deepest despair, joined the elders in their grief. But even though his greatest ambition had been dashed, he praised the bravery and virtues of the Greeks whom he had tried in vain to conquer.

PERSUASION

Type of work: Novel
Author: Jane Austen (1775-1817)
Type of plot: Comedy of manners
Time of plot: Early nineteenth century
Locale: Somersetshire and Bath, England
First published: 1818

Principal characters:

SIR WALTER ELLIOT, owner of Kellynch Hall
ELIZABETH ELLIOT, his oldest daughter
ANNE ELLIOT, his second daughter
MARY MUSGROVE, his youngest daughter
CHARLES MUSGROVE, her husband
HENRIETTA, and
LOUISA, Charles Musgrove's sisters
CAPTAIN FREDERICK WENTWORTH, a naval officer
MRS. CLAY, Elizabeth Elliot's friend
WILLIAM ELLIOT, Sir Walter's cousin; heir to Kellynch Hall

Critique:

Persuasion may be called an autumnal novel. It is Jane Austen's last work, and the tone is mellow. Even the satire is gentler than in her other works. Anne Elliot is Jane Austen's sweetest heroine. The book has a certain melancholy throughout, even though the final outcome is a happy one.

The Story:

Sir Walter Elliot, a conceited man, vain of both his good looks and his title, lived at his countryseat, Kellynch Hall, with two of his daughters, Elizabeth and Anne. Elizabeth, handsome and much like her father, was the oldest and her father's favorite. Anne, sweet, self-effacing, and quietly intelligent, was ignored, neglected, and underrated by both. Mary, the youngest daughter, was married to an agreeable young man named Charles Musgrove, and lived in an untidy house at Uppercross, three miles from Kellynch Hall.

Living beyond his means had brought financial disaster upon Sir Walter, and on the advice of his solicitor and of a family friend, Lady Russell, he was persuaded to rent Kellynch Hall and take a smaller house in Bath. Anne would have preferred to take a modest house near home, but as usual her father and sister had their way in the matter.

Reluctantly, Sir Walter let his beloved countryseat to Admiral and Mrs. Croft. Mrs. Croft was the sister of a former suitor of Anne, Captain Frederick Wentworth of the navy. Anne and Captain Wentworth had fallen in love when they were both very young, but the match had been discouraged. Anne's father felt that the young man's family was not good enough for his own and Lady Russell considered the engagement unwise because Captain Wentworth had no financial means beyond his navy pay. Also, she did not like or understand Captain Wentworth. Anne had followed their advice and broken the engagement. But it had been poor advice, for Wentworth had advanced and had become rich in the navy, just as he had said he would. Anne, at twenty-seven, had not forgotten her love at nineteen. No one else had taken Captain Wentworth's place in her affection.

With all arrangements completed for the renting of Kellynch Hall, Sir Walter, Elizabeth, and her friend, Mrs. Clay, were off to Bath. Before they departed, Anne warned Elizabeth that Mrs. Clay's was not a disinterested friendship, and that she was scheming to marry Sir Walter if she could. Elizabeth would not believe such an idea, nor would she agree to dismiss Mrs. Clay.

Anne was to divide her time between her married sister, Mary Musgrove, and Lady Russell until Christmas. Mary and her family lived also near her husband's father and mother and their two daughters, Henrietta and Louisa. During her visit to the Musgroves, Anne met Captain Wentworth again, while he was staying with his sister at Kellynch Hall. She found him little changed by eight years.

The Musgroves at once took the Crofts and Captain Wentworth into their circle, and the captain and Anne met frequently. He was coldly polite to Anne, but his attentions to the Musgrove sisters were such as to start Mary matchmaking. She could not decide, however, whether he preferred Henrietta or Louisa. When Louisa encouraged Henrietta to resume a former romance with a cousin, Charles Hayter, it seemed plain that Louisa was destined for Captain Wentworth.

The likelihood of such a match was increased when, during a visit to friends of Captain Wentworth at Lyme Regis, Louisa suffered an injury while the captain was assisting her to jump down a steep flight of steps. The accident was not his fault, for he had cautioned Louisa against jumping, but he blamed himself for not refusing her firmly. Louisa was taken to the home of Captain Wentworth's friends, Captain and Mrs. Harville, and Captain Benwick. Anne, quiet, practical, and capable during the emergency, had the pleasure of knowing that Captain Wentworth relied on her strength and good judgment, but she felt certain of a match between him and the slowly recovering Louisa.

Anne reluctantly joined her family and the designing Mrs. Clay at Bath. She was surprised to find that they were glad to see her. After showing her the house, they told her the news — mainly about how much in demand they were, and about a cousin, Mr. William Elliot, who had suddenly appeared to make his peace with the family. Mr. William Elliot was the heir to Sir Walter's title and estate, but he had fallen out with the

family years before because he did not marry Elizabeth as Sir Walter and Elizabeth felt he should have. Also, he had affronted Sir Walter's pride by speaking disrespectfully of his Kellynch connections.

Now, however, these matters were explained away, and both Sir Walter and Elizabeth were charmed with him. Anne, who had seen Mr. Elliot at Lyme Regis, wondered why he chose to renew a relationship so long neglected. She thought it might be that he was thinking of marrying Elizabeth, now that his first wife was dead; Lady Russell thought Anne was the attraction.

About that time news came of Louisa Musgrove's engagement to Captain Benwick. Joy, surprise, and a hope that Captain Wentworth had lost his partiality for Louisa were mingled in Anne's first reaction. Shortly after she had heard the news, Captain Wentworth arrived in Bath. After a few meetings Anne knew that he had not forgotten her. She also had the pleasure of knowing that he was jealous of Mr. Elliot. His jealousy was groundless.

Even if Anne had felt any inclination to become Lady Elliot, the ambition would have been short-lived, for Mr. Elliot's true character now came to light. Anne learned from a former schoolmate, who had been friendly with Mr. Elliot before he basely ruined her husband, that his first design in renewing acquaintance with Sir Walter's family was to prevent Sir Walter from marrying Mrs. Clay and thus having a son who would inherit the title and estate. Later, when he met Anne, he had been genuinely attracted to her. This information was not news to Anne, since Mr. Elliot had proposed to her at a concert the night before. She, of course, gave him no encouragement.

Her patience in waiting for Captain Wentworth was soon to be rewarded. Convinced that Anne still loved him as he did her, he poured out his heart to her in a letter, and all was settled happily between them. Both Musgrove girls were also married shortly afterward. Neither of their husbands was as rich as Anne's, much to Mary's satisfaction. Mrs. Clay, sacrificing ambition for love, left Bath with Mr. William Elliot, and went to live under his protection in London. Perhaps she hoped some day to be Lady Elliot, though as the wife of a different baronet.

PETER IBBETSON

Type of work: Novel
Author: George du Maurier (1834-1896)
Type of plot: Historical romance
Time of plot: Mid-nineteenth century
Locale: France and England
First published: 1891

Principal characters:
PETER IBBETSON, a confessed murderer
COLONEL IBBETSON, his guardian
MIMSY SERASKIER, his dearest friend; later the Duchess of Towers
MR. LINTOT, his employer
MRS. DEANE, a widow

Critique:

Peter Ibbetson has become a minor classic in its particular field. It is a story composed of the elements of love, friendship, and kindness, but they are so mixed that we have a completely new plot. It is difficult to be sure of the author's purpose in writing this story. Certainly it was not to question the creation or eternity. Perhaps it was merely to show what might be possible if the world would "dream true." The story has been dramatized both for the stage and motion pictures, and it is also the subject of a popular opera.

The Story:

(After his death in a criminal lunatic asylum, Peter Ibbetson's autobiography was given to his cousin, Madge Plunket, who arranged for the publication of the manuscript. Through her efforts the strange and beautiful story was preserved.)

Peter Pasquier moved from England to Paris when he was five years old. His father was a dreamy-eyed inventor, his mother a soft-spoken woman devoted to her family. During his childhood Peter had many friends, but the dearest were Mimsy Seraskier and her beautiful mother, who lived nearby. Mimsy was a delicate, shy child, as plain as her mother was beautiful. She and Peter were inseparable friends, making up their own code language so that no one could intrude on their secret talks.

When Peter was twelve years old, his father was killed in an explosion, and his mother died giving birth to a stillborn child less than a week later. His mother's cousin, Colonel Ibbetson, came from England to take Peter home with him. Peter wept when he took leave of his friends, and Mimsy was so ill from her grief that she could not even tell him goodbye.

Colonel Ibbetson gave Peter his name, and he became Peter Ibbetson. The colonel sent him to school, where he spent six years. Events at the school touched him very little, as he spent most of his time dreaming of his old life in Paris.

When he left school, Peter spent some time with Colonel Ibbetson. The colonel's only request was that Peter become a gentleman, but Peter began to doubt that the colonel himself fitted the description. He learned that Colonel Ibbetson had a very poor reputation among his acquaintances, due largely to his vanity and gallantry. His latest victim was Mrs. Deane, a woman he had ruined with malicious lies. The colonel seemed also to derive great pleasure from telling scandalous tales about everyone he knew, and Peter grew to hate him for this habit. After a time he ran away to London and joined the cavalry for a year. Following his term in the army, he was apprenticed to Mr. Lintot, an architect whom he had met through Colonel Ibbetson. He took rooms in Pentonville and there began a new chapter in his life.

He worked industriously for Mr. Lin-

2816

tot and achieved some success, but his outer life was lonely and dull. The only real joy he found was in the arts, and of these only music inspired him deeply. He saved carefully that he might occasionally attend a concert. His nightly dreams were still of his childhood in Paris and of Mimsy, but his dreams were becoming blurred.

Viewing with skepticism the belief in a creator and a life after death, Peter believed man would have to work back to the very beginning of time before he could understand anything about a deity. He believed it was possible to go back, if only he knew the way. His ideas on sin were unorthodox, for to Peter the only real sin was cruelty to the mind or body of any living thing.

During this period of his life his only acquaintances were the friends of Mr. and Mrs. Lintot, for Peter was a shy young man, too much concerned with his speculations and dreams for social gaiety. At one party, however, he saw a great lady who was to be his guiding star for the rest of his life. He was told she was the Duchess of Towers, and although he was not presented to her, he saw her looking at him in a strange manner, almost as if she found his a familiar face.

Some time after his first sight of the Duchess of Towers, Peter revisited Paris, where he found his old home and those of his friends replaced with modern bungalows. The only news he had of his old friends was that Madame Seraskier had died and Mimsy and her father had left Paris many years ago. He returned to his hotel that night, exhausted emotionally from the disappointments of the day.

But that night his real and true inner life began, for he learned how to dream true. When he fell asleep, the events of the day passed before him in distorted fashion. He found himself surrounded by demon dwarfs. As he tried to escape them, he looked up and saw standing before him the Duchess of Towers. She took his hand and told him he was not dreaming true, and then a strange thing happened.

He was transported back to the happy days of his childhood, and he saw himself as he was then. But at the same time he retained his present identity. He was two people at the same time, his adult self looking at his child self. The duchess told him he could always transport himself into any scene he had experienced if he would only dream true. To do this he must lie on his back with his arms over his head, and as he went to sleep he must never cease thinking of the place he wanted to be in his dreams. Also, he must never forget in his dream who and where he was when awake; in this way his dream would be tied to reality. She had learned the trick from her father and could revisit any place she chose.

When he awoke, he knew that at last one of his greatest desires had come true; he had looked into the mind of the duchess. But the matter puzzled him, for he had always thought such a fusion would be possible only between two people who knew and loved each other. The duchess was a stranger to him.

He returned to Pentonville and outwardly resumed his normal life. But his inner self was his real life, and he mastered the art of dreaming true and reliving any experience he wished. He visited with his mother and Mimsy frequently in his dreams, and his life was no longer bleak and lonely.

One day he again met the Duchess of Towers in his outer life. Then he discovered why she had been in his true dream. She was Mimsy, grown and married to a famous duke. She had had the same dream as he when she had rescued him from the dwarfs, and she too had been unable to understand why a stranger had invaded her dreams.

Although he did not again meet the grown Mimsy in his dreams, Peter saw the child Mimsy almost every night. So his life went along without interruption until he met Mrs. Gregory, formerly Mrs. Deane, whom Colonel Ibbetson had tried to ruin with slander. She told him that

Colonel Ibbetson had told her and many others that he was Peter's real father. The recorded marriage and birth dates proved he was lying; the story was another product of the colonel's cruel mind. Peter was so enraged he went to the colonel's house to force an apology. The two men fought, and Peter in his fury struck blindly at Colonel Ibbetson and killed him.

Peter was tried and sentenced to be hanged for the murder of his uncle. While he was in prison, the grown Mimsy came into his dream again and told him his sentence had been changed to life imprisonment because of the circumstances under which the murder had been committed. She promised Peter she would continue to come to him in his dreams and thus they would spend the rest of their lives together.

Peter in his prison cell was the happiest man in England. Attendants were kind to him during the day, and at night he was with Mimsy. At last they learned they were distant cousins, and then they discovered that they could project themselves into the past through the character of any of their direct ancestors. Either of them, not both at once, could become any ancestor he chose, and thus they relived scenes in history which had occurred hundreds of years before. They went back to the days when monsters roamed the earth and might have gone back to the beginning of time, but Mimsy died.

She came back to Peter seven times after she had died, urging him to continue his search for the beginning of time. She could come to him now only because he was the other half of her soul. She asked him to write down his method and to urge others to follow him, and she gave him some books in their secret code, telling him of things she had learned.

But before he could begin to write the secrets she told him, he died in his cell, and his cousin, Madge Plunket, felt that she would remember until her own death the look of happiness and peace upon his face.

PETER PAN

Type of work: Drama
Author: James M. Barrie (1860-1937)
Type of plot: Romantic fantasy
Time of plot: Anytime
Locale: England
First presented: 1904

Principal characters:
PETER PAN, the boy who would not grow up
WENDY, his friend
TINKER BELL, Peter's fairy
HOOK, a pirate captain
NURSE NANA, a dog

Critique:

Loved by adults as much as by children, *Peter Pan* portrays the joys of perpetual childhood. Even in a realistic age few can resist the mischievous Peter and his followers, for in him adults can live again those carefree days filled with dreams and unending joys. The special magic of James Barrie was his ability to make dreams real, and for that reason his charming, whimsical play marks the high point of pure fantasy in the modern theater. The play has had a successful stage history, with many famous names listed in its cast. Barrie later retold the story in his novel, *Peter and Wendy* (1906).

The Story:

In the nursery of the Darling home, a dog was the Nana. Perhaps that was one reason there was so much joy there. Nana bathed the three children and gave them their suppers and in all ways watched over them. One night Mrs. Darling, on Nana's night off, sat with the children as they slept. Drowsing, she was awakened by a slight draught from the window, and looking around she saw a strange boy in the room. As she screamed, Nana returned home and made a lunge for the intruder, but the boy leaped out of the window, leaving only his shadow behind. He had been accompanied also by a ball of light, but it too had escaped. Mrs. Darling rolled up the

shadow and put it in a drawer. She thought that the boy would come back for it one night soon and thus could be caught.

Mr. Darling considered the affair a little silly, his thoughts being more concerned with getting a different nurse for the children. Believing that the dog Nana was getting too much authority in the house, Mr. Darling dragged her out of the house and locked her up.

When the Darlings went out that night, they left only a maid to look in on the children occasionally. After the lights were out and the children asleep, the intruder returned. The boy was Peter Pan. With him was the fairy, Tinker Bell, the ball of light. Peter found his shadow after searching in all the drawers, but in his excitement he shut Tink in one of the dressers. Peter could not get his shadow to stick to him again, and the noise he made in trying awakened Wendy, the daughter of the household. Peter told Wendy that he had run away the day he was born because he heard his parents talking about all the things he would do when he was a man, and he went to live with the fairies so that he would never have to grow up. Suddenly he remembered Tink, whom he looked for until he found her in the dresser. Tink, a ball of light no bigger than a fist, was so small that Wendy could hardly see her. She was not a very

PETER PAN OR THE BOY WHO WOULD NOT GROW UP by James M. Barrie, from THE PLAYS OF J. M. BARRIE. By permission of the publishers, Charles Scribner's Sons. Copyright, 1914, 1928, by Charles Scribner's Sons. Copyright, 1918, 1919, 1920, 1922, 1924, 1928, by J. M. Barrie.

polite fairy, for she called Wendy horrible names.

Peter told Wendy, the only girl of the three children and instantly his favorite, that he and Tink lived in Never Land with the lost boys, children who fell out of their prams and were never found again. He had come to Wendy's house to listen to her mother tell stories to the others. Peter, begging Wendy and her brothers to go back to Never Land with him, promised to teach them to fly. The idea was too much for the children to resist. After a little practice they all flew out the window, barely escaping the Darlings and Nana, who had broken her chain to warn them of the danger to the children.

In Never Land the lost boys were guarded against the mean pirates, led by Captain Hook, by the Indians and their chief and princess. It was Hook's greatest desire to capture Peter Pan, for Peter had torn his arm off and fed it to a crocodile. The crocodile had so liked the taste of the arm that he followed Hook everywhere, waiting for the rest of him. But the crocodile had, unhappily, also swallowed a clock, and its ticking warned Hook of his approach.

To this queer land Wendy and her brothers flew with Peter Pan. The lost boys, seeing Wendy first, thought her a giant bird and shot her with a bow and arrow. Jealous Tink had suggested the deed. But when Peter arrived he saw that Wendy was only stunned, and after banishing Tink for a week he told the others that he had brought Wendy to them. They promptly built her a house and asked her to be their mother. Wendy thought so many children a great responsibility, but she quickly assumed her duties by telling them stories and putting them to bed.

Jealous, the pirates planned to steal Wendy and make her their mother; the other children they would force to walk the plank. But Peter overheard their plan and saved the children and Wendy. He himself escaped by sailing out to sea in a bird's nest.

Wendy and her brothers, beginning to worry about their parents, thought that they should return home. The lost boys, delighted at the thought of a real grown-up mother, eagerly accepted Wendy's invitation to come live with her and her brothers and parents. Peter refused to go, for he wanted always to be a little boy and have fun. But he sent Tink to show them the way.

The Pirates had learned of the proposed journey, and as the children ascended from Never Land Hook and his men seized them and bound them fast, all but Peter. When Peter found that Hook had all his friends, he vowed to get revenge on the pirate, once and for all.

On the pirate ship the children prepared to walk the plank. They were all taken on the deck and paraded before Wendy, who was tied to the mast. Unknown to the pirates, however, Peter was also on board, and by tricks and false voices he led first one pirate and then another to his death. These strange happenings were too much for Hook. When he knocked the seat from under Peter and then saw the boy calmly sitting on air, the pirate threw himself overboard, into the waiting jaws of the patient crocodile.

Meanwhile, in the nursery of the Darling home, Mrs. Darling and Nana waited hopelessly for the children. They had left the window open so that their loved ones might get back easily should they ever return. Peter and Tink flew ahead of the other children and closed the window so that Wendy and the others would think they were not wanted. But Peter did not know how to get out of a door, and thus he was forced to fly out the window again, leaving it open behind him. Wendy and her brothers flew in and slipped into their beds. Mrs. Darling and Nana were overcome with joy when they found their darlings safe again.

The lost boys, adopted by Wendy's

family, had great fun romping with her father. Peter returned and tried to get Wendy to fly away with him, but she refused to leave her parents again. She did go once each year to clean his house for him, but each time she saw him a little less clearly. Once or twice she tried to get him to see her as something more than a mother, but Peter did not know what she meant. Then came the day when Wendy could no longer fly without a broomstick to help her. Peter, watching her, sadly wished he could understand all she said. He picked up his pipes and played softly, perhaps too softly to awaken humans in a grown-up world.

PETER SIMPLE

Type of work: Novel
Author: Frederick Marryat (1792-1848)
Type of plot: Adventure romance
Time of plot: Early nineteenth century
Locale: England, France, various ships at sea
First published: 1834

Principal characters:
 PETER SIMPLE, a naval officer
 ELLEN SIMPLE, his sister
 TERENCE O'BRIEN, a fellow officer
 LORD PRIVILEGE, Peter's rascally uncle
 CAPTAIN HAWKINS, Lord Privilege's illegitimate son
 CELESTE O'BRIEN, in love with Peter
 COLONEL O'BRIEN, her father, a French army officer

Critique:

Captain Marryat's novels of the sea are part of a long line extending from those of Smollett in the eighteenth century to those of C. S. Forester in the twentieth, and, like the latter, Marryat laid his in the period of the Napoleonic wars, in which the author himself saw service as an officer of the British Navy. It is unfortunate that Marryat's novels have descended from the reputation of adult fiction to become, in reputation, books for adolescents. The novels, redolent of sea lore, the traditions of the British Navy, and the Napoleonic wars deserve a better fate than that to which they have been committed, for about the turn of the century they were replaced as standard juveniles by works of such authors as Robert Louis Stevenson. Marryat's books richly deserve a renewed reputation among adult readers of fiction. In particular, *Peter Simple,* one of his best novels, deserves that renewal of interest.

The Story:

Peter Simple was the younger son of the younger son of Lord Privilege, an English viscount. Because there was apparently no chance of the lad's inheriting any money, he was sent to sea at the age of fifteen as a midshipman so that he could earn a living for himself.

Coming from a country home, Peter knew almost nothing of the world, but fortunately for him he served at first under a very gentlemanly captain. He was also befriended by an older midshipman, Terence O'Brien. During his first days aboard the *Diomede,* a British man-of-war, Peter was hazed by his fellow midshipmen because he seemed at times as simple as his surname, but under the tutelage of the crew in general, and O'Brien in particular, he soon learned to become a good sailor. Before many months had passed he became fairly proficient in seagoing matters and earned the approval of his officers.

At every opportunity Peter went where there was trouble and excitement. Having no fears, he got into tight places several times, but serious trouble did not occur until he stowed away in a boat which was sent ashore to spike a gun battery on the French coast. French infantry surprised the raiding party, and Peter and his friend O'Brien were captured; they had remained behind to finish the spiking of the guns while the rest of the sailors made their escape.

Peter having been wounded in the escapade, the colonel of the regiment and his young daughter nursed him back to health before he was sent to prison. The daughter, Celeste O'Brien, was devoted in her attentions to Peter, even though he was, an enemy. After his recovery, Peter and his friend O'Brien, who was no relation to the French colonel, were sent to a prison at Givet. Although that military prison was the stoutest in France, they finally made their escape, thanks to O'Brien's ingenuity, and crossed France in two sets of disguises. At first O'Brien dressed as a policeman and escorted Peter as his prisoner. When that ruse was discovered, they disguised themselves as traveling performers. As they passed through one town they accidentally met Celeste O'Brien and the colonel, who not only kept their secret but gave them a purseful of money. After some difficulty the two fugitives made their way to England. Peter's grandfather, Lord Privilege, invited the boy to visit him. Several deaths had occurred in the family, and Peter was now third in line for the title, after his father and uncle, and the latter had no legal male heir. Thanks to his grandfather's assistance, O'Brien was commissioned a lieutenant. The two were assigned to a frigate and went on a cruise to the West Indies.

During the second cruise word came to Peter that his uncle was very unhappy over the grandfather's patronage and help for the young man, but Peter, busy at sea, paid little attention to the news. At last, his sea duty ended, Peter returned to England. There he studied for examinations which would lead to his own commission as a lieutenant. He almost failed to pass, however, because he appeared at his examination dressed in a very unmilitary fashion. He was excused, however, when the military examiners learned that his appearance was the result of saving a soldier from drowning.

Thanks to a deception passed upon his now senile grandfather, Peter was given his commission. While Peter was still home on leave, the old man died. When his will was read, it was discovered that Peter and his father had not been left any money, because of the interference of Peter's rascally uncle, who now succeeded to the title of Lord Privilege. The shock made Peter's father partially insane. Peter was forced to return immediately to duty.

On his third tour of duty Peter was separated from his friend O'Brien, who now commanded a ship of his own. Peter's new captain was a man named Hawkins, who was, as it turned out, the illegitimate son of Peter's uncle. At his father's request, Captain Hawkins made life miserable for Peter. Lord Privilege wanted to discredit Peter because he had discovered that his uncle, anxious to keep the family fortune for his own children, had replaced his fourth daughter with a male infant at the time of her birth. The uncle, fearful lest Peter's investigations bring the truth to light, hoped to discredit Peter so that any charges the young man might bring against him would be scornfully rejected.

When the troublesome voyage was over and Peter's ship was back in an English port, Captain Hawkins had Peter court-martialed on a series of counts, and Peter was relieved of his duties, although the court-martial board sympathized with him. Peter was not sorry. Having learned of his father's death, he wished to help his sister. On his way home across England Peter was robbed and taken ill. Lord Privilege went to get him, and while Peter was still delirious the uncle had him committed to Bedlam asylum.

For twenty months Peter was an inmate in the asylum. One day Celeste O'Brien and her father happened to visit the place and recognized him, and with the help of an English nobleman they had him released. Peter immediately started a suit against his uncle for false imprisonment. While the suit was pending, his friend O'Brien arrived back in England, bringing with him the wife of the soldier whose life Peter had saved years before. The woman, it turned out, was the mother of the child whom Peter's uncle had substituted for his own daughter.

A short time later Lord Privilege was exclaiming to his lawyer that he hated his nephew and wished to see him dead. At that moment the uncle's substitute son fell from a window and was killed. The shock of the event was so great that the uncle had a fit of apoplexy from which he never recovered. Within a matter of hours he too died. The title then passed to Peter, along with a large fortune and vast estates.

Peter's happiness at his good luck was increased when he and his friend O'Brien found Peter's sister Ellen a few days later. She, left penniless at her father's death, had gone through great troubles and when found had become a singer on the stage.

A few weeks later Peter, firmly entrenched in his new title and fortune, married Celeste O'Brien, the girl who had befriended him on several occasions. Peter's sister married his friend O'Brien, who had been made a baronet for his outstanding services as a naval officer. They lived quietly thereafter, satisfied to exchange family life for the rigors of the service.

PETER WHIFFLE

Type of work: Novel
Author: Carl Van Vechten (1880-   )
Type of plot: Simulated biography
Time of plot: 1907-1919
Locale: New York, Paris, Italy
First published: 1922

Principal characters:
 PETER WHIFFLE, a would-be writer
 CARL VAN VECHTEN, his friend
 EDITH DALE, friend of Peter and Carl
 MAHALAH WIGGINS, Peter's friend

Critique:

A first reading of *Peter Whiffle* may leave the impression that here is an ordinary biographical novel of a pseudosophisticated young man who did not know what he wanted from life. But there is more to the story than that. Peter Whiffle learned, before he died, that not everyone is meant to accomplish great things, that some are meant to enjoy and appreciate the work of others. To tell his readers this fact was apparently Van Vechten's motive for writing the story.

The Story:

Carl Van Vechten saw Peter Whiffle for the first time in Paris, in the spring. They were both young. Carl was naïve and unworldly; Peter was sophisticated and knowing. Theirs was a strange friendship. Often they did not see one another for several years. But Carl knew that he was one of the few people whom Peter called his friend. They had spent many enjoyable hours in Paris that spring and together had seen all the famous places of which they had read. Peter wanted to write, and at that point in his life he thought that subject was unimportant, that style and form were the only important things. In fact, it was his plan to write a book containing nothing but lists of Things. When he wrote, he used colored papers to express his moods.

After that spring in Paris, six years passed before Carl saw Peter again. Carl was back in New York at the time, and while walking in the Bowery one night he met Peter. He hardly recognized his friend when he saw Peter in rags, unshaven and unkempt. Carl learned that the rags were only another phase of Peter's life, for Peter was a rich man. After he had learned Peter's history, Carl began to understand him better.

Peter Whiffle, the son of a banker, was born and raised in Toledo, Ohio. From infancy, Peter found it almost impossible to make decisions. Whether to do this or that was a problem that he could seldom solve, and so, preferring inactivity to decision, he usually did nothing. But there was one thing about which he knew his own mind. He hated work in any form. When Peter could no longer stand his work in his father's bank, he left home and went to New York. There he often slept in the park and went for days without food. He took a few odd jobs in order not to starve. He lived in this fashion until his mother's brother died and left him a fortune. On the night he learned of his inheritance he decided to become a writer. A few days later he left for Paris.

When they met in New York, Carl learned from Peter that although he was still a wealthy man he had joined a group of Socialists and with them was plotting an American revolu-

PETER WHIFFLE by Carl Van Vechten. By permission of the author and the publishers, Alfred A. Knopf, Inc. Copyright, 1922, by Alfred A. Knopf, Inc.

tion against capitalism. He was full of plans to barricade the rich in their homes and starve them to death, or bomb them, or hang them. Carl was not much disturbed, for he recognized this idea as another stage in Peter's life. When Carl asked Peter about his book, he learned that Peter now believed subject, rather than style or form, was all-important. He was planning to write about the revolution, to have as his heroine a girl with a clubfoot, a harelip, and a hunched back. The book would be bloody and dirty, for that was the way life was.

When Carl took Peter to see Edith Dale, a woman of wealth, Peter and Edith became friends. At Edith's house Peter met Mahalah Wiggins, a young girl whom he found interesting. But he could not make up his mind whether he wanted to marry her, and so he did nothing. He did change his living habits, however, and the next time Carl saw him Peter was clean and neat in appearance. He still talked of the revolution, but half-heartedly, and Carl knew another phase of Peter's life was almost over.

Deciding at last to marry Mahalah, Peter asked Carl to be his attendant. But on the wedding day Peter sent Carl a note saying that he could not go through with the wedding; it was too big a decision for him to make. Instead, Peter went to Africa.

Four months later Carl was in Italy, visiting Edith Dale at her villa in Florence. One night, while they were dining in the city, they saw Peter again. His father had died and his mother was traveling with him. Peter told them that he had almost died in Africa, that while he lay at the point of death he had had a vision. An angel from hell and an angel from heaven had waited for him to make up his mind about the place to which he wanted to go when he died. It had been a terrible moment, until he remembered that he did not have to make a decision; he could stay right where he was. Then he recovered.

He had again changed his mind about the book he planned to write. He claimed that everything about the characters must be put down, but he admitted that it would be quite a task to record all emotions, impressions, actions, and speech. Having sent his mother home, Peter went to stay with Carl and Edith. The days at the villa were peaceful and happy ones, so happy, in fact, that one day Peter told Carl that he was going to leave the villa at once, without telling Edith goodbye. He wanted to leave in the midst of his happiness so that his memory would not have one blot on it. He could not tell Carl where he was going because he had not yet made up his mind.

A few months later Carl found Peter sitting on a park bench in New York. Peter did not want Edith to learn that he was there, for he was in the middle of a new experiment and Edith might distract him. Interested in black magic, Peter was trying to discover the mystery of life and death. He took Carl to his apartment and showed him his laboratory. He also persuaded Carl to join him in an experiment. The magic brew exploded and they woke up in the hospital.

Carl sustained only minor injuries and left the hospital before Peter, who was dangerously hurt. But Peter recovered and returned to Toledo with his mother. Carl did not see him again until after the war, in 1919. By that time Peter was very ill from some incurable disease. He never mentioned his illness, but Carl knew that his friend's time was not long. One afternoon in December, while the two friends were in Peter's apartment, Carl learned that Peter had at last found himself. He told Carl that his book had never become a reality because he had attempted to do something that he was never intended to do. He was not meant to be a writer or a worker—he was meant only to appreciate and love the work of others, the art, the literature, the ability. He would make art greater and people better by bestowing upon them his appreciation and his affection. He would never have to make a decision; he would be himself. He told Carl that now he was happy and that he was a success. Then he closed his eyes. When Carl spoke to him again, Peter Whiffle did not answer.

PHAÈDRA

Type of work: Drama
Author: Jean Baptiste Racine (1639-1699)
Type of plot: Classical tragedy
Time of plot: Remote antiquity
Locale: Troezen, in Ancient Greece
First presented: 1677

Principal characters:
THESEUS, King of Athens
PHAÈDRA, his wife
HIPPOLYTUS, Theseus' son
ARICIA, an Athenian princess

Critique:

Phaèdra represents the classic tradition of the French stage. In the seventeenth century France, then at her apex, demanded great things of her artists to support the glory of the armies and the royal house, and the writers of the period assaulted the past in an effort to arouse the minds of their contemporaries to past glories and to stimulate them to greater efforts. The vast storehouse of classic legends became the source of countless plots and themes. In whole or in part, ancient plays and myths were constructed into plays which adhered as closely as possible to the classic tradition. Racine stands foremost among the neo-classicists of his century.

The Story:

After the death of his Amazon queen, Theseus, slayer of the Minotaur, married Phaèdra. the young daughter of the King of Crete. Phaèdra, seeing in her stepson, Hippolytus, all the bravery and virtue of his heroic father, but in more youthful guise, fell in love with him. In an attempt to conceal her passion for the son of Theseus, she treated him in an aloof and spiteful manner until at last Hippolytus decided to leave Troezen and go in search of his father, absent from the kingdom. To his tutor, Theramenes, he confided his desire to avoid both his stepmother and Aricia, an Athenian princess who was the daughter of a family which had opposed Theseus.

Phaèdra confessed to Oenone, her nurse, her guilty passion for Hippolytus, saying that she merely pretended unkindness to him in order to hide her real feelings.

Word came to Troezen that Theseus was dead. Oenone talked to Phaèdra in an attempt to convince the queen that her own son, not Hippolytus, should be chosen as the new king of Athens. Aricia hoped that she would be chosen to rule.

Hippolytus, a fair-minded young man, told Aricia that he would support her for the rule of Athens. He felt that Phaèdra's son should inherit Crete and that he himself should remain master of Troezen. He also admitted his love for Aricia, but said that he feared the gods would never allow it to be brought to completion. When he tried to explain his intentions to his stepmother, she in turn dropped her pretense of hatred and distrust and ended by betraying her love for Hippolytus. Shocked, he repulsed her, and she threatened to take her own life.

The people of Athens, however, chose Phaèdra's son to rule over them, to the disappointment of Aricia. There were also rumors that Theseus still lived. Hippolytus gave orders that a search be made for his father.

Phaèdra, embarrassed by all she had told Hippolytus, brooded over the injury she now felt, and wished that she had never revealed her love. Phaèdra was proud, and now her pride was hurt beyond recovery. Unable to overcome her passion however, she decided to offer the kingdom to Hippolytus so that she might keep him near her. Then news came that Theseus was returning to his home. Oenone warned Phaèdra that now she must hide her true feeling for Hippolytus. She even suggested to the queen that Theseus be made to believe that Hippolytus had tempted Phaèdra to adultery.

When Theseus returned, Phaèdra greeted him with reluctance, saying that she was no longer fit to be his wife. Hippolytus made the situation no better by requesting permission to leave Troezen at once. Theseus was greatly chagrined at his homecoming.

When scheming Oenone told the king that Hippolytus had attempted to dishonor his stepmother, Theseus flew into a terrific rage. Hippolytus, knowing nothing of the plot, was at first astonished by his father's anger and threats. When accused, he denied the charges, but Theseus refused to listen to him and banished his son from the kingdom forever. When Hippolytus claimed he was really in love with Aricia, Theseus, more incensed than ever, invoked the vengeance of Neptune upon his son.

Aricia tried to convince Hippolytus that he must prove his innocence, but Hippolytus refused because he knew that the revelation of Phaèdra's passion would be too painful for his father to bear. The two agreed to escape together. Before Aricia could leave the palace, however, Theseus questioned her. Becoming suspicious, he sent for Oenone to demand the truth. Fearing that her plot had been uncovered, Oenone committed suicide.

Meanwhile, as Hippolytus drove his chariot near the seashore, Neptune sent a horrible monster, part bull and part dragon, which destroyed the son of Theseus.

When news of his death reached the palace, Phaèdra confessed her guilt and drank poison. Theseus, glad to see his guilty queen die, wished that memory of her life might perish with her. Sorrowfully he sought the grief-stricken Aricia to comfort her.

2829

PHILASTER

Type of work: Drama
Authors: Francis Beaumont (1584?-1616) and John Fletcher (1579-1625)
Type of plot: Tragi-comedy
Time of plot: The romantic past
Locale: Sicily
First presented: 1610

Principal characters:
PHILASTER, heir to the crown of Sicily
THE KING OF SICILY, a usurper
ARETHUSA, his daughter
PHARAMOND, a pompous Spanish prince
DION, a Sicilian lord
EUPHRASIA, his daughter, disguised as page, Bellario

Critique:

Philaster, Or, Love Lies A-Bleeding was the first successful production, if not actually the first collaboration, resulting from the happy association of Beaumont and Fletcher. The play is pure romance. It is believed by scholars that this play was written for the most part by Beaumont, but echoes of Shakespearean themes and rich imagery would tend to substantiate the participation of Fletcher, who served his dramatic apprenticeship under the master. The drama passed from popular favor because Restoration audiences did not favor Philaster. Modern readers feel that Euphrasia deserved a better fate than she received. Yet *Philaster* remains a beautiful and pathetic play, soundly constructed and admirable in style—a masterpiece of its period.

The Story:

The King of Calabria had usurped the crown of Sicily from Prince Philaster's father, now dead. Because the Sicilian people loved their young prince, however, the king did not dare imprison him or harm him in any way. Meanwhile the king planned to marry his daughter Arethusa to Pharamond, a Spanish prince, who would thereby become heir to both thrones. Pharamond proved to be a pompous, conceited man. When Philaster, who was quite free and outspoken in his manners, told Pharamond that he could marry Arethusa and ultimately become king only over Philaster's dead body, the king admonished Philaster to restrain himself. Philaster, acting strangely, declared that he would restrain himself only when he was better treated; he believed that he was suddenly possessed by the spirit of his late father. Philaster was promised aid by the loyal Lord Dion and by two noble gentlemen, Cleremont and Thrasilene.

At an audience with the Princess Arethusa, Philaster could not believe his ears when he heard Arethusa profess deep love for him, and he declared his love for her in return. In order to avoid detection under the suspicious eyes of the court, he promised to send Arethusa his servant to act as their messenger. When Pharamond entered Arethusa's apartment, Philaster departed with words of scorn for the boastful Spanish prince. Later he had difficulty in persuading his servant, Bellario—actually Euphrasia, daughter of Lord Dion, in disguise—to enter Arethusa's service.

At court, meanwhile, Pharamond attempted the virtue of Galatea, a court lady who led him on but refused to yield to his base suggestions. Later he made an assignation with Megra, a court lady of easy virtue. Galatea, having overheard the conversation between Pharamond and Megra, reported the prince's dissolute ways to Arethusa.

That night the king, told about Pharamond's conduct, discovered Megra in the prince's apartment. Pharamond was in disgrace. Megra, however, managed to extricate herself to some extent by insinuating that Arethusa was as wicked as she and that Bellario was more than a mere servant to Arethusa. The princess, unfortunately, had made much of Bellario because the page had been a gift from Philaster. The king, who had not even heard of Bellario's existence, was confounded by Megra's suggestions of evil.

Megra's story convinced even Philaster's friends that Arethusa was unfaithful to the prince, but when they told Philaster what had happened he refused to believe them. Nevertheless, his trust in Arethusa was shaken. When Bellario delivered a letter from Arethusa to Philaster, who was still in doubt, the disguised girl innocently damned herself by speaking in praise of Arethusa and by describing Arethusa's virtuous affection for the page. Philaster accused Bellario of perfidy and, overcome with the passion of jealousy, threatened to take the page's life. At Bellario's sincere protestations of innocence, Philaster, although still not convinced, spared his servant.

Meanwhile the king had ordered Arethusa to discharge her young page. When Philaster found Arethusa depressed over Bellario's dismissal, he revealed his suspicions and declared that he would give up his claim to the throne and become a hermit. The wretched Arethusa, knowing that she was guiltless, could do nothing to prevent the departure of Philaster.

Philaster went to a nearby forest and there wandered about disconsolately. At the same time the king and the court entered the forest to hunt. During the chase Arethusa disappeared. The hunters found her riderless horse but no trace of the princess. Bellario, having been banished from the court, had also gone into the forest. Encountering Philaster, the page was brusquely ordered away. In another part of the forest Arethusa, stunned by recent events and without direction in her wandering, sat down to rest and suddenly fainted. Bellario appeared in time to revive her, only to be told by Arethusa that efforts to help her in her distress were

wasted; the princess was prepared to die.

Philaster in his own wanderings came upon the pair. Thinking that their meeting had been planned, and that Bellario and Arethusa were lovers, he told the page to take his wretched life. When Bellario disregarded his order, Philaster angrily dismissed the page and then, assuming the role of an agent of justice, attempted to kill Arethusa. He only wounded her, however, in his attempt. A peasant then came upon the scene of violence. In the fight that followed, Philaster was seriously wounded. The young prince fled when he heard horsemen approaching.

When Pharamond, Lord Dion, and others of the hunting party arrived to find Arethusa wounded, they immediately went in search of her attacker. In his flight Philaster, hurt and bleeding, came upon Bellario asleep. Distractedly, Philaster wounded the page before collapsing from loss of blood. Faithful Bellario administered gently to Philaster and convinced the prince that he had made a mistake in his belief that Arethusa had been unfaithful to him. Hearing Philaster's pursuers, they fled. Bellario was captured, but not before the page had led them away from the prince. In order further to protect the fugitive, Bellario confessed to the attack on Arethusa. When Philaster overheard this confession, he came out of hiding to defend Bellario. The king ordered that both be imprisoned, but Arethusa, somewhat recovered from her hurt, prevailed upon her father to give her the custody over the prince and the page.

In prison Philaster, about to be executed, and Arethusa, his guard, pledged their troth. The king disavowed his daughter when he learned of the marriage. Meanwhile the people of Sicily, aroused by Philaster's imprisonment and impending execution, seized Pharamond and threatened total revolt. The king, fearful for his safety and at last repentant for his usurpation of the throne, promised to restore the crown of Sicily and to approve Arethusa's marriage to Philaster, if the prince would only calm the enraged citizens. The people returned quietly to their homes when Philaster assured them that he was now quite free and that he was their new ruler.

The king, still not satisfied with the relationship between Arethusa and Bellario, commanded that Bellario be tortured in order that he might learn the truth. Philaster protested vehemently against the order. As the king's servants prepared to strip Bellario for the ordeal, the page revealed that she was, in reality, Euphrasia, daughter of Lord Dion. Having loved Philaster from childhood and despairing, because of a difference in rank, of ever marrying him, she had allowed everyone to think that she had gone overseas on a pilgrimage. Instead, she had disguised herself as a boy and had taken service with Philaster in order to be near him. Philaster and Arethusa, moved by Euphrasia's devotion, made her a lady in waiting to the queen.

THE PHILIPPICS

Type of work: Orations
Author: Demosthenes (384-322 B.C.)
First transcribed: Fourth century B.C.

Occasionally in history, perhaps more often than we realize, genius and a crisis in human affairs unite to produce a great man whose name then rings down through the ages long after the particular events which produced him have faded into the dimness of antiquity Such a man was Demosthenes. Almost every educated person has heard of him and knows that he was a famous Greek orator. But the events and the crisis in ancient Greece which helped make him famous are unknown, except to students of ancient history.

As an Athenian lawyer and orator, Demosthenes might have won but little fame had it not been for Philip of Macedon, whose ambition was to conquer and rule as much of the world as he could; and to a great extent he succeeded in his aim. When the danger to Athens became great, Demosthenes did all he could to arouse his fellow Athenians to the defense of their city-state. The crisis was one that has recurred in various forms throughout history. On the one hand was Philip of Macedon, a tyrant who sought control of many lands and peoples: on the other, Demosthenes, a believer in democracy and local sovereignty who did all that one person could to arouse his contemporaries to fight against Philip and, later, his son, Alexander the Great. In this conflict between democracy and tyranny there is no doubt of Demosthenes' sincerity; it rings out from his orations almost as clearly today as it must have more than twenty-three centuries ago.

By common consent of his contemporaries and later generations, Demosthenes was the greatest of the Greek orators, in a culture that produced a great many able men in rhetoric and oratory. Scholars of all periods have praised his speeches, and the number of manuscripts found in Egypt containing fragments of his speeches has been second only to papyri containing fragments of the Homeric epics. In modern times we can see but dimly the greatness of the speeches from the standpoint of formal rhetoric as the Greeks knew and used it. What Cicero praised in the orations is now to be found only by the serious student of Greek language and culture.

On the other hand, modern readers can find something in the speeches that his admirers in the ancient world seem to have overlooked or ignored. We can see that Demosthenes was an able and sincere statesman laboring for democratic ideals at a time when his fellow citizens in Athens were inclined to do little to oppose the forces of tyranny led and symbolized by Philip of Macedon. Demosthenes knew human nature as he knew his art, and he brought the two together to speak out forcefully what he believed in. He spoke out, not for the sake of his rhetoric, but for the sake of Athens; he spoke not to a select group, to no aristocracy, but to all Athenians. He wished to persuade them to rise to the defense of their city and the way of life and government that it represented. In the orations there is, at least as they are translated, little flamboyance. Demosthenes spoke plainly and sincerely; his art was like all great art, hiding beneath the cloak of apparent simplicity great care in production. Demosthenes' tone is serious, even to the point of sobriety.

As in the case of so many ancient authors, the authenticity of work supposedly done by Demosthenes is open to question. More than sixty orations, as well as some letters and poems have been attributed to him; but scholars nowadays accept only about forty of the speeches as authentic. Many of the orations accepted as his are nonpolitical, having been composed for delivery in cases at law. These orations furnish a great deal of material about Greek culture, as Cicero's orations furnish information about Roman culture at a later time. Demosthenes' true fame rests on the speeches called the *Philippics*. These were not the only orations on political subjects that he made, nor were they the only speeches he gave which had to do with the threat of Philip to Athens. Quite a number of other orations, like the *Olynthiacs*, deal with Philip's depredations in the Greek peninsula and other portions of the eastern Mediterranean world.

The first *Philippic* was delivered in 351 B.C. At that time Philip, stopped at Thermopylae, had sent his armies into Thrace, dispatched a fleet to attack the islands of Lemnos and Imbrus, and interfered with the commerce of Athens by attacking shipping. Demosthenes spoke that the Athenians might be made aware of the danger and take steps to defend themselves. The orator obviously felt that Athens in 351 B.C. had more to fear from the Macedonian king than its traditional enemy, Thebes, or from a combination of other unfriendly city-states. It was not as an alarmist that Demosthenes spoke; he spoke, rather, to awaken his fellow Athenians to an awareness of the need for watchfulness and preparedness. In this first *Philippic* he encouraged his city to meet the danger, pointing out its advantages and strengths. In practical fashion, he suggested ways in which the city could economically take steps to meet the danger, which at that time was not as great as it would become in passing years. It was not enough, as Demosthenes knew, merely to hope that Philip had died, as rumor had it. Demosthenes realized that failure to provide for defense through inaction sets up circumstances which are an invitation to strong-armed tyranny. Later history has shown that leaders have often failed to realize this truism of politics. Demosthenes realized, as leaders sometimes have failed to do, that free people do not have a choice between action and inaction. To oppose Philip, to warn him that Athens was prepared to defend itself, the orator suggested a military force of moderate size, with good officers to lead it. He recommended that at least twenty-five percent of the personnel be Athenians, the rest mercenaries. Knowing that to equip, pay, and keep in the field a large force was beyond the economic power of the city, he urged a small, but efficient military force. The answer to the problem, he said, lay in making the best use of what could be afforded, not in hitting blindly only at places where Philip had already struck.

Nothing was done by the Athenians. In 344 B.C., seven years later, he again spoke pointedly in the second *Philippic*. By that time Philip, allied with the Messenians, had become a more powerful threat to Athens. Demosthenes himself had headed an embassy to Messene and Argos to warn those cities against the oppressor, to no avail. Philip, in turn, had sent an emissary to Athens to complain about Demosthenes' charges and to vindicate his conduct. Demosthenes spoke to explain carefully what Philip was doing and what the pro-Macedonian group in Athens was doing to endanger the city. He ended by pointing out that Philip's conduct now made the Athenians' problem one of defending their city and homes, not merely of looking after claims and interests abroad. Philip's benevolence was shown to be double-edged.

In the third of the *Philippics*, delivered in 341 B.C., Demosthenes cried out that Athenians had to learn that a state of war existed, even though Philip talked of peace. Philip aimed at the Chersonese, which controlled the route of grain ships between Athens and the Euxine. Demosthenes urged that the Chersonese be protected as a means of protecting Athens. He was right in his predictions: Philip attacked the Propontine cities in the following year. The Athenians, to their credit and Demosthenes', played their part in resisting the tyrant. The fourth and last of the *Philippics* was also delivered in 341 B.C., just before Philip laid siege to the Propontine cities. In this oration, as he had in the third *Philippic*, Demosthenes urged resistance, even advocating an alliance with Persia. Although the fourth *Philippic* is generally accepted as authentic, some scholars have viewed it with suspicion, claiming for several reasons that it is spurious and not really a product of Demosthenes' own hand.

PHILOCTETES

Type of work: Drama
Author: Sophocles (c. 496-406 or 405 B.C.)
Type of plot: Classical tragedy
Time of plot: The Trojan War
Locale: The island of Lemnos
First presented: 409 B.C.

Principal characters:
PHILOCTETES, an abandoned Greek warrior
NEOPTOLEMUS, Achilles' son
ODYSSEUS, King of Ithaca
A SAILOR, disguised as a trader
HERAKLES, a Greek immortal
CHORUS OF SAILORS, under the command of Neoptolemus

Critique:

Philoctetes is Sophocles' penultimate play. It is interesting that it is in theme markedly similar to his last play, *Oedipus at Colonus.* In both plays the protagonist has become hateful to his society and has been rejected by it, and in both plays the hero again becomes necessary to the society which had cast him out, is restored by the gods, and resumes his powers. In this play the attitude of Odysseus to the sufferings of the hero, like that of Creon in the Oedipus plays, is completely inhuman. *Philoctetes* varies from all of Sophocles' other plays, however, in having a happy ending. This circumstance is achieved only after Philoctetes has been lovingly accepted as a fellow man by Neoptolemus. The myth of the Wound and the Bow, although it has not received the overwhelming attention that has been accorded the Oedipus myth, has interested modern writers and critics. The crux of the myth is the fact that the unacceptable man and his remarkable and essential powers are inseparable. Only when this fact is understood by others can he take his place and play his part in society.

The Story:

Odysseus had abandoned Philoctetes on the barren island of Lemnos after the warrior had been bitten on the foot by a snake while preparing to make a sacrifice at the shrine of Chrysa. The wound never healed, and the smell that came from it and the groans of suffering Philoctetes were the reasons Odysseus gave for making him an outcast. But Philoctetes, with his invincible bow, once the property of Herakles, had become indispensable to the Greeks in their war against Troy. Landing for the second time on Lemnos, Odysseus described the cave in which Philoctetes lived. Neoptolemus identified it by the stained bandages drying in the sun, the leaf-stuffed mattress, and the crude wooden cup he found.

Instructed by Odysseus, Neoptolemus was to lure Philoctetes on board with his bow by declaring that he too hated Odysseus because the king had deprived him of the weapons of his father Achilles. Neoptolemus was disgusted by this deception, but wily Odysseus pleaded necessity and promised him honor and glory after this one day. When Neoptolemus had agreed to obey, Odysseus left him.

The chorus of sailors reported that they heard the painful approach of Philoctetes. He asked who they were and whether they too were Greeks. Imploring their pity, he told them not to fear him, although he had become a savage through solitude and great suffering. Neoptolemus answered Philoctetes, who asked who he was and why he had come. The young warrior said that he was the son of Achilles and that he did not know Philoctetes, who replied that he must indeed be vile if no word of him had reached the

Greeks. His wound had grown worse and because he was alone on the island he had to use all his energy to keep alive. He shot birds with his great bow, and in order that he might drink in winter he was forced to build a fire to melt the ice. He cursed the Atreidae and Odysseus, who had abandoned him, and wished that they might suffer his agony. Neoptolemus, answering as he had been instructed, said that he too had cursed Odysseus, who had deprived him of his rights and robbed him of his father's arms. He asserted that he intended to sail for home. Philoctetes, declaring that their grief was equal, wondered also why Ajax had allowed these injustices. He was told that Ajax was also dead. Philoctetes was certain that Odysseus was alive, and this fact Neoptolemus confirmed. After hearing of the death of other friends, Philoctetes agreed with Neoptolemus that war inevitably killed the good men but only occasionally and by chance killed the bad. Neoptolemus stressed his determination never to return to Troy. He then said goodbye to Philoctetes, who implored them not to abandon him and to suffer for one day the inconvenience of having him on board the ship on which Neoptolemus was sailing. When he begged on his knees not to be left alone again, the chorus expressed their willingness to take him with them. After Neoptolemus agreed, Philoctetes praised the day that had brought them together and declared himself bound in friendship to the young warrior for all time.

As Odysseus had planned, a sailor disguised as a trader came to help Neoptolemus in tricking Philoctetes. He said, hoping to persuade Philoctetes to go quickly on board, that Odysseus was pursuing him in order to compel him to rejoin the Greek army, for Helenus, Priam's son, had prophesied that Philoctetes was the one man who would defeat Troy. Philoctetes swore that he would never go with his most hated enemy, and the disguised trader returned to his ship. Neoptolemus asked permission to hold

the mighty bow while Philoctetes prepared to leave the island. Suddenly the wound in Philoctetes' foot began to pain him beyond endurance. He handed the bow to Neoptolemus and writhed on the ground until the abscess burst and the blood flowed. The sailors advised Neoptolemus to leave with the bow while the exhausted man slept. Neoptolemus refused, for the bow was useless without Philoctetes.

When Philoctetes awoke, Neoptolemus revealed to him that he had come to take the warrior to fight against Troy. Philoctetes refused to go. When Neoptolemus insisted on keeping the bow, Philoctetes, enraged and despairing, cursed such treachery and declared that he would starve without his weapon. Neoptolemus' loyalties were divided between duty and compassion, but before he had decided on the course to pursue, Odysseus arrived and demanded that Philoctetes should accompany them. When he remained adamant, Odysseus and Neoptolemus left, taking with them the bow.

The chorus of sailors assured Philoctetes that it would be best to fight with the Greeks, but out of pride he was determined not to fight with men who had made him an outcast. He begged for a sword to kill himself. Then Neoptolemus, followed by Odysseus, returned; he had decided to redress the wrong he had done Philoctetes and to return the bow. Odysseus, unable to change the young warrior's decision, went to tell the other Greeks of this act of treachery. Meanwhile, Neoptolemus again tried to persuade Philoctetes to join them. When Philoctetes again refused, Neoptolemus, in spite of the return of Odysseus, gave back the bow. He was then forced to keep Philoctetes from killing Odysseus.

When Odysseus had again left them, Neoptolemus revealed the whole of Helenus' prophecy, which foretold that the wound would be cured when Philoctetes returned and that, together with Neoptolemus, he would conquer Troy. Philoctetes, declaring Odysseus had been faithless once and would be so again, implored Neoptolemus to take him home, as he had first promised. But Neoptolemus was afraid that the Greeks would in retaliation attack his country. Philoctetes swore that he would defend the country with his bow.

Before they could leave, Herakles, from whom Philoctetes had inherited the bow, appeared on the rocks above the cave. He informed Philoctetes that Zeus had spoken: Philoctetes should return to the Greek army, where he would be healed. Also, with Neoptolemus, he would kill Paris and take Troy. Philoctetes, heeding the voice of the immortal, willingly left Lemnos to fulfill his destiny.

PHILOSOPHIAE NATURALIS PRINCIPIA MATHEMATICA

Type of work: Scientific and philosophical treatise
Author: Sir Isaac Newton (1642-1727)
First published: 1687

One of the most seminal and influential books in the English language has been Newton's *Philosophiae Naturalis Principia Mathematica* (*The Mathematical Principles of Natural Philosophy*). Published in 1687, the book immediately led to intellectual controversy among the scientists and philosophers of the day. Men as distinguished as Leibniz, Dr. Robert Hooke, and John Flamsteed, the British Astronomer-Royal, felt it necessary to argue with many of the propositions and conclusions Newton advanced. In spite of these arguments, the *Principia* remained the principal document in the field of physics for two hundred years and a highly revered work of philosophy throughout the eighteenth century. Newton became one of the most honored figures in Western culture, one of the first formulators of scientific method and the man whose work formed the basis for scientific study and application of principles. Physics, as a field of theory and knowledge did not exist before Newton's work.

Newton published a preface to the *Principia* in which he announced that he was interested in the laws of mathematics as a means of discovering nature, or getting at philosophical truth. He felt that mathematics was not a pure, abstract system, but rather a human and rational means for discovering the principles of the universe, for making a kind of universal order out of man's disparate experience. In fact, he felt this function of mathematics so strongly that, in the body of the *Principia*, every experiment or demonstration is concluded with a "Scholium." The "Scholium" is a short essay giving the philosophical implications or the speculative use of the mathematical or physical principle just demonstrated.

After the preface, Newton supplied a series of definitions for such terms as motion, force, and quantity, terms necessary for even an elementary understanding of his work. These definitions are still standard among students of physics. After the definitions, Newton stated his famous three axioms or laws of motion. These axioms, like the tendency of a body at rest to remain at rest or the fact that every action has an equal and opposite reaction, are still relevant in any account of the physical forces operating with respect to the earth. Newton stated these laws as axioms on which his whole account of the universe rested. It was not that he could prove them universally; rather, these axioms became the cornerstone of his system, the principles which explained the various facts and data that men found in physical phenomena around them. The axioms, like the definitions, were necessary beginnings, points which must be accepted in order that all the physical data could make rational sense. The axioms had six corollaries, propositions which could be established from the axioms and be used in turn to establish other propositions.

In the first book of the *Principia*, Newton deals with the motion of bodies. In order to simplify and explain his theories, in the first book he confines his observations and proofs to bodies moving in a vacuum. He begins with the more purely mathematical: establishing ratios (demonstrating the logic of the number system), determining the vectors of forces, tracing and proving how bodies move in various arcs, parabolas, and ellipses. For all these geometric demonstrations he gives mathematical proof by inventing and proving his equations and by making frequent reference to his many diagrammatic figures. He also develops and proves equations dealing with the ascent and descent of bodies, again confining his work to bodies in a vacuum. He also devises mathematical explanation for the oscillations of a pendulum. Finally, at the end of the first book, Newton deals with the attractions of bodies for one another, setting up equations to demonstrate this necessary and universal principle of attraction and repulsion.

In the second book he deals with the motion of bodies in resisting mediums. Because of the natures of the resisting mediums, such as water or air, the proofs become more intricate and complicated. Newton usually attempts to simplify his demonstrations by assuming that the medium is constant. These experiments allow Newton to calculate and, more important, to explain the resistance of substances like water or air to the motion of bodies. He gives further demonstrations of motion, analyzing some of the problems dealt with in his first book. He brings up, for example, the oscillations of the pendulum and charts the equations for the motion of a pendulum through air. His consideration of the resistance to bodies allows Newton to present and demonstrate the solution to other problems in the physical universe. In this section, dealing with means of determining the density and compression of fluids, he develops equations to explain the behavior of fluids: the density they offer as resistance and the force they exert when compressed. This work on fluids permitted Newton to establish his equations to determine the velocity of waves.

Newton called his third book the "System of the World," his specific intention in this book being to develop the philosophical principles which he believed followed directly from his mathematical proofs and his experimentation. He begins the book by stating his rules for accurate reasoning, based on his belief that there are no superfluous causes in nature. Each cause that man can talk of sensibly has direct effects which man is able to observe and subdue to order with his mathematical and rational equipment. In other words, Newton thought that the simplicity of the design of the universe is a basic rule; causes are never extraneous, only the basis for observable and frequently calculable phenomena.

Another significant rule is Newton's belief that all conclusions are based on induction: Man reasons from the observable facts and always needs to refer his conclusions or theories to the observable facts around him. In this complete devotion to scientific method, to the necessity of constant reference of the theory to all of the data, Newton fully realized, however, that theories might well have to be altered to provide explanations for new or accumulated data. Changes in post-Newtonian physics would not have surprised Newton, for he always acknowledged that scientific theories could be no more than the best conclusions available from the data at hand at the moment the conclusion was made.

The third book sets forth Newton's mathematical demonstrations of the periodic times and movements of the planets. Again, he derives many new equations to demonstrate, with a good deal of accuracy, the movements of the planets and to correlate this knowledge with the system of time on earth. He also proves that gravity applies to all bodies and calculates the ratio of gravity. Much of the third section is devoted to lunar motion, establishing equations and calculating, in terms of time, the various changing relationships between the moon and the earth. These matters lead Newton into consideration of the effect of the sun and the moon on the waters of the earth, and he devises means of measuring the tides. He also computes the times and ranges of recurrent comets.

In a long, final "Scholium" designed to tie the extensive parts of the *Principia* together, Newton develops the basis for his belief in God. He asserts that such a perfect, and perfectly simple, system must have, as its ultimate or final cause, a perfect, and perfectly simple, Being. This Being must embody all the intelligence, the rationality, the perfection, of the system itself. Newton views God as this ultimate principle, not as a personal God or a larger edition of a human being. Firm in his devotion to his principle, he answered, in later editions of the *Prin-*

cipia, charges of atheism brought against his system. This principle, the final cause, is the perpetrator of the whole Newtonian universe, the perfectly rational origin of all the laws, mathematics, and reason that man can use in order to develop and describe the meaningful pattern in his universe. And God, the perfect Being, having set this vast plan in constant motion, is constantly at hand to make sure the universe does not run down, or to repair any defects in the system.

This concept of God became, during the eighteenth century, one of the principal concepts held by intellectuals. The religion of Deism, of viewing God as the perpetrator and final cause of a complete, perfect, mechanistic universe, was derived from Newton's thorough and systematic explanation.

As science and as philosophy, the *Principia* is one of man's great achievements. The book vastly increased the store of human knowledge and derived a sound and rational basis for making conclusions about the physical universe. In addition, Newton, in his *Principia,* both illustrated and defined the method by which man could continue to test his observations, developed a whole new and important area for the human intellect, and established a metaphysical system which governed a great deal of human thinking and scientific investigation for over a century.

PHILOSOPHY OF ART

Type of work: Aesthetic philosophy
Author: Hippolyte Taine (1828-1893)
First published: 1865

Hippolyte Taine, author of *The History of English Literature* (1863-1869) and of *The Origins of Contemporary France* (1875-1894), combined a historical interest in his subjects with a philosophical one. He was able to do this because he regarded both history and philosophy as sciences; he believed that a study of the nature of art and of art production could proceed, in the manner of any scientific study, by attention to the observable facts and by the framing of inductive generalizations Consequently, his *Philosophy of Art* is to some extent a description of some predominant art periods and to some extent an attempt to generalize philosophically from the data of his historical inquiries. Other Taine volumes present studies of the art of Greece, the Netherlands, and Italy.

Taine's working assumption is that no work of art is isolated and that the only way to understand a particular work of art or the nature of art in general is by attending to the conditions out of which works of art come.

This theory holds that the character of a work of art is determined by the artist but that the artist himself is what he is in virtue of a number of cultural influences which are inescapable. Taine believed that works of art present, in perceptible form, the essential character of the time and place in which the artist works. In his words, "The work of art is determined by an aggregate which is the general state of the mind and surrounding manners." To illustrate his point, Taine refers to the art of Greece, reflecting in its nude statues the Grecian preoccupation with war and athletics and with the development of the healthy human animal; the art of the Middle Ages, reflecting the moral crisis resulting from feudal oppression; the art of the seventeenth century, reflecting the values of courtly life; and the art of industrial

democracy, expressing the restless aspirations of man in an age of science.

The work of art itself is conditioned by the wholes of which it is a part and product. In the first place, according to Taine, the work of art exhibits the artist's style, that prevailing mode of aesthetic treatment which runs through all the works of an artist, giving them a family resemblance to one another. Secondly, the work of art reflects the prevailing manner of the school of artists to which the individual artist belongs. It expresses, in the third place, the world of the times, the social milieu of taste, conviction, and manners within which the artist must work and by which he must be affected. Taine believed, then, that "in order to comprehend a work of art, an artist or a group of artists, we must clearly comprehend the general social and intellectual condition of the times to which they belong."

In addition to the influence of taste and style, one must consider "moral temperature," the spiritual milieu, whether mystic or pagan or something foreign to both, which infects the artist and, consequently, his work. The philosophy of art, as Taine understood it, is the attempt to study the art of various countries and ages in order to discover the conditions under which the art of a particular place and time was created, and, finally, the conditions in general for any art whatsoever. A report of those general conditions would be a philosophy of art.

In examining actual works of art, the first step in scientific aesthetics, Taine found that imitation was an important feature of most works of art, particularly of works of poetry, sculpture, and painting. Taine wondered whether exact imitation was the end of art, for he was interested in arriving by inductive means at a theory of the nature of art. He concluded that it is not since exact imitation does not produce the finest works of art. Photography, for example, is useful as a means of making accurate reproductions of scenes, but no one supposes that it can be ranked with such fine arts as painting and sculpture. Another reason for concluding that works of art are not essentially concerned with exact imitation is that many works of art are intentionally inexact.

There is a kind of imitation, however, which is essential to art, according to Taine, and that is the imitation of what he calls "the relationships and mutual dependence of parts." Just as a painter, even when reproducing a human figure, does not represent every feature of the body, its exact size, color, and weight, but rather what might be called the *logic* of the body, so artists in general, in creating works of art, do not aim at deception through exact representation but, rather, at presenting the essential character of an object. Since the essential character of an object is simply the predominant feature of the object as affected by the place and time of its existence, we may say that the artist's objective, according to Taine's analysis, is to put into perceptible form that principal feature of the object. In painting a lion, for example, the important thing is to represent him as carnivorous; in painting the Low Countries the artist must imitate its alluvial character.

Taine was aware of the fact that the artist is often doing something quite different from making the dominant feature of nature the predominant feature of the work of art, but he believed that all art can be explained as the imitation of essential quality. What the artist presents may be not the essential character of some physical scene or object; it may be the prevailing temper of his times. This view is made clear in Part II of the book, in which Taine considers artistic production. Part I, on the nature of art, concludes with the summary statement that "The end of a work of art is to manifest some essential or salient character, consequently some important idea, clearer and

more completely than is attainable from real objects. Art accomplishes this end by employing a group of connected parts, the relationships of which it systematically modifies."

The law of art production—that a work of art is determined by the general state of mind and surrounding circumstances—Taine defends in two ways. He refers to experience in order to argue that the law of production applies to all works of art; and then he analyzes the effects of "a general state of mind and surrounding circumstances" in order to claim that the law reveals a necessary connection.

As an example, Taine considers the effect of melancholy as a state of mind, together with the circumstances which made melancholy characteristic of an age. He argues that in a melancholy age the artist is inevitably melancholy. As a result, the artist portrays all objects as being predominantly melancholy; he "paints things in much darker colors. . . ."

During a renaissance, when there is "a general condition of cheerfulness," the works of art will express a joyful condition. Whatever the combination of moods in an age, the art of that age will reflect the combination. It could not be otherwise, Taine argues, because the artist cannot isolate himself from his age.

As historical examples, the Greek period, the feudal age, the seventeenth century, and the nineteenth century are referred to.

A "general situation" resulting from a condition of wealth or poverty, or of servitude or liberty, or from a prevailing religious faith, or from some other feature of the society, has an effect on the individual artist, affecting his aptitudes and his emotions. Thus, "In Greece we see physical perfection and a balance of faculties which no manual or cerebral excess of life deranges; in the Middle Ages, the intemperance of over-excited imaginations and the delicacy of feminine sensibility; in the seventeenth century, the polish and good breeding of society and the dignity of aristocratic salons; and in modern times, the grandeur of unchained ambitions and the morbidity of unsatisfied yearnings."

The four terms of a causal series by reference to which the production of art can be explained are: 1. The general situation, 2. The tendencies and special faculties provoked by that situation, 3. A man, representing and embodying the tendencies and faculties, and 4. The material—such as sounds, forms, colors, or language—by the use of which the man gives the character sensuous form.

Taine argues that the artist imitates the prevailing quality of his age because he cannot escape being a part of his age, because nothing else would be accepted, and because the artist works for accept-ance and applause.

Taine's *Philosophy of Art* is a clear and sensible defense of the idea that art reflects the spirit of the times. In opposition to his position there are those theories which emphasize the role of the extraordinary man, the eccentric who by his genius transcends the perspectives and sentiments of his age. The attempt to reconcile these two basic philosophical perspectives only hides the truth that resides in each. The moral seems to be to read Taine for an appreciation of the influence of the social milieu, and someone else, say Nietzsche, for an aesthetics in which the artist is shown as an individual rebel who falsifies nature.

PHINEAS FINN

Type of work: Novel
Author: Anthony Trollope (1815-1882)
Type of plot: Political romance
Time of plot: Mid-nineteenth century
Locale: The British Isles
First published: 1869

Principal characters:

PHINEAS FINN, a personable young Irishman
LORD BRENTFORD, an important Whig
LORD CHILTERN, his profligate son
LADY LAURA STANDISH, Brentford's beautiful daughter
MR. KENNEDY, a very rich Member of Parliament
VIOLET EFFINGHAM, a charming girl of large fortune
MADAME MARIE MAX GOESLER, a pretty and wealthy young widow
MARY FLOOD JONES, a pretty Irish girl

Critique:

Phineas Finn, the Irish Member is an objective account of the successful but brief parliamentary career of a guilelessly opportunistic young man who lacks the fortune which could give him independence from his party. The novel is rewarding for its dispassionate account of the passing of the important English Reform Bill, but the author's approach both to that and to his hero is so completely objective that it is difficult for the reader to feel much enthusiasm for either. As usual, Trollope's characterizations are excellent, but the loose and episodic plot structure prevents *Phineas Finn* from equaling the best of the Barsetshire series.

The Story:

Young Phineas Finn, just admitted to the bar, was tempted to postpone his career as a barrister by an offer to run for election as a member of Parliament from the Irish borough of Loughshane. Phineas' father, a hard-working Irish doctor, reluctantly agreed to give Phineas enough money to enable him to live, for a Member of Parliament received no salary and could only hope that his party, when in power, would reward him with a lucrative office.

Phineas was elected. Among those to whom he said goodbye before leaving for London was pretty Mary Flood Jones, a girl devoted to Phineas, but no richer than he.

Phineas' well-wishers in London included Lady Laura Standish, daughter of Lord Brentford, an influential Whig. Phineas, falling in love with Laura, saw a rival in the aloof and unprepossessing but rich Mr. Kennedy, also a Whig and a member of Parliament. Laura tried to encourage a friendship between Phineas and her brother Lord Chiltern, a violent young man who had quarreled with their father. Lord Brentford would be reconciled with his son if Chiltern were to marry rich, lovely, and witty Violet Effingham, a friend from childhood. Chiltern, loving her deeply, had proposed repeatedly; but Violet was level-headed and, though fond of Chiltern, she did not intend to ruin herself deliberately.

At Laura's recommendation, Phineas accepted an invitation to visit Loughlinter, the Kennedy estate in Scotland. There Phineas made friends with several Whig leaders and became the special disciple of Mr. Monk, a cabinet minister with independent views. Phineas proposed to Laura, who told him she was engaged to marry Kennedy. Against her father's wishes, she explained, she had exhausted her personal fortune by paying her brother's debts and was consequently obliged to marry someone with money.

Last-minute fright prevented Phineas from carrying out his elaborate plans for his first speech in Parliament. Laura, now several months married, began to find life with her strict, demanding husband oppressive. Chiltern, having unsuccessfully proposed to Violet once more, invited Phineas to hunt with him. Cared for by Phineas after a hunting injury, Chiltern became his intimate friend. The young nobleman confided that, although he could no longer hope for success with Violet, he would fight any other aspirant for her hand.

In the voting on the Reform Bill, the question of the ballot divided Parliament, and the government was dissolved. The capriciousness of Lord Tulla, who had insured Phineas' original success, prevented his running again for Loughshane. Lord Brentford, however, who had the English borough of Loughton "in his pocket," offered it to Phineas, who was easily elected.

Phineas, who had rescued Kennedy from two attackers late one night, was again visiting at Loughlinter. Gradually he had transferred his affections from Laura to Violet, but his plan to confide in Laura was prevented by her confession to him that life with her husband had grown intolerable. Phineas, despairing of an opportunity to see Violet, found his excuse in a letter from Chiltern which contained a conciliatory message for his father. Phineas took the letter to Lord Brentford, at whose house Violet was staying. Lord Brentford agreed to forgive his son if Chiltern resumed his courtship of Violet. Phineas sent this message to Chiltern and, to avoid duplicity, added that he himself hoped to win Violet's hand. He later found the opportunity to propose to Violet. Rejected, he felt that her negative answer was not really conclusive.

Because Phineas refused to give up his courtship of Violet, Chiltern challenged him to a duel. Though they fought secretly in Belgium, the news leaked out, partly because of Phineas' injury; he had

been wounded before he could fire. At last Phineas confided in Laura, who was angered by his news—as much because of her own affection for him as because of her brother's claims on Violet.

Phineas met the beautiful and charming widow, Madame Goesler, who became interested in him. Phineas, who had been left a legacy of three thousand pounds, soon received an even more substantial income on being appointed to an office which paid one thousand pounds annually. Feeling she had wronged Phineas, Laura took it upon herself to urge his suit with Violet. But Violet, knowing that Phineas had first courted Laura, disliked being in second place. She refused when Phineas proposed to her again.

When the English Reform Bill was passed, redistributing parliamentary representation to conform to actual population, the borough of Loughton, among others, was voted out of existence. Phineas, having shown himself an able and loyal Whig, was promoted to a higher office paying two thousand pounds a year. Having no borough to run for, he despaired of keeping the office after the next election. But Loughshane was made available again by the caprice of Lord Tulla, and Phineas was assured success.

Chiltern proposed to Violet once more and was accepted, and he and his father were at last reconciled. Phineas, miserable over Violet's engagement, confided in Madame Goesler. He also told Laura of his heartbreak, but she chided him, saying he would soon forget Violet just as he had forgotten her.

Lord Brentford finally learned of the duel between his son and Phineas, whom he accused of treachery. Phineas discovered the real cause of Lord Brentford's anger: Chiltern and Violet, quarreling over Chiltern's unwillingness to work, had broken their engagement.

Madame Goesler had made a conquest of the elderly and all-respected Duke of Omnium. Though tempted to accept, she finally refused his proposal of marriage.

Not the least of her motives was her own attachment to Phineas.

Because he accused her of taking Phineas as a lover, Laura decided to leave her husband. Phineas again asked Violet to marry him. She answered that, although she and Chiltern had quarreled, she could not love anyone else.

Phineas caused a great sensation at home by bringing Mr. Monk to Ireland with him. Caught up with Mr. Monk in political fervor, Phineas pledged himself to support Irish tenant rights in Parliament. Mr. Monk had warned him against such promises, saying that Phineas, voting in opposition to his party, would be forced to resign his office. Then, without means of support, he would have to give up his promising career. Phineas confided this danger and his unsuccessful love of Violet to Mary Flood Jones, who now won him to herself completely. They became engaged.

After Laura had taken up residence with her father, Kennedy sought legal aid to get her to return to him. To escape persecution, Laura decided to live abroad. She confessed to Phineas that she had always loved him and worked for him, even though heartbroken when he had revealed his love for Violet. Laura urged him to assure his career by marrying Madame Goesler for her money. Phineas did not mention his engagement to Mary. When Madame Goesler offered her hand and money to Phineas, he could only refuse. His first feeling was one of bitter disappointment.

Chiltern and Violet were reconciled. The Irish Reform Bill was passed, abolishing Phineas' borough of Loughshane. Phineas' career in Parliament was over. The intervention of governmental friends, however, gave Phineas a permanent appointment, that of a poor-law inspector in Ireland. It paid a yearly salary of a thousand pounds, enabling Phineas and Mary to plan an immediate wedding.

PHINEAS REDUX

Type of work: Novel
Author: Anthony Trollope (1815-1882)
Type of plot: Political romance
Time of plot: Mid-nineteenth century
Locale: England
First published: 1874

Principal characters:
PHINEAS FINN, an Irish politician, a widower
MADAME MARIE MAX GOESLER, a wealthy and pretty widow
LADY LAURA KENNEDY, in love with Phineas
MR. KENNEDY, her estranged husband
LORD CHILTERN, Laura's brother
VIOLET CHILTERN, his wife
MR. BONTEEN, a conniving politician

Critique:

Phineas Redux is the second of Trollope's parliamentary novels. It is a sequel to *Phineas Finn*, which was an entertaining account of events which never seemed really momentous. *Phineas Redux* is even more entertaining; the characterization is equally good, and the well-constructed plot encompasses accusations of adultery and a trial for murder. These events fully exploit Trollope's genius for detailing the exasperatingly logical thought processes which lie behind false rumors and misinformation.

The Story:

The conservatives had been in control of the government for over a year. In planning their return to power, the liberals wanted to get every good man they could muster.

Phineas Finn, now thirty, who had retired from politics two years before to marry his childhood sweetheart and to settle down in a modest but permanent position in Ireland, was invited back to resume his political career. His wife had died in the interval and he had saved enough to let him live two or three years without being given an office. Because the urging of his friends seemed to imply that he would not have to wait long for an office, he agreed to give up his security for the more exciting life of a member of Parliament. He was to run for the borough of Tankerville, held until then by a corrupt conservative named Browborough.

While awaiting the election, Phineas visited Chiltern and Violet, now happily married. Chiltern had at last found the occupation perfectly suited to his temperament and enthusiasm for hunting—Master of the Brake Hounds. Also visiting the Chilterns were Adelaid Palliser and Mr. Maule, a gloomy and idle but rather pleasing young man, devoted to and loved by Adelaid.

In the Tankerville election Phineas campaigned for separation of church and state. Although Browborough won by seven votes, the seat was to be contested on evidence that Browborough had bought votes. The conservative leader, in a desperate effort to keep his party in power, also declared for separation of church and state.

Phineas, on his way to visit Lady Laura Kennedy and her father in Dresden, was summoned by her husband to his estate. Kennedy's mind had become deranged; his one purpose in life was to get his wife back. He forbade Phineas to visit her, and accused him of adultery. Although he knew himself to be guiltless, Phineas could not reason with Kennedy. Later, in Dresden, Laura confided that her love for Phineas had been the real reason behind the failure of her marriage; however, Phineas had long felt nothing but friendship for Laura.

On his next visit to the Chilterns Phineas saw Madame Goesler. The first meeting was awkward because of their earlier relationship, but soon they were old friends again. She told Phineas that she had been acting as unofficial companion and nurse to the old Duke of Omnium, now on his deathbed. Lady Glencora, the duke's niece, had become her intimate friend.

Adelaid's thoroughbred qualities attracted the uncouth squire and fox hunter Spooner, who, unaware of the subtleties of social behavior, felt himself more eligible than Maule, whose income was very small. Spooner's proposal of marriage was refused with horror, and Maule's was accepted. Maule and Adelaid felt that they could marry if his father would let them live in Maule Abbey, now abandoned. But Mr. Maule, Sr., opposed to his son's marriage to a fortuneless girl and, angry at the implied reminder that the property would be his son's after his death, refused the request.

Quintus Slide, representative of all that is bad in journalism, brought to Phineas a letter written to his newspaper by Kennedy. The letter was a madman's accusation, implying that Phineas and Laura were guilty of adultery. Slide, who intended to print the letter, enjoyed the feeling of power its possession gave him; believing that he was interested only in upholding the institution of marriage, he offered to give Phineas a day to persuade Laura to return to Kennedy. Actually, Phineas went to Kennedy's hotel to urge him to retract the letter. Kennedy shot at Phineas and missed. In spite of efforts to keep the affair hushed up, the news leaked out later. When Phineas obtained an injunction against Slide, forbidding him to print the letter, the journalist, enraged, wrote an editorial in which, though he could not quote, he referred to the letter. Because he made the story seem even worse than it was, the whole affair was damaging to Phineas' career.

In the meantime Mr. Bonteen, long disliked by and jealous of Phineas, had achieved advancement through party loyalty. After the death of the old Duke of Omnium the new duke had given up his former office of Chancellor of the Exchequer, a post which Bonteen was now expected to fill as soon as the liberals returned to power. Since Bonteen was using his influence against Phineas, who despaired of getting an office, Madame Goesler and her friend Lady Glencora, now Duchess of Omnium, resolved on a counter-intrigue. But the duchess, while able to prevent Bonteen's being made chancellor, was unable to secure an office for Phineas.

Normally the liberal party was for separation of church and state, but now they officially opposed it, knowing that the conservatives took the unnatural side only to keep control of the government. Phineas, although with some misgivings at first, went along with his party. The conservatives were defeated.

Bonteen and his wife had been befriending a woman victimized by a fortune-hunting Bohemian Jew turned preacher and named, variously, Emilius or Mealyus. Mealyus hoped to get half his wife's fortune as a settlement, but Bonteen was working to prove a rumor that Mealyus was a bigamist. One night, after Phineas had been publicly insulted by Bonteen in their club, Bonteen was murdered. Phineas and Mealyus were both arrested, but the latter was released when he proved he could not have left his rooming-house that night.

Circumstances looked dark for Phineas. Laura, Madame Goesler, the Duchess of Omnium, Phineas' landlady, and the Chilterns were the only ones convinced of his innocence.

When Kennedy died, leaving everything to Laura, she dreamed that she might be happy with Phineas at last, even though she sensed at the same time that her hope was impossible.

Madame Goesler, on the trail of evidence to help Phineas by destroying Mealyus' alibi, went to Prague; she suspected Mealyus of having another rooming-house key made there during a recent trip. Then Mealyus' first wife was discovered and he was arrested for bigamy. At Phineas' trial the circumstantial evidence against him broke down when Madame Goesler wired from Prague that she had found proof of Mealyus' duplicate key. Laura, realizing that Madame Goesler had saved Phineas, hated her as a rival.

The late Duke of Omnium had willed a handsome fortune to Madame Goesler. Not needing the money, and afraid of suspicion that she had been the duke's mistress, she had refused to accept it. The duchess took up the cause of Maule and Adelaid, who were too poor to marry, it being out of the question to expect Maule to work. Adelaid had been a niece of the old duke, and the duchess persuaded Madame Goesler to let Adelaid have the fortune she herself would not accept. Adelaid and Maule were able to marry, and Mr. Maule, Sr., was so pleased with her fortune that he turned Maule Abbey over to them after all. Spooner, who had clung to his hope of marrying Adelaid, was so miserable that he gave up fox hunting for a time. Quintus Slide, who had consistently denounced Phineas and Laura in his newspaper, was sued for libel by Chiltern. Chiltern won the suit

and Slide was forced to leave the paper.

Phineas was the hero of the day—overwhelmingly reëlected in Tankerville, sought by the ladies, acclaimed everywhere—but the knowledge that he had been suspected by friends as well as by strangers made him miserable and bitter. Gradually, as his spirits improved, he was able to meet people and to resume his seat in the House. Also, he was offered the same office he had filled so well in his earlier parliamentary career. Although he was almost at the end of his funds and needed the position, the knowledge that the offer was made simply because he had not committed murder prompted him to refuse.

While visiting Laura at her request, he felt it only honorable to tell her that he planned to propose to Madame Goesler. At first Laura was violent in her denunciation of Madame Goesler, but she was at last calmed. Hers was the unhappiness of knowing that she had brought all her misery on herself by marrying one man while loving another. Now deeply in love with Madame Goesler, Phineas proposed marriage and was joyfully accepted. No longer a poor man, Phineas would be able to continue his career in Parliament without being the slave of his party.

THE PHOENICIAN WOMEN

Type of work: Drama
Author: Euripides (c. 485-c. 406 B.C.)
Type of plot: Classical tragedy
Time of plot: Time of the War of the Seven against Thebes
Locale: Thebes
First presented: c. 410 B.C.

Principal characters:
JOCASTA, Oedipus' wife
ANTIGONE, Oedipus' daughter
POLYNICES, Oedipus' exiled son
ETEOCLES, brother of Polynices and King of Thebes
CREON, Jocasta's brother
MENOECEUS, Creon's son
TIRESIAS, the blind prophet
OEDIPUS, deposed King of Thebes
CHORUS OF PHOENICIAN MAIDENS

Critique:

The Phoenician Women (Phoenissae) probably incorporates more lines of dramatic development and is more packed with incident than any other Greek play, possibly because the text has been supplemented by one or more later hands. It may be said that Aeschylus The Seven against Thebes and the entire Oedipus cycle of Sophocles are embodied in it, although Euripides does not underscore the religious or moral significance of the action. In presenting the entire history of the line of Cadmus, Euripides has made a play that is polyproposon, in which none of the characters (no less than eleven, not counting the chorus) can be said to be the tragic hero or the focus of attention. Nevertheless, the play is extremely well constructed, with each action leading directly to the next, and uniformly serious throughout, with no deviations into satire or comedy.

The Story:

Before the royal palace of Thebes, Jocasta, the mother of King Eteocles, prayed to the sun god for aid in reconciling her two sons and avoiding fratricidal war over the kingdom of Thebes. In her supplication she recalled that her family had already suffered unbearable horrors when her husband Oedipus plucked out his eyes upon discovering that in marrying her he had married his own mother and had conceived two sons

and two daughters by her. At first the sons had confined their father in the palace in order to hide the family shame and had decided to rule the kingdom between them in alternate years. However, Eteocles had refused to yield the throne to Polynices, who, after marrying the daughter of Adrastus, King of Argos, had raised a host from seven city-states ᵻnd was already at the gates of Thebes to win his rightful place by force of arms.

Antigone, viewing the besieging armies from the palace tower, recognized the justice of Polynices' claim but prayed that Thebes would never fall. In desperate fear, Jocasta cut off her hair and dressed in mourning. Then. in the hope that the war could be averted, she arranged a meeting under a truce between her two sons. Eteocles was willing to receive Polynices back in Thebes, but not as an equal to share the throne; Polynices, on the other hand, unable to endure exile and equally unable to accept such ignoble terms, remained bent on war.

Eteocles then sent for his uncle Creon to work out battle strategy. The two, agreeing that the situation was grave, finally decided not to attempt any counterattack with their vastly outnumbered troops but to post men at the seven gates in defensive action. Creon also sent his son Menoeceus to summon the prophet Tiresias for further advice. The blind prophet, after warning Creon that the means for saving Thebes would be one he would be unwilling to accept, announced that Menoeceus must be sacrificed. Horror-stricken Creon refused and urged his son to flee at once. Menoeceus pretended to agree, but shortly after his departure a messenger hurried to Creon with the news that his son had plunged a sword into his own throat at the very moment that the Argive hosts launched their first fruitless assault against the gates of the city.

Jocasta, upon hearing that her two sons had decided to determine the fate of Thebes by a single combat apart from their armies, rushed off with Antigone to the battlefield to stop them if she could. As she departed, Creon entered carrying the corpse of his dead son and seeking Jocasta's aid in the funeral preparations. But a second messenger brought him word that Jocasta had gone outside the walls of Thebes and had found her two sons dying, each the other's victim. Eteocles, unable to speak, bade his mother farewell with his eyes, and Polynices with his dying breath begged his mother to bury him in Theban soil. Then the grief-stricken Jocasta seized a sword and thrust it through her throat. Upon that stroke the Theban warriors fell upon the surprised Argives and drove them from the field. Menoeceus' sacrifice had not been in vain.

Antigone, returning with servants bearing the bodies of her mother and her two brothers, was met by blind King Oedipus, who had emerged from his confinement in the palace and who began to express his grief in groans and lamentations. Creon, resolutely taking over the rule bequeathed to him by Eteocles, commanded him to cease and to prepare for exile. Determined to restore order in the tragic city, Creon was compelled to put aside personal feelings in submitting to the prophecies of Tiresias. Antigone, the new king insisted, must prepare to marry his son Haemon; furthermore, while the body of Eteocles was to be given burial fit for a king, Polynices' corpse must be left to rot, a prey to birds, as a warning to all who might contemplate taking up arms against the city. Oedipus, refusing to beg from Creon, prepared to leave at once, but Antigone flouted his commands. Rather than marry Haemon, she was determined to accompany her father into exile and to bury the body of Polynices with proper religious rites. As father and daughter set out from Thebes, Oedipus lamented the sad history of his life but courageously submitted to the fate that the gods had decreed for him.

PHORMIO

Type of work: Drama
Author: Terence (Publius Terentius Afer, c. 190-159 B.C.)
Type of plot: Comedy of intrigue
Time of plot: Second century B.C.
Locale: Athens
First presented: 161 B.C.

Principal characters:
CHREMES, a rich gentleman of Athens
DEMIPHO, Chremes' rather miserly brother
ANTIPHO, Demipho's son
PHAEDRIA, Chremes' son
GETA, a slave
PHORMIO, a parasite
NAUSISTRATA, Chremes' wife

Critique:

Phormio, a tricky parasite and one of the most fascinating rogues in all literature, is the chief character in this play by Terence. It is he who engineers all the solutions to the problems involved in the comedy and sees to it that each young man is permitted to have the woman of his choice. Phormio's plotting, acting as he does on behalf of two young men, involves a double plot, with many attending complexities. But complex as the plot becomes, especially when a mistaken identity theme is also introduced, the play is not confusing. As in other dramas by Terence, there are no digressions; each part of the play is closely knit into the structure and furthers the development of both plots. In addition, the comedy is even more restrained than that of earlier comedies by Terence. Never slapstick, the humor of this play should be sufficient to please even the most sophisticated modern audiences.

The Story:

Demipho and Chremes, two wealthy Athenian brothers, left the city on journeys and entrusted the welfare of their two sons to Geta, a slave belonging to Demipho. For a time Antipho and Phaedria, two young men of exemplary habits, gave the slave little trouble. When both fell in love, however, before their fathers returned, Geta's troubles began. His sympathy for Antipho and Phaedria caused him to help both of them in their amours, but he realized only too well that both fathers would be angry when they learned what had happened.

Phaedria, the son of Chremes, had fallen in love with a lovely young harp player owned by a trader named Dorio, who refused to part with the girl for less than thirty minae. Unable to raise the money, Phaedria was at his wits' end. His cousin Antipho had fallen in love with a young Athenian girl of a good but penniless family.

Antipho had already married the girl, even though he knew that his father, who was something of a miser, would be furious to learn that his son had married a girl who brought no dower. Geta, in an effort to smooth out the problem, had contacted a parasite named Phormio. Phormio, a lawyer, had brought suit against Antipho under an Athenian law that made it mandatory for an unprovided-for girl to be married to her nearest relative. Antipho did not contest the suit, and so he had the excuse that he had been forced by the court to marry the young woman.

Shortly after the wedding, the two older men returned. As soon as he learned what had happened, Demipho ordered his son to give up his wife. Antipho and Geta again called upon Phormio for assistance. Phormio warned the old man that he would be unable to avoid keeping the girl, even though Demipho claimed that the girl was not actually a relative. Phormio

2853

contended that the girl was a relative, the daughter of Demipho's kinsman, Stilpo, who had lived in Lemnos. Demipho said he never had a relative by that name.

In the meantime Phaedria tried desperately to raise the thirty minae that would purchase his beloved harpist from Dorio. Dorio had given him three days to find the money. Then Phaedria learned from a slave that a sea captain, about to sail, wanted to purchase the girl and that Dorio, anxious to make a sale, had promised to sell the girl to him. Phaedria appealed to Dorio, but with no success. Dorio would promise only to hold off the sale of the slave girl until the following morning.

After seeing Phormio, Demipho went to his brother Chremes and talked over the situation with him. They finally agreed that the only answer to the problem of Antipho's wife was to send her away with a sum of money. Chremes agreed to have his wife, Nausistrata, tell the girl that she was to be separated from her husband. While they were planning, Geta went to Phormio once again.

Phormio hatched out a plan to satisfy everyone and make some money for himself. He offered to marry Antipho's cast-off wife, if he were given a large sum of money. With part of that money he expected to have a good time, and with the rest, which he was to turn over to Phaedria, that young man was to purchase his beloved harpist. Geta presented the first part of Phormio's plan to the brothers, who readily acquiesced, even though Demipho hated to see Phormio receive payment for marrying the girl.

After the arrangements had been made, Chremes was horrified to learn that the girl he was advising his brother to cast off was his own daughter by a second wife whom he had married in Lemnos. Even worse was the fact that his Athenian wife, Nausistrata, did not know of the other marriage. Chremes took his brother into his confidence and told him what had happened. They both agreed to let the marriage stand, and Chremes offered to add a dower to the girl.

The only difficulty, as the old men saw it, was how to redeem their money from Phormio, who no longer needed to marry the girl. Phormio, having given part of the money to Phaedria, was unwilling to return that part of the money which was to have been his for his trouble.

While the old men were hunting for Phormio, he was in conversation with Antipho. Geta went to them with the news that Antipho's uncle was also his father-in-law and that Antipho's troubles were at an end. Asked where he had learned this fact, Geta replied that he had overheard a conversation between Chremes and a servant. The information made both Antipho and Phormio happy, Antipho because he would be able to keep his wife, Phormio because he had information to use in keeping the money he had received from Chremes and Demipho.

When Chremes and Demipho confronted Phormio, he refused to give back the money, and in answer to their threats he replied that if they tried to bring a suit against him he would tell Nausistrata about Chremes' affair in Lemnos and the true identity of Antipho's wife. During the argument the brothers laid hands on Phormio. Phormio, infuriated by their treatment of him, called out to Nausistrata. When she came out of the house, Phormio told her about Chremes' other wife. She was somewhat mollified, however, when she realized that the other woman was dead and that she would have something to hold over her husband's head.

Seeing that Nausistrata had been converted to his side, Phormio told them also that he had given thirty minae to Phaedria so that he might purchase the harpist from Dorio. Chremes began to protest, but Nausistrata silenced him with the statement that it was no worse for the son to have such a mistress than for the father to have two wives. Nausistrata, pleased at the turn events had taken—for her son had his beloved and her rival was dead—asked Phormio if there were anything she could do for him. Fun-loving Phormio said that he would be vastly pleased, and her husband much exasperated, if she would ask the lawyer to dinner. Nausistrata, proud of her newly-found power over her husband, agreed.

THE PHYSICAL BASIS OF LIFE

Type of work: Essay in scientific philosophy
Author: Thomas Henry Huxley (1825-1895)
First published: Written in 1868; published in *Method and Results,* 1896

"The Physical Basis of Life," together with the other essays that compose Huxley's *Method and Results,* reveals a nineteenth-century man of science attempting to go beyond the limits prescribed by authoritarian scientists and churchmen and making an effort to bring the clarity of philosophy to the interpretation and expression of the results of empirical observation. This particular essay is among Huxley's most famous. Its subject matter is protoplasm, and its claim is that all life has as its physical basis protoplasmic substance.

Such a claim, which to twentieth-century man seems so trivial as not to be worth making, was revolutionary in an age which demanded that all studies of man find him unique, possessed of a life-giving principle ·by reference to which he could be distinguished from all those animals that were merely animals. Huxley realized that his contention would be novel, even shocking, to many of his contemporaries. It was bad enough to suggest that life is not independent of matter but has a physical basis; it was even worse to insist that there is but one physical basis of life for all living things. To reduce man to the material and to equate him with the beast—that was intolerable even to those who respected science.

In his essay Huxley was careful to state that even though all life has protoplasm as its physical basis, it by no means follows that materialism—the philosophical theory that everything is nothing but matter—is true; in fact, he argued that materialism involved "grave philosophical error."

Huxley's objections to a strict materialism are made in the spirit of Hume's philosophy. Referring to Hume as "the most acute thinker of the eighteenth century," Huxley argues that we mean by the terms "matter" and "spirit" either

something that can be explained by reference to matters of our scientific experience, or else names for unknown, even imaginary, causes. He joins Hume in objecting to the idea that it makes sense to talk about a necessity that is anything more than the observed order of events. "Fact I know; and Law I know," wrote Huxley, "but what is this Necessity, save an empty shadow of my own mind's throwing?" Since both materialism and spiritualism (or idealism) depend on unfathomable senses of the terms "matter," "spirit," and "necessity," Huxley concluded that such unscientific philosophies were unsatisfactory.

In opposition to metaphysical philosophies, Huxley proposed what he called the "New Philosophy," the attempt to limit philosophical thought and inquiry to matters that could be verified experimentally or explained by reference to matters of experience. In doing this he anticipated the most significant direction of twentieth-century philosophy, the logical empiricist movement as amended by pragmatism and linguistic analysis.

Huxley made a plea for limiting the consideration of problems to those matters about which something can be known. Agreeing with Hume in the rejection of theology and metaphysics, he argued that progress in scientific philosophy is possible on the basis of two assumptions: "the first, that the order of Nature is ascertainable by our faculties to an extent which is practically unlimited; the second, that our volition counts for something as a condition of the course of events." In a footnote Huxley explained that it would be more accurate to say that not volition but "the physical state of which volition is the expression" may condition the course of events.

He then went on to point out the practical advantages, from the scientific

2856

point of view, that resulted from using the language of materialism. The materialistic terminology allowed the scientist to relate thought and life to experienceable phenomena and permitted a kind of expression which facilitated the human control of events. The language of those who held that all is spirit and idea—the spiritualists—was barren and confusing, according to Huxley.

Nevertheless, despite the practical advantages of the terminology of materialism, it would be a mistake, Huxley wrote, to slide into metaphysical materialism.

The reader who asks what Huxley was, if he was neither a materialist nor an idealist, makes the mistake of supposing that Huxley's rejection of two opposing metaphysical positions is somehow a sign of his having adopted a third. The truth is that Huxley had no sympathy for metaphysics. He wanted to use an empirically meaningful language to talk about events that came within the scope of scientific inquiry; hence he had no metaphysics.

In arguing that protoplasm is the physical basis of life, Huxley was making a much more radical claim than the theory that without protoplasm there is no life. He argued that the matter of life is composed of ordinary matter; life is not an indestructible and unchangeable substance. Furthermore, the vital properties of protoplasm are the result of molecular changes. He concluded that his thoughts, and the thoughts of the audience, were the expression of molecular changes in protoplasm.

In his analysis Huxley found a unity in three respects among all living organisms: "a unity of power or faculty, a unity of form, and a unity of substantial composition." The faculty which all living matter has in common is contractility; as to form, protoplasm is usually a nucleated mass, and it is composed of carbon, hydrogen, oxygen, and nitrogen. The line between plants and animals is not at all precise—there are borderline cases—but both forms of living matter are alike in the respects mentioned.

The essays collected under the title *Method and Results,* also to be found in Huxley's *Collected Essays* (1898), are intended to outline "the indispensable conditions of scientific assent" as defined by Descartes in his *Discourse on Method,* and to show the results of applying the method to various problems. In an essay written in 1870 concerning Descartes' method, Huxley praised Descartes as the thinker from whose works the philosophy and science of the modern world stem. Huxley agreed with Descartes in valuing doubt as the first critical operation in science and philosophy, as the beginning of what Goethe called "the active scepticism whose whole aim is to conquer itself." Although he found fault with Descartes' acceptance of "I think; therefore, I am" as an indubitable truth, he credited the Frenchman with having made a reconciliation of physics and metaphysics possible. According to Huxley, Descartes' analysis suggests what physics must admit: that "all the phaenomena of Nature are, in their ultimate analysis, known to us only as facts of consciousness. . . ." But metaphysics must admit, Huxley adds, that the facts of consciousness make sense, practically speaking, only as interpreted by physics. The ideas in this essay are very similar to those which William James was later (1906-1907) to present as the basis of pragmatism in his lectures at Columbia University.

Devotion to skepticism and to the benefits of natural science was shown and defended by Huxley in his essay "On the Advisableness of Improving Natural Knowledge" (1866). The essay is a defense of the advantage of finding out about the world by studying the world itself, a sensible procedure from the twentieth-century point of view. But the tentative, practical, empirical character of natural science was believed by many critics of Huxley to be antipathetic to religion. Huxley himself argued that science need not conflict with religion, although it could not tolerate meaningless metaphysics and theology. Huxley concluded that science must refuse to acknowledge authority; for the scientist "scepticism is the highest of duties; blind faith the one unpardonable sin." Justification for the scientist is not by faith, but by verification.

These ideas led Huxley to argue bitterly against churchmen who proclaimed that belief in God or in the particular dogmas of a church was the duty of every man. The duty of a man, according to Huxley, is to face the facts, to test his ideas by reference to the course of natural events, and to know the limits of his inquiry. It cannot be his duty, then, to believe what he has no reason to believe.

Almost a century after Huxley wrote "The Physical Basis of Life," it seems clear that the value of the essay results from the clear and temperate defense of scientific method which it contains. Resisting the impulse to deify science, Huxley indicated its method and results; and he rested secure in the conviction that the progress of science would justify his faith. There is every reason to suppose that from Huxley's point of view, that of a man concerned with the practical search for knowledge, he was right in his belief.

PICKWICK PAPERS

Type of work: Novel
Author: Charles Dickens (1812-1870)
Type of plot: Comic romance
Time of plot: Nineteenth century
Locale: England
First published: 1836-1837

Principal characters:
MR. PICKWICK, founder of the Pickwick Club
MR. WINKLE,
MR. SNODGRASS, and
MR. TUPMAN, members of the club
MR. WARDLE, owner of Manor Farm
RACHAEL WARDLE, his sister
EMILY WARDLE, his daughter
MRS. BARDELL, Mr. Pickwick's housekeeper
MR. PERKER, a lawyer
SAM WELLER, Mr. Pickwick's servant
ARABELLA ALLEN, in love with Mr. Winkle
MR. ALFRED JINGLE, a rascal

Critique:

Mr. Pickwick, the lovable, generous old gentleman of Dickens' novel, is one of the best-known characters of fiction. Mr. Pickwick benignly reigns over all activities of the Pickwick Club, satisfied, under every circumstance, that he has helped his fellow creatures by his well-meaning efforts. The height of this Dickensian comedy, however, lies in Sam Weller and his father. Sam's imperturbable presence of mind and his ready wit are indispensable to the Pickwickians. The novel has importance beyond humorous incident and characterization. It is the first novel of a literary movement to present the life and manners of lower and middle-class life.

The Story:

Samuel Pickwick, Esquire, was the founder and perpetual president of the justly famous Pickwick Club. To extend his own researches into the quaint and curious phenomena of life, he suggested that he and three other Pickwickians should make journeys to places remote from London and report on their findings to the stay-at-home members of the club. The first destination decided upon was Rochester. As Mr. Pickwick, Mr. Tracy Tupman, Mr. Nathaniel Winkle, and

Mr. Augustus Snodgrass went to their coach, they were waylaid by a rough gang of cab drivers. Fortunately the men were rescued by a stranger who was poorly dressed but of a magnificently friendly nature. The stranger, who introduced himself as Alfred Jingle, appeared to be going to Rochester also, and the party mounted the coach together.

After they had arrived at their destination, Mr. Tupman's curiosity was aroused when Mr. Jingle told him that there was to be a ball at the inn that very evening and that many lovely young ladies would be present. Because his luggage had gone astray, said Mr. Jingle, he had no evening clothes and so it would be impossible for him to attend the affair. This was a regrettable circumstance because he had hoped to introduce Mr. Tupman to the many young ladies of wealth and fashion who would be present. Eager to meet these young ladies, Mr. Tupman borrowed Mr. Winkle's suit for the stranger. At the ball Mr. Jingle observed a doctor in faithful attendance upon a middle-aged lady. Attracting her attention, he danced with her, much to the anger of the doctor. Introducing himself as Dr. Slammer, the angry gentleman challenged Mr. Jingle to a duel.

The next morning a servant, identifying Mr. Winkle from the description given of the suit the stranger had worn, told Mr. Winkle that an insolent drunken man had insulted Dr. Slammer the previous evening and that the doctor was awaiting his appearance to fight a duel. Mr. Winkle had been drunk the night before, and he decided he was being called out because he had conducted himself in an unseemly manner which he could no longer remember. With Mr. Snodgrass as his second, Mr. Winkle tremblingly approached the battlefield. Much to his relief, Dr. Slammer roared that he was the wrong man. After much misunderstanding, the situation was satisfactorily explained and no blood was shed.

During the afternoon the travelers attended a parade, where they met Mr. Wardle in a coach with his two daughters and his sister, Miss Rachael Wardle, a plump old maid. Mr. Tupman, being quite taken with the elder Miss Wardle, accepted for his friends Mr. Wardle's invitation to visit his estate, Manor Farm. The next day the four Pickwickians departed for the farm, which was a distance of about ten miles from the inn where they were staying. Having difficulties with their horses, they arrived at Manor Farm in a disheveled state, but they were soon washed and mended under the kind assistance of Mr. Wardle's daughters. In the evening they played a hearty game of whist, and Mr. Tupman squeezed Miss Wardle's hand under the table.

The next day Mr. Wardle took his guests rook hunting. Mr. Winkle, who would not admit himself unable to cope with any situation, was given the gun to try his skill. He proved it by accidentally shooting Mr. Tupman in the arm. Miss Wardle offered her aid to the stricken man. Observing that their friend was in good hands, the others went off to a neighboring town to watch the cricket matches. There Mr. Pickwick unexpectedly encountered Mr. Jingle, and Mr. Wardle invited the fellow to return to Manor Farm with his party.

Convinced that Miss Wardle had a great deal of money, Mr. Jingle misrepresented Mr. Tupman's intentions to Miss Wardle and persuaded the spinster to elope with him. Mr. Wardle and Mr. Pickwick pursued the couple to London. There, with the assistance of Mr. Wardle's lawyer, Mr. Perker, they went from one inn to another in an attempt to find the elopers. Finally, through a sharp-featured young man cleaning boots in the yard of the White Hart Inn, they were able to identify Mr. Jingle. They indignantly confronted him as he was displaying a marriage license. After a heated argument, Mr. Jingle resigned his matrimonial designs for the sum of one hundred and twenty pounds. Miss Wardle went tearfully back to Manor Farm. The Pickwickians returned to London, where Mr. Pickwick engaged as his servant Sam Weller, the sharp, shrewd young bootblack of the White Hart Inn.

Mr. Pickwick was destined to meet the villainous Mr. Jingle soon again. A Mrs. Leo Hunter invited the learned man and his friends to a party. There Mr. Pickwick spied Mr. Jingle, who, upon seeing his former acquaintance, disappeared into the crowd. Mrs. Hunter told Mr. Pickwick that Mr. Jingle lived at Bury St. Edmonds. Mr. Pickwick set out in pursuit in company with his servant, Sam Weller, for the old gentleman was determined to deter the scoundrel from any fresh deceptions he might be planning. At the inn where Mr. Jingle was reported to be staying, Mr. Pickwick learned that the rascal was planning to elope with a rich young lady who stayed at a boarding-school nearby. Mr. Pickwick fell in with the suggestion that in order to rescue the young lady he should hide in the garden from which Mr. Jingle was planning to steal her. When Mr. Pickwick sneaked into the garden, he found nothing of a suspicious nature; in short, he had been deceived, and the blackguard had escaped.

Mr. Pickwick had for housekeeper Mrs. Bardell, a widow. When he was about to hire Sam Weller, Mr. Pickwick had spoken to her in such a manner that she had mistaken his words for a proposal of marriage. One day Mr. Pickwick was resting in his rooms when he received notice from the legal firm of Dodgson and Fogg that Mrs. Bardell was suing him for breach of promise. The summons was distressing, but first Mr. Pickwick had more important business to occupy his time. After securing the services of Mr. Perker to defend him, he went to Ipswich upon learning that Mr. Jingle had been seen in that vicinity. The trip to Ipswich was successful. The Pickwickians were able to catch Mr. Jingle in his latest scheme of deception and to expose him before he had carried out his plot.

At the trial for the breach of promise suit brought by Mrs. Bardell, lawyers Dodgson and Fogg argued so eloquently against Mr. Pickwick that the jury fined him seven hundred and fifty pounds. When the trial was over, Mr. Pickwick told Dodgson and Fogg that even if they put him in prison he would never pay one cent of the damages, since he knew as well as they that there had been no true grounds for suit.

The Pickwickians shortly afterward went to Bath, where fresh adventures awaited Mr. Pickwick and his friends. On that occasion Mr. Winkle's weakness for the fair sex involved them in difficulties. In Bath the Pickwickians met two young medical students, Mr. Allen and Mr. Bob Sawyer. Mr. Allen hoped to marry his sister, Arabella, to his friend, Mr. Sawyer, but Miss Allen professed extreme dislike for her brother's choice. When Mr. Winkle learned that Arabella had refused Mr. Sawyer because another had won her heart, he felt that he must be the fortunate man because she had displayed an interest in him when they had met earlier at Manor Farm. Kindly Mr. Pickwick arranged to have Mr. Winkle meet Arabella in a garden, where the distraught lover could plead his suit.

Mr. Pickwick's plans to further his friend's romance were interrupted, however, by a subpoena delivered because he had refused to pay money to Mrs. Bardell. Still stubbornly refusing to pay the damages, Mr. Pickwick found himself returned to London and lodged in Fleet Street prison. With the help of Sam Weller, Mr. Pickwick arranged his prison quarters as comfortably as possible and remained deaf to the entreaties of Sam Weller or Mr. Perker, who thought that he should pay his debt and regain his freedom. Dodgson and Fogg proved to be of lower caliber than even Mr. Pickwick had suspected. They had taken Mrs. Bardell's case without fee, gambling on Mr. Pickwick's payment to cover the costs of the case. When they saw no payment forthcoming, they had Mrs. Bardell arrested also and sent to the Fleet Street prison.

While Mr. Pickwick was trying to decide what to do, Mr. Winkle with his new wife, Arabella, came to the prison and asked Mr. Pickwick to pay his debts so that he could visit Mr. Allen with the news of Mr. Winkle's marriage to Arabella. Arabella herself felt that Mr. Pickwick was the only person who could arrange a proper reconcilliation between her brother and her new husband. Kindness prevailed; Mr. Pickwick paid the damages to Mrs. Bardell so that he would be free to help his friends in distress.

Winning Mr. Allen's approval of the match was not difficult for Mr. Pickwick, but when he approached the elder Mr. Winkle, the bridegroom's father objected to the marriage and threatened to cut off his son without a cent. To add to Mr. Pickwick's problems, Mr. Wardle came to London to tell him that his daughter Emily was in love with Mr. Snodgrass and to ask Mr. Pickwick's advice. Mr. Wardle had brought Emily to London with him.

The entire party came together in Arabella's apartment. All misunderstandings happily ended for the two lovers, and a jolly party followed. The elder Mr.

Winkle paid a call on his new daughter-in-law. Upon seeing what a charming and lovely girl she was, he relented his decision to disinherit his son, and the family was reconciled.

After Mr. Snodgrass had married Emily Wardle, Mr. Pickwick dissolved the Pickwick Club and retired to a home in the country, with his faithful servant, Sam Weller. Several times Mr. Pickwick was called upon to be a godfather to little Winkles and Snodgrasses, but for the most part he led a quiet life, respected by his neighbors and loved by all his friends.

THE PICTURE OF DORIAN GRAY

Type of work: Novel
Author: Oscar Wilde (1856-1900)
Type of plot: Fantasy
Time of plot: Late nineteenth century
Locale: England
First published: 1891

Principal characters:
DORIAN GRAY, a Faustian young man
LORD HENRY WOTTON, his tempter
BASIL HALLWARD, an artist
SIBYL VANE, an actress
JAMES VANE, her brother

Critique:

The Picture of Dorian Gray is definitely a period piece, but the central idea of the story is so typical of its author and the elements of the plot are so carefully worked out that the novel is sure to attract readers for many years to come. Wilde has written that there is no such thing as a moral or unmoral book, that a book can be judged only as it is well written or badly written. The Picture of Dorian Gray should be judged with this statement in mind.

The Story:

One day, in his London studio, Basil Hallward was putting a few last finishing touches on a portrait of his handsome young friend, Dorian Gray. Lord Henry Wotton, a caller, indolently watched the painter at work. In reply to his friend's admiration for the painting, the artist explained that Dorian was his ideal of youth. For this reason he asked Lord Henry never to meet Dorian because the older man's influence on the boy would be absolute and evil.

While they were talking, Dorian himself came to the studio, and he and Lord Henry met, much against Hallward's wishes. Half seriously, half jokingly, Sir Henry began to exert his influence on Dorian. Hallward signed the portrait and announced it was finished. When Lord Henry offered to buy the picture, the painter said it was not his property, that it belonged to Dorian, to whom he was

presenting it. Looking at his portrait, after listening to Lord Henry's witty conversation, Dorian grew sad. He would become old and wrinkled, he said, while the picture would remain the same. He wished, instead, that the portrait might grow old while he remained forever young. He said he would give his soul to keep his youth.

Dorian and Lord Henry became close friends. One of the gifts Lord Henry gave the boy was a book about a young man who attempted to realize in his brief lifetime all the passions of man's history. Dorian made the book a pattern for his own life, and the first lesson from its pages was the lesson of love. In a third-rate theater he saw Sibyl Vane, a young actress who played the role of Juliet with such sincerity and charm that he fell in love with her on the spot. After he had met her, Dorian dreamed of taking her away from the cheap theatrical troupe and making her a great actress who would thrill the world. One night he took Lord Henry to watch her performance. That night Sibyl was listless and wooden, so uninspired in her acting that the audience hissed her. When Dorian went to her dressing-room after the final curtain, she explained that before meeting him she had thought acting her only reality. Now, she said, Dorian's love had taught her what reality actually was, and she could no longer act. Dorian coldly and cruelly told her she had killed his love and he

THE PICTURE OF DORIAN GRAY by Oscar Wilde. Published by The Viking Press, Inc.

never intended to see her again.

In the meantime, Hallward had delivered the painting to Dorian. When the young man returned to his home after the theater that night he saw that the appearance of his portrait had changed. There was a new, faint line of cruelty about the mouth. Looking at his own features in a mirror, he found no such line on his own lips. His wish had evidently been granted. He would remain young and untouched — the portrait would take on an appearance of experience and age.

Disturbed, he resolved to reform, to see no more of Lord Henry, to ask Sibyl Vane's forgiveness and marry her. Accordingly, he wrote her a passionate letter declaring his love. Before he could post the letter, however, Lord Henry visited him the next morning, bringing the news that Sibyl had killed herself in her dressing-room the night before.

After his friend had gone, forgetting all his good resolutions Dorian decided on a life of sensation and pleasure. The portrait only was to bear the burden of his shame. That night he attended the opera with Lord Henry. The next day, when Basil Hallward attempted to reason with him over scandalous reports beginning to circulate, Dorian refused to show any emotion over Sibyl's suicide. His part in her tragic story would never be revealed, for she had known him only as Prince Charming. Before he left, Hallward asked to see his painting. Dorian refused to show it. In sudden rage, he shouted that he never wished to see Hallward again. Later he hung the portrait in an old schoolroom upstairs, locked the door, and put the key where only he could find it.

London continued to gossip about the friendship of Lord Henry and Dorian Gray. The young man was suspected of strange vices, and gentlemen walked out of their club rooms when he entered them. He was invited to fewer balls and parties at country houses. Many of his former friends refused to recognize him when they met. It was reported he had been seen in low dives with drunken sailors and thieves. Meanwhile Dorian's features did not change; only the portrait reflected his life of crime and debauchery. For Dorian's life, like that of the hero in the book Lord Henry had given him, became a frenzied quest for fresh experiences and new sensations. In turn, he became interested in religious rituals, perfumes, music, jewels. He frequented opium dens. He had sordid affairs with women. His features in the portrait became the terrible record of his life.

On the eve of Dorian's thirty-eighth birthday, Basil Hallward visited him again. Though the two had been estranged for years, Hallward came in a last attempt to persuade Dorian to change his dissolute ways. He was still unable to believe many of the stories he had heard about Dorian. With a bitter laugh, Dorian said that Hallward should see what he had truly become. He took Hallward to the schoolroom and unveiled the portrait. The artist was horrified, for only by signature could he identify his own handiwork. In anger that he had betrayed his true self to his former friend, Dorian seized a knife which lay nearby and stabbed Hallward in the neck and back.

Dorian relocked the door and went down to the drawing-room. Because Hallward had intended to leave for Paris that night, Dorian knew the painter would not be missed for some time. Removal of the body, he decided, was not enough. He wanted it completely destroyed. Suddenly he thought of Alan Campbell, a young chemist who had once been his intimate. By threatening the young scientist with exposure for some secret crime, Dorian forced Campbell to destroy the body with fire and chemicals. After that night, the hands of the portrait were smeared with blood.

Late one night, commonly dressed, Dorian visited an opium den. As he was leaving the place, a drunken woman addressed him as Prince Charming. A sailor followed him out. The sailor was James Vane, Sibyl's brother, who had sworn revenge on his sister's betrayer. The sailor would have killed Dorian but for the fact that he looked so young. Sibyl had committed suicide eighteen years before, and Dorian seemed no more than twenty years old. When Vane, convinced that Dorian could not have known his sister, returned to the den, the woman told him that Dorian Gray had ruined her many years before, and that he had not changed in appearance since then.

Some time later, at his country home, Dorian saw James Vane watching him outside a window. During a hunt on the estate Vane was accidentally shot and killed. In the meantime, Alan Campbell had committed suicide under strange circumstances, and Basil Hallward's disappearance was being investigated.

Back in London, Dorian, having decided to destroy the picture which stood as an awful record of his guilt, went to the old schoolroom. The portrait now had an appearance of cunning and triumph. Using the knife with which he had murdered Basil Hallward, Dorian stabbed the frightful portrait. The servants in the house heard a horrible cry of agony. When they forced open the locked door of the room, they found, hanging on the wall, a fine portrait of their master as he had always looked. On the floor was a dead body, withered, wrinkled, in evening dress, with a knife in its breast. Only by his jewelry did they recognize Dorian Gray, who, in his desperate attempt to kill his conscience, had killed himself.

PIERRE

Type of work: Novel
Author: Herman Melville (1819-1891)
Type of plot: Philosophical tragedy
Time of plot: Early nineteenth century
Locale: New York
First published: 1852

Principal characters:
PIERRE GLENDINNING, a wealthy, cultivated young man
MRS. GLENDINNING, his mother
LUCY TARTAN, his fiancée
ISABEL, his illegitimate half-sister
GLEN STANLY, his cousin
DELLY ULVER, a farm girl

Critique:

Pierre, Or, The Ambiguities, the seventh novel published by Herman Melville, is probably the least read of his works because of obscure and at times confused symbolism which repels the reader who prefers less philosophical and tortuous fiction. Scholars have declared that Pierre was an experiment on Melville's part, an attempt to turn away from the materials of his earlier volumes: the sea, the romantic islands of the Pacific, and man's struggles against fate. Yet Melville, as he had in his earlier volumes, used materials from his own experience. Many of the incidents and much of the background of this novel reflect Melville's life and experiences of members of his family. Those incidents and that background are woven together with fiction, however, as the author had woven fact and fiction in his greatest novel, Moby Dick. This novel, like Moby Dick, was very probably an attempt to prove himself something more than the fabulous author of Typee, a man who had lived among the cannibals.

The Story:

Pierre Glendinning was a young man who lived amid luxury and ease, the heir to vast estates that formed the larger portion of two counties in New York State. His time was taken up with outdoor recreation, reading, and the courting of beautiful and well-to-do Lucy Tartan, a girl of whom Pierre's mother approved completely. Mrs. Glendinning,

who was jealous of her influence over her son, saw nothing to fear in quiet, unaggressive Lucy Tartan.

One evening, however, a strange incident occurred when Mrs. Glendinning and Pierre visited a sewing bee in a nearby home. One of the girls who was there shrieked and fainted when she saw Pierre. The incident bothered the young man, but he was totally unprepared for a note which he received from the girl a short time later. In the note she requested that Pierre visit her in the evening at the farm where she was employed. Pierre, disturbed by the mystery involved, went to the farm and discovered that the girl, Isabel, was his half-sister, the illegitimate child of his father and a young Frenchwoman. Pierre resolved immediately to acknowledge Isabel as his sister, but the question of how to accomplish the acknowledgment was a weighty one.

At first Pierre intended to tell his mother of his discovery, but his mother's attitude toward Delly Ulver, a farm girl who had been born an illegitimate child, warned Pierre that he could expect no sympathetic understanding from Mrs. Glendinning. He next thought of approaching his minister for help with his problem, but the discovery that the minister followed his mother's opinion caused Pierre to fall back on his own thinking. He realized also that his mother could not bear to have it proved that her husband had been an adulterer, nor could he bring himself to dishonor his father's name. The only road which seemed open to Pierre was to acknowledge Isabel as his wife rather than his sister.

When Pierre told his mother that he had been married secretly, she ordered him to leave the house immediately. Disowned and cast forth from his mother's affections, he also told Lucy Tartan that he had married another girl. His story threw Lucy into an almost fatal illness.

Having been disowned by his family, Pierre took Isabel from her home at the farm and went to New York City. They were accompanied by Delly Ulver, whom Pierre had decided to help. Although he had announced that he and Isabel had been married, Pierre and his half-sister had entered into no such union; the announcement was only a means to permit them to live together. In New York City they found life barren and difficult, for Pierre had only a small supply of money. He had hoped to find a haven for himself and the two girls with his wealthy cousin, Glen Stanly, but the cousin refused to recognize Pierre and had him thrown out of his home.

Forced to rely upon his own resources, Pierre resolved to become an author. He had, he thought, acquired quite a reputation by publishing some short poems and some essays in various periodicals. He also thought he had great talent, sufficient, at least, to enable him to write a philosophical work. After much difficulty he managed to find a publisher who agreed to take his unwritten novel and to advance him enough money to live. For months Pierre, struggling to write his great work, lived in three miserable, unheated rooms in a vast tenement, along with Isabel and Delly Ulver, who acted in the capacity of servant to them both.

One day word came to Pierre that his mother had died just a few weeks after he had left for New York City; her heir was Pierre's cousin, Glen Stanly. The news made Pierre very bitter, particularly when he discovered that his cousin was a suitor for the hand of Lucy Tartan, whom Pierre still loved dearly. Despite the feeling of utter helplessness which the news created in his mind, Pierre kept at work upon his book. Because he was unable to keep Isabel from realizing that she was not alone in his affections, the girl became jealous and disliked the fact that another woman could claim his attentions and love. Her attachment for Pierre went much deeper than ordinary love for a brother by a sister.

Some time later Pierre received a letter from Lucy. She had rebuffed Glen Stanly's suit, and she wrote to tell Pierre that he alone had her affections. She told Pierre that, even though he was married, she wished to travel to New York City to live near him. Pierre could not prevent her from joining his household, although he lied to Isabel and told her that Lucy was his cousin. Lucy arrived the next day. As she entered the tenement where Pierre lived, her brother and Glen Stanly tried to take her away by force. Pierre interfered on her behalf, and the two men had to leave without the girl.

Lucy, listening only to the promptings of her heart, refused to leave Pierre, even though he told her that Isabel was his wife. Having brought along her painting materials, she intended to support herself as a painter of portraits. Isabel disliked the idea of a third woman in the home, but she was powerless to turn Lucy out. The two women lived in a state of distrustful and watchful truce.

Glen Stanly and Lucy's brother, not wishing to see Lucy remain near Pierre, sent him a letter of premeditated insults in hopes of provoking him. Angered by their message, Pierre found two pistols in the apartment of a friend and set out to find Stanly and Lucy's brother. He encountered them on a crowded street. When they met, Stanly lashed at Pierre with a whip, whereupon Pierre drew his pistols and killed his cousin. The police immediately seized Pierre and took him to prison.

In prison, Pierre had no hope of life.

Nor did he care to live, for he felt that fate had been too cruel to him. One evening Isabel and Lucy were allowed to visit him for a few hours. When Isabel revealed that she was Pierre's sister, the shock of her announcement killed Lucy immediately. Pierre, driven mad by her death, seized a vial of poison which he knew Isabel carried in her bosom. He drank a portion of the poison, and Isabel emptied the vial of the remainder.

A short time later Lucy's brother came looking for her, still hoping to rescue her from Pierre's influence. When the turnkey opened the cell door, Pierre was already dead, lying close to Lucy. Isabel still had sufficient life to say that no one had known the real Pierre. Then she too died, completing the tragedy of their ambiguous relationships.

PILGRIMAGE

Type of work: Novel
Author: Dorothy M. Richardson (1873-1957)
Time: 1893-1911
Locale: England, Germany, Switzerland
First published: Pointed Roofs, 1915; Backwater, 1916; Honeycomb, 1917; The Tunnel, 1919; Interim, 1919; Deadlock, 1921; Revolving Lights, 1923; The Trap, 1925; Oberland, 1927; Dawn's Left Hand, 1931; Clear Horizon, 1935; Dimple Hill, 1938

> *Principal characters:*
> MIRIAM HENDERSON
> HARRIET,
> SARAH, and
> EVE, her sisters
> GERALD, Harriet's husband
> FRÄULEIN PFAFF, a German schoolmistress
> DR. ORLY, head of a dental clinic
> DR. HANCOCK, a dentist
> "HYPO" WILSON, a writer and socialist
> ALMA, his wife
> ELEANOR DEAR, a nurse
> MRS. BAILEY, a boarding-house keeper
> DR. DENSLEY, Miriam's friend
> MICHAEL SHATOV, a young socialist
> AMABEL, Miriam's young friend, later Mrs. Shatov

Of the writers who added to the dimensions and technical resources of fiction in the first half of this century, Dorothy Richardson is the least read and the most inaccessible. The single novels of her twelve-part sequence, *Pilgrimage*, are now out of print and five, except for some imported sheets of the four-volume collected edition, have never been published in this country. Critical material on her writing is negligible—an early monograph by John Cowper Powys, brief discussions in histories of the English novel, two or three scattered articles, a handful of reviews. For all critical purposes her career ended in 1938, so that when she died in 1957 she had outlived both her work and her minor reputation. Yet in all that has been written about her there is general agreement that she contributed significantly to the stream-of-consciousness technique of the modern novel. Critical neglect of her books is all the more remarkable in view of the adulation accorded fellow pioneers like James Joyce and Virginia Woolf. Certainly Dorothy Richardson has never received the attention which her position

as an innovator warrants.

It was John Middleton Murry who first called attention to the historical and critical importance of her first novel. In "The Break-up of the Novel," printed in *The Yale Review* in 1923, he called attention to the fact that between 1913 and 1916 three books calling themselves novels but trying in a new way to present character and the texture of experience had quietly appeared. In France, Marcel Proust had published *Du Côté de chez Swann* in 1913. Two years later came Dorothy Richardson's *Pointed Roofs*, followed by Joyce's *A Portrait of the Artist as a Young Man* in 1916. (Virginia Woolf, who would now be bracketed with these three, did not begin her own assault on the conventions of the naturalistic tradition until 1919.) In these novels the writers, working independently, were shown in the process of creating new techniques for recording the development of consciousness without the mediation of story or plot. This was the narrative method to which May Sinclair, reviewing Dorothy Richardson's novels in 1918, applied the term "stream-of-consciousness," after a phrase from William James.

In a sense Miss Richardson's method is an elaborate but logical extension of Henry James's theory of the "point of view"—with one important difference. Although James tried by every means at his command to identify himself with one or another of his characters, he nevertheless remained unobtrusively on the scene to direct that character's view of things and to control the flow of time. But in Miss Richardson's novel the scene as a dramatic unit has disappeared and time has become only a pattern of impressions and sensations arranged not in chronological sequence but by a process of immediate perception or association. The result is a record of experience lived wholly from within, a sensitively conceived, extended internal monologue presenting what is in many ways the most complete and revealing portrait of a woman in all literature.

The novel may be called a portrait because in the world of Miss Richardson's fiction character is the beginning and end of all experience. *Pilgrimage* presents no view of the individual in relation to family or society, or to some great concept like good or evil. There is only the view of personality in relation to itself in the life of the heart or the life of the mind. This is not the world of feminine perception we find in the ironic propriety of Jane Austen, the emotional intensity of the Brontës, the moral earnestness of George Eliot, or the quicksilver play of fancy and fact in the novels of Virginia Woolf. It is something more somber and primitive dredged from the depths of being and thrown upon the page without selection, order, or comment.

Dorothy Richardson makes no break with tradition, however, in the substance of her novel. *Pilgrimage* "tells" the rather conventional story, partly by inference through references to things past, partly by direct impressionism, of Miriam Henderson through an eighteen-year period during which she progresses from the awkwardness and confusion of adoles-cence to the calm of maturity. In *Pointed Roofs* she appears as one of four sisters —Harriet, Miriam, Eve, and Sarah—in a middle-class family of some means living in a pleasant suburban home. When the novel opens the family is facing a crisis. Mr. Henderson, who has lived on an inherited income, has, in a way never made clear, lost most of his money, and his daughters are about to be thrown on their own resources. Harriet becomes engaged to Gerald. Miriam and Eve plan to teach. Sarah will stay at home with her parents. At seventeen Miriam secures a post in Fräulein Pfaff's private school in Germany; her intention is to familiarize herself with the language and later to return to teach German in England. Her stay in Germany lasts only a year. Unknowingly she has attracted the interest of Pastor Lahmann, a friend of Fräulein Pfaff's, and the headmistress, jealous, dismisses her.

Returning to England, Miriam becomes a teacher at Wordsworth House, a school conducted by the Misses Perne in London. There she meets Grace and Florrie Bloom, who are to become her lifelong friends. She meets Ted, but because she spends so much time with Max at a dance she loses him. Later Max dies in New York. Although the Misses Perne are pleased with her instruction, she becomes dissatisfied and leaves Wordsworth House at the end of the year to become a governess in the Corrie household in the country. Harriet finally marries Gerald. Miriam is forced to give up her position in order to go to Brighton with her mother, who is dying of cancer.

After her mother's death Miriam feels that she is at last free to find a different life for herself. Harriet and Sarah are married, and Eve has become a governess in the home of a wealthy family in Wales. Miriam becomes the assistant in a dental clinic conducted by Dr. Orly, his son, and Dr. Hancock. Through them she meets new people and forms new friendships. She also renews her association with Alma, a former school friend now married to "Hypo" Wilson, who is gaining some fame as a writer. Miriam goes to visit them at their house in the country. She also finds herself looking after Eleanor Dear, a neurotic nurse suffering from tuberculosis. Through Eve she meets Dr. Densley, who is to become another lifelong friend. During this time she lives in a boarding-house owned by Mrs. Bailey in Tansley Street.

At Mrs. Bailey's she meets Michael Shatov, a young Russian Jew, and through him she becomes interested in literature and in socialism. When Shatov proposes to her she accepts, even though she cannot bring herself to marry him because of his race. Meanwhile, Mr. Henderson has died, Harriet and Gerald have apparently lost their money, and Eve has moved back and forth between London and Wales. She finally opens a shop in the suburbs where Harriet and her husband have a rooming-house. Through Shatov and "Hypo" Wilson, Miriam has become interested in a socialist organization called the Lycurgans. She breaks her engagement to Shatov because, as we learn later, he has become Eleanor Dear's lover. Miriam herself has fallen in love with Wilson.

After Dr. Orly's retirement Miriam becomes Dr. Hancock's assistant when he opens an office of his own. To supplement her income she begins to write literary reviews. She also leaves Mrs. Bailey's for a time and shares a flat with Selina Holland, a social worker. The two women quarrel and she returns to the boarding-house. At Dr. Densley's suggestion she goes to Switzerland for a vacation. On her return to London she hears that Eleanor Dear is dead. Dr. Densley wants her to marry him, but she refuses. Instead, she becomes "Hypo" Wilson's mistress. When the affair fails to bring her the peace and happiness she desires, she becomes more disturbed than ever, and on Shatov's recommendation she goes to stay for six months in the country with a family named Rescorla, at Dimple Hill. There she finds the freedom from self she has dreamed of Shatov falls in love with Amabel, a young girl

in whom Miriam has taken an interest; the two are married. Back in London, Miriam meets "Hypo" Wilson again at a Lycurgan meeting. This time she sends him on his way.

This bald outline can give no idea of the quality of the novel or of Dorothy Richardson's method. Through the twelve volumes everything remains in flux, a constantly shifting kaleidoscopic pattern of emotion, observation, situation, and reflection. The time of the action, like the story, must be inferred from the clues Miss Richardson scatters casually through the work. In *Pointed Roofs* she makes references to music, particularly to that of Wagner. There are references to Oscar Wilde's trial in *Honeycomb*. Joseph Conrad's *Typhoon* is mentioned in *Revolving Lights*, Arnold Bennett's *Clayhanger* in *Dawn's Left Hand*. Automobiles appear in *Clear Horizon*. From these instances it may be gathered that the time covered falls approximately between 1893 and 1911. In somewhat the same way certain of Miss Richardson's characters supply the authenticity of a *roman à clef*. "Hypo" Wilson, for example, is obviously a portrait of H. G. Wells, as one of his biographers has testified, just as the Lycurgans are plainly modeled on the Fabian Society. On an intensely personal level, the experiences of Miriam Henderson reflect the personalities and the spirit of English social and intellectual life between the Victorian Age and World War I.

These links with the realities of time, place, and personality do not serve Miss Richardson's purpose as they would a less experimental writer; her novel remains a roughhewn segment of experience extracted from the flux of time passing. In spite of the writer's originality and those qualities within the work which make for greatness in fiction, *Pilgrimage* suffers in the end from an excess of its virtues. To follow one woman's interior life through twelve volumes puts a strain on even the most patient and appreciative reader. One has a vision of Miss Richardson resolutely hacking her way through the waste

2871

and clutter of material things in the naturalistic tradition of the novel in order to reveal the essence of character, but she leaves only a rough trail behind her. Beside the myth-making quality and the resourcefulness of language that we find in Joyce or the poetry of perception and mood in the novels of Virginia Woolf, her effects appear curiously static. Nevertheless, the reader gets from *Pilgrimage* the impression of something vast, at times impenetrable, and, at last, meaningful. A resolute experiment, if not always a successful one, in the creation of a new kind of fiction, the work seems likely to stand as a milestone in the development of the novel in our time.

THE PILGRIMAGE OF CHARLEMAGNE

Type of work: Poem
Author: Unknown
Type of plot: Heroic legend
Time of plot: c. 800
Locale: Paris, Jerusalem, Constantinople
First transcribed: c. 1100

Principal characters:
CHARLEMAGNE, the Frankish king, Emperor of the West
HUGO, Emperor of Greece and of Constantinople
ROLAND,
OLIVER,
WILLIAM OF ORANGE,
NAIMES,
OGIER OF DENMARK,
GERIN,
BERENGER,
TURPIN THE ARCHBISHOP,
ERNAUT,
AYMER,
BERNARD OF BRUSBAN, and
BERTRAM, Charlemagne's twelve peers

Critique:

The Pilgrimage of Charlemagne, a legend from the Middle Ages, is an old French poem titled *Pèlerinage de Charlemagne,* probably the product of some minstrel or group of storytellers who passed the legend, in poetic form, from one to the other and embellished it. The poem presents Charlemagne as the champion of Christianity, undertaking a pilgrimage to Jerusalem in order to return with holy relics for the churches of France. The fact is that Charlemagne never went on a pilgrimage to Jerusalem, but the legend is not confined to facts. It reaches its most amusing highpoint with the recital of the "gabs," the fantastic boasts, of the twelve peers of Charlemagne; it seems not at all surprising that God sees to it that enough of the "gabs" come true to satisfy Hugo of Constantinople, Charlemagne's angry host on the return journey from Jerusalem.

The Story:

At the Abbey of Saint Denis, Charlemagne boasted to his queen that he looked handsome and powerful wearing his crown and carrying his great sword at his side. The queen chided him for boasting and declared that she knew of a king who was even more handsome when wearing his crown. Charlemagne angrily answered that he would have the French lords compare him to such a king, and if it turned out that Charlemagne was handsomer the queen would lose her head. She tearfully begged his pardon, insisting that she had not meant to insult him; and she attempted to pacify him by saying that the other king was not as brave as Charlemagne. But Charlemagne threatened to cut off the queen's head at once if she did not tell him who the king was whom she believed handsomer than he. The queen at last confessed that she had been talking about King Hugo of Constantinople, Emperor of Greece and much of Persia.

Charlemagne returned to Paris and announced to the peers that he would undertake a pilgrimage to Jerusalem to worship the Cross and the Holy Sepulchre. He also intended to visit King Hugo. For the journey the emperor's

THE PILGRIMAGE OF CHARLEMAGNE, from THE MERRY PILGRIMAGE. Translated by Merriam Sherwood. By permission of the publishers, The Macmillan Co. Copyright, 1927, by The Macmillan Co. Renewed. All rights reserved.

attendants were dressed in pilgrims' robes, and the pack animals were loaded with gold and silver.

During the pilgrimage Charlemagne boasted to Bertram that there were eighty thousand pilgrims in the forefront alone; he declared that whoever led such a force must be a great leader.

In Jerusalem, Charlemagne visited the great cathedral, and he and his twelve peers sat in the chairs of Christ and the twelve apostles. When the Patriarch of Jerusalem heard that a great man was sitting in Christ's seat, and that twelve men filled the other places, he went to Charlemagne to learn who the visitor might be. The Patriarch named the emperor Charles Magnus and granted the king's request for holy relics. He gave Charlemagne a handkerchief that had covered the head of Jesus, one of the nails with which He had been crucified, the crown of thorns, a knife, a chalice, and a bowl. When the relics were given to Charlemagne, a cripple nearby was immediately cured.

Charlemagne spent four months in Jerusalem; then he departed for Constantinople after having promised the Patriarch to destroy the Saracens.

Charlemagne and his company were awed by the grandeur of Constantinople. They saw beautiful gardens in which twenty thousand knights played chess and backgammon, and thirteen thousand maidens worked on embroidery with golden threads.

Charlemagne discovered King Hugo driving a golden plow and riding on an ornamented cushion. The king welcomed him and invited him and his followers to be his guests. The palace was magnificent with paintings and hangings and decorations in silver, gold, and rich jewels. The palace turned with the wind so that Charlemagne and his men could not keep their feet. When the wind ceased and the Frenchmen were able to stand, dinner was served. Oliver, one of Charlemagne's peers, was charmed by King Hugo's daughter. The feast was luxurious.

The king led Charlemagne and his twelve peers to a splendid bedchamber where they would spend their nights. While the Frenchmen drank their wine and told boasting stories, according to the old custom, they were spied upon by one of King Hugo's men, who hid under a staircase.

Charlemagne began the boasting with the remark that were King Hugo to select his strongest knight and dress him in two hauberks and two helmets, Charlemagne would cut through the armor with King Hugo's sword, burying the sword so far in the ground that it would be necessary to dig down a spear's length to draw it out.

Roland boasted that he would take one of Hugo's ivory horns and blow it so loudly that all the doors in the city would be blown down, and King Hugo would have his cloak torn from him.

Turpin the Archbishop said that he would leap over two running horses and land on the back of a third while juggling four apples.

William of Orange claimed that he would take a mighty ball which thirty men could not move and throw it through the palace, knocking down a hundred and sixty cubits of wall.

Ogier, the Duke of Denmark, made his gab by declaring that he would crush the pillar on which the castle turned in the wind.

Naimes boasted that he would wear a heavy hauberk and leap over the palace, while Berenger said that he would jump from the palace onto the swords of King Hugo's knights while the blades were sticking up from the earth.

Bernard of Brusban said that he would divert the river and flood the city, sending King Hugo in flight to the highest tower in Constantinople.

Ernaut claimed that he would leap into a vat of molten lead and sit there until it hardened, when he would shake himself free.

Aymer declared that he would take his invisible cap and eat King Hugo's food and drink his wine, capping it all by knocking the king so that he would fall onto the table.

Bertram boasted that he would take two shields and use them as wings, and that while in flight he would make a cry that would frighten all the animals and birds of the forest.

Gerin said that he would throw a spear from a league's distance and so shake the palace as to cause a farthing to fall from the top of the tower without disturbing another farthing on which the first coin rested.

The spy reported to King Hugo that Charlemagne and his men were boasting that they could overcome the king in various ways, and that they were making fun of him. King Hugo was angry, and in the morning he called his knights together. Confronting Charlemagne as the emperor was leaving the mass, he declared that unless the gabs were shown to be true he would have Charlemagne and his peers beheaded.

Charlemagne prayed before the relics, and an angel appeared, assuring him that the gabs would be carried out. The angel warned him, however, never to make gabs about any man again.

William of Orange, challenged to throw the mighty ball as he had boasted he could, picked it up and threw it through the palace. Bernard of Brusban then diverted the river and sent King Hugo in flight to the highest tower. God made the waters withdraw, and King Hugo became one of Charlemagne's vassals.

When the two kings passed before the French knights, all declared that Charlemagne was the handsomer. He returned to France in such good humor that he forgave his queen and did not behead her.

THE PILGRIM'S PROGRESS

Type of work: Novel
Author: John Bunyan (1628-1688)
Type of plot: Religious allegory
Time of plot: Any time since Christ
Locale: Anywhere
First published: 1678

Principal characters:
CHRISTIAN
FAITHFUL
HOPEFUL
MR. WORLDLY WISEMAN
EVANGELIST
DESPAIR
IGNORANCE
APOLLYON, a giant devil

Critique:

This famous story of man's progress through life to heaven or hell has often been rated next to the Bible in importance as a Christian document. In any case, it remains one of the most pleasing allegories of the Christian way ever written. Bunyan, an early Puritan, wished to write a book which would be popular with the common people as well as with intellectuals. His characters are more than simple symbols; they are real people. The story can be read as a symbolic narrative, a picaresque romance, and a realistic novel.

The Story:

One day, according to Bunyan, he lay down in a den to sleep, and in his sleep dreamed that he saw a man standing in a field and crying out in pain and sorrow because he and his whole family as well as the town in which they lived were to be destroyed. Christian, for that was his name, knew of this catastrophe because he had read about it in the book he held in his hands, the Bible. Evangelist, the preacher of Christianity, soon came up to Christian and presented him with a roll of paper on which it was written that he should flee from the wrath of God and make his way from the City of Destruction to the City of Zion. Running home with this hope of salvation, Christian tried to get his neighbors and family to go away with him, but they would not listen and thought he was either sick

or mad. Finally, shutting his ears to his family's entreaties to stay with them, he ran off toward the light in the distance. Under the light he knew he would find the wicket gate which opened into Heaven.

On his way he met Pliant and Obstinate, who so distracted Christian that he fell in a bog called the Slough of Despond. He could not get out because of the bundle of sins on his back. Finally Help came along and aided Christian out of the sticky mire. Going on his way, he soon fell in with Mr. Worldly Wiseman, who tried to convince Christian he would lead a happier life if he gave up his trip toward the light and settled down to the comforts of a burdenless town life. Fearing that Christian was about to be led astray, Evangelist came up to the two men and quickly showed the errors in Mr. Worldly Wiseman's arguments.

Soon Christian arrived at a closed gate where he met Good-Will, who told him that if he knocked the gate would be opened to him. Christian did so. Invited into the gatekeeper's house by the Interpreter, he learned from him the meaning of many of the Christian mysteries. He was shown pictures of Christ and Passion and Patience; Despair in a cage of iron bars; and finally a vision of the Day of Judgment, when evil men will be sent to the bottomless pit and good men will be carried up to Heaven.

Having seen these things, Christian was filled with both hope and fear. Continuing on his journey, he came to the Holy Cross and the Sepulchre of Christ. There his burden of sins fell off, and he was able to take to the road with renewed vigor.

Soon he met Sloth, Simple, Presumption, Formalism, and Hypocrisy, but he kept to his way and they kept to theirs. Later Christian lay down to sleep for a while. When he went on again, he forgot to pick up the roll of paper Evangelist had given him. Remembering it later, he ran back to find it. Running to make up the time lost, he suddenly found himself confronted by two lions. He was afraid to pass by them until the porter of the house by the side of the road told him that the lions were chained, and that he had nothing to fear. The porter then asked Christian to come into the house. There he was well-treated and shown some of the relics of Biblical antiquity by four virgins, Discretion, Prudence, Piety, and Charity. They gave him good advice and sent him on his journey armed with the sword and shield of Christian faith.

In the Valley of Humiliation, Christian was forced to fight the giant devil, Apollyon, whose body was covered with the shiny scales of pride. In this battle Christian was wounded, but after he had chased away the devil, he healed his wounds with leaves from the Tree of Life which grew nearby. After the Valley of Humiliation came the Valley of the Shadow of Death in which Christian had to pass one of the gates to Hell. In order to save himself from the devils who issued out of that terrible hole, he recited some of the verses from the Psalms.

Having passed through this danger, he had to go by the caves of the old giants, Pope and Pagan, and when he had done so he caught up with a fellow traveler, Faithful. As the two companions went along, they met Evangelist, who warned them of the dangers in the town of Vanity Fair.

Vanity Fair was a town of ancient foundation which since the beginning of time had tried to lure men away from the path to Heaven. Here all the vanities of the world were sold, and the people who dwelt there were cruel and stupid and had no love for travelers such as Christian and Faithful. Having learned these things, the two companions promised to be careful and went on down into the town. There they were arrested and tried because they would buy none of the town's goods. Faithful was sentenced to be burned alive and Christian was put in prison. When Faithful died in the fire, a chariot came down from Heaven and took him up to God. Christian escaped from the prison. Accompanied by a young man named Hopeful, who had been impressed by Faithful's reward, he set off once more.

They passed through the Valley of Ease, where they were tempted to dig in a silver mine free to all. As they left the valley, they saw the pillar of salt which had once been Lot's wife. Becoming lost, they were captured by a giant, Despair, who lived in Doubting Castle, and were locked in the vaults beneath the castle walls. There they lay until Christian remembered he had a key called Promise in his pocket, and with this they escaped from the prison.

They met the four sheperds, Knowledge, Experience, Watchful, and Sincere, who showed them the Celestial Gate and warned them of the paths to Hell. Then the two pilgrims passed by the Valley of Conceit, where they were met by Ignorance and other men who had not kept to the straight and narrow path. They passed on to the country of Beulah. Far off they saw the gates of the city of Heaven glistening with pearls and precious stones. Thinking that all their troubles were behind them, they lay down to rest.

When they went on toward the city, they came to the River of Death. They entered the river and began to wade through the water. Soon Christian became afraid, and the more afraid he became the deeper the waters rolled.

Hopeful shouted to him to have hope and faith. Cheered by these words, Christian became less afraid, the water became less deep, and finally they both got across safely. They ran up the hill toward Heaven. Shining angels led them through the gates.

THE PILLARS OF SOCIETY

Type of work: Drama
Author: Henrik Ibsen (1828-1906)
Type of plot: Psychological realism
Time of plot: Nineteenth century
Locale: Norwegian seaport
First presented: 1877

Principal characters:
CONSUL BERNICK, the leader of the town
MRS. BERNICK, his wife
OLAF, their son
MARTHA, the consul's sister
JOHAN TÖNNESEN, Mrs. Bernick's brother
LONA HESSEL, her stepsister
DOCTOR RÖRLUND, a schoolmaster
DINA DORF, Bernick's charge
AUNE, a foreman shipbuilder

Critique:

The Pillars of Society is a play concerned only with everyday realities, and it is one of the few plays by Ibsen in which the plot is more important than the characters. At times the plot is cumbersome, for so many characters are required to tell the story that the cast becomes unwieldy. The plot is almost too mechanical in arrangement and solution. Conscience triumphs almost automatically, just in time to bring the play to a close. But there are touches of Ibsen's genius throughout, and these justify a technique less perfect than that which we expect from a master dramatist.

The Story:

Consul Bernick was the unquestioned leader of the town, with his wealth and influence extending into every enterprise. He owned the large shipyard which was the source of most of the townspeople's income, and he had successfully fought the project of building a seacoast railway. But he had introduced machines into the yards, and Aune, his foreman, was stirring up the workmen because the machines meant the loss of jobs. Bernick, not wishing to have his authority questioned, threatened Aune with loss of his job if he did not stop his speaking and writing against the machines.

There was only one breath of scandal about Consul Bernick, and that concerned his wife's family. Many years before Johan Tönnesen, her brother, had been seen leaving the rear window of the house of Mrs. Dorf, a married woman. Later Johan left town and went to America. It was said that before he left he stole the strongbox containing Bernick's mother's fortune. What made the matter worse was that Mrs. Bernick's stepsister, Lona Hessel, had followed her younger stepbrother to America and had been like a mother to him. Only Bernick's standing in the town prevented his ruin, and he had made it clear to his wife that her family was a disgrace to him.

Mrs. Dorf's husband deserted her and their daughter. When Mrs. Dorf died soon afterward, Bernick's sister Martha took the child into their home. The girl, Dina, was a constant annoyance to Bernick. Not only did she have a disgraceful background, but she talked constantly about exercising her own free will and acting independently of his desires. Dr. Rörlund, the schoolmaster, loved Dina, but he would not marry her or let anyone know his attachment because he was afraid of the town's feelings about her. His beautiful words about goodness and kindness concealed his moral cowardice. He promised that when he could improve her position they would be married.

In the meantime Bernick had changed his mind about allowing a railroad to come to the community. Formerly the proposed road would have competed with his shipping. Now he realized that a spur line through the town would bring timber and minerals to his shipyard. The railroad would be a good thing for the town because it was a good thing for Bernick. He was aiding the town, a pillar of society.

There was constant trouble at the shipyard. The American owners of a ship he was repairing had cabled him to get her under way immediately, although the ship was so rotted that it would require several weeks to make her safe. Bernick was torn between the profits to be gained by getting her afloat at once and the conscience that kept him from sending her crew to certain death.

He grew even more disturbed because Lona and Johan had returned from America and the town had revived the old gossip. Many tried to ignore the pair, but Lona refused to be ignored. She felt no disgrace, nor did Johan.

Johan and Dina were at once drawn to each other, and she begged him to take her back to America so that she could be free and independent. Bernick and his wife would not hear of this plan, but for quite different reasons. Mrs. Bernick still felt her brother's disgrace. Bernick, however, knew that Johan was blameless. It had been Bernick, not Johan, who had been forced to flee the married woman's house. Johan had taken the blame because he had no great reputation to save and he was anxious to leave the town and strike out for himself. What he did not know was that Bernick had spread the story about the theft of his mother's money.

Johan, thinking that the town would soon have forgotten a boyish escapade with another man's wife, renewed his promise not to tell that it was Bernick who had been involved. He told Bernick that Lona knew the true story but that she would not reveal the secret. Johan was grateful to Martha, Bernick's sister, for caring for Dina. Martha had refused several offers of marriage in order to care for the younger

girl who had been so disgracefully orphaned.

Johan learned also that Martha had not married because she had always loved him and had waited for him to return. Martha told Johan that her brother's strict moral principles had made him condemn Johan and try to turn her against him. Johan was puzzled, for he thought Bernick had been grateful to him for assuming Bernick's own guilt. Johan could not understand his brother-in-law's attitude.

Lona, too, forgave Bernick for his past acts, even his jilting of her in favor of her rich stepsister. Bernick told her why he had acted as he did. His mother's business had been in great danger, and he had needed money to avoid bankruptcy. For that reason he had renounced Lona, whom he loved, for her wealthier relative. For the same reason he had spread the story that Johan had taken old Mrs. Bernick's money. In reality, there had been no money at all; had the town learned the truth, it would have meant ruin for Bernick. Bernick completely justified himself by saying that as the pillar of the town he had been forced to act deceitfully and maliciously.

Lona begged him to tell the truth at last, to keep his life from being built on a lie. Bernick said that the cost was too great; he could not lose his money and his position. In addition, the railway project would fail if a whisper of scandal were heard. The railway was to make Bernick a millionaire.

While he struggled with his conscience over this problem, repair of the American ship still confronted him. He forced Aune to get her ready to sail in two days, even though her unseaworthiness meant death for her crew. At the same time he laid plans to pretend that it was Aune who had failed to take proper time and precautions to make the vessel safe. Then he would stop the sailing and take credit for losing his profit rather than risk the lives of the sailors. He needed public acclaim, for soon the town would learn that he had bought up all the land through which the railroad would run. It would be hard to convince the townspeople that they would benefit from his wealth.

To make matters worse, Johan became difficult. He had not known about the story of the theft, but he would forgive the lie if Bernick would now tell the truth. Johan wanted to marry Dina, but his name must first be cleared. Bernick refused the pleas of both Johan and Lona, lest he be ruined. He would not release Johan from his promise of secrecy. Lona would not tell the true story because she still loved Bernick. Besides, she thought he himself should tell the truth so that he would be whole again. When Johan, planning to leave on the American ship, vowed to return in two months and to tell the truth at that time, Bernick decided to allow the ship to sail. If it sank, he would be free of Johan forever.

On the night of the sailing Bernick arranged for a celebration in his honor for the purpose of getting the citizens into the proper frame of mind before they learned that he had bought property along the railroad route. Shortly before the celebration he learned that his son Olaf had stowed away on the unseaworthy ship. He tried to call it back, but it was already out to sea. Then he was told that Johan had taken Dina with him to America, but that they had sailed on a different ship. He would lose his son and gain nothing.

He was overjoyed when he learned that his wife had found the boy on board and brought him home before the ship sailed. Word came also that Aune stopped the sailing of the ship and brought her back to the harbor. Bernick, saved from the evil of his deeds, stood up before the townspeople and confessed that he and not Johan had been the guilty man. He promised also that he would share the profits from the railroad. Lona was happy. She told Bernick that at last he had found the real pillars of society—truth and freedom. Only on them could society build a firm foundation.

THE PILOT

Type of work: Novel
Author: James Fenimore Cooper (1789-1851)
Type of plot: Historical romance
Time of plot: Revolutionary War
Locale: Northeastern coast of England
First published: 1823

Principal characters:

LT. RICHARD BARNSTABLE, commander of the Ariel
MR. EDWARD GRIFFITH, an officer aboard an American frigate
LONG TOM COFFIN, coxswain of the Ariel
MR. MERRY, a midshipman
MR. GRAY, the pilot, in reality John Paul Jones
COLONEL HOWARD, a Tory
KATHERINE PLOWDEN, his niece
CECILIA HOWARD, another niece of Colonel Howard
CAPTAIN MANUAL, an officer of the Marine Corps
CAPTAIN BORROUGHCLIFFE, a British officer
CHRISTOPHER DILLON, kinsman of Colonel Howard
ALICE DUNSCOMBE, friend of Katherine and Cecilia

Critique:

While a number of earlier poems and stories had presented fragmentary pictures of seafaring life and some details of the handling of ships, it was not until 1823, when Cooper's sea romance appeared, that the first genuine sea novel was published. For the technical material of his story Cooper drew upon his six years of service in the United States Navy. Since the time of its publication the novel has been popular with readers of many lands and all ages. While Cooper never names the pilot whose activities give the novel its title, it is generally understood that the unknown seaman was John Paul Jones.

The Story:

Toward the close of a bleak wintry day during the American Revolution, a small schooner and a frigate sailed through shoal waters off the northeastern coast of England and anchored in a small bay beneath some towering cliffs. As darkness settled, a whaleboat was put ashore from the schooner Ariel. The boat was in charge of the Ariel's commander, Lieutenant Richard Barnstable, who had been ordered to make a landing near the cliffs and bring off a pilot known only as Mr. Gray.

With the aid of a weather-beaten old Nantucket whaler, Long Tom Coffin, Barnstable climbed the cliff and there met his mysterious passenger, a man of middle height and sparing speech. Before he had completed his mission, however, he also encountered Katherine Plowden, his fiancée, who gave him a letter and a signal book. The girl was staying temporarily at the St. Ruth's Abbey manor house, the home of her uncle, Colonel Howard, a wealthy South Carolina Tory who had fled from America at the outbreak of the war. From her Barnstable learned that another niece, Cecilia Howard, and her friend, Alice Dunscombe, were also guests at the abbey. Cecilia was in love with Lieutenant Edward Griffith, first officer aboard the frigate. Alice Dunscombe was reported to be in love with the mysterious pilot, but she refused to marry him because she was completely Loyalist in her sympathies.

Darkness had fallen by the time the pilot had been put aboard the deck of the frigate, and a storm was rising. Captain Munson of the frigate alone knew the pilot's identity, a secret concealed from everyone else aboard the ship and its escort, the Ariel. Captain Munson, seeing the pilot by the light of the battle-lanterns on deck, thought him greatly changed in appearance since their last meeting.

As the storm rose, the pilot guided the frigate safely through dangerous, wind-lashed shoal waters and out to open sea. At sunrise the frigate signaled the *Ariel* and ordered Barnstable to go aboard the larger ship for a council of war. There plans were made to harass the English by sending landing parties ashore to raid the mansions and estates of the gentry in the neighborhood.

Barnstable wanted these expeditions to serve another purpose, for he hoped to rescue Katherine Plowden and Cecilia Howard from the abbey, where they lived unhappily with Colonel Howard, their uncle and guardian.

Meanwhile, at the abbey, Colonel Howard was holding a conference with Christopher Dillon, a kinsman, and Captain Borroughcliffe, a British officer in charge of a small detachment of troops stationed at the abbey. Dillon, an impoverished gentleman, hoped to marry, with the colonel's approval, one of his wealthy cousins. The three men discussed the progress of the American Revolution, other political questions, and the piracies of John Paul Jones. They agreed that extra precautions should be taken, for there were rumors that Jones himself had been seen in the neighborhood.

That night Griffith and the pilot, accompanied by a Marine Corps captain named Manual, went ashore on a scouting expedition. Because of Griffith's imprudent conduct, they were seen and seized. When a sentry reported the arrest of strange seamen lurking in the neighborhood, Captain Borroughcliffe ordered them brought to the abbey for examination.

On their arrival at the abbey the prisoners would say only that they were seamen out of employment, a suspicious circumstance in itself. When the seamen offered no further information of any consequence, they were imprisoned to await Borroughcliffe's pleasure. Katherine and Cecilia bribed the sentry on duty and obtained permission to visit the prisoners. They recognized Griffith in disguise. Alice Dunscombe also went to visit the pilot, whom she recognized. After drinking too much wine at dinner, Borroughcliffe began to interview the men and in his intoxicated condition unwittingly helped them to escape.

Believing that the men had come from a ship lying offshore, Dillon mounted a horse and rode to a neighboring bay, where the war cutter *Alacrity* lay at anchor. Alarmed at the possible presence of an American ship in the neighborhood, the cutter put out to sea, with Dillon among its volunteer crew. Barnstable and Long Tom Coffin, waiting in the *Ariel's* whaleboat, engaged the cutter in a furious battle that ended when Coffin pinned the captain of the cutter to the mast with his whaler's harpoon. Dillon was among the prisoners taken. Frightened, he offered to return to the abbey and, in return for his own freedom, secure the release of the Americans held there.

After their escape, the pilot left Griffith and Manual, who rejoined a party of marines that had remained in hiding while their captain went with Griffith and the pilot to reconnoiter the abbey. Attacked by Borroughcliffe and his troops, the marines were surrounded. Griffith was recaptured and Manual was forced to surrender.

Trusting Dillon's word of honor, Barnstable had sent Long Tom Coffin with Dillon to the abbey to arrange for the transfer of prisoners. But Dillon, dishonoring his parole, had Coffin held prisoner while he and Borroughcliffe planned to trap Barnstable and his men. When Borroughcliffe boasted of his intentions, Coffin made a surprise attack upon him and seized and bound the British officer. He then followed Dillon to the apartments of Katherine and Cecilia and there took Dillon prisoner. He succeeded in getting Dillon aboard the *Ariel* as a British battery on the shore opened fire on the schooner. A lucky shot wrecked her mainmast as the schooner put out to sea, where a heavy storm completed the *Ariel's* destruction.

Before the schooner sank, Barnstable, a true captain, decided to go down with his ship, and he ordered Mr. Merry, a midshipman, to take charge of the crew and lower the boats. Coffin threw Barnstable overboard and in this manner saved his commander's life. The ship went down with Coffin and Dillon aboard. When Dillon's body was later washed up by the sea, Barnstable ordered his burial.

Shortly afterward Mr. Merry appeared at the abbey in the disguise of a peddler. Barnstable himself signaled by means of flags to Katherine, using signals from the code book which she had given him. Later they met secretly and laid plans for surprising the abbey and the soldiers who guarded it. Borroughcliffe had wind of the plot, however, and Barnstable walked into Borroughcliffe's ambush. But at this juncture the pilot arrived with a party of marines from the frigate and made prisoners of the Tories and the British.

Later Griffith released Borroughcliffe and his soldiers because Borroughcliffe had behaved in an honorable manner toward his prisoners. There was a final interview between Alice Dunscombe and the pilot. During their talk she addressed him as John and said that if she should speak his real name the whole country-side would ring with it. The pilot insisted that he would continue his activities for the cause of patriotism, regardless of the unsavory reputation it might gain for him in England. Colonel Howard and his two nieces were taken aboard the frigate for the return voyage to America.

But the American ship was not yet out of danger. The next morning a man-of-war broke through the morning mists, her decks cleared for action. There was tremendous activity aboard the frigate in preparation for the battle, and the women were taken below for safety as the English ship of the line blazed a three-tiered broadside at the American vessel. One shot struck Captain Munson and cut him down. Griffith, who now knew the pilot's identity begged for permission to reveal it to the crew, to encourage them in the fight, but the pilot refused. Meanwhile the British ship had been reinforced by two others, but the Americans were lucky enough to disable the smallest of their attackers. Then, as the other ships closed in upon the battered American ship, the pilot took the wheel and daringly guided her through the shoal waters that only he knew well. Out-maneuvered, the pursuing British ships dropped behind.

Colonel Howard, wounded during the engagement, lived long enough to see his nieces married by the ship's chaplain to their lovers. He died insisting that he was too old to change his politics and blessing the king.

The frigate sailed to Holland, where the pilot was put ashore. To all but Griffith, among those who watched his small boat dwindling to a speck against the horizon, his identity remained a mystery.

THE PIONEERS

Type of work: Novel
Author: James Fenimore Cooper (1789-1851)
Type of plot: Historical romance
Time of plot: 1793
Locale: New York State
First published: 1823

Principal characters:
JUDGE TEMPLE, a frontier landowner
ELIZABETH TEMPLE, his daughter
NATTY BUMPPO, an old hunter, sometimes called Leatherstocking
OLIVER EDWARDS, in reality Edward Oliver Effingham, Natty's young friend
INDIAN JOHN, Natty's Indian companion
HIRAM DOOLITTLE, a local magistrate

Critique:

The Pioneers, or Thē Sources of the Susquehanna was the first of the Leatherstocking Tales written by Cooper. A romantic story of life in upstate New York ten years after the Revolutionary War, it has historical importance as the first true romance of the frontier in American literature. The novel is filled with scenes of hunting and trapping life, the description of Templeton being drawn from Cooper's memories of his own boyhood in Cooperstown. Although romantic in effect, the novel presents with considerable realism the character of Natty Bumppo, the old hunter and frontiersman. His fate and the death of Indian John point to the tragedy of the Indian and the wilderness scout; neither had a place in the life of a developed frontier.

The Story:

On a cold December day in 1793, Judge Temple and his daughter Elizabeth were traveling by sleigh through a snow-covered tract of wilderness near the settlement of Templeton. Elizabeth, who had been away from her home attending a female seminary, was now returning to preside over her father's household in the community in which he had been a pioneer settler after the Revolutionary War. Hearing the baying of hounds, the judge decided that Leatherstocking, an old hunter, had started game in the hills, and he ordered his coachman to stop the sleigh so he could have a shot at the deer if it came in his direction. A few minutes later, as a great buck leaped into the road, the judge fired both barrels of his fowling piece at the animal, but apparently without effect. Then a third report and a fourth were heard, and the buck dropped dead in a snowbank.

At the same time Natty Bumppo, the old hunter, and a young companion appeared from the woodland. The judge insisted that he had shot the buck, but Leatherstocking, by accounting for all the shots fired, proved the judge could not have killed the animal. The argument ended when the young stranger revealed that he had been wounded by one of the shots fired by the judge. Elizabeth and her father then insisted that he accompany them into the village in their sleigh, so he could have his wound dressed as soon as possible.

The young man got into the sleigh with obvious reluctance and said little during the drive. In a short time the party arrived at the Temple mansion, where his wound was treated. In answer to the judge's questions, he gave his name as Oliver Edwards. His manner remained distant and reserved. After he had departed, a servant in the Temple home reported that Edwards had appeared three weeks before in the company of old Leatherstocking and that he lived in a nearby cabin with the hunter and an Indian known as Indian John.

Judge Temple, wishing to make amends for having accidentally wounded

Edwards, offered him a position as his secretary. When Elizabeth added her own entreaties to those of her father, Edwards finally accepted the judge's offer, with the understanding that he would be free to terminate his employment at any time. For a while he attended faithfully and earnestly to his duties in Judge Temple's mansion during the day, but his nights he spent in Leatherstocking's cabin. So much secrecy surrounded his comings and goings, and the reserve of Leatherstocking and his Indian friend, that Richard Jones, the sheriff and a kinsman of the judge, became suspicious. Among other things, he wondered why Natty always kept his cabin closed and never allowed anyone except the Indian and Edwards to enter it. Jones and some others decided that Natty had discovered a mine and was working it. Jones also suspected that Edwards was an Indian half-breed, his father a Delaware chief.

Hiram Doolittle, the local magistrate, prowled around the shack and set free the dogs guarding it. In the meantime Elizabeth and Louisa Grant, the minister's daughter, went walking in the woods. There they were attacked by a savage panther and were saved only by the timely arrival of Leatherstocking, who shot the animal. But Natty had also shot a deer, in defiance of Judge Temple's strict game laws. With the charge that the old hunter had killed a deer out of season as his pretext, Doolittle persuaded Judge Temple to sign a warrant so that the magistrate could gain entrance to the cabin and search it. Jones was more convinced than ever that Leatherstocking was secretly smelting ore he had mined.

But when Doolittle went to the cabin, Leatherstocking, rifle in hand, refused him entrance. Then the magistrate attempted to force his way over the threshold, but the old hunter seized him and threw him twenty feet down an embankment. As the result of his treatment of an officer, Leatherstocking was arrested. Found guilty, he was given a month's jail sentence, a fine, and placed in the stocks for a few hours. When Elizabeth went to see what assistance she could give the humiliated old woodsman, she learned he was planning to escape. Edwards, who had given up his position with the judge, was planning to flee with his aged friend; he had provided a cart in which to carry the old hunter to safety. Elizabeth promised to meet Leatherstocking the following day on the top of a nearby mountain and to bring with her a can of gunpowder he needed.

The next day Elizabeth and her friend Louisa started out on their expedition to meet Leatherstocking. On the way Louisa changed her mind and turned back, declaring that she dared not walk unprotected through the woods where they had lately been menaced by a panther. Elizabeth went on alone until she came to a clearing in which she found old Indian John, now dressed in the war costume and feathers of a great Mohican chief. When she stopped to speak to the Indian, she suddenly became aware of dense clouds of smoke drifting across the clearing and discovered that the whole mountainside was ablaze. At that moment Edwards appeared, followed by Leatherstocking, who led them to a cave in the side of the mountain. There the old Indian died of exhaustion, and Elizabeth learned that he had been in earlier days Chingachgook, a great and noble warrior of the Mohican tribe.

When danger of the fire had passed, Edwards conducted Elizabeth down the mountainside until she was within hearing of a party of men who were looking for her. Before they parted, Edwards promised he would soon reveal his true identity.

The next day the sheriff led a posse up the mountain in search of Leatherstocking and those who had aided him in his escape from jail. Leatherstocking was again prepared to defend with his rifle the cave to which he had taken Elizabeth the day before, but Edwards declared that the time had now come to let the truth be known. He and Natty brought from the depths of the cave an old man seated in a chair. The stranger's face was grave and dignified, but his vacant eyes showed that his mind was gone. Edwards announced that the old man was really the owner of the property on which they stood. Judge Temple interrupted with a shout of surprise and greeted the old man as Major Effingham.

The young man told his story. His name, he said, was Edward Oliver Effingham, and he was the grandson of the old man who sat before them. His own father had been, before the Revolutionary War, a close friend of Judge Temple. They had gone into business together, but the outbreak of the war found them on opposite sides during the struggle. Judge Temple had some money entrusted to him by his friend, money which actually belonged to his friend's father, but when he received no reply to letters he wrote to the Effinghams he at last decided that all the family had been lost in a shipwreck off Nova Scotia. The money he had invested in his own enterprises.

The judge had never met Major Effingham; he would not have recognized him if he had seen the helpless old man who had for years been hidden in the cabin on the outskirts of Templeton. During those years he was nursed faithfully by Leatherstocking and his Indian friend; by Leatherstocking because he had served with the major on the frontier years before, by Indian John because the major was an adopted member of the Mohican tribe.

Judge Temple ordered that the old man be carried to the Temple mansion at once, where he would receive the best of care. Old Major Effingham thought himself back home once more, and his eyes gleamed with joy. He died, happy and well cared for, soon afterward.

Edward Effingham also explained his belief that Judge Temple had stolen his father's property and the money left in trust years before. In his resentment he had come to Templeton to assist his grandfather and regain in some manner the property which he believed Judge Temple had unrightfully possessed. Now the judge was happy to return that part of the property which belonged to the Effinghams, and there was a reconciliation between the two men. As it turned out, however, the property stayed in the family, for Elizabeth and Edward Effingham were married within a short time.

Elizabeth and Edward Effingham wanted to build a new cabin for Leatherstocking, but the old hunter refused their offer. He intended to go off into the woods to hunt and trap in the free wilderness until he died. Settlements and towns were not for him. He would not listen to their pleas but set out soon afterward on his long journey, pausing only long enough to view the stone tablet on Indian John's grave, a monument Edward Effingham had erected. Then he trudged off toward the woods, his long rifle over his shoulder. Elizabeth and her husband watched him go. Tears were in their eyes as they waved a last farewell to the old hunter just before he disappeared into the forest.

THE PIRATES OF PENZANCE

Type of work: Comic opera
Author: W. S. Gilbert (1836-1911)
Type of plot: Humorous romance
Time of plot: Nineteenth century
Locale: England
First presented: 1879

Principal characters:
MAJOR GENERAL STANLEY, of the British Army
RICHARD, the pirate king
FREDERIC, the pirate apprentice
MABEL,
EDITH,
KATE, and
ISABEL, General Stanley's daughters
RUTH, a pirate maid of all work

Critique:

The Pirates of Penzance, Or, The Slave of Duty is another entertaining and perennially popular operetta by the team of Gilbert and Sullivan. The hero was such a noble lad that he killed and plundered with the pirates because it was his duty. Altogether delightful, this libretto is one of the favorites of light opera lovers throughout the world.

The Story:

Frederic, the pirate apprentice, had reached his twenty-first birthday, and at midnight he would be free of his indenture. The pirate king announced that Frederic would then become a full-fledged member of the band. But Frederic said that he had served them only because he was a slave to duty; now he was going to leave the pirates. Astounded, the king asked for reasons. Frederic would not tell, but Ruth, the pirate maid of all work, confessed that she had been Frederic's nurse when he was a baby. She had been told to apprentice him to a *pilot*, but being hard of hearing she had thought the word was *pirate*. Afraid to reveal her mistake, she too had joined the pirates to look after her charge.

Frederic also announced that when he left the pirates he was going to do his best to exterminate the whole band. Individually, he loved them all, but as a crew of pirates they must be done away with. The pirates agreed that they were

such unsuccessful pirates that they could not blame him for leaving. Frederic told them why they were such poor pirates. When they reminded him that he would still be one of them for half an hour, he felt that it was his duty to give them the benefit of his knowledge. The trouble was that they were too kindly. They would never attack a weaker party and were always beaten by a stronger one. Then, too, if any captive said he was an orphan, he was set free; the pirates themselves had all been orphans. Word about the soft-hearted pirates had spread, and now everyone who was captured declared himself an orphan. The pirates knew that Frederic was right, but they hated to be grim and merciless.

Asked what Ruth would do when he left their band, Frederic said he would take her with him. He wondered if she was attractive. Ruth declared that she was, but since he had had no opportunity to see another female face, Frederic could not be sure. The king assured him that she was still a fine-appearing woman, but when Frederic tried to give her to the king, he would not have her.

Ruth had him almost convinced that she was a fair woman when Frederic saw approaching a bevy of beautiful maidens. Ruth, realizing that her cause was lost, admitted that she had deceived him; she was forty-seven. Frederic cast her aside.

Frederic hid himself as the girls approached, but he felt that he ought to reveal himself again as the girls, believing themselves alone, prepared for a swim. When they heard his story, they were filled with pity for his plight and admiration for his handsome figure. From a sense of duty, one of the sisters, called Mabel, accepted his affection. Her sisters, Kate, Edith, and Isabel, wondered whether her sense of duty would have been so strong had Frederic been less handsome.

Frederic warned the other girls about the pirates. Before they could escape, however, the band, led by their king, appeared and seized them. At the same time their father, Major General Stanley, appeared in search of his daughters. He bragged of his great knowledge—he knew everything but military skill. As soon as he learned something of military tactics he would be the greatest general ever. When the pirates told him they were going to marry his daughters, the general, much to their sorrow, begged them not to take his lovely girls from him because he was an orphan. Unhappily the pirates gave up their prizes; they could not harm an orphan.

Later, at his home, a ruin which he had purchased complete with ancestors, the general grieved because he had lied to the pirates. He knew that his falsehood about being an orphan would haunt him and his ancestors, the newly purchased ones. Frederic consoled him by telling him that the lie was justified to save his daughters from the pirates. At midnight he, Frederic, would lead the police who would capture the outlaw band. He must wait until then because he was still one of them.

When the police entered, the girls praised them for going so nobly to their deaths. The police, not cheered by the praise, agreed that theirs would be a noble death. At midnight Frederic prepared to lead them to the the pirate hideout. At that moment the pirate king and Ruth appeared, laughing at a joke they had just discovered. Frederic had been born on February twenty-ninth in leap year. Thus he was not twenty-one but only five years old. His apprenticeship would not be up until 1940. Frederic, thinking that he looked more than five, also laughed at that paradox.

And, since Frederic was again one of the pirate band, he felt it his duty to tell the pirates that Major General Stanley was not an orphan, that he had lied. The pirates went at once to capture the villain and to torture him for his falsehood. A struggle took place between the pirates and the police. The pirates won, but when the police challenged them to surrender in the name of Queen Victoria, the pirates yielded, for they loved their queen. But before the police could take them away, Ruth entered and told all assembled that the pirates were really noblemen gone wrong. Then the general forgave them their youthful fling and sent them back to their ranks, giving them his daughters for their brides.

THE PIT

Type of work: Novel
Author: Frank Norris (1870-1902)
Type of plot: Naturalism
Time of plot: 1890's
Locale: Chicago
First published: 1903

Principal characters:
CURTIS JADWIN, a speculator in wheat
LAURA DEARBORN, later his wife
SHELDON CORTHELL, an artist in love with Laura
MR. AND MRS. CRESSLER, friends of the Jadwins
GRETRY, Jadwin's broker

Critique:

The Pit, A Story of Chicago, is an exciting story about the Board of Trade in Chicago and a man who for a time cornered the wheat market of the world. Norris, who intended to write a trilogy about wheat, completed the first two books. The second novel of the planned trilogy, The Pit tells how wheat is bought and sold on the Board of Trade. Along with the interest in the financial explorations of the novel, there is presented a moving love story of two strong but very human characters.

The Story:

From the first evening that Laura Dearborn met Curtis Jadwin she knew that she interested him. She had attended the opera with her sister Page and her Aunt Wess, as the guests of some very old friends, the Cresslers. Jadwin had also been a guest that evening, and she found the marked attention which he paid her so flattering that she listened only absently to avowals of love from her old and devoted suitor, Sheldon Corthell. Corthell was an artist. The life of the capitalist who made and broke fortunes and human lives from the floor of the Board of Trade seemed to Laura more romantic than painting.

The next day Mrs. Cressler told Laura part of Jadwin's story. He had been born into a poor family, had worked to educate himself. When, in default of a loan, he gained possession of some land in Chi-

cago, he sold it, bought more real estate, and by shrewd dealings now owned a portion of one of the wealthiest sections of real estate in Chicago. He was also speculating in the wheat market, and he was a familiar figure on the floor of the Board of Trade.

Jadwin, stopping by the Board of Trade one morning in answer to the summons of his broker, Gretry, paused in the Pit—the huge room downstairs in which all the bidding took place—to watch the frenzied excitement of bidders and sellers. Gretry had advance information that in a few days the French government would introduce a bill placing heavy import duties on all foreign goods. When this news became widespread, the price of wheat would drop considerably. Gretry urged Jadwin to sell his shares at once and Jadwin agreed.

The deal was a tremendous success. Jadwin pocketed a large profit. The Cresslers tried to persuade Jadwin to stop his speculating. Mr. Cressler had almost ruined himself at one time through his gambling with wheat, and he feared that the same thing might eventually happen to his friend.

But Jadwin was too much interested in Laura to pay attention to the warning or even to hear the words of his friends. One evening at the Cresslers he asked Laura to marry him. Laura, in a capricious mood, said that although she loved no one as yet she might some day come

THE PIT by Frank Norris. By permission of the publishers, Doubleday & Co., Inc. Copyright, 1903, by Doubleday & Co., Inc. Renewed, 1930, by Jeannette Preston.

to love him. She had given Sheldon Corthell the same encouragement. That night, ashamed of her coquetry, she wrote to both men telling them that she did not love either, and that if they were to continue friends they must never speak of love to her again. Corthell accepted her refusal and left for Europe. Jadwin came to call on Laura while she was out and refused to leave until he had spoken to her. He was successful in his suit and they were married in July.

The early years of their marriage were completely happy. Their home was a mansion, exquisitely furnished and with beautiful grounds. At first Laura found it difficult to adjust herself to her luxurious surroundings, but as time passed she found great pleasure in satisfying her interest in art, decorating her home, and entertaining her friends.

Jadwin, caught up once more in the excitement of the Pit, invested all his money in successful speculative enterprises. For some time he had aligned himself with the bears in the wheat market. But now, as he saw that the country was becoming more prosperous and the wheat crops were increasing, he decided to change to the side of the bulls. He resolved to buy as much wheat as he could and, if possible, to corner the market. Luck was with him. One year, when European crops were very poor, Jadwin bought a tremendous amount of wheat at a low price and determined to hold it until he could ask his own price.

Laura was worried by his constant attendance at the Board of Trade, and he promised to give up speculating as soon as he concluded an important deal.

One evening Laura had dinner with Sheldon Corthell, who had returned from Europe. Late that night Jadwin came home with the announcement that the deal had been concluded and that he had cleared five hundred thousand dollars. He kept his promise to give up speculating in the Pit, but within a short time he grew restless. He began again to try his luck in the wheat market.

Because he kept his activities hidden from the public, he was spoken of as the unknown bull. After he had purchased as much wheat as he could, it suddenly became evident that he was in a position to corner the world's wheat and name his own price. Cressler, meantime, had been drawn into speculation by the group of bears who were certain that they could break the unknown bull. He had no idea that the bull was his own friend, Jadwin.

Weeks went by while Laura saw her husband only at breakfast. He spent his days and many of his nights at the board. Laura, lonely and unhappy, began to see more and more of Corthell. Corthell, still in love with Laura, finally declared his feelings to her. Laura was kind in her dismissal, but she still loved her husband.

In cornering the market, Jadwin had risen upon a wave of power and prosperity. But he began to have strange, irritating headaches which he attempted to ignore, just as he disregarded his moods of loneliness and depression.

Mrs. Cressler confided that her own husband was not well. She invited Laura to call on her one afternoon. When Laura arrived, Mrs. Cressler was not yet home. She wandered into the library and saw Mr. Cressler sitting there. He had shot himself through the temple.

Jadwin was horrified when he realized that Cressler had lost all his money in speculation with the bears, and he felt that he was responsible for his friend's death. But Jadwin himself was in a tight spot. Having forced the price of wheat to a new high, he was now faced by the necessity of cornering a bumper crop in addition to the millions of bushels he already owned. His enemies were waiting for the time when the unknown bull could buy no more wheat. At that moment the price would drop considerably. Jadwin put every penny he owned into his attempt to keep wheat cornered, but he was defeated by the wheat itself. The grain flowed in, millions of bushels at a time. Almost out of his mind, he bought and bought, and still the wheat harvest continued. He no longer controlled the market. He was ruined.

He walked into his home one night a broken man. Laura nursed him through days and nights of illness. When he was well enough, the two set out for the West to begin life again. Although they had lost their money, the Jadwins were much happier than they had been for many years.

THE PLAGUE

Type of work: Novel
Author: Albert Camus (1913-1960)
Type of plot: Impressionistic realism
Time of plot: The 1940's
Locale: Oran, Algeria
First published: 1947

Principal characters:
DR. BERNARD R. RIEUX, a young physician
JEAN TARROU, a traveler
COTTARD, a fugitive
JOSEPH GRAND, a clerk
RAYMOND RAMBERT, a journalist
FATHER PANELOUX, a priest

Critique:

Camus in this novel exhibits those traits so frequently attributed to him: classical clarity, independence, and logic. The Plague has been very well received here and abroad; in fact, it has been called the best novel to come out of postwar Europe. In structure the work is compact, covering only the duration of the plague. The characters are projected with insight. But characters and plague alike are subordinated to a search for meanings. From the frightful course of events Rieux finds an answer to the eternal question, Why are we here?

The Story:

For a few days Dr. Bernard Rieux gave little thought to the strange behavior of the rats in Oran. One morning he found three on his landing, each animal lying inert with a rosette of fresh blood spreading from the nostrils. The concierge grumbled about the strange happening, but Rieux was a busy doctor and just then he had personal cares. Madame Rieux was going away from Oran. She suffered from a lingering illness and Rieux thought that a sanatorium in a different town might do her some good. His mother was to keep house for him while his wife was absent. Rambert, a persistent journalist, cut into his time. The newsman wanted to do a story for his metropolitan paper on living conditions among the workers in Oran. Rieux refused to help him, for he knew an honest report would be censored.

Day by day the number of dead rats increased in the city. After a time truckloads were carried away each morning. People stepped on the furry dead bodies whenever they walked in the dark. Rieux's first case of fever was the concierge who had grumbled about having to clean up the rats on the stair landing. He had a high temperature and painful swellings. Rieux was apprehensive. By telephoning around he learned that his colleagues had similar cases.

The prefect was averse to taking any drastic action because he did not want to alarm the population. Only one doctor was sure the sickness was bubonic plague; the others reserved judgment. When the deaths rose to thirty a day, however, even officialdom was worried. Soon a telegram came instructing the prefect to take drastic measures, and the news became widespread; Oran was in the grip of the plague.

Rieux had been called to Cottard's apartment by Grand, a clerk and former patient. Grand had cut down Cottard just in time to prevent his suicide by hanging. Cottard could give no satisfactory reason for his attempt to kill himself. Rieux was interested in him; he seemed rather an eccentric person.

THE PLAGUE by Albert Camus. Translated by Stuart Gilbert. By permission of the publishers, Alfred A. Knopf, Inc. Copyright, 1948, by Stuart Gilbert.

Grand was another strange man. He had for many years been a temporary clerk, overlooked in his minor post, whom succeeding bureaucrats kept on without investigating his status. Grand was too timid to call attention to the injustice of his position. Each evening he worked hard on his manuscript and seemed to derive much solace from it. Rieux was surprised when he saw the work. Grand in all those years had only the beginning sentence of his novel finished, and he was still revising it. He had once been married to Jeanne, but she had left him.

Tarrou was an engaging fellow, a political agitator who had been concerned with governmental upheavals over the whole continent. He kept a meticulous diary in which he told of the ravages and sorrows of the plague. One of his neighbors was an old man who each morning called the neighborhood cats to him and shredded paper for them to play with. Then, when all the cats were around him, he would spit on them with great accuracy. After the plague grew worse, the city authorities killed all cats and dogs to check possible agents of infection. The old man, deprived of his cats as targets, stayed indoors, disconsolate.

As the blazing summer sun dried the town, a film of dust settled over everything. The papers were meticulous in reporting the deaths by weeks. When the weekly total, however, passed the nine hundred mark, the press reported only daily tolls. Armed sentinels were posted to permit no one to enter or leave the town. Letters were forbidden. Since the telephone lines could not accommodate the increased traffic, the only communication with the outside was by telegraph. Occasionally Rieux had an unsatisfactory wire from his wife.

The disposal of the dead bodies presented a problem. The little cemetery was soon filled, but the authorities made a little more room by cremating the remains in the older graves. At last two pits were dug in an adjoining field, one for men and one for women. When those pits were filled, a greater pit was dug and no further effort was made to separate the sexes. The corpses were simply dropped in and covered with quicklime and a thin layer of earth. Discarded streetcars were used to transport the dead to the cemetery.

Rieux was in charge of one of the new wards at the infirmary. There was little he could do, however, for the serum from Paris was not effective. He observed what precautions he could, and to ease pain he lanced the distended buboes. Most of the patients died. Castel, an older physician, was working on a new serum.

Father Paneloux preached a sermon on the plague in which he called Oran's pestilence a retribution. M. Othon, the judge, had a son under Rieux's care by the time Castel's new serum was ready. The serum did the boy little good; although he did show unexpected resistance, he died a painful death. Father Paneloux, who had been watching as a lay helper, knew the boy was not evil; he could no longer think of the plague as a retribution. His next sermon was confused. He seemed to be saying that man must submit to God's will in all things. For the priest this view meant rejection of medical aid. When he himself caught the fever, he submitted to Rieux's treatment, but only because he had to. Father Paneloux died a bewildered man.

Rambert, because he was not a citizen of Oran, tried his best to escape. Convinced that there was no legal means of leaving the city, he planned to leave with some illicit smugglers. Then the spirit of the plague affected him. He voluntarily stayed to help Rieux and the sanitation teams, for he realized that only in fighting a common evil could he find spiritual comfort.

Tarrou had left home early because his father was a prosecutor; the thought of the wretched criminals condemned to death because of his father's zeal horrified him. After he had been an agitator for years he finally realized that the workings of politics often resulted in similar executions. He had fled to Oran just before the plague started. There he found an answer to his problem in organizing and directing sanitary workers.

Cottard seemed content with plague conditions. Wanted for an old crime, he felt safe from pursuit during the quarantine. When the plague eased a little, two officers came for him but he escaped. He was recaptured in a street gun fight.

Grand caught the fever but miraculously recovered to work again on his manuscript. Tarrou, also infected, died in Rieux' house. As the colder weather of January came, the plague ended. Rieux heard by telegram that his wife had died.

The streets became crowded again as lovers, husbands, and wives were reunited. Rieux dispassionately observed the masses of humanity. He had learned that human contact is important for every one. For himself, he was content to help man fight against disease and pain.

LES PLAIDEURS

Type of work: Drama
Author: Jean Baptiste Racine (1639-1699)
Type of plot: Satiric comedy
Time of plot: Seventeenth century
Locale: Normandy, France
First presented: 1668

Principal characters:
DANDIN, a judge
LEANDRE, his son
CHICANNEAU, a bourgeois
ISABELLE, Chicanneau's daughter
LA COMTESSE, a litigant
PETIT JEAN, a porter
L'INTIME, a secretary
LE SOUFFLEUR, the prompter

Critique:

Racine first planned Les Plaideurs as a French adaptation of Aristophanes' The Wasps, to be presented by an Italian company in Paris. As it turned out, he received some collaboration from a group of friends who dined together regularly, a circumstance which may explain the spontaneity of the comedy. The action, unimportant in itself, becomes the occasion for a series of amusing scenes which ridicule doctors and lawyers. Like Aristophanes, Racine took the greatest liberties with the logic of his plot. The play occupies an interesting place in Racine's work, for it shows a master of tragedy equally at ease in a drama of completely different effect.

The Story:

Early one morning Petit Jean stood in front of Dandin's house while he complained about the sad state of affairs created by his master's madness. Judge Dandin suddenly wanted to sit in judgment on his own family and to go to bed with his robes on. He had even ordered his rooster killed, saying that a defendant had bribed the bird to wake him up too late.

It was necessary for Leandre to have his father watched day and night, and this was the reason why Petit Jean could not sleep and was complaining. Leandre

also insisted that Judge Dandin should not be allowed to go into court, but Dandin was constantly attempting to escape the watchfulness of his family in order to do so. When L'Intime and Petit Jean caught him trying to climb out the window, the noise awakened Leandre, who tried to persuade his father to go back into the house. Finally Petit Jean took Dandin into the house by force.

Leandre confessed to L'Intime his wish to have a note delivered to Isabelle, daughter of their neighbor, Chicanneau, and L'Intime promised to help him. At that moment Chicanneau arrived and insisted on seeing Dandin about one of his trials; the bourgeois was constantly engaged in lawsuits. Petit Jean firmly refused to let him enter. During the argument La Comtesse arrived; she also was always suing someone. Chicanneau tried to advise her about one of her lawsuits. When she misunderstood him and they began to quarrel, both asked Petit Jean to act as a witness. He tried his best to pacify them.

In order to deliver the note to Isabelle, L'Intime disguised himself as a process server and insisted that Leandre dress as a police commissioner. The idea was to give Isabelle the letter while serving La Comtesse' writ on Chicanneau. Finding Isabelle alone, they succeeded in giving her the letter just as Chicanneau arrived home. Isabelle, pretending that it was a legal paper, tore up the note and declared that she detested lawsuits. In order to convince Chicanneau, L'Intime produced the actual document from La Comtesse. Chicanneau, doubting that L'Intime was a process server, administered a sound thrashing.

When Leandre arrived in his disguise, L'Intime complained bitterly about the bad treatment he had received and the defiance of the law exhibited by both Chicanneau and Isabelle. Leandre, seizing upon this situation as an opportunity to "question" Isabelle, tricked her into admitting her feelings toward him. Chicanneau, bewildered, failed to understand what was happening and signed what he thought was a police report, but which was actually a marriage contract between Leandre and Isabelle.

Dandin, meanwhile, was running from one window of his house to another. Insisting on giving audience to Chicanneau and La Comtesse, he succeeded in pulling Chicanneau inside the house through a cellar window. When he next tried to escape, Leandre suggested that he preside at the trial of Citron, a dog that had eaten a chicken.

Declaring that he had never seen them before, Chicanneau complained to Leandre about the process server and the police commissioner. Leandre suggested that Chicanneau and Isabelle demand justice from Dandin.

Meanwhile, Leandre staged the trial of Citron, with Petit Jean and L'Intime acting as lawyers. Petit Jean, as the prosecutor, had difficulty in playing his role in spite of help from Le Souffleur, the prompter, at every other word. L'Intime, acting as the defense lawyer, was so eloquent that Dandin fell asleep. On awakening, he decided to condemn the dog to the gallows. L'Intime then produced a basket of puppies and, swearing that they would become orphans if the dog were executed, pleaded their cause. Dandin, greatly perplexed, discussed this situation with everyone.

Chicanneau and Isabelle arrived. When Leandre produced the marriage contract, Chicanneau threatened to go to court over the agreement. Leandre assured him, however, that he had no interest in Isabelle's dowry. Mollified, Chicanneau finally agreed to the marriage. Then, as a welcoming present to Isabelle, Dandin decided to acquit Citron.

THE PLAIN DEALER

Type of work: Drama
Author: William Wycherley (1640?-1716)
Type of plot: Comedy of manners
Time of plot: Seventeenth century
Locale: London
First presented: c. 1674

Principal characters:
> CAPTAIN MANLY, a misanthropic gentleman in the king's service
> FREEMAN, Manly's lieutenant
> OLIVIA, Manly's mistress
> VERNISH, Manly's only trusted friend
> WIDOW BLACKACRE, a rich widow gulled by Freeman
> FIDELIA, Manly's page, an heiress in disguise

Critique:

In Wycherley's own time *The Plain Dealer* was regarded as his best play. It is, at any rate, an important, if sardonic, account of the times when Holland and England were at war during the reign of Charles II. Manly, the plain dealer in all situations, displays as much bitterness as the misanthropes of Molière's drama and the plays of Marston and others in the earlier seventeenth century. The picture of contemporary life, complete with scenes showing Westminster Hall, bookseller's stalls, eating houses, and private homes, is anything but enticing. The people, except for Manly and his page, are portrayed as evil, grasping, litigious, and belligerent characters or, like the two sailors, as simpletons incapable of a thought of their own. Yet the social message of the play is not oppressive, for Wycherley also employed a tricky plot, brilliant dialogue, and realistic stage business.

The Story:

The plain dealer, Captain Manly, returned to London after his ship had been sunk in a battle with the Dutch. He sought another ship because he disliked the hypocrisy of the age and wished to be away from the sycophancy of court and social life. Among the acquaintances who called at his quarters in London was Lord Plausible, who attempted to persuade the captain to seek his ship through influential people instead of waiting for an assignment to be made. Manly demonstrated his

love of plain dealing by showing Lord Plausible the door.

After Lord Plausible's departure Manly instructed the two sailors who served him not to admit anyone to his lodgings except his ship's lieutenant, Freeman. When Freeman came, he and Manly discussed the relative merits of plain dealing and hypocrisy. Freeman held that no one could have a successful career without being hypocritical, but he could not convince Manly that such a policy was better than telling the truth at all costs.

While they talked, Widow Blackacre broke past the sailors and entered Manly's rooms. Manly made her welcome because she was a cousin of his fiancée, Olivia. The widow, who was of an extremely litigious nature, wanted Manly to appear on her behalf at a court hearing the following day. She warned Manly that if he did not appear she would have him subpoenaed. Freeman, well aware that the widow had a great deal of money, started a courtship for her hand. The widow, who had a son Jerry, almost Freeman's age, ridiculed the idea because she wanted to manage her own affairs and could not do so if she were married.

Manly then went to seek information about Olivia, whom he had entrusted with most of his fortune while he was at sea.

Meanwhile Olivia had heard of Manly's arrival in London. She was none too anxious to see him because she had kept his fortune for her own and had

2898

married Vernish, the only man Manly trusted and called his friend. Olivia pretended to be a plain dealer like Manly. When visited by her cousin Eliza, Lord Plausible, and others, she belabored them for their hypocrisy, saying they spoke only ill of people in their absence but praised the same persons to their faces. Her cousin reminded her that her comments about people were much worse, and that she did not go out in company often enough to have an opportunity to say anything good about people to their faces.

Olivia, going on to speak plainly about Captain Manly, revealed that she did not love him and wished to be rid of his attentions. No one present knew as yet of her secret marriage to Vernish. In the meantime Manly had entered her apartment unnoticed. After the others left Manly and Olivia had words, and Manly told Olivia that he detested her. Freeman and Manly's page reminded him to recover his money and jewels from Olivia, and so Manly went back to request them. Olivia then announced to all three that she was married but did not say to whom. She told Manly that she could not return the money because her husband had it.

Olivia, noticing Manly's page, became infatuated and told Manly to send the young page as messenger if they were to have any further dealings. As Manly left, Widow Blackacre, accompanied by her son, entered, and Freeman once more began his suit for her hand. When she repulsed him, he decided to use law instead of ordinary courtship to gain his ends.

The following morning Manly, Freeman, and the page appeared at Westminster Hall as witnesses in Widow Blackacre's lawsuit. While away from Freeman for a time, Manly instructed his page to go to Olivia and arrange an assignation for him, for Manly had decided to get revenge by making her unknown husband a cuckold. That was a bitter errand for the page, who was actually a young woman in disguise. She had some time before fallen in love with Manly and had disguised herself as a boy in order

to be near him.

At the court session Freeman found Widow Blackacre's son and befriended him by giving him some money. The boy told Freeman that his mother refused to let him have any money until he came of age. Learning that the boy had not yet appointed a guardian for himself, Freeman persuaded the boy to name him as guardian, an act which put Widow Blackacre's money into his hands instead of the widow's. In addition, Freeman had the boy leave all the widow's legal documents in his care.

Manly, returning to his lodgings, was informed by his page that she had succeeded in getting an assignation with Olivia; Manly could substitute himself for the page in the darkness. When Manly heard the comments Olivia had made about him, he became even more furious and eager to have revenge. A little later Widow Blackacre arrived, hoping to find Freeman and her son. When she confronted them, they told her that she was helpless, since they had her documents and Freeman had been appointed the boy's guardian. The widow threatened then to prove that her son was illegitimate and so could not inherit her husband's estate.

That evening the page went to Olivia's home. When Vernish appeared, the page escaped without being discovered, only to return later with Manly after Olivia had sent her husband away. Manly, refusing to seduce Olivia, left. The page, trapped when Vernish returned unexpectedly, escaped by disclosing herself to Vernish as a woman, incapable of cuckolding him. Vernish's attempt to ravish her was foiled by the entrance of his wife.

The page, escaping through a window, returned to Manly. Later Manly and Vernish met. Manly was not yet aware that Vernish was Olivia's husband, and Vernish was unaware that Manly was trying to seduce Olivia. Because they still trusted one another as the best of friends, Manly told Vernish he had been intimate with Olivia before her marriage, a fact which made Vernish all the more certain she had cuckolded him after marriage. The page, entering during the conversation, took Manly aside and told him another assignation with Olivia had been set for that evening. When they parted, Vernish told himself that he would pretend to leave town and thus trap the unknown man who was seducing Olivia.

In the meantime Freeman and some bailiffs overheard Widow Blackacre plan with some court hangers-on to prove that her son was born out of wedlock. Rather than marry Freeman and lose control of her estate, the widow finally granted an allowance to the boy and an annuity to Freeman. The lieutenant was satisfied; the money was all he wanted.

That evening Manly and the page went to Olivia's apartment. There Manly overcame Vernish in a duel. Olivia, in shame, tried to escape with the jewels and money, but Manly took them from her. In the scuffle the page's wig came off, disclosing her as a woman. Manly, impressed by her faithfulness and beauty, immediately asked her to marry him. She, on her part, told Manly she was Fidelia, heiress to a large fortune. They planned to begin a new life in the West Indies.

PLATERO AND I

Type of work: Prose poems
Author: Juan Ramón Jiménez (1881-1958)
First published: 1914-1917

About his life Juan Ramón Jiménez said very little. He was born in the small Spanish village of Moguer, in Andalusia, and educated at a Jesuit school. A few poems published in a Madrid magazine brought him an invitation to visit the capital where the poet Rubén Darío and others befriended him. But violent critical attacks on a volume of his poetry and the death of his father so upset him that he spent some time in a French sanitarium. From then on, in spite of enthusiastic reception of later volumes of verse, he lived almost a recluse either in Spain or as a political refugee, after the Spanish Civil War, in Cuba and Puerto Rico. By the time he was thirty-five, he had published twenty volumes of what he called *borradoras* (rough drafts); the rest of his life was spent polishing them, beginning with his *Selected Poems* in 1917.

In prose, his best-known work is *Platero and I*, a series of brief, unconnected sketches, 138 in all, about life in Moguer, the whole given unity by the presence of a silver gray donkey, Platero. There are both narrative and descriptive sections in poetic prose. The subtitle is "Andalusian Elegy," making the donkey a symbol of the simplicity and purity of the soul. Like Sancho Panza's donkey in *Don Quixote*, Platero seems headed for immortality in a volume "capable of giving back to people their childhood soul."

Platero was a hairy donkey, so soft that he might have been made of cotton, without bones. Only his eyes were hard, like two scarabs of black crystal. He fed on oranges, grapes, and figs when he was not nibbling the grass of the meadow. To the country people he looks like steel as the narrator, telling his story in the first person, rides him through the town of Moguer on Sundays. Coming back at

dusk, he tells the customs collector that all they have brought with them are white butterflies. Then he rides on through the miserable streets down by the river, where poor children are playing games of make-believe.

Unconnected episodes are presented. Once Platero and the author saw an eclipse of the sun. In the eerie light, the town seemed to shrink and even the donkey appeared diminished.

At the age of four, Platero should have entered kindergarten, but there were no chairs big enough for him. The wisest plan, in the opinion of his master, was to take Platero to the fields where he could learn about flowers and stars. There no one would ever put a dunce cap on him or call him an ass.

Riding his donkey, the author, with his long brown beard and small black hat, must have looked strange, for ragged children ran after him, shouting "Crazy man!" Later the children were the ones who seemed crazy on the day before Easter, as they celebrated their feast by shooting at Judas, to the terror of the little donkey.

The lengthening days, as the year went on, brought the ripening of the first figs, and Jiménez and Platero went to Rica to pick them. Everybody raced to see who could get there first and arrived panting and excited. The author picked a few of the ripe ones and put them on a tree trunk for Platero. Somehow a fig fight started; the pickers threw the bluish fruit at everybody, including the donkey. On another occasion, Jiménez, with a book of prints that he had received the day before from Vienna, told the children that he would give it as a prize to the first one who reached the violets at the end of the meadow. Seeing them running, Platero took off after them and

PLATERO AND I by Juan Ramón Jiménez. Translated by Eloise Roach. Excerpts reprinted by permission of the publishers, University of Texas Press. Copyright, 1957, by Juan Ramón Jiménez.

easily outdistanced them. Panting their protests, the children gathered around the author. He told them that Platero had won and demanded a prize. Because the book would be of no use to him, Jiménez took some parsley and made a crown with which to adorn the victor.

In a serious moment Jiménez tried to comfort his donkey by promising that he would not be thrown into a pit when he died, or abandoned beside the road; he would be buried beside the tall pine in the orchard. More immediate problems occupied the donkey, however. As he entered the pasture, he began limping. Immediately his master jumped off. Platero showed his right forefoot, in which Jiménez found a long orange-tree thorn stuck into it like a little emerald dagger. After the wound had been washed in a brook they continued on toward the sea, the master now walking ahead and Platero, still limping, gently nudging him in the back.

The swallows arrived early, chirping as if to tell everybody about their two sea crossings and the flowers they had seen in Africa. Because of the unseasonal cold, the birds nearly froze to death.

Sometimes, in their conversations, Jiménez would reminisce over his childhood days, the people who lived across the street from him, the striped doorway of the confectioner's house, and the little idiot boy who sat, ugly and unable to speak, in the doorway of his house to watch the people pass. The boy had died, and must now be in heaven watching the promenade of heavenly souls.

Another memory was the story of Anilla, who used to dress in a sheet, put flour on her face, and walk about carrying a lantern to scare children. One September night, during a severe storm, lightning struck and a eucalyptus tree fell on the tool shed. When the moon came out, the dog began barking so loudly that everybody went out to see what was wrong. There was Anilla, still dressed in a sheet and with her lantern burning, but now she really was a ghost.

The author also communed with his earthbound donkey about the joys of height. He described climbing to the flat roof and the sights to be seen: the gardens, the houses, the people working in them, and even the far-off river with its boat. Looking into the distance gave him the same feeling that he felt when, as a child, he went to the locked gate in the city walls and saw the winding road with its promise of romance.

Many of the inhabitants of Moguer pass through these pages: the French doctor whose parrot comforted patients with "It's nothing! Nothing!"; the gipsies who would sometimes visit the town and scandalize its inhabitants: Don José, the priest who rode a female donkey; Darbón, the veterinarian. Children, in particular, play an important part in the life of Platero and his master. There is much talk over plans to celebrate the Day of the Magi, when the children would put their shoes on the balconies in hopes of presents from the Wise Men and all the older people would have a parade; Platero would be adorned with a Colombian flag and his master, wearing a cotton beard, would impersonate one of the Three Kings.

There are tragedies as well. One day Platero, while drinking at the fountain, got a leech on his tongue. With the help of Raposo, a farmer, Jiménez pried open the donkey's mouth and removed the leech with sticks. At another time horseflies left him covered with blood.

Sometimes Platero could be helpful, as when he gave a ride to a little sick girl, or when he and his master helped a little girl and her donkey with their cart which was stuck in the mud. She rewarded them with two oranges, one of which Platero ate; the other little donkey got the second orange.

Finally came the morning when the author found Platero "lying on his bed of straw, his eyes soft and sad." Darbón, the veterinarian, could do nothing for him. "Something he ate, perhaps a poison root." By noon Platero was dead. Later, when his master went with some children to his grave and asked whether the donkey was carrying angel children through the heavenly meadows, a white butterfly appeared.

At the end, in "To Platero, in the heaven of Moguer," Jiménez dedicated the book to the donkey, and concluded: "You, Platero, are alone in the past. But you also live in a period of no time, for you possess. as I do, a new sun with the dawn of each day, red as the heart of the everlasting God."

THE PLAYBOY OF THE WESTERN WORLD

Type of work: Drama
Author: John Millington Synge (1871-1909)
Type of plot: Realistic comedy
Time of plot: Early twentieth century
Locale: County Mayo, Ireland
First presented: 1907

Principal characters:
CHRISTOPHER MAHON, a braggart
OLD MAHON, his father
MARGARET FLAHERTY (PEGEEN MIKE), his sweetheart
WIDOW QUIN, a villager
SHAWN KEOGH, a young farmer in love with Pegeen

Critique:

This play is the most outstanding of John Millington Synge's Irish dramas, and in it Synge has used the beautiful lyrical Irish language to the finest effect. *The Playboy of the Western World* is tender, ironical, and humorous drama.

The Story:

One evening a young man arrived at a small inn on the wild Mayo coast of Ireland and announced that he had run away from home. He said his name was Christopher Mahon and that he was running away because he had killed his father during a fight. The farmers who were passing the time in the inn were very much pleased by his exhibition of courage. Christopher was especially admired by Pegeen, the pretty young daughter of Michael Flaherty, the innkeeper. She, along with the others, pressed the young man to tell his story over and over again.

At home Christopher had been a meek and obedient son, domineered by his father. He accepted the insults of his parent until the latter tried to force him into marrying a rich old woman. At last, in desperation, he hit his father over the head with a loy. Seeing the old man fall, Christopher presumed that he was dead.

The experience at the inn was something new for Christopher, who for the first time in his life was looked upon as a hero. When the news of his story spread among the villagers, they flocked to look at this paragon of bravery. The young women were particularly interested in him—and the not so young as well. Dame Quin, a middle-aged widow, was much taken with the young taproom hero.

But Christopher was attracted to pretty Pegeen. He was flattered by her admiration, and in an attempt to live up to her opinion of him he began to adopt an attitude of bravado. Before long he himself believed that he had done a courageous deed.

Each year the village held a festival in which the men competed with each other in various sports. Christopher was naturally expected to take part. His early timidity having long since disappeared, he made every effort to appear a hero in the eyes of Pegeen, to whom he was now openly betrothed. She had broken her engagement with a young farmer, Shawn Keogh, soon after Christopher arrived on the scene.

While her Playboy, as Pegeen called him, was taking part in the sports, an old man came to the inn. He was looking for a young man whose description fitted Christopher's appearance. Dame Quin, who still had designs on the boy, deliberately misdirected the stranger. But when the man returned from his wild goose chase, he arrived in time to see Christopher hailed as a hero because he had just won the mule race. Old Mahon,

THE PLAYBOY OF THE WESTERN WORLD by John Millington Synge. By permission of Random House, Inc. Published by The Modern Library, Inc. Copyright, 1935, by The Modern Library, Inc.

not dead from Christopher's blow, recognized his son and flew into a rage. He insisted that Christopher go home with him, and by his angry tirade he humiliated his son in front of the spectators.

But the Playboy had enjoyed too long the thrill of being a hero. He did not give in timidly as he would have done at an earlier time. Much to his father's astonishment, he struck the old man over the head. Once again it appeared that old Mahon was dead. But the reaction of the people was not at all what Christopher might have expected. Killing one's father some miles away was one thing. Killing him in front of a number of spectators who might be involved in the affair was another. The people muttered angrily among themselves, and even Pegeen joined with them in denouncing the murderer.

Deciding at last that the only thing to do was to hang Christopher for his crime, they tied up the struggling young man and prepared to lead him away. But Old Mahon had proved himself a tough fellow once before, and he did so again. The first blow that Christopher had given him had only stunned him, so that soon after the boy ran away his father was able to follow him to the village. Now the second blow had merely knocked him unconscious for a short time. As Christopher struggled and the noose was slipped over his head, Mahon crawled through the door on his hands and knees.

While the villagers stood around dumbfounded, he walked over to his son and quickly untied him. Far from being angry with Christopher for hitting him, he was pleased to discover that his son was not the timid weakling he had thought him to be. The two left the inn, arm in arm, deaf to the pleas of Pegeen, both of them jeering at the foolishness of the people on the Mayo coast.

2905

THE PLOUGH AND THE STARS

Type of work: Drama
Author: Sean O'Casey (1884-   )
Type of plot: Social criticism
Time of plot: 1916
Locale: Dublin, Ireland
First presented: 1926

Principal characters:
FLUTHER GOOD,
PETER FLYNN,
MRS. GOGAN,
MOLLSER GOGAN,
BESSIE BURGESS,
THE COVEY,
NORA CLITHEROE, and her husband,
JACK CLITHEROE, neighbors in a Dublin tenement house
CAPTAIN BRENNAN, of the Irish Citizen Army
CORPORAL STODDART, and
SERGEANT TINLEY, of the Wiltshires

Critique:

Sean O'Casey's bitter childhood and early manhood accounted for his adherence to the Marxist idea of class war. He believed that the Irish would have to reckon with the problem of Irish poverty before they could ever hope to win independence. It is with this problem of some poor people caught in the midst of the famous Easter Rebellion of 1916 that O'Casey deals in The Plough and the Stars. Here the desperate situation of a group of tenement dwellers overshadows the dream of national independence. The Covey seems always to give O'Casey's own views on humanity versus nationality. The play was the cause of a patriotic riot when it was first produced by the Abbey Theatre in Dublin.

The Story:

Fluther Good had put a new lock on the Clitheroes' door when Mrs. Gogan brought in a hatbox, just delivered for Nora Clitheroe. Mrs. Gogan was convinced that Nora was putting on airs and buying too many new clothes to hold on to her husband.

Nora's Uncle Peter Flynn drifted in and out, getting ready his uniform of the Irish National Foresters. Peter had a chip on his shoulder which all the tenement dwellers took turns knocking off. He was an ineffectual man and he knew it.

When the Covey, Nora's cousin, came in, telling them that he had been laid off from work because the boys had mobilized for a demonstration for independence, he aroused both Peter and Fluther. The Covey was less inclined to follow the flag of the Plough and the Stars than to go ahead with his work.

Peter and the Covey were arguing away when Nora came home and quieted them, declaring that there was small hope of ever making them respectable. She was pleased with the way Fluther had put on the lock, but Bessie Burgess, a vigorous but rather coarse woman, scornfully berated Nora for treating her neighbors shamefully, not trusting them. As Fluther broke up the women's wrangling, Jack Clitheroe came home and sent Bessie away. He told Nora that he would speak to Bessie when she was sober again.

Jack was despondent because the Citizen Army was to meet that night. He had

THE PLOUGH AND THE STARS by Sean O'Casey. By permission of the publishers, The Macmillan Co. Copyright, 1926, by The Macmillan Co.

lost the rank of captain to Ned Brennan and, sulking, had refused to attend meetings. Wanting to be a leader, he did not have strength of leadership. Nora tried to get his mind off the meeting by making love to him. They were interrupted by the new Captain Brennan with a dispatch from the general telling Jack where to report. Jack did not understand why he was to report until Brennan told him that the boys had given him the title of Commandant, word of which had been in a letter Nora had never delivered. Disturbed because Nora had withheld the letter, Jack went off to the meeting with Brennan.

Mollser Gogan, a child in the last stages of tuberculosis, asked Nora if she might stay with her, since everyone else had gone to the demonstration.

Fluther and Peter, overwhelmed by the oratory of the speakers at the demonstration, repaired to a bar to pour in more courage. Even in the public house, the voice of the speaker followed them, urging bloodshed and war. Bessie and Mrs. Gogan were engaged in a verbal battle when they entered. Bessie, drunk, was ready for a hair-pulling, but the barman sent both women away. Peter was left holding Mrs. Gogan's baby, for she had forgotten the child when she was piloted out of the bar. He hurried out to find her.

Fluther, though he had intended to give up drinking before the meeting, decided the time had come for all the liquor he could hold, and he was generous enough to stand treat, even to the Covey and Rosie, a prostitute. Fluther and the Covey got into an argument on the labor movement and the barman had to separate them. Rosie and Fluther left when Jack, Brennan, and other officers, their eyes shining with excitement, came in for a drink before moving off with the Citizen Army.

The next day Mollser was so much weaker that Mrs. Gogan put her out in the sun in front of the house; they could hear shooting in the distance. Looking

for Jack, Nora and Fluther had spent the night going to all the barricades without finding him. When they came back to the house, Nora was leaning heavily on Fluther. Bessie shouted down curses from her window. The Covey sighed that the fight would do the poor people no good.

Bessie brought Mollser a mug of milk when she came downstairs. The men began to gamble to keep their minds off the shooting, but they stopped when Bessie reappeared, laden down with booty, to say that looting had begun in the shops. Fluther and the Covey went off immediately. The guns scared Mollser so much that Bessie took her into the house. Even timid Peter started to follow Bessie and Mrs. Gogan when they set out with a baby carriage to hold their loot, but the sound of the big guns again stopped him. He was envious, however, when he saw the Covey, then Bessie and Mrs. Gogan, return with piles of loot.

Brennan and Jack stopped at the steps to let a wounded comrade rest. It was with difficulty that Jack got away from Nora, who had run down to him when she heard his voice. When the two officers finally took their man away, Nora was ready to faint.

Fluther came back with a jug of whiskey. Roaring drunk, he was too fuddled to go out for a doctor for Mollser, who was suddenly very sick. Bessie, praying when she heard the guns, went off toward the shooting to find a doctor.

A few days later the rebellion was still going on. Mollser had died, and Nora had had a stillborn baby. Both bodies were in the same coffin in Bessie's room, the only room in the tenement that seemed safe from the shooting. Fluther, the Covey, and Peter, having taken refuge there, played cards to while away the time.

Nora was on the verge of insanity. Bessie had stayed up with her for three nights and was herself almost dead for sleep. Each time Bessie sat in the chair in front of the fireplace for a nap, Nora would wake up. Once, when Nora got up, Brennan, in civilian clothes, was in the room telling the men how Jack had died. Nora did not recognize him. Brennan wanted to stay with the others; he said there was nowhere to go any more. Corporal Stoddart, an English soldier, came in to escort the coffin out of the house. Mrs. Gogan was the only one allowed to go with it. As she was thanking Fluther for making the funeral arrangements, the soldier heard a sniper nearby shoot another English soldier. The English, trying to find the sniper, were rounding up all the men in the district, and so Fluther, the Covey, Peter, and Brennan were forced to go with the corporal to spend the night in the Protestant church.

Bessie had again fallen asleep. Nora got up to prepare tea for Jack. As she stood at the window looking for him, the soldiers below shouted for her to go away. Bessie, awakened, tried to pull her back, but Nora struggled so hard that Bessie fell back against the window frame as she pushed Nora. Two shots, fired quickly, struck Bessie. She was dead before Mrs. Gogan came home.

Two English soldiers, investigating the room for snipers, found the mistake they had made in killing Bessie. They calmly poured themselves cups of tea while Mrs. Gogan took Nora downstairs to put her into Mollser's bed.

THE PLUMED SERPENT

Type of work: Novel
Author: D. H. Lawrence (1885-1930)
Type of plot: Symbolic romance
Time of plot: Twentieth century
Locale: Mexico
First published: 1926

Principal characters:
KATE LESLIE, an Irishwoman
DON RAMÓN CARRASCO, a Spanish-Indian scholar and the reincarnated
Quetzalcoatl
GENERAL CIPRIANO VIEDMA, the reincarnated Huitzilopochtli, god
of war
DOÑA CARLOTA, Don Ramón's first wife
TERESA, his second wife
OWEN RHYS, Kate Leslie's cousin

Critique:

D. H. Lawrence was a writer driven by deep, personal need in his search for values that would redeem his vision of a disordered modern world and a brittle, crumbling civilization. *The Plumed Serpent*, the impressive novel of his later period, is the result of his American pilgrimage. Brilliantly colored in style and symbolic in theme, it is his tortured confession of faith in an atavistic mysticism which would restore to contemporary man the primitive virtues of potency and blood unity. In this novel the symbols of quest and discovery are the gods of ancient Mexico, Quetzalcoatl and Huitzilopochtli, whom Don Ramón Carrasco and General Cipriano Viedma attempt to revive as living deities. These dark gods of the primitive spirit alone can revitalize the earth, for Christianity had failed to do so: this is Lawrence's message. Kate Leslie, involved in the efforts of the two Mexicans, is a woman bred in a tradition dominated by industrial and mechanical controls, but her submission is inevitable when she finds herself in a strange world of masculine domination, symbolized by the Indian drum and the dance as expressions of that ancient, instinctive life which civilization has almost destroyed. *The Plumed Serpent*, a tremendous fable of sexual,

political, and religious rebirth, is a stirring and disturbing book, a great, even though imperfect, work of the creative imagination.

The Story:

Kate Leslie was the widow of an Irish patriot. Restless after her husband's death, she had gone to Mexico with Owen Rhys, her American cousin. But Mexico oppressed her. Dark and secretive, the arid land weighed upon her spirit like a sense of doom. She saw it as a country of poverty, brutality, and bloodshed.

Owen and one of his friends took her to a bullfight. It was a distressing experience, for to her that ritual of death was like modern Mexico, vulgar and cruel, without m?ster or passion. At last, unable to endure the spectacle and the reek of warm blood, she announced that she was returning alone to the hotel. A downpour of rain began as she was leaving the arena and she was forced to wait in the exit tunnel with a crowd whose speech and gestures filled her with alarm. She was rescued from her predicament by a small, authoritative man in uniform who introduced himself as General Cipriano Viedma. A full-blooded Indian, he was impassive and withdrawn, yet vitally

THE PLUMED SERPENT by D. H. Lawrence. By permission of the publishers, Alfred A. Knopf, Inc. Copyright, 1926, 1951, by Alfred A. Knopf, Inc.

alert. While they talked, waiting for the automobile he had summoned to take Kate to her hotel, she felt unaccountably drawn to him.

The next day Mrs. Norris, widow of a former English ambassador, invited Kate and Owen to her house for tea. The general and his friend, Don Ramón Carrasco, were among the guests. Don Ramón was a landowner and a distinguished scholar. There were reports of a strange happening near his estate at Sayula. A naked man was supposed to have risen from the Lake of Sayula and told the villagers that Quetzalcoatl and the old gods of Mexico were soon to return to earth. Don Ramón had promised an investigation. The story appealed to Kate's Celtic imagination; she wanted to go to Sayula and see the lake from which the Aztec gods were to be reborn.

Kate and Owen dined with Ramón before his return to Sayula. The guests talked about Mexican politics and the happening at the lake. One impassioned young man declared that only a great miracle, like the return of Quetzalcoatl, could save Mexico. Cipriano seldom spoke but sat, his eyes black and unfathomable, looking from Kate to his host. After dinner he and Kate walked in the garden. In the darkness she felt that he was a man of strange, almost primitive potency and impulses.

When Owen returned to the United States, Kate decided to go to Sayula for a time. There she found an old Spanish house that pleased her. With the house went a servant, Juana, and her two sons and two daughters. Liking the house and its surroundings, Kate rented it for an indefinite stay.

The people of Sayula were restless, filled with a spirit Kate had not seen elsewhere in Mexico. One night she heard drums beating in the village plaza. Men naked to the waist were distributing leaflets printed with a hymn to Quetzalcoatl. Later the peons began to dance to the savage, insistent rhythms of the drums. In the torchlight the dance looked like a ritual out of old, almost forgotten times, a ritual men remembered in their blood rather than in their minds. Some said that Don Ramón was behind the new cult of Quetzalcoatl that was springing up.

Several weeks after Kate arrived in Sayula, Don Ramón and his wife, Doña Carlota, came to call. Doña Carlota was devoutly pious and eager to be friendly. When Kate visited Jamiltepec, Don Ramón's hacienda, she found soldiers guarding the gates. A drum was beating in the patio. Doña Carlota, hating the sound, told Kate that she was afraid because her husband was involved in the business of Quetzalcoatl. He wished to become a god, she confided, the reincarnation of the Plumed Serpent that the Aztecs had worshipped. Cipriano arrived at the hacienda for supper. That night there was a dance in the patio. Don Ramón promised that the reborn gods would bring new life to the country. The rains began, ending the hot, dry season.

Doña Carlota, refusing to witness her husband's heresies, as she called them, returned to Mexico City. Meanwhile the work of the Men of Quetzalcoatl continued. During one of his visits Cipriano asked Kate to marry him, but she put him off. Don Ramón continued to write and publish his hymns to Quetzalcoatl. Cipriano's soldiers distributed them. After he had been denounced by the clergy Don Ramón had the holy images removed from the church at Sayula and burned.

One day a group of his political and religious enemies, disguised as bandits, attacked Jamiltepec and tried to assassinate Don Ramón. Kate, who happened to be at the hacienda when the raiders appeared, killed one of the attackers and saved Don Ramón's life after he had been seriously wounded. Afterward she stayed much to herself, afraid of her own disturbed emotions. But she was being drawn slowly toward the dark, powerful forces of primitive awareness and power that she found in Don Ramón and Cipriano. The general now believed himself the living Huitzilopochtli, god of war. Fascinated and repelled, Kate yielded at last to his masculine dominance. Don Ramón married them with pagan rites and she became Malintzi, bride of the red-knifed god of battles.

When Don Ramón reopened the church, which he had converted into a sanctuary of the old Aztec gods, Doña Carlota appeared to protest against his blasphemy. Overcome by hysteria and fear of his implacable will, she suffered a stroke and died a short time later. Meanwhile Cipriano had been spreading the new doctrines among his soldiers. On an appointed night he was declared the living Huitzilopochtli, god of the knife, and in the rites of his assumption he sacrificed three of the prisoners captured after the attack on Don Ramón some weeks before.

Don Ramón married again. His bride was Teresa, daughter of a dead landowner of Jalisco. Watching Teresa's passive, female submission to her husband, Kate began to fear the dark potency, the upsurge of blood with which Don Ramón and Cipriano were arousing all Mexico. Men wearing the white and blue serapes of Quetzalcoatl and the red and black serapes of Huitzilopochtli were seen everywhere. When the Church excommunicated the leaders, revolt broke out. The President of Mexico declared the Church outlawed, and the faith of Quetzalcoatl became the official religion of the republic. Kate viewed these happenings with a sense of horror. Because the pride and strength of the old gods seemed to menace her spirit and her womanhood, she decided to return to Ireland.

But in the end she could not go. Cipriano with his black, impassive eyes and dark maleness was stronger than her European sensibility and her woman's will. Afraid of his violence but awed by the strength of a spirit stronger than her own, she felt wanted but not needed. The need, she realized, was her own, not Cipriano's. He had revealed to her the deep, dark, hot life of the senses and the blood, and she was trapped in his primitive world. She could never escape.

PLUTUS

Type of work: Drama
Author: Aristophanes (c. 448-385 B.C.)
Type of plot: Satiric comedy
Time of plot: Fifth century B.C.
Locale: Athens
First presented: 388 B.C.

Principal characters:
CHREMYLUS, a poor, but honest farmer
CARIO, his servant
BLEPSIDEMUS, his friend
PLUTUS, the god of wealth

Critique:

Plutus is a dramatized moral fable marked by a debate on the advantages of poverty against the advantages of wealth, by delightfully irreverent humanizing of gods, and by pungent satire on ill-gotten wealth and ingratitude. The utter nonsense which takes place in the temple of Asclepius is a high point in the comedy.

The Story:

Chremylus, a Greek farmer, went to the temple of Apollo in Athens. There he asked the oracle how his son might attain affluence without having to resort to knavery. The oracle directed him to follow the first man he encountered on his emerging from the temple and to take the stranger home with him.

The first man Chremylus saw was a blind beggar, whom he followed impatiently. At first the beggar refused to reveal his identity to Chremylus, but when Cario, Chremylus' servant, threatened to push the blind man over a cliff, he fearfully revealed that he was Plutus, the god of riches, blinded by Zeus when he told the god that he would favor only good men. Zeus did not want Plutus to discriminate among men. The unhappy Plutus declared to Chremylus that had he his sight back again he would favor only the good and shun the wicked.

When Chremylus offered to restore his sight to him, Plutus expressed fear of the wrath of Zeus. But Chremylus declared that if Plutus had his sight back, even for a moment, Zeus would be superseded, because the dispensation of all

wealth, upon which Zeus was dependent for his authority, would be in the power of Plutus, even money paid for sacrifices offered up to Zeus. Indeed, it would then be Plutus, according to Chremylus, not Zeus, who would be all things to all men. Plutus was delighted to hear these words.

Chremylus, after sending Cario to summon the neighboring farmers, ushered Plutus into his house. When Cario told the farmers that Plutus was at Chremylus' house and that he would lift them out of their poverty, they were delirious with joy. Chremylus, welcoming them, noticed that his friend Blepsidemus was skeptical of Cario's report; he suspected that Chremylus had stolen a treasure. Chremylus declared that Plutus was truly in his house and that all good and deserving people would soon be rich. Even Blepsidemus was convinced, and he agreed that it was essential to restore to Plutus his eyesight.

As Chremylus prepared to take Plutus to the Temple of Asclepius, there to have his sight restored, the goddess of poverty, a hideous old woman, appeared and objected to the prospect of being cast out of Chremylus' house after having lived with him for many years. Blepsidemus and Chremylus were terrified at the sight of her. But Chremylus quickly regained his composure and engaged the goddess in a debate over which deity, the god of riches or of poverty, was more beneficial to mankind. Chremylus declared that with Plutus once again able to see, those who deserved it would receive money. Thus

2912

society would be benefited. The goddess of poverty answered that progress would come to a halt because Plutus would distribute money equally. The pair then argued the difference between beggary and poverty; the goddess maintained that men who entertained her were brave, alert, and strong, while those who entertained Plutus were soft, fat, and cowardly. She declared that men were virtuous when she was their guest, but were corrupted when Plutus was their guest. Chremylus was not convinced by her arguments.

The goddess, having been defeated, departed in sorrow and anger. Chremylus now took Plutus to the temple of Asclepius, the god of healing. He observed every detail of the ritual and laid Plutus on a couch. A priest told them to sleep. Plutus' eyes were wiped with a cloth; then a purple mantle was placed over his head. At a signal from Asclepius, two serpents came forth from the sanctuary and slithered under the mantle. In a short time, Plutus, his sight restored, arose from the couch.

Now, those people who had got their wealth by unfair means looked with fear upon Plutus, but the poor rejoiced at their new good fortune. Plutus was happy; he vowed to correct all of the mistakes he had made when he was blind. Chremylus was rewarded with great wealth for his service to the god.

While Plutus was a guest in the house of Chremylus, a just man came to petition the god. He had helped his friends when they were in need, but they had not responded in kind when he himself had become indigent. The man became wealthy again through the power of Plutus. He offered an old cloak and a worn-out pair of sandals as tribute to the god.

Soon afterward an informer came to the house and complained that he had been ruined by the change wrought in Plutus. Cario stripped the informer of his fine coat and bedecked him in the just man's threadbare cloak.

An old woman, presuming to be a young one, came to see the god. She was distressed because her young lover, who had flattered her in order to get money from her, had deserted her now that Plutus had made him independent. The youth appeared with a wreath to give to Plutus in appreciation.

Hermes, the messenger of the gods, appeared and reported that Zeus and the other gods were furious because men no longer made oblations to them. He declared that he himself was actually starving since there were no more offerings in the form of cakes or figs or honey, and he urged Cario to succor him. Cario condescended to retain Hermes to preside at the games which Plutus surely would sponsor.

A priest of Zeus came and complained of hunger; when everyone was rich, there were no more offerings to the gods. Chremylus, calling attention to the fact that Plutus had now taken the place of Zeus in human fortunes, hinted that the priest of Zeus would do well to become the priest of Plutus. Zeus having been deposed, Plutus was installed as the supreme god.

POEM OF THE CID

Type of work: Poem
Author: Unknown
Type of plot: Heroic epic
Time of plot: c. 1075
Locale: Fief of Bivar, to the north of Burgos, Spain
First transcribed: Twelfth century

Principal characters:
RUY DÍAZ, sometimes called My Cid, Lord of Bivar
ALFONSO, King of León, by whom the Cid was exiled
DOÑA XIMENA, the Cid's wife
MARTÍN ANTOLÍNEZ, one of the Cid's chief lieutenants
DOÑA ELVIRA, and
DOÑA SOL, the Cid's daughters
MINAYA ALVAR FÁÑEZ, the Cid's chief lieutenant and companion
FÉLIX MUÑOZ, the Cid's nephew and rescuer of his daughters
GARCÍA ORDÓÑEZ, Lord of Grañón, and the Cid's enemy
DIEGO, and
FERNANDO GONZÁLEZ, the princes of Carrión, suitors and husbands to
  the Cid's daughters, two villains
GONZALO ANSÚREZ, Count of Carrión, father of Diego and Fernando
  González

Critique:

In this national epic of eleventh-century Spain, the poet writes in irregular verse; there are 3735 lines of uneven length in three Cantos which relate in succession the major events in the Cid's life. The poem, rich in Homeric flavor, with frequently repeated descriptions of the principal characters, is more or less historically correct. Such a man did live (he died in 1099)· however, his character and exploits have been embroidered, amplified, and distorted to earn him the unquestioned position of the most heroic figure in Spanish history and legend. Of all the epics of the Cid, the *Poem of the Cid*, dating from the twelfth century, is unique in its qualities of realism, verity, and poetic excellence. The Cid is drawn as a typical Spanish warrior, proud, ruthless, realistic, and calculating. At the same time he shrewdly deals out praise to his vassals and is generous to a fault. In victory, he is quick to do honor—even to overdo it—to his loyal lieutenants. Although exiled by King Alfonso VI he continued to hold the position of the king, if not the man himself, in high regard.

The Story:

By royal edict, the Cid was banished from Christian Spain by King Alfonso VI of Castile. The royal edict allowed him nine days in which to leave the kingdom but forbade him from taking with him any of his wealth and goods. Anyone in the kingdom who would offer aid to the Cid would forfeit his estate.

Nevertheless, the Cid enlisted the aid of Martín Antolínez in swindling two money-lenders, Raquel and Vidas, in exchange for two large sealed coffers, supposedly loaded with the Cid's riches but containing only sand. The Cid and a small force of vassals then rode away and made a secret camp. On the morning of his actual departure from the country, with a fair-sized group of loyal vassals, mass for all was said at the abbey where Doña Ximena, the Cid's wife, and his two infant daughters, Doña Elvira and Doña Sol, had been ordered to remain.

Becoming a soldier of fortune, the knight led his host in conquest of one Moorish territory after another, each time with a generous sharing of spoils and booty among his knights and vassals, even the lowliest. Thus he built up a larger and stronger force with every foray, and after each victory mass was said in thanks-

2914

giving.

The Cid fought his way to the eastern side of the peninsula, where he fought his most crucial battle and won his greatert victory when he took as his prisoner Count Ramón of Barcelona. After Count Ramón had been humbled and forced to give up all his property, he was granted his liberty.

Although Minaya Alvar Fáñez returned to King Alfonso with gifts and a glowing report of the Cid's successes, the king did not revoke his decree of banishment. Minaya's estates were restored, however, and he was granted freedom to come and go without fear of attack.

The Cid continued his campaigns against the Moorish territories in order to increase his favor with King Alfonso. After he had conquered the provinces of Valencia and Seville, his men grew tired of fighting and many wished to return to Castile. The Cid, although still generous and understanding, proved himself master by threatening all deserters with death.

Again the Cid sent Minaya to King Alfonso with a gift of one hundred horses and a request that Doña Ximena and her daughters be permitted to join him in Valencia. Visibly softened by the Cid's obvious power, King Alfonso granted this request. In addition, he returned their former estates to the Cid's men.

Shortly after a triumphant reunion with his family in Valencia, the Cid overcame the King of Morocco. As a gesture of victory he sent the Moroccan's tent to King Alfonso. This dramatic gift earned the Cid's pardon and the request that he give his daughters in marriage to Diego and Fernando, the princes of Carrión.

At the victory feast, many marveled at the great length and abundance of the Cid's beard, for he had sworn at the time of his banishment that his beard would never again be cut and that it would grow very long. A mystical significance of power and success was now attached to the fullness of his beard.

The Cid had reservations about giving his daughters to the princes of Carrión. They were, he thought, too young for marriage. Also, he distrusted the two men. However, with a great show of humbleness and subservience, he returned Doña Elvira and Doña Sol to the king with word that Alfonso would honor the Cid by disposing of his daughters' future as the monarch saw fit.

After the weddings, the elaborate wedding feast, to which all the Cid's vassals as well as those of the territory of Carrión had been invited, lasted for more than two weeks. The Cid expressed some satisfaction in having his family united with noblemen as rich as Prince Diego and his brother Fernando. Two years of happiness followed.

One day one of the Cid's pet lions escaped. Far from showing valor in the emergency, Diego hid from the lion under the bench on which the Cid was asleep, while Fernando fled into the garden and hid behind a wine press. After the Cid's vassals had easily subdued the lion, the favored princes became the butt of much crude humor and scorn, but the Cid, choosing to ignore the evident cowardice of his daughters' husbands, made excuses for their pallor.

Once again the Cid was forced to war with the Moroccans, this time against mighty King Bucar. After a great battle, Bucar was killed and his vassals were subdued. The Cid was jubilant. As the spoils were divided, he rejoiced that at last his sons-in-law had become seasoned warriors. His vassals were half-amused, half-disgusted, because it was common knowledge among them that neither Diego nor Fernando had shown the slightest bravery in the conflict, and at one time the Cid's standard-bearer had been forced to risk his life in order to cover for Fernando's shocking cowardice.

Diego and Fernando were richly rewarded for their supposed valor, but their greed was not satisfied. Resentful and injured by the insults and scorn heaped on them by the Cid's vassals, they began a scheme for revenge by telling the Cid that, proud of their wives and their wealth, they would like to make a journey to Carrión in order to show off their wives and to sing the Cid's praises. In secret, they planned not to return. The noble and generous Cid, always ready to think the best of anyone, granted their request without question.

The Cid added further to the princes' treasure and sent them off with a suitable company of his own vassals as an escort of honor. Then, belatedly concerned for the safety of his daughters, he also sent with them his nephew, Félix Muñoz, after charging the young nobleman with the care of Doña Elvira and Doña Sol.

When they were safely away from Valencia, the princes sent the company on ahead and took their wives into the woods. There, with viciousness, they stripped the women of their rich garments and their jewels, whipped them, and left them, bleeding and wounded, to die. His suspicion aroused by the desire of the princes to separate their wives from the rest of the party, Félix Muñoz followed the princes' tracks and found the women. He nursed them back to consciousness and returned them to the Cid.

The princes' scheme of revenge rebounded to their further disgrace. Word of their wicked and dishonest acts spread quickly, and King Alfonso, in his great displeasure with the Carrións, swore to try them in Toledo. The Cid swore that he, to avenge the treatment his daughters had received, would marry them to the richest in the land.

At the trial, the princes were first ordered to return the Cid's valued swords, which he had given them as tokens of his high regard. Then they were ordered to return his gold. Having squandered it all, they were forced to give him equal value in horses and property.

In the meantime ambassadors from Aragón and Navarre had arrived to ask for the Cid's daughters as queens for their kings. The Cid was jubilant, but still he demanded that the princes of Carrión pay in full measure for their brutality: trial by combat with two of the Cid's chosen knights. King Alfonso charged the princes that if they injured their opponents in the least, they would forfeit their lives. Proved cravens in the fight, the princes were stripped of all honor and wealth.

The Cid rejoiced that, once banished, he could now count two kings of Spain among his kinsmen. He died, Lord of Valencia, on the Day of Pentecost.

POEMS, CHIEFLY IN THE SCOTTISH DIALECT

Type of work: Poetry
Author: Robert Burns (1759-1796)
First published: 1786

Since the first publication of Burns's verse in the famous Kilmarnock edition entitled *Poems, Chiefly in the Scottish Dialect*, the poet's fame has increased and spread. Other editions of his work, containing later poems, only enhanced his reputation. Unlike many writers who achieve early fame only to see it fade, Burns is still widely read and appreciated.

At least part of the reason for this continuing appreciation is the fact that Burns was essentially a transitional figure between the eighteenth-century neo-classicists and the Romantics who were soon to follow. Possessing some of the qualities of each school, he exhibits few of the excesses of either. He occasionally used the couplet that had been made a skillful tool by Pope and his followers, but his spirit was closer to the Romantics in his attitude toward life and his art.

Although he occasionally displayed a mild conservatism, as in the early "The Cotter's Saturday Night," he was fundamentally a rebel — and rebellion was a basic trait of the Romantics. It would have been hard for Burns to be a true neo-classicist because his background, which figures constantly in his poems, simply did not suit him for this role. He had a hard early life and a close acquaintanceship with the common people and the common circumstances of life. He was certainly not the uneducated, "natural" genius that he is sometimes pictured — having had good instruction from his father and a tutor and having done considerable reading on his own — but he lacked the classical education that earlier poets thought necessary for the writing of true poetry.

Like the neo-classicists, however, he was skillful in taking the ideas and forms of earlier poets, in Burns's case, particularly, the Scottish poets Ramsay and Fergusson as well as the anonymous balladists and writers of folk songs, and treating them in his own individual way. Thus his verse has a wide variety of stanza forms and styles.

Despite the variety of his techniques, his basic outlook in his poems is remarkably consistent. This outlook also may have a great deal to do with his popularity. Perhaps more than any other poet since Chaucer, Burns possessed the personal insight and the instinct for human feelings that can make a poem speak to all men's hearts. Burns always saw the human aspect of things. His nature poetry, for instance, marks a departure from the precise appreciation of the eighteenth-century poets; Burns's lines about nature treat it primarily as a setting in which people live.

The warmth of his verse arises from this attitude combined with the experience he had of being in close personal contact with the people about whom he wrote. His writing never deals with subjects that he did not know intimately. Burns loved several women and claimed that they each served as great poetic inspiration. The reader may well believe this statement when he encounters the simple and clearly sincere little poems "Highland Mary," "Mary Morison," and the well-known song "Sweet Afton." It was this quality of sincerity that another great Scot, Thomas Carlyle, found to be Burns's greatest poetic value.

Burns was not an original thinker, but he had a few strong convictions about religion, human freedom, and morality. His condemnation of Calvinism and the hypocrisy it bred is accomplished with humor and yet with sharpness in two of his best poems, "The Holy Fair" and the posthumously published "Holy Willie's Prayer." In these and several other poems Burns pokes occasionally none too gentle fun at the professional religionists of his time without ever seeming didactic. Here his intensely personal viewpoint saved him from preaching in the style of earlier eighteenth-century versifiers. It is to be expected that the few poems that contain examples of his rare attempts to be lofty are unsuccessful.

Having grown up in a humble environment, Burns was especially sensitive to social relations and the value of human freedom and the equality of men. On this subject, too, he is never didactic, but few readers have remained unmoved by the lines of probably his most famous poem in defense of the lower classes, "A Man's a Man for A' That":

Is there, for honest poverty
   That hings his head, an' a' that?
The coward slave, we pass him by—
   We dare be poor for a' that!
For a' that and a' that,
   Our toil's obscure and a' that;
The rank is but the guinea's stamp,
   The man's the gowd for a' that.
. . . .
Then let us pray that come it may,
   As come it will for a' that,
That sense and worth, o'er a' the earth,
   Shall bear the gree, an' a' that.
For a' that, an' a' that,
   It's coming yet for a' that,
That man to man, the warld o'er,
   Shall brithers be for a' that.

It was this powerful feeling for democracy that led Burns, in his later years, to a tactless advocation of the principles of the French Revolution, a crusade that did his career as a minor government official no good.

It is questionable whether Burns's heated protest against Calvinism and the strict morality it proclaimed was simply a rationalization of his own loose behavior. However many the romances he had, and however many the illegitimate children he fathered, there can be little doubt of Burns's sincere devotion, at least at the time, to the woman of his choice. In a larger sense, too, the poet's warm sympathy for his fellow man is evidence of a sort of ethical pattern in his life and work that is quite laudable.

The poetic techniques in Burns's poems are unquestionably a chief reason for his popularity. Few poets have so well suited the style to the subject, and his use of earlier stanza forms and several kinds of poetic diction has a sureness and an authority that are certain to charm even the learned student of poetry.

There are three types of diction in his poetry: Scottish dialect, pure English, and a combination of the two. In "Tam O' Shanter," a later work that is perhaps his masterpiece, Burns used dialect to tell an old legend of the supernatural with great effect. The modern reader who takes the trouble to master the dialectal terminology will be highly rewarded. In this, as in most of Burns's poems, the pace and rhythm of the lines are admirably well suited to the subject.

His use of the purely English idiom, as in "The Vision," was seldom so successful. Usually Burns wrote in pure English when he had some lofty purpose in mind, and with the exception of "The Cotter's Saturday Night" this combination was nearly fatal to the poetic quality of these poems.

For the general reader, probably the most enjoyable and rewarding reading consists of the poems and songs that Burns did in English, with occasional Scottish touches here and there in the lines. Most happy is this joining of language and dialect in such a poem as the famous little love lyric, "A Red, Red Rose." These three kinds of poetic diction can be found side by side in one of Burns's best poems, the highly patriotic "The Jolly Beggars," which gives as fine a picture of Scottish low life as can be found anywhere.

Naturally, Burns was most at home when he wrote in his native dialect; and, since one of the most striking characteristics of his verse is the effortless flow of conversational rhythms, it is not surprising that his better poems are those that came as natural effusions in his most familiar diction.

The total achievement of Burns is obviously great, but it should not be misunderstood. Burns lacked the precision and clarity of his predecessors in the eighteenth century, and he never was able to reach the exalted heights of poetic expression attained by Shelley and Keats not long after him. For vigor and the little touches that breathe life into lines of poetry, however, he was unexcelled by earlier or later poets.

The claim that Burns wrote careless verse has been perhaps too much emphasized. His poems and songs are surely not carefully carved jewels, but neither are they haphazard groupings of images and rhymes. The verses seem unlabored, but Burns worked patiently at them, and with considerable effort. That they seem to have been casual utterances is only further tribute to his ability.

It may be that the highest praise of all was paid to Burns, both as man and poet, by Keats when the great Romantic said that we can see in Burns's poems his whole life; and, though the life reflected was not an altogether happy one, the poet's love of freedom, people, and of life itself appears in nearly every line.

THE POETICAL WORKS OF EDWARD TAYLOR

Type of work: Poetry
Author: Edward Taylor (c.1645-1729)
First published: 1939

> Lord, let thy Glorious Body send such
> rayes
> Into my Soule, as ravish shall my
> heart,
> That Thoughts how thy Bright Glory
> out shall blaze
> Upon my body, may such Rayes thee
> dart.
> My Tunes shall dance then on these
> Rayes, and Caper
> Unto thy Praise: when Glory lights
> my Taper.
> —Meditation Seventy-Six, Second
> Series.

Edward Taylor, an orthodox Puritan minister, was New England Puritanism's sweetest singer before the Lord, but for more than two hundred years after his death his poems were unknown since he did not allow their publication and directed that his heirs should not publish them. The 400-page manuscript containing his poetical works was presented to Yale University in 1883 by Henry Wyllys Taylor. Thomas H. Johnson, a specialist in American literature, discovered the poems and received permission from the university to publish them. *The Poetical Works of Edward Taylor*, published in 1939, contains what Mr. Johnson regards as the best of Taylor's poems.

The *Poetical Works* contains a long verse sequence titled "God's Determinations Touching His Elect," a group of five occasional poems, and selected poems from two long series of "Sacramental Meditations." "God's Determinations" is largely in dialogue form; and the speakers—Mercy, Justice, Christ, Satan, the Soul, and a Saint—are reminiscent of characters in early English morality plays. The several poems in the sequence are written in a variety of stanzaic patterns; and the style (as in all of Taylor's poems) is that of the seventeenth-century English

metaphysical poets like John Donne and George Herbert. The lines abound in homely comparisons and metaphors drawn from New England life and in extravagant conceits which are a distinguishing mark of all metaphysical poetry.

This long work, which embodies a contest between Christ and Satan for mankind, is typically Puritan in thought in that it attempts to justify the Calvinistic doctrine of the Covenant. According to this doctrine, God made a covenant with Adam that he and his descendants would possess eternal happiness if they did not eat of the tree of the knowledge of good and evil. By disobeying, Adam and Eve lost their immunity to suffering and death. But through a new Covenant of Grace, God gave men another chance to save themselves from condemnation. If they would believe in Christ, who had willingly died for them, certain elect souls would be saved. They would not really earn this salvation through any good works they might do, but they would receive it out of God's abounding grace. No one knew how many of these elect there were, but each believer in Christ might hope that he was included.

Though Calvinism, greatly modified, is still present in the doctrines of many of the Protestant churches of today, most modern readers find tedious the long discussions of grace, faith, redemption, and damnation which course through the poetry and prose of the New England Puritans. For this reason, much of "God's Determinations" is of less interest than Taylor's other poems, in which the poet's lyricism and fanciful turns of thought are not subdued or distracted by theological argument.

There is nothing to distinguish many of Taylor's lines in "God's Determinations" from the writing of perhaps a

THE POETICAL WORKS OF EDWARD TAYLOR. Excerpts reprinted by permission of the publishers, Princeton University Press. Copyright, 1939, by Rockland Editions. Copyright, 1943, by Princeton University Press.

dozen of his poetizing Puritan contemporaries in America and England. Mercy's reply to Justice, for example, concerning the respective fates of the Devil's disciples and of the true believers is no more than rhymed Calvinism:

I will not onely from his Sin him free,
But fill him with Inherent grace also.
Though none are Sav'd that wickednesse imbrace,
Yet none are Damn'd that have Inherent Grace.

If Taylor were capable of nothing better than this, he would never have been hailed as America's best poet before the appearance of William Cullen Bryant in the nineteenth century.

But Taylor possessed more than the inherent grace of Calvin's theology; he was also gifted with the inherent grace (in a different sense) of the true poet. In the "Prologue" to "God's Determinations," he humbly seeks aid from the great God whom he would praise. He asks:

Lord, Can a Crumb of Earth the Earth outweigh:
Outmatch all mountains, nay the Chrystall Sky?
Imbosom in't designs that shall Display
And trace into the Boundless Deity?

Even if this "Crumb of Earth" had an angel's quill dipped in liquid gold, he says, "It would but blot and blur: yea, jag and jar," unless God made both "Pen and Scribener." He then admits that he himself is

this Crumb of Dust which is design'd
To make my Pen unto thy Praise alone,
And my dull Phancy I would gladly grinde
Unto an Edge on Zions Pretious Stone:
And write in Liquid Gold upon thy Name
My Letters till thy glory forth doth flame.

He prays that God will not laugh to scorn his attempts and that He will overlook any failings as "being Slips slipt from thy Crumb of Dust." If God will but guide his pen he may then write,

To Prove thou art, and that thou art the best,
And shew thy Properties to shine most bright.
And then thy Works will shine as flowers on Stems,
Or as in Jewellary Shops, do jems.

One of the most charming passages in "God's Determinations" is found in the opening stanzas of Christ's lengthy reply to a soul who "groans for succour" in his struggles against the fierce assaults of Satan, characterized as a cur who "bayghs and barks . . . veh'mently." As Christ begins to speak, He is not God's Son clothed in majesty or dignity but simply a loving father comforting a frightened child:

Peace, Peace, my Hony, do not Cry,
My Little Darling, wipe thine eye,
Oh, Cheer, Cheer up, come see.
Is anything too deare, my Dove,
Is anything too good, my Love,
To get or give for thee?

The cur barks, Christ explains, only because this soul belongs to Him, and "His barking is to make thee Cling/Close underneath thy Saviours wing." To make it clear that fright is needless, Christ uses a simile from New England rural or village life:

As Spot barks back the sheep again,
Before they to the Pound are ta'ne,
So he, and hence 'way goes.

Continuing with other endearing names ("Fear not, my Pritty Heart. . . ,. Why did my sweeten start?"), Christ even employs New England dialect:

And if he run an inch too fur,
I'le Check his Chain, and rate the Cur.
My chick, keep close to me.

Suddenly, in the next line, Christ's language is transformed, and it is as though John Donne or George Herbert had taken

2921

over the pen to finish Taylor's stanza for him:

> The Poles shall sooner kiss and greet,
> And Parallels shall sooner meet,
> Than thou shall harmed bee.

Of Taylor's occasional poems included in the *Poetical Works*, the best known (through many reprintings in anthologies) is "Huswifery," a poem of three six-line stanzas of the type which Taylor uses in his "Sacramental Meditations." Also, as in the "Meditations," the whole poem develops a single "conceit" or extended metaphor. The poet prays to his Lord, "Make me . . . thy Spin[n]ing Wheele compleat," and the process of becoming a Christian is described in terms of the making of clothing which he will wear. When, with Distaff ("Thy Holy Worde"), Swift Flyers ("mine Affections"), Spool ("my Soule"), and Reel ("My Conversation"), the yarn has been spun, the poet prays again:

> Make me thy Loome then, knit therein
> this Twine:
> And make thy Holy Spirit, Lord,
> winde quills:
> Then weave the Web thyselfe. The
> yarn is fine.
> Thine Ordinances make my Fulling
> Mills.
> Then dy the same in Heavenly Colours Choice,
> All pinkt with Varnish't Flowers of
> Paradise.

When the poet's Understanding, Will, Affections, Judgment, Conscience, Memory, Words, and Actions have been dressed in this God-made cloth,

> Then mine apparell shall display before yee
> That I am Cloathd in Holy robes for
> glory.

Taylor's "Sacramental Meditations" were written over a period of forty-four years, 1682 to 1725. His purpose in writing them is suggested in his complete manuscript title: "Preparatory Meditations before my Approach to the Lords Supper. Chiefly upon the Doctrin[e] preached upon the Day of administration." Each meditation is in Taylor's favorite six-line stanza, rhyming *ababcc*; and each is numbered, with a Biblical text to provide the theme. In view of the sensuousness in the language and imagery of so much of Taylor's poetry—despite his Puritan religious orthodoxy—it is significant that of ninety-seven texts which he chose from the Old Testament, seventy-six are from the *Song of Solomon* (Taylor uses the alternate name Canticles), which is filled with the passion and imagery of Oriental love poetry. The orthodox interpretation of the book as an allegory describing Christ's love for the Church permitted Taylor to return repeatedly to it without a twinge of his Puritan conscience, but the modern reader may wonder whether it was not Taylor's own natural ardor which drew him so often to Canticles for his texts. Yet, reading the "Meditations," one never questions the sincerity of his love for Christ in such lines as these:

> Oh! that my Heart, thy Golden Harp
> might bee
> Well tun'd by Glorious Grace, that
> e'ry string
> Screw'd to the highest pitch, might
> unto thee
> All Praises wrapt in sweetest Musick
> bring.
> I praise thee, Lord, and better praise
> thee would,
> If what I had, my heart might ever
> hold.

Though the "Sacramental Meditations" are often awkward and uneven in development and sometimes repetitious in phrasing or imagery, they form altogether a remarkable group of poems, filled with light and warmth and beauty and proclaiming the poet's love for the Christ whom he served devotedly for so many years.

THE POETICS

Type of work: Philosophical essay
Author: Aristotle (334-322 B.C.)
First transcribed: Fourth century B.C.

Although Aristotle's reputation as one of the greatest philosophers of all time rests principally on his work in metaphysics, he nowhere shows himself more the master of illuminating analysis and style than in the *Poetics*. The conception of tragedy which Aristotle developed in this work has perpetuated the Greek ideal of drama through the ages.

Aristotle begins his essay with an exposition of the Greek idea that all poetry, or art, is representative of life. This conception—that art is imitative—is also to be found in Plato's *Republic*, a work in which Plato, who was Aristotle's teacher, portrays Socrates as urging that poets be banned from the ideal state for, as imitators, they are too far removed from reality to be worthy of attention. For the Greeks the idea of poetry as imitative or representational was a natural one since, as a matter of fact, a great deal of Grecian art was representational in content. Furthermore, by "representation" was meant not a literal copying of physical objects, although it was sometimes that, but a new use of the material presented by sense.

Aristotle's intention in the *Poetics* is to analyze the essence of poetry and to distinguish its various species. The word "poetry" is used in translation as synonymous for "fine art." Among the arts mentioned by Aristotle are epic poetry, tragedy, comedy, dithyrambic poetry, flute-playing and lyre-playing. These arts are regarded as all representative of life, but they are distinguished from each other by their means and their objects. The means include rhythm, language and tune; but not all the arts involve all three, nor are these means used in the same way. For example, flute-playing involves the use of rhythm and tune, but dancing involves rhythm alone.

When living persons are represented,

Aristotle writes, they are represented as being better than, worse than, or the same as the average. Tragedy presents men somewhat better than average, while comedy presents men somewhat worse. This point alone offers strong evidence against a narrow interpretation of Aristotle's conception of art, for if men can be altered by the poet, made better or worse than in actual life, then poetry is not a mere uncreative copying of nature. Furthermore, a comment later on in the *Poetics* tells us that the poet in representing life represents things as they are, or as they seem to be, or as they should be. This concept certainly allows the artist a great deal more freedom than "imitation" suggests.

The origin of poetry is explained by Aristotle as the natural consequence of man's love of imitation and of tune and rhythm. We enjoy looking at accurate copies of things, he says, even when the things are themselves repulsive, such as the lowest animals and corpses. The philosopher accounts for this enjoyment by claiming that it is the result of our love of learning; in seeing accurate copies, we learn better what things are. This view is in opposition to Plato's idea that art corrupts the mind since it presents copies of copies of reality (physical objects being considered as mere copies of the universal idea or kind). Aristotle believed that universals, or characteristics, are to be found only in things, while Plato thought that the universals had some sort of separate existence.

Comedy represents inferior persons in that, laughable, they are a species of the ugly. The comic character makes mistakes or is in some way ugly, but not so seriously as to awaken pity or fear.

Epic poetry differs from tragedy in that it has a single meter and is narrative in form. A further difference resulted from the Greek convention that a tragedy encompass events taking place within a single day, while the epic poem was unlimited in that respect.

Tragedy is defined by Aristotle as a representation of a heroic action by means of language and spectacle so as to arouse pity and fear and thus bring about a catharsis of those emotions.

The relief, or catharsis, of the emotions of pity and fear is the most characteristic feature of the Aristotelian conception of tragedy. According to Aristotle, tragedy arouses the emotions by bringing a man somewhat better than average into a reversal of fortune for which he is responsible; then, through the downfall of the hero and the resolution of the conflicts resulting from the hero's tragic flaw, the tragedy achieves a purging of the emotions in the audience.

The audience feels pity in observing the tragic hero's misadventures because he is a vulnerable human being suffering from unrecognized faults, and then fear results from the realization that the hero is much like ourselves: we, too, can err and suffer.

Aristotle defines "plot" as the arrangement of the events which make up the play, "character" as that which determines the nature of the agents, and "thought" as what is expressed in the speeches of the agents. "Diction" is the manner of that expression.

The plot is the most important element in the tragedy (the others being character, diction, thought, spectacle, and song) because a tragedy is a representation of action. The characters exist for the sake of the action, not the action for the sake of the characters.

The two most important elements of the tragedy and of its plot are "peripety" or reversal and "discovery." By "peripety" is meant a change of a situation into its opposite state of fortune—in tragedy, a change from a good state of affairs to the bad. A "discovery" is a revelation of a matter previously unknown. The most effective tragedy, according to Aristotle, results from a plot which combines peripety and discovery in a single action, as in Sophocles' *Oedipus*.

To modern readers Aristotle's definitions of the "beginning," "middle," and "end" of a tragedy may seem either amusing or trivial, but they contain important dramatic truths. The philosopher defines the beginning as that which does not necessarily follow anything else but does necessarily give rise to further action. The end necessarily follows from what has gone before, but does not necessarily lead to further events. The middle follows the beginning and gives rise to the end.

The sense of Aristotle's definitions is found once we realize that the important thing about the beginning of a play is not that it is the start, but that relative to the audience's interest and curiosity no earlier event is needed, but further events are demanded. Similarly, for the ending, the closing events of a play should not be merely the last events presented, but they should appear necessary as a result of what has already happened, and, furthermore, they should not give rise to new problems which must be solved if the audience is to be satisfied.

Aristotle writes that anything that is beautiful must not only have parts orderly arranged, but must also have parts of a large enough, but not too large, size. An animal a thousand miles long or something too small to be seen cannot be beautiful. A play should be as long as possible, allowing a change of fortune in a sequence of events ordered in some apparently inevitable way, provided the play can be understood as a whole.

In his conception of unity Aristotle emphasizes a point that continues to be useful to all who compose or criticize works of art: if the presence of a part makes no difference, it has no place in the work.

A good tragedy should not show worthy men passing from good fortune to bad, for that is neither fearful nor pitiful but shocking. But even worse is to show bad men acquiring good fortune, for such a situation irritates us without arousing pity and fear.

The tragic hero, consequently, should be a man better than ourselves, but not perfect; and he should suffer from a flaw which shows itself in some mistaken judgment or act resulting in his downfall. There has been considerable discussion about the kind of flaw Aristotle meant, but it seems clear from the examples he gives, like the *Oedipus*, that the flaw should be such that, given it, a man must inevitably defeat himself in action; nevertheless, it is not inevitable that man have that flaw. All men are liable to the flaw, however; hence, the tragic hero arouses fear in all those who see the resemblance between the hero's situation and their own. The hero arouses pity because, as a human being, he cannot be perfect like the gods; his end is bound to be tragic.

Aristotle concludes his *Poetics* with a careful discussion of diction and thought, and of epic poetry. Among the sensible comments he makes is one to the effect that what is believable though not possible is better in a play than an event which is possible but not believable.

Throughout the *Poetics* Aristotle offers remarkably clear analyses of what Greek tragedy actually was and of what, according to Aristotle, it ought to be. He shows not only an adroit analytical intellect but also an understanding of the practical problems of the art of poetry; and he is sophisticated enough to realize that most questions as to the value, length, beauty, and other features of a work of art are settled relative to the kind of audience the judge prefers.

THE POETRY OF AUDEN

Type of work: Poetry
Author: W(ystan) H(ugh) Auden (1907-   )
Principal published works: Poems, 1930; The Orators, 1932; The Dance of Death, 1933;
Poems, 1934; Look, Stranger, 1936; Spain, 1937; Another Time, 1940; The Double Man,
1941; For the Time Being, 1944; Collected Poetry, 1945; The Age of Anxiety, 1947;
Nones, 1951; The Shield of Achilles, 1955; The Old Man's Road, 1956

W. H. Auden, for twenty years ranked among the best modern poets, is, like his contemporary T. S. Eliot, the product of both the English and the American traditions. Auden was raised in the industrial midlands of England and educated at Oxford during the bleak 1930's. There he became one of a group of young poets, including C. Day Lewis, Louis Mac-Neice, Stephen Spender, and Christopher Isherwood, who directed their writing toward a search for meaning in a world which seemed to them empty and mechanical.

Growing up during the great depression, when unemployment was at a peak in England, Auden and his contemporaries, in sympathy with the problems of the working class, looked to Marxism as a possible solution to social conditions and to Sigmund Freud and George Walther Groddeck for answers to the spiritual barrenness resulting from these conditions. Auden's continual search for meaning and faith during this period led him away from these ideas to the orthodox Christianity of theologians like Reinhold Niebuhr and Søren Kierkegaard. The most complete expression of his Christianity is his Christmas Oratorio, *For the Time Being*, possibly his finest, most cohesive work.

Auden's acceptance of Christianity coincided approximately with his move to New York, just before the outbreak of World War II. His more recent work combines American images, rhythms, and colloquialism with English ones, but his poetry is almost always universal rather than regional.

Auden's wide reading is reflected in the development of his technique and his

philosophy. In the inaugural address delivered when he became Professor of Poetry at Oxford in 1956 he named Thomas Hardy as his first real model; the younger poet found in his master's work an expression of the disillusionment he himself felt. Hardy wrote of an apparently meaningless universe, governed by chance, and Auden found men going through life as a ritual in which there is no meaning. The soldiers of "Which side am I supposed to be on?" are "aware of our rank and alert to obey orders." but they have no idea of what they fight for. Like Hardy, Auden often speaks in abstract tones, and he may have acquired his fondness for experimenting with verse forms from the late-Victorian poet.

William Blake's concern for the mistreated laboring class and the paradoxical religious views expressed in *The Marriage of Heaven and Hell* are reflected in Auden's poetry. Blake's *Songs of Innocence* and *Songs of Experience* also suggest the form of many of the poems in "Songs and other musical pieces" in Auden's *Collected Poetry*. Especially reminiscent of Blake is:

> Now the leaves are falling fast,
> Nurses flowers will not last;
> Nurses to the graves are gone,
> And the prams go rolling on.

Auden's rhythms also reflect his interest in Anglo-Saxon and Middle English verse. *The Age of Anxiety*, "a Baroque Eclogue," is written almost entirely in the old alliterative four-stress line, which is used also in the lines of the Voices of the Desert in *For the Time Being*. The colloquial style of William Butler Yeats's later poetry also influ-

THE POETRY OF W. H. AUDEN. Excerpts reprinted from THE COLLECTED POETRY OF W. H. AUDEN by permission of the publishers, Random House, Inc. Copyright, 1945, by W. H. Auden.

enced some of Auden's work. Critics have pointed out the similarity between Yeats's "September 1913" and Auden's "September 1, 1939":

> I sit in one of the dives
> On Fifty Second Street
> Uncertain and afraid
> As the clever hopes expire
> Of a low dishonest decade.

It is difficult to assess the effect of T. S. Eliot on Auden: the latter is reported to have told his Oxford tutor that Eliot was the only poet to be seriously considered by the prospective writer. The social criticism of *The Waste Land* and *The Hollow Men* was certainly an inspiration to the young poet who felt the same cultured barrenness that Eliot had described. Auden has adopted a few of Eliot's symbols: the desert is a recurrent image of the present civilization for both men.

A particularly striking similarity between Eliot and Auden is their acceptance of Anglo-Catholic Christianity. However, Eliot writes in *Ash Wednesday* and *The Four Quartets* of a contemplative ideal, while Auden preaches the necessity for human relationships and mutual concern. His view is well expressed in these lines from *For the Time Being*:

> Space is the Whom our loves are needed by,
> Time is our choice of How to love and Why.

Several related themes run throughout Auden's work. He sees man as an individual isolated in society: a "lonely." "Musée des Beaux Arts" emphasizes this separation: suffering, Auden says, "takes place while someone else is eating or opening a window or just walking dully along":

> In Brueghel's *Icarus*, for instance; how everything turns away
> Quite leisurely from the disaster; the ploughman may,
> Have heard the splash, the forsaken cry,
> But for him it was not an important failure . . .

The Wanderer is another recurrent figure in Auden's poetry. The isolated man searches. sometimes aimlessly, for meaning in life. An early poem, "Doom is Dark and Deeper Than Any Sea Dingle," whose title comes from a Middle English poem translated by Auden, describes the strange impulse which drives a man away from home to wander "a stranger among strangers." Man's quest is portrayed more elaborately in *The Age of Anxiety*, in the section called "The Seven Stages." The four characters. three men and a woman, travel, sometimes together, sometimes separately, through different scenes, passing through the pitfalls of modern culture and their own dreams, but they lack the courage to cross the desert which is the final stage. They cannot take the "leap of faith" in which Auden found the end to his own quest. Only Rosetta. who possesses the vestiges of her Jewish heritage, has roots and conviction enough to allow her to face the future; whatever happens. she believes that peace lies in reconciliation with her earthly and heavenly fathers. Malin, the Air Force officer, expresses the paradoxes which confront the prospective Christian and the tension which is an integral part of Auden's faith:

> For the others, like me, there is only the flash
> Of negative knowledge. . . .

In both his pre-Christian and Christian poems Auden writes of love as the saving force for mankind, but both humanistic and Christian love in his poetry are extremely impersonal. Concern for others is a familiar theme, but there are almost no descriptions of personal relationships. Even the so-called love lyric, "Lay Your Sleeping Head My Love," is strangely abstract.

Auden is a highly skilled technician. His volume of collected poems includes sonnets, lyrical songs, colloquial meditations, and complex medieval and Renaissance stanza forms like the sestina. His long poems—*The Sea and The Mirror*, in which he discusses the place of the artist in society, using the characters from Shakespeare's *The Tempest,* and *For the Time Being*—contain passages of excellent prose. This virtuosity, one of the poet's greatest assets, is also a defect; verbal tricks intended to produce striking effects succeed only in seeming slick and insincere in some of his work. Many a potentially good poem is marred by the intrusion of a too clever phrase or forced aural effects. Nevertheless, Auden's skill makes his best work* inimitable. In the elegiac "In Memory of William Butler Yeats" he interweaves imagery from several of Yeats's own poems and uses three rather different styles of his own to produce one of the finest elegies of the twentieth century. In the concluding lines of this poem one will find Auden's concept of the function of the poet.

Auden has adopted a long, free verse line for many of his more recent poems including parts of *The Shield of Achilles* and "In Praise of Limestone," a "moral landscape" published in 1951. His limestone hill is not the habitat of "saints-to-be" or of "intendant Caesars"; the water-carved stone attracts the men of imagination who see statues, vineyards, in the natural formations, those who climb "arm in arm, but never, thank God, in step."

It is too early to evaluate Auden's work as a whole; he may yet write the masterpiece which his best poems indicate he is capable of creating. But whatever the future direction his work may take, he will certainly be remembered, on the basis of his published poetry and criticism, as one of the outstanding literary men of our time.

THE POETRY OF BASHÔ

Type of work: Verse and poetic prose
Author: Matsuo Bashô (1644-1694)
First published: 1672-1748

No poet in Japan has had a greater effect upon his contemporaries or his posterity or has been accorded greater acclaim and honor than Matsuo Bashô. Throughout Japan, wherever his poetic wanderings took him there are stone memorials, more than three hundred altogether, inscribed with his compositions and many mounds believed to contain objects he owned. Although his remains were buried in a Buddhist temple, on his centennial and sesquicentennial anniversaries he was deified in at least three Shintô shrines, one of which was actually named after two of the words in his famous poem:

> Furu-ike ya
> Kawazu tobi-komu
> Mizu no oto.

Many have tried it, but no one has successfully translated this poem. However, it seems to refer to the sound of the water when a frog jumps into a pond. Thus, the name of the shrine might be translated as "Shrine of the Jump-sound."

Born the third (some say the second) son of a warrior family, Bashô not only studied *haikai* poetry, but also read widely in the Japanese and Chinese classics and poetry. He was a student of Zen Buddhism, calligraphy, and painting, and had at one time been a student of Taoism and of medicine. With this rich and varied background Bashô, after a few youthful indiscretions common to his age and society, developed into a man of high virtue, possibly because of the shock he experienced at the death of his feudal lord and fellow poet, the privations he met during his wanderings, and his serious studies in Zen Buddhism.

Haikai, the origins of which may be traced back to the very beginnings of Japanese poetry, developed from a form in which a series of seventeen-syllable verse were linked together. During the middle of the sixteenth century, this form split into the seventeen-syllable *haiku* and linked verse (*renga*), the former a humorous, sometimes bawdy, type of epigram. By the middle of the seventeenth century, *haiku* had again split into two schools, one emphasizing the form itself, the other seeking greater freedom for the expression of wit and the unusual at the expense of form. Ibara Saikaku (q.v.) was in his verse a follower of the latter school. Neither school, however, produced superior poetry.

Bashô lived in a peaceful period following a century of wars and internecine strife. More than half a century before, Ieyasu had unified Japan under the rule of his house. The warriors who had fought under him and their descendants now were busy with peaceful enterprises. There was also a rising moneyed class made up of merchants in the urban trading centers of Osaka and Edo, now Tokyo. The concentration of power and resources in the shogunate, the concentration of cash money among the merchants, the philosophical clashes between the rigid codes of feudal loyalty on the one hand and the power of money on the other, and peaceful times, produced three of the greatest literary figures in Japanese history almost at the same time. Bashô was the poet among them, and the only one who forsook material wealth for matters of the spirit.

In 1666, when Bashô was twenty-three, his feudal lord died. Bashô left feudal service in spite of the fact that such a step made him a semi-outcast from his society, and in 1672 he arrived in Edo already versed in the two schools of the *haiku*. For the rest of his life he devoted himself to bringing this form back to true poetry and, in the course of this effort, created a third school which is named after him. In the three centuries since, *haiku* poetry has had its vicissitudes, but each revival has been a movement back to Bashô. His influence is felt not only in his own school, but also in the other two. His death anniversaries are still strictly observed by his followers, and admiration for him amounts to bare idolatry. The latest revival was begun by Masaoka Shiki (1867-1902), *haiku* poet and novelist, in the 1890's.

There is no single adequate word for the essence of Bashô's poetry, but it has been described as the illustration of an old man girding on his armor and fighting on the battlefield, or clothing himself in the richest brocades to attend a banquet. In either case he cannot hide the fact that he is beyond his physical prime. The gayest of Bashô's *haiku* contain an element of lingering pathos, but such pathos is not to be gained by seeking it *per se*. It must be a development of one's nature as the result of the varied experiences of life.

The best of the poems by Bashô and his disciples are collected in the *Haikai Shichibu-shû* (*Seven Collected Works*) in twelve volumes compiled by Sakuma Ryûkyo (1686-1748). The seven collections contained are: *Fuyu no Hi* (*Winter Days*); *Haru no Hi* (*Spring Days*); *Arano* (*Fields of Wilderness*); *Hisago* (*The Gourd*); *Saru Mino* (*Coats of Straw for Monkeys*); *Sumi-dawara* (*Bags of Charcoal*); and *Zoku Saru Mino* (*Saru Mino, Continued*).

Other well-known collections of his verse and prose writings are the following: *Kai-oi*, a collection of sixty *haiku* in pairs, each like the two shells of a clam, which gives this collection its title. The verse of thirty-seven persons is contained, as well as Bashô's comments. The preface is dated 1672, when Bashô was twenty-eight. The poems combine snatches of popular songs and expressions of the time, and Bashô's comments indicate that if he himself did not indulge in a gay life in his youth, he was at least in sympathy with those who did. This work is representative of his earlier years.

The remaining books are accounts of his wanderings and journeys, each liberally sprinkled with poems. These include *Nozarashi Kikô* (*In the Face of Wind and Rain*), 1685, an account of a trip from Edo to the Kyoto-Nara-Ise area, particularly Nagoya in 1684-1685; *Kashima Kikô* (*Moon Viewing to Kashima*), 1687; *Oi no Obumi* (*Scraps from my Letterbox*), 1687, an account of a journey in the Yamato area, believed to show Bashô at his peak as a poet and philosopher; *Sarashina Kikô* (*Moon Viewing to Sarashina*), 1688, a brief work like the *Kashima Kikô* and similar in style; *Oku no Hoso-michi* (*The Narrow Road of Oku*), an account of a trip in 1689 from Edo to Sakata in northeastern Japan via Nikkô and Matsushima, and thence down toward the Japan Sea to Kanazawa, Tsuruga and then southward to Ise, covering about 1,467 miles in seven months. This work, the greatest of Bashô's travel accounts, inspired numerous followers, both of his own time and later (including at least one American), to make trips by the same route. The *Saga Nikki* (*Diary at Saga*), 1691, is Bashô's diary written during a month's stay in 1691 at the Rakushi-sha, a modest residence in Saga, near Kyoto. The style reveals Bashô at his best in describing his enjoyment of a simple, uncluttered life.

Some examples of Bashô's prose and poetry have been translated into English, German, and Spanish. Among the English translations, his *Genjû-an no ki* ("*Prose Poem on the Unreal Dwelling*") is included in Donald Keene's *Anthology of Japanese Literature* (New York, 1955). There are two translations into German of the *Kashima Kikô*. The *Oku no Hoso-michi* has been translated by Isobe Yaichirô (Tokyo, 1933). A partial translation is included in the Keene *Anthology*. It also appears as "Bashô, the Wanderer," by Richard Lane, in the *Journal of Oriental Literature* (IV, 1951). The *Saru Mino* appears in "Bashô (1644-94) and the Japanese Political Epigram," by Basil Hall Chamberlain, in the *Transactions of the Asiatic*

Society of Japan (XXX, 2, 1902). Harold G. Henderson has a number of unique translations of Bashô's poems in his *An Introduction to Haiku: an Anthology of Poems and Poets from Bashô to Shiki* (New York, 1958).

THE POETRY OF BLAKE

Type of work: Poetry
Author: William Blake (1757-1827)
Principal published works: Poetical Sketches, 1783; *There Is No Natural Religion,* c. 1788-1794; *All Religions Are One,* c. 1788-1794; *Songs of Innocence,* 1789; *The Book of Thel,* 1789; *The Marriage of Heaven and Hell,* c. 1790; *The French Revolution,* 1791; *For the Sexes: The Gates of Paradise,* 1793; *Visions of the Daughters of Albion,* 1793; *America, A Prophecy,* 1793; *Songs of Experience,* 1794; *Europe, A Prophecy,* 1794; *The First Book of Urizen,* 1794; *The Song of Los,* 1795; *The Book of Ahania,* 1795; *The Book of Los,* 1795; *Milton,* 1804-1808; *Jerusalem, The Emanation of the Giant Albion,* 1804-1820; *Laocoön,* c. 1820; *The Ghost of Abel,* 1822

The poetry of William Blake, an artist, printer, prophet, and revolutionary, varies widely in style and substance, from youthful imitations of Spenser to lyrics of seemingly naïve childish wonder to obscure and pretentious mysticism. Apart from his earliest productions, his work shows a powerful originality in form, images, and technique.

His juvenile work, written between the ages of twelve and twenty, was published in 1783 as *Poetical Sketches.* The poems, which are slight and at times even crude, show a strong Elizabethan influence. Occasional flashes of lyrical brilliance are visible, however, such as this stanza from a song known to have been written before he was fourteen:

> With sweet May dews my wings were wet,
> And Phoebus fir'd my vocal rage;
> He caught me in his silken net,
> And shut me in his golden cage.

Although he remained poor and generally unknown throughout his life, Blake was well acquainted with a number of leading social and political radicals, and he belonged to a discussion group which included Henry Fuseli, Thomas Holcroft, Mary Wollstonecraft, Thomas Paine, and others. Through such stimulation he was able to develop his own radical views about Christianity, Swedenborgianism, and the American and French revolutions. His dual concern with mysticism and political radicalism about 1788-1789 marks his intellectual and artistic maturity. These two strains were immediately evident in Blake's two major collections of lyrics, *Songs of Innocence* (1789), and *Songs of Experience* (1794), printed together in 1794 as *Songs of Innocence and Experience.* All three volumes were illustrated by the author's powerfully imaginative engravings, which contribute greatly to the reader's appreciation of the text. By "innocence" and "experience" Blake meant two contrary, though not clearly defined, states of the human soul. The two groups of poems directly oppose their subject matter. We are given "Infant Joy" against "Infant Sorrow," "The Blossom" against "The Sick Rose," "The Lamb" against "The Tiger," "The Divine Image" against "The Human Abstract," and opposed treatments of "The Chimney Sweeper," "A Little Boy Lost," and others. The poems are remarkable for their simple grace and direct emotional expression. "Innocence" is something like happiness, a state of wonder and acceptance and endurance of life. The "innocent" chimney sweep, for example, although aware of his misery, retains his vision and faith:

> There's little Tom Dacre, who cried when his head,
> That curled like a lamb's back, was shaved: so I said
> "Hush Tom! never mind it, for when your head's bare
> You know that the soot cannot spoil your white hair."

In contrast, the chimney sweep of the opposed poem in *Songs of Experience* understands the earth-bound social cause and the destructive aspects of life. His complaint is bitter:

And because I am happy and dance
and sing,
They think they have done me no
injury,
And are gone to praise God and His
Priest and King,
Who make up a Heaven of our misery.

The poet's opposition of "innocence" and "experience" reflects the development of his Doctrine of Contraries, a philosophical view which was to dominate his poetry for the rest of his life. He defines this doctrine in *The Marriage of Heaven and Hell* (c. 1790): "Without Contraries is no progression. Attraction and repulsion, reason and energy, love and hate, are necessary to human existence." Elsewhere in the same work he cas·s these oppositions as a "Prolific Force" against a "Devouring Force":

But the Prolific would cease to be prolific unless the Devourer, as a sea, received the excess of his delights. Some will say: 'Is not God alone the Prolific?' I answer: 'God only acts and is in existing beings, or men.'

Blake apparently viewed progress as cyclical, as a period of creation following one of destruction. Such a view is present in the mythology of his later works. Specifically, *The Marriage of Heaven and Hell* attacks the rationalism of eighteenth-century Protestantism, which, Blake felt, reduced complex moral problems to oversimplified formulas. By means of paradox he hoped to stress a truer and more complicated awareness of the human condition. In "The Little Vagabond," for example, a later lyric associated with *Songs of Experience*, the young narrator complains: "Dear mother, dear mother, the Church is cold,/But the Ale-house is healthy and pleasant and warm." Although apparently uncomplicated, Blake's lyrics are written in a complex vision.

Blake's prophetic and mystical writings include *The Book of Thel* (1789); *Tiriel* (c.1789); *Visions of the Daughters of Albion* (1793); *America, A Prophecy* (1793); *Europe, A Prophecy* (1794); *The First Book of Urizen* (1794): *The*

Song of Los (1795); *The Book of Ahania* (1795); *The Four Zoas* (c.1797); *Milton* (1804-1808); *Jerusalem* (1804-1820); and *The Ghost of Abel* (1822). These poems generally employ a kind of free verse, although there are some memorable lyrical passages, and an obscure and at times incomprehensible personal mythology. Various critics have produced widely differing interpretations.

These writings may be profitably divided into four groups which indicate different directions in the author's thought. The first such group contains *Thel* and *Tiriel*, works that are allegorical rather than symbolic. *Thel* argues for a benevolent providence found in all things. *Tiriel* is an Ossianic imitation with the theme of defiant children against a tyrannical father. Neither poem shows the paradoxical views Blake was soon to develop.

The second group marks the beginning of Blake's characteristic mystical thought. It includes the prose work. *The Marriage of Heaven and Hell*, and two subgroups of related poems. The first group, consisting of *A Song of Liberty; Visions of the Daughters of Albion; America, A Prophecy; Europe, A Prophecy;* and *The Song of Los,* employs relatively uncomplicated symbolism. They stress the doctrine of man's regeneration through a revolt against common moral standards to produce an apparently anarchical society. The second group, which includes *The First Book of Urizen, The Book of Los* (1795), and *The Book of Ahania,* introduces a myth which challenges the Hebraic-Christian and Miltonic views of cosmology, man, and sin. These poems are intellectually significant in that the action is set against a background of blind fate. The power of God to direct the universe is implicitly denied.

Vala, an earlier form of *The Four Zoas,* is representative of a third development in Blake's mythology. To his earlier symbolism he added new qualities and powers. Urizen, Luvah, Tharmas, and Urthona or Los are associated respectively with the intellect or the Brain, the affections or the Heart, the appetite or the Tongue, and the Ear or the prophetic and creative activity. He apparently wished either to base his myth in psychology or to include human attributes in a story about the origins of the universe.

About 1797, however, while still working on *Vala*, Blake radically shifted his views to a belief in a beneficent God, although he maintained his attack against conventional theology and moral codes. *The Four Zoas*, *Milton*, and *Jerusalem* belong to the fourth group, which features a more extensive use of symbols derived from Christianity and a more elaborate view of his theories about reality and knowledge. His theory of salvation through revolt, as well as Orc, its symbol, finally disappears. At the same time Blake more closely identifies his mysticism with art. Instead of creating a new mythology to express his new views, Blake rewrote and patched up the old symbolism, inevitably confusing it still further. He left no fully coherent myth.

Milton consists of two separate parts, the obscure and shadowy Satan-Palamabron myth, and the descent of Milton into the world to correct his theological errors in *Paradise Lost*, such as having regarded Satan as punished by God for his sins. Blake often claimed to have spoken to Milton in visions. Crabb Robinson, an acquaintance of Blake, wrote to Dorothy Wordsworth: "Now, according to Blake, atheism consists in worshipping the natural world, which same natural world, properly speaking, is nothing real but a mere illusion produced by Satan. Milton was for a great part of his life an atheist, and therefore his fatal errors in *Paradise Lost*, which he often begged Blake to refute." *Milton* is also noteworthy for the striking lyric with which it begins, "And did those feet in ancient time."

Jerusalem deals with Albion's (man's) conquest of error on earth and with his return to Eternity. It celebrates the law of Forgiveness of Sins. The text as we have it is obscured by many revisions, but in 1809 the poet published a clear description of its theme: "(The Strong Man, the Beautiful Man, and the Ugly Man) were originally one man who was fourfold; he was self-divided, and his real humanity slain on the stems of generation, and the form of the fourth was like the Son of God . . . it is voluminous, and contains the ancient history of Britain and the world of Satan and of Adam."

THE POETRY OF BRYANT

Type of work: Poetry
Author: William Cullen Bryant (1794-1878)
Principal published works: The Embargo, or Sketches of the Times: A Satire, 1808; *Poems,*
1821, 1834, 1836, 1839; *The Fountain and Other Poems,* 1842; *Poems,* 1854; *The
Poetical Works of William Cullen Bryant,* 1876

William Cullen Bryant was one of the first authentic voices of the Romantic Movement in America. At his best, he combined the essential simplicity and emotion of a romantic with careful observation of and allegiance to the world of nature about him. His poems demonstrate this minute observation and this simple care, fashioned into verse that is clear, sometimes moving, and easily communicated.

Bryant was a precocious boy who demonstrated an early interest in politics and literature. In 1808, before he was fourteen years old, his first volume of poetry, *The Embargo, or Sketches of the Times: A Satire,* was published. "The Embargo," the principal poem in this volume, was an attack on President Jefferson in which the young poet set down in heroic couplets all the slanderous epithets he had heard his elders use against Jefferson. Bryant's next poem was "Thanatopsis." First written in 1811, and published in the *North American Review* in 1817, it is an instance of genuine precocity. A meditation in blank verse, developing its theme with quiet power and a simple sense of movement, the poem reflects movingly on the spectacle of man going to his death secure in the knowledge that ultimate salvation is his. Avowedly moral in purpose, it became one of the most frequently read poems in American literature.

Bryant never lost his tendency to use poetry as a vehicle for his explicit moral and religious convictions. He felt that poetry should uplift and ennoble; and his work is filled with poems enjoining man to recognize the truths of nature and of God and to live his life in accordance with them. Bryant's poems indicate that the author felt no shame or self-consciousness in preaching to his fellows.

For contemporary readers, however, Bryant is remembered far more for his simple and direct observation of nature than for his moral teaching. Poems like "The Yellow Violet," "To A Waterfowl" and "To the Fringed Gentian," verse acute, precise, and unpretentious, seem now to represent Bryant's highest poetic achievement. The simplicity and ease of stanzas like the following from "To the Fringed Gentian" demonstrate something of the ease and directness of Bryant's nature poetry:

Thou comest not when violets lean
O'er wandering brooks and springs
    unseen,
Or columbines, in purple dressed,
Nod o'er the ground-bird's hidden nest

Bryant is often thought of as the American Wordsworth, the Nature Poet extraordinary. Like Wordsworth, he could be didactic in his moral certainty, direct and simple in his treatment of nature. If Bryant's best work has not the power and the simple force of Wordsworth at his best, neither does Bryant have long sections of poems as completely prosaic and undistinguished as sections of *The Prelude.*

Bryant wrote in a variety of stanza forms. Although he often used blank verse, he also frequently wrote his nature poems in simple quatrains. He also attempted other stanza forms; in fact, he experimented, at one time or another, with most of the forms regularly used in English poetry. An early poem, "The Ages," written for delivery before the Phi Beta Kappa Society at Harvard in 1821, was written in the nine-line Spenserian stanza; other poems attempted various forms used in the ode. Although not an innovator, Bryant served a genuine function in making Americans more aware of the structural variety in English poetry, of incorporating into the American tradition the forms and the possibilities of the English tradition. Bryant's work, as he himself was well aware, was, by its example, the work of the conscientious and enlightened teacher.

Bryant, in his effort at romantic simplicity and smoothness, often was distinguished for his sure sense of poetic diction. His aim was, like Wordsworth's, to use simple language and to avoid the stylized or "poetic." Yet his poetry demonstrates that, along with his belief in simplicity of diction, he felt a strong allegiance to the notion of propriety. He attempted to get a certain elevation or majesty into his poetic language, a quality that, at its best, succeeded, although at other times it led him into vast and flat abstractions. In a poem called "The Poet," he both articulated and illustrated his sense of language as the combination of the concrete and the majestic in a carefully wrought passage:

> Yet let no empty gust
>   Of passion find an utterance in thy lay,
> A blast that whirls the dust
>   Along the howling street and dies away;
> But feelings of calm power and mighty sweep,
> Like currents journeying through the windless deep.

Despite the apparent calm, this passage shows that Bryant had a great deal of variety and power within his simple language. At other times, inversion and abstract pretense mar what might otherwise be simple and moving poetry, as in the poem called "October, 1866," written just after his wife's death:

> Yet was the home where thou wert lying dead
> Mournfully still, save when, at times, was heard,
> From room to room, some softly-moving tread,
> Or murmur of some softly-uttered word.

Feared they to break thy slumber? As we threw
A look on that bright bay and glorious shore,
Our hearts were wrung with anguish, for we knew
Those sleeping eyes would look on them no more.

Bryant's poetry covered a great number of themes. In addition to his interest in nature, he also demonstrated his sympathy for various causes throughout the world: the fight for freedom in Italy, the Greek revolt for independence from the Turks. His opinions on social and political questions were generally on the liberal side (he was, for example, an ardent abolitionist), but these opinions, on domestic issues, seldom found their way into his verse. He also frequently mourned the death of friends and famous contemporaries in verse and used his foreign travels as the motivation for other poems. But his most frequent theme was nature; the change of the seasons, the appearance of flowers, the beauty of the familiar world were all his constant preoccupation.

For Bryant, nature was never very far from God, a merciful and forgiving God whose bounty was evident in all his works. He wrote a number of hymns which demonstrate the same simple and genuine devotion, the same sense of pervading goodness, that emanates from his poems on nature. No human tragedy seemed to him so deep or meaningful that the calm, the peace, the divine reason behind it could not be seen. His poetry was full of a generous and pervasive faith.

Bryant was also a translator of many poems from the Spanish and German lyrics of his time. Late in his career he translated Homer's *Iliad* and *Odyssey*, but unfortunately his versions do not convey the boldness, sweep, and power of the Homeric style. Bryant's peaceful faith, particularly as it functioned in his later poetry, was not an effective filter through which to convey Homer's grandeur.

Bryant's poetry has had a great influence on poetry in America. His variety, his enthusiasm for expressing individual emotions, his genuine interest in nature, and his interest in many forms of poetic expression helped to educate generations of American poets and readers. Although his influence has been far less notable during the past thirty or forty years, he helped to introduce poetry to a young country that would have been highly suspicious of more sophisticated practitioners. In his poems he seemed an ordinary man developing simple emotions in a variety of styles, managing each in a clear, clean, dignified way. For American poetry in the middle of the nineteenth century, no more was required: before his time, no one had accomplished as much.

In addition to his historical value, Bryant still merits the modern reader's attention for his careful diction and his simple observation of nature. At its best, his verse has a simple power and precision. If the contemporary reader cannot appreciate Bryant's easy assurances about ultimate peace and justice or is disturbed about the poet's lapses into flat and banal language, he can still appreciate the fact that Bryant was often a poet of skill and simple directness, still acknowledge the poetic achievement of lines such as the following from "The Burial Place":

> Yet here,
> Nature, rebuking the neglect of man,
> Plants often, by the ancient mossy stone,
> The brier-rose, and upon the broken turf
> That clothes the fresher grave, the
> strawberry plant
> Sprinkles its swell with blossoms, and
> lays forth
> Her ruddy, pouting fruit. . . .

As these lines show, Bryant could often describe what he saw with clarity, emotion, and poetic force.

THE POETRY OF CARDUCCI

Type of work: Poetry
Author: Giosuè Carducci (1835-1907)
Principal published works: Rime, 1857; Inno a Satana. 1865 (*Hymn to Satan*); Levia
Gravia, 1868; Odi barbare, 1877-1889 (*Pagan Odes*); Rime e ritmi, 1899

Rarely has a poet in modern times been awarded the admiration and adulation during his lifetime that was accorded by the people of Italy to Giosuè Carducci. Regarded as a national prophet, as well as the unofficial poet laureate of Italy, he was for many years prior to his death, something of an Italian institution. In addition to his career as poet and essayist, he was a highly successful member of the academic world. For more than forty years he served as a professor of literature at the University of Bologna. He was awarded the Nobel Prize for literature in 1906.

As a poet Carducci was a nonconformist in his time, a fact which accounts for much of his popularity in Italy and his importance in the history of Italian literature. When he began his career, Italian poetry was and had been for many years inferior to Italian prose. A romantic interest in the past and its glories had become a curse to poetry. Carducci pointed the way to a new view. however. by looking at contemporary events and the possibilities of the future: the greatness of Italy, its culture and its national unity, in the nineteenth century. Carducci felt that poetry had a part to play in the great awakening—political, religious, and literary—that seemingly was about to break in his native country.

From the beginning, Carducci reacted consciously against romanticism. As a member of the "Amici Pedanti." a circle of young Italian writers, he worked to return Italian poetry to classicism. This change, hoped Carducci, would revitalize the poetry of his native land. The poetry he wrote at the time is typical in many ways of work produced throughout his career. His verse is simple, but at the same time heroic and solemn in tone. There is none of the excessive verbiage, emotion. or metaphor typical of romantic

literature. All is restrained and controlled.

Carducci also tried to revive the classical meters. This interest may be explained partly by the strong humanistic element in his education and academic environment. In his first volume of poems, Rime, he presented a collection which decried two influences on Italian culture: romanticism and Christianity. Carducci expressed through his early poems a belief that classicism in art and paganism in religion were needed to invigorate Italian art and culture.

Two volumes of poems, mainly about contemporary political events. followed. They were Levia Gravia and Giombi ed Epodi (1882). Critics in Italy and abroad have felt that the political slanting of the poems in these volumes weakened the effort and that the two volumes represent the least valuable in his work. One of Carducci's best-known and most controversial poems. Hymn to Satan, was published in 1865. Invoking Satan as other poets had invoked the muses, Carducci complained that Christianity was moribund and was carrying the world to death with it, that rust was gnawing at the mystical sword of the Archangel Michael. He went on to call back paganism as a means of freeing man and his mind. Satan in the poem was made a spirit of paganism, the spirit that evoked the marbles, the pictures, the literature of classical antiquity, as well as the pantheon of gods and goddesses. Carducci wrote, too, that this was the spirit behind such great rebels against the Roman Catholic Church as Wycliffe, Huss, Savonarola, and Martin Luther, men who unbound human thought from the fetters with which orthodoxy had, according to Carducci, bound it. Satan became in the poem not one symbol, but many. He symbolizes progress, intellectuality, anti-clericalism, the idea of progress, and the good influence of classical thought. Satan becomes for Carducci more a helper than an adversary of man.

The political aspects of Italian culture and life were never far from Carducci's mind and art. Sometimes he favored those in power and sometimes he did not. In the 1850's he was for a time the darling of the monarchists because of such poems as "La Croce di Savoia" and the "Canzone a Vittorio Emanuele," for as the years went by, Carducci tended away from his earlier republicanism and became satisfied with a monarchy for his beloved Italy. That he was finally reconciled is evident in the poems, especially such a poem as "Piedmonte," an ode which appeared in 1890 and was included in Rime e ritmi.

Carducci did not, on the other hand, change his mind very much about the Church. Although he became less bitter about the cultural significance of the Roman Catholic Church in Italy, he could not reconcile his views of art with Christian theology, as the "Hymn to Satan" had proved. Carducci believed that beauty had reached its best expression in Greek and Roman art. It was this belief that caused him to try to return to classical expression, even the meters of classical poetry. It was in this pagan view of the world, which he tried to express, that the poet found tranquil loveliness. When Carducci wrote of his native land, he found in pagan religion and its spirit something which welcomed the reality of the land and its creatures, instead of repressing the things of this world as Christianity seemed to do, with its emphasis on another, more spiritual world. In Carducci's poems about the Italian countryside there is a suggestion of the early Vergil. It is as if the poet, sometimes tired of struggling in political and cultural battles, retired to the country for peace, security, and contentment.

Carducci differs, however, from the English poets of the nineteenth century. Unlike Wordsworth, Carducci does not moralize about what he finds in nature and the rural life; unlike Keats, he shies away from the sensuous, from the emotional, and the subjective. Carducci seems merely to have looked for and found contentment of a kind. Such expression is found, for example, in "Il Bove," a poem about the mild, strong, and patient ox, whose eyes mirror for the poet the green and divine silence of the fields. It is not strange to find that the poet says in a poem to Vergil that the Roman poet's verse is to him like the sea, a line of mountains, or the breeze in tall trees. Again, in "A un Asino," Carducci used the donkey as a symbol of ancient patience and asks, at the same time, if it may not be love that moves the donkey to bray. Even "Presso una Certosa," a poem written about landscape near a monastery, is a poem on the loveliness of the countryside, a loveliness which leads the poet to think of pagan times and things, and ends with the hope that the poet may be visited by the spirit of Homer.

At times Carducci seems to feel that he could have chosen a better life by living in the countryside, instead of writing about the disturbances of his native land. His "Idyl of the Maremma" finds him writing of a vigorous countrywoman meant for bearing vigorous sons and daughters. Better to have loved and won her, to have lived with such a one in the country amidst a large and healthy family, writes the poet, than to sweat in small rhymes, to write painfully of sad and miserable things, and to seek out the ambiguous answers to the riddles of the universe.

Although he was a reformer in poetry and the foe of slavish imitation of the past, Carducci revered the great poets, as his poems to Dante, to Vergil, and to Homer testify. The poet of nineteenth-century Italy did not deny the greatness of his predecessors; he simply wished to find his own vein of work which might be as productive for him and his age as those the great poets of the past had found for themselves and their ages. Even though he could not use the same materials as Dante, Carducci realized the greatness of *The Divine Comedy* and praised Dante for it. But, wrote Carducci, the greatness of Dante's time was gone and only the greatness of the song remained.

Few American readers know Carducci and his poetry. He was essentially a lyric poet, and too much is lost when a lyric is taken from one language and remade in the words of another. In Carducci's case this is particularly true. His materials, spirit, and style remain essentially Italian, resistant to adequate translation in another tongue.

THE POETRY OF CHRISTINA ROSSETTI

Type of work: Poetry
Author: Christina Rossetti (1830-1894)
Principal published works: Goblin Market and Other Poems, 1862; *The Prince's Progress and Other Poems,* 1866; *Sing Song,* 1872; *A Pageant and Other Poems,* 1881; *Verses,* 1893; *New Poems,* 1896

The sister of Dante Gabriel Rossetti, one of the founders of the Pre-Raphaelite Brotherhood, Christina Rossetti began writing poetry in her early teens. Her verse, always simple, pure, direct, never lost some of the childlike and direct quality evident in her earliest work. Indeed, she later wrote a nursery rhyme book (*Sing Song*), full of pleasant and sharp little rhymes for children. She even included a rhymed alphabet, containing six or eight onomatopoetic references for each letter. Her skill and facility in light verse can be seen in the lines like the following from "An Alphabet":

K is a King, or a Kaiser still higher;
K is a Kitten, or quaint Kangaroo.
L is a Lute or a lovely-toned Lyre
L is a Lily all laden with dew.

Her deftness in children's verse and in slight lyrics lasted throughout her poetic career.

Christina Rossetti is, however, far more frequently remembered for her religious or devotional poetry. Living in partial seclusion with her family (primarily with her mother until the latter's death in 1886), Christina Rossetti saw little of the London around her but lived intensely within her own private world of religious contemplation and meditation. Her poetry, the product of inward contemplation rather than a weapon for a public cause like that of the Pre-Raphaelites, was most frequently devotional. Her themes were faith and the peace of the eternal spiritual life.

Her religion was not theological or doctrinal, however, in the manner of many Victorians, for she concentrated on simple faith and applied her simple and pure lyrics to celebration of that faith. In this simple faith, Jesus being the object of much of her devotion; she wrote a

number of poems on the incidents in His life and used Good Friday and the Resurrection as a subject for several of her best poems. In devoting her poems, the products of her faith, to Jesus, she idealized the peace that the individual could find in his dedication to Christianity and the life of the spirit. She seemed, often, to picture herself as humble and unworthy, to long for the peace of eternal rest without ever being sure she could obtain it. She made religion a haven, frequently in her poetry presenting religion as a resting place from the cares of a troubled life. This theme, along with her simple diction, is evident in the following passage from "I Do Set My Bow in the Cloud":

Then tell me: is it not enough
To feel that, when the path is rough
And the sky dark and the rain cold,
His promise standeth as of old?
When heaven and earth have past away
Only His righteous word shall stay,
And we shall know His will is best.
Behold: He is a haven-rest,
A sheltering-rock, a hiding place,
For runners steadfast in the race;
Who, toiling for a little space,
Had light through faith when sight
    grew dim,
And offered all their world to Him.

This passage illustrates many of Miss Rossetti's frequent attitudes: the darkness and difficulty of this world, usually portrayed in wintry images; the sense of God's promise to man emanating through all human experience; the idea of the "sheltering-rock," the haven of faith in which the poor human being could "hide"; the sense that religious faith, without question, is more important for man than are any of his own attempts to see and understand the world about him.

In her devotional poetry she frequently presents simple images of nature through which she demonstrates her devotion. Flowers, the coming of spring and hope, the simple natural details of the world around her, form the pattern of images through which her faith is conveyed. The fields and the meadows, like her simple reflections, all demonstrate the power of God and man's necessary faith in the mercy and forgiveness of Christ. The most common symbol in her poetry is the rose. Standing for a kind of spiritual beauty, an emanation of the spirit of Christ, the rose figures centrally in her work. Roses are, in a poem like "Three Nuns," the flowers planted in paradise, the sure indications of the existence of divine love. The rose is also, in this and other poems, the symbol of purity, of a virginal and spiritual beauty that emanates from the divine. In addition, the rose is often solitary, blooming alone in a dark and wintry landscape. As a figure of solitary beauty, the rose becomes an emblem for faith and virtue in the midst of a dark and corrupt world.

Christina Rossetti's faith was not simply a private matter. In her poetry she demonstrated a great deal of concern for her family and her small circle of friends, and she included them in her poetic requests for the blessings of a merciful Christ. Many of her poems mark family occasions: birthday greetings, valentines to her mother, hopes that her talented brothers could find the peace and rest latent in the true faith. Sometimes she questions her worthiness for salvation, although she generally concludes that Christ is sufficiently merciful to receive her in paradise. In these poems she often comments on the vanity of worldly ambition and the folly of man's pride. Although she humbly includes her own inclination to judge others as one of the most damning of sins, she often speaks out against those less faithful to the divine spirit than she, giving her work qualities of precision and sharpness.

Not all of Christina Rossetti's verse is religious or devotional. She can be light and witty; some of her early epigrams

have the flavor of Jane Austen's quiet, civilized, cutting comments. She also wrote a few satirical poems, like one called "The P.R.B." which begins:

The two Rossettis (brothers they)
And Holman Hunt and John Millais,
With Stephens chivalrous and bland,
And Woolner in a distant land—
In these six men I awestruck see
Embodied the great P.R.B.
D.G. Rossetti offered two
Good pictures to the public view;
Unnumbered ones great John Millais,
And Holman more than I can say

William Rossetti, calm and solemn,
Cuts up his brethren by the column.

Some of this sharpness and directness also appears in the poems she wrote about neighboring farm girls. These poems sometimes begin with a simple characterization or a simple account of the circumstances in which the farm girl lived. From this point, the writer goes on, as in "Margery," to demonstrate that the unhappy girl should not have been so obvious in letting her boy friend know that she loved him, or she may urge the simple farmer to speak up and tell his love. These poems have a direct, homely quality of easy and unpretentious diction. If they frequently add a didactic tag that spoils them for modern ears, the moral is also kept in the language and the area of concern in the poem. Wit and homely common sense distinguished much of Christina Rossetti's nonreligious poetry, an indication that her observation of the world around her was as sharp, though restrained, as her allegiance to the world of spirit was thorough and genuine.

Praised in her own time for the clarity and sweetness of her diction as well as for the purity of her faith, Christina Rossetti was widely read, although not widely imitated, for she introduced little in the way of technical innovation or a new area of poetic subject matter. Faith is often more bitter in the twentieth century, and the simplicity of her faith seems remote and unworldly to many contemporary readers. Yet the simplicity of her diction and the ability to state a perception with ease and grace and point are still qualities that endear this writer to many modern readers. Although her public is not wide, it is faithful and appreciative.

THE POETRY OF DANTE GABRIEL ROSSETTI

Type of work: Poetry
Author: Dante Gabriel Rossetti (1828-1882)
Principal published works: Poems, 1870; *Ballads and Sonnets,* 1881; *Collected Works,* 1886

Some glimpse into Rossetti's ideas on poetry can be obtained from the statement made, at almost the end of his life, to Hall Caine, that when, as a youth, he had first encountered early English ballad literature, he had said to himself, "There lies your line." He read the collections made by Thomas Percy (1765) and by Sir Walter Scott (1802-1803) as well as Scott's original poetry, and he spent many hours in the British Museum poring over medieval romances in a search for words to use in poems that he planned to write.

He began his career, however, as a painter, and entered literature through the coterie which called itself the Pre-Raphaelite Brotherhood. This loosely-knit group, formed in 1848 by Rossetti, Holman Hunt, and J. E. Millais, had as its artistic goal the return to the "fidelity to nature" of medieval Italian painters prior to Raphael. Thus both as painter and as poet Rossetti was directed towards medievalism. The new group soon needed a periodical through which the members could make their views known; so, in 1850, they founded *The Germ.* Its life was short—only four numbers appeared —but in it some of Rossetti's early work was printed.

Surely no manuscript in all of English literature had a stranger or more macabre history than did Rossetti's first volume of poems. When, on a February night of 1862, he returned to his home to find his wife dead from an overdose of laudanum, he was so conscience-stricken by the possibility that her death had been suicide that he resolved on the melodramatic gesture of placing the manuscript in her coffin under her famous red-gold hair. Even his brother William, who knew that of some of the poems no other copies existed, while of others there

were but imperfect copies, was sufficiently influenced by the tension-charged atmosphere to approve the act. The manuscript contained some of Rossetti's most famous poems: "The Blessed Damozel," "Jenny," "Sister Helen" (first titled "The Witch"), and "Love's Nocturn." But further melodrama was to come. In October, 1869, Rossetti, who now wished to publish the poems and had even advertised their appearance, had the grave opened and the manuscript disinterred by C. A. Howell and Dr. Llewellyn Williams. For this exhumation, which he somewhat lamely tried to justify, Rossetti has been much criticized, one biographer even calling him a "changeable widower rifling his dead wife's grave at the dictate of literary ambition."

The pieces that Rossetti included in this first volume can be divided, at least roughly, into three classes: "medieval" poems, love poems, and sonnets for pictures. By the first category is meant those verses employing medieval settings or imitations of medieval techniques. Rossetti derived his literary medievalism from two sources, the romance and the ballad. From the romance he obtained the colorful background of knights, ladies, and castles found in "The Staff and Scrip"; from the ballad he got the terse, tragic story as well as such devices as the refrain and the question and answer method of narration. These two technical devices, which were common enough in the traditional border ballads, Rossetti—as well as the other Pre-Raphaelite poets—developed into artistic elements of considerable effectiveness. From the simple refrain of the old ballads they created what has been called the "incremental" refrain—that is, a refrain which, by changing with the progress of the narrative and its emotional pattern, helps to build up the climax of the story. The trick is best seen in "Sister Helen," which has been considered one of the best literary ballads of the nineteenth century. This poem has the starkness of the traditional ballad plus modern psychological handling. Usually, however, Rossetti tended to overlay the simplicity of the old ballads with the luxuriant detail so dear to the Pre-Raphaelites.

Another side of Rossetti's medievalism appears in his three translations from Villon, one of which, the "Ballad of Dead Ladies," is perhaps the most famous short piece of translation in English.

Rossetti's love poetry, both of this time and later, presents a difficult problem. To understand the work of any poet, one must know something of his life; and this statement is particularly true of Rossetti. Even on the surface, his love poems are not easy reading, for they are densely woven, at times enigmatic. The mystery turns on his attitude toward his dead wife, Elizabeth Siddall and on the circumstances of her death. It is now fairly well agreed among Rossetti biographers that her death was an act of suicide, and that the suspicion—or even the knowledge —of this fact haunted Rossetti for the rest of his life and was responsible for the gloom of his later years. Some critics even go so far as to say that he never wrote a good poem or painted a good picture after 1862. On the other hand, it seems also true that his brief marriage, after a prolonged engagement, was unhappy. It has been customary to say that these passionate, even sensuous, love poems were inspired by Elizabeth or that they expressed a yearning for a reunion with her; but in recent years it has been claimed that the real inspiration of the poems was Jane Burden, who married William Morris in 1859. She, it is said, was the woman Rossetti really loved. Having married Elizabeth out of a sense of duty and having seen Jane become the wife of one of his best friends, he poured his frustrated love for Jane into "The Stream's Secret" and the sonnet sequence "The House of Life." So anxious was he, according to the proponents of this theory, to conceal the autobiographical aspects of these poems that he deliberately falsified the dates of composition so as to throw readers off the scent. Since all the facts, even after so many years, have never been made public, the matter must remain conjectural.

Rossetti's poetry was, on its publication, generally well received by critics. But a storm was brewing. In 1871 there appeared in the *Contemporary Review* an article, over an assumed name, called "The Fleshly School of Poetry." Twenty years earlier, Rossetti, along with the other Pre-Raphaelites, had been attacked for his paintings; now he was to be attacked for his poetry. The writer of this article was one Robert Buchanan, an almost unknown Scotsman. The whole situation was complicated by personal feuds and animosities. But the (to us) almost unbelievable prudery of Victorian England made Rossetti peculiarly vulnerable to this kind of attack. His poems were, for those days, extremely frank; his sonnet "Nuptial Sleep" and especially "Jenny," the description of a prostitute, with such lines as

Your silk ungirdled and unlac'd
And warm sweets open to the waist,

were genuinely shocking to the contemporary reading public. Also, Rossetti's well-known friendship with Swinburne, the real *enfant terrible* of the period, added to the suspicions of the Victorian public. It is certainly true that Rossetti's love poems were far more sensuous than nineteenth-century poetry had been used to. But Buchanan's attack hurt Rossetti deeply and increased his tendency toward melancholia.

Few styles are as out of fashion these days as the Pre-Raphaelite. To the modern mind, these men seemed far too self-conscious and artificial in their medievalism. But both as poet and painter Rossetti exercised a considerable influence over the artistic taste of the subsequent decades. He and the other Pre-Raphaelites were in part responsible for the "aesthetic movement" of the 1880's and 1890's, the chief ornament of which was Oscar Wilde. Perhaps the most important contribution of Rossetti as a poet was his part in shattering the prudery that had strangled so much of Victorian literature.

THE POETRY OF DONNE

Type of work: Poetry
Author: John Donne (1572-1631)
Principal published works: An Anatomy of the World: The First Anniversary, 1611; *Of the Progress of the Soule: The Second Anniversary,* 1612; *Poems by J.D.,* 1633

It was in the early years of the twentieth century that John Donne was first acknowledged to be a major English poet, and his achievement meaningfully evaluated. Pope "translated" Donne's *Satires* so thoroughly that they were unrecognizable, and Dryden misleadingly declared that he wrote "nice speculations of Philosophy" and not love poetry at all. The poets of the nineteenth century show, with the exception of Gerard Manley Hopkins, the influence of Milton rather than of the metaphysical poets. The poets of this century have learned much from Donne's poetic method, by which emotions are expressed by ideas and ideas defined in their emotional context. Ironically, both Donne and Dryden, by writing in what are essentially speech rhythms and not in the current poetic mode revitalized the language of poetry in their generation.

Dryden was in error when he called Donne's poetry philosophical. Donne was not committed to a particular philosophic system, but he was interested in the fascinating, conflicting, and often disturbing philosophies of his period. The scholastic way of thought, in which systems tended towards synthesis and unity, was giving way to the European scientific renaissance, which was analytical. Ptolemaic astronomy was challenged by Copernicus; Aristotle was challenged by Galileo. What interested Donne, however, was not the ultimate truth of an idea but the fascination of ideas themselves. His images are drawn from whatever belief best expressed the emotion he had to communicate.

Donne was not the first man to write metaphysical poetry. That is, he was not the first poet to describe an emotional state by its intellectual equivalent. However, before Donne wrote, this technique was confined, with the exception of some of Shakespeare's sonnets and Ben Jonson's poetry, to the drama and was most frequently found in the plays of Ford, Jonson, and Webster. Also, the Elizabethan tradition of love poetry had already begun to be rivaled by witty and cynical courtly verse. Donne's own reaction against the Elizabethan tradition was as successful as it was complete.

In some poems, as in "The Indifferent," Donne celebrated variety in love, and in "Go and Catch a Falling Star" he insisted that no woman remained faithful. As well as in these poems of wit and fancy, where Donne directly mocked literary convention, there are serious love poems in which he is seen to have absorbed and surpassed it. In "A Feaver" the world would not merely be a place of darkness after the lady's death; it would disintegrate:

> But yet thou canst not die, I know;
> To leave this world behind, is death,
> But when thou from this world wilt goe,
> The whole world vapours with thy breath.

A further departure from the tradition in which the lady was invariably unattainable is the glory Donne finds in sexual as well as spiritual love. In only two or three poems does he praise platonic relationships, and the poems that describe a relationship in which the beloved woman is not the poet's mistress are extremely bitter and mocking, as, for example, in "The Apparition."

The element of hyperbole in these poems is central also in the poems of consummated love and continued devotion, where it is one of the means by which the strength and sincerity of the poet's passion is conveyed. "The Good-Morrow" begins:

I wonder, by my troth, what thou and I
Did, till we lov'd? were we not wean'd
till then?

and continues:

For love, all love of other sights con-
troules,
And makes one little roome, an every
where.

At first Donne's images may amaze rather
than delight; however, they communicate
effectively the idea through which the
emotion is conveyed.

The areas from which Donne's images
were drawn—astronomy, geography, philosophy, and alchemy among others—
were those of interest to educated readers
of his time. Donne's images do not evoke
general or remembered sensation, but explain the particular one of which he
wrote. In "A Valediction: forbidding
mourning," the central idea is that love
is not destroyed by death. Donne compares his love to "the trepidation of the
spheres" which on earth is not destructive, although the lesser "moving of the
earth brings harms and fears." Further,
his love is beyond the ordinary love and
includes the soul (love to Donne always
involved the entire being); thus separation by death is not a "breach" but an
"expansion"—"Like gold to airy thinness
beat." The most striking image in this
poem is that of a pair of compasses: the
mistress who stays alive is the "fixt foot"
around which the dead soul revolves and
which, invisibly, circles with it. The
poem ends:

Thy firmness drawes my circle just,
And makes me end where I begunne.

The circle in Donne's poetry is always a
symbol for infinity.

The rhythm of Donne's poetry is as
varied and accurate in conveying the
sense as the imagery he employs. Its texture is sinewy and often irregular. The
speech cadences of the verse are heard
in the mind and are essentially dramatic.
It is not smooth verse, but it is exact and
musical. The opening of "The Sunne

Rising" is illustrative of his quick, tense
quality:

Busie old foole, unruly Sunne,
Why dost thou thus,
Through windowes, and through cur-
taines call on us?
Must to thy motions lovers seasons
run?

Compare these lines with the tranquility
and sensuousness of his close:

Thine age askes ease, and since thy
duties bee
To warme the world, that's done in
warming us.
Shine here to us, and thou art every
where;
This bed thy center is, these walls, thy
spheare.

"Aire and Angels" has lines in which
the vowel sounds are long and the con-
sonants soft, when love is contemplated,
and short-voweled monosyllabic lines
which express love's actuality. The sound
in Donne's poetry not only echoes the
sense but in part communicates the emotion.

The power and beauty of Donne's
poetry is its synthesis of emotion, passion, and thought. "The Anniversarie,"
which was presumably written to his wife
Ann More, is a triumphant expression
of confidence in love. In the opening
stanza of this poem Donne contrasts the
mutability of kings, courts, and even the
sun with their love:

Only our love hath us decay;
This, no to morrow hath, nor yesterday,
Running it never runs from us away,
But truly keeps his first, last, everlasting
day.

The discussion of death in the second
stanza of this poem is not, here or in
other of his lyrics, a morbid preoccupation but, as is true of all Donne's poetry,
an illustration of the all-embracing and
inquiring quality of his mind. Death will
not destroy love; love will increase in
the souls released from the grave. In the
third stanza the lovers themselves are
kings and thus they will know physical

2948

change and decay; however, since the love in their souls after death is inviolate, so are they, while they live. The evolution of this paradoxical idea and the simplicity and directness of the language carry dramatic conviction. The poem ends:

Let us love nobly, and live, and adde
  againe
Yeares unto yeares, till we attaine
To write threescore; this is the second
  of our raigne.

Probably the *Songs and Sonets* are the best known of Donne's poems, but some of the *Elegies* and religious verse are of the same quality. In 1615, Donne was ordained an Anglican priest and became Dean of St. Paul's Cathedral in London. The poetry that Donne wrote after his ordination was as passionate, as intellectually inquiring, and often as tormented as his love poetry. He spoke of God and the Church in the same terms as he spoke of secular love. For many years before he became a priest he had studied theology and was converted to Protestantism, from the Catholic faith to which he had been born. He discussed the difficulty of finding true religion in his poetry and was apparently almost overwhelmed by the knowledge of his sinfulness.

The "Holy Sonnets" are vibrant and impassioned cries, infused with the knowledge of the need for grace. They, too, are highly personal and dramatic. Number XIV begins:

Batter my heart, three person'd God;
  for, you
As yet but knocke, breathe, shine, and
  seeke to mend;
That I may rise, and stand, o'erthrow
  mee, and bend
Your force, to breake, blowe, burn and
  make me new.

It ends:

Take mee to you, imprison mee, for I
Except you enthrall mee, never shall be
  free,
Nor ever chast, except you ravish mee.

Sometimes the paradoxes in the religious poetry are superb and convincing, but occasionally the ideas are pursued to the point of tedium and a seeming detail is over-elaborated. One of Donne's most successful devotional poems is "A Hymnne to God the Father," on sin, fear, and forgiveness, which, with its repeated phrase "Wilt thou forgive," has a simplicity and humility which is equaled only by the poetry of George Herbert.

Donne was the greatest of the metaphysical poets. In some few of their poems he was equaled by Vaughan and Marvell and in religious poetry by Herbert. But the body of his work is poetry of a quality which, when compared with that of any other of these poets, is unsurpassed. When his images are understood in their function of communicating a state of mind, and his ideas in their power to give expression to emotions, Donne's poetry is appreciated for its wit, beauty, and perception.

THE POETRY OF DRAYTON

Type of work: Poetry
Author: Michael Drayton (1563-1631)
Principal published works: The Harmonie of the Church, 1591; Idea, the Shepherd's Garland, 1593; Piers Gaveston, 1593; Idea's Mirror, 1594; Matilda, 1594; Endimion and Phoebe, 1595; The Tragical Legend of Robert, Duke of Normandy, 1596; Mortimeriados, 1596; England's Heroical Epistles, 1597; Legend of the Great Cromwell, 1607; Poly-Olbion, 1612-1622; Nimphidia, 1627; Shepherd's Sirena, 1627; The Muses' Elizium, 1630

Held in high esteem by his contemporaries, Michael Drayton was one of the first professional poets whose entire life was devoted to his muse. He was thought to have been with Shakespeare during the last merry evening of the playwright's life, or so legend has it. Drayton is almost as elusive a figure for the biographer. According to his own word, he turned to poetry at the age of ten, when he was a page in the service of Sir Henry Goodere —a connection he maintained by worshipful devotion to Goodere's youngest daughter Anne throughout his bachelor lifetime.

His first published work, *The Harmonie of the Church*, is seldom read now even by scholars, so much like the weaker works of his contemporaries is this collection of Biblical studies in verse. But some of the prayers, the songs of thanksgiving, and especially his rendition of the Song of Solomon give indications of his latent talent. His admiration for Spenser led to the writing of a pseudo-*Shepheardes Calender*, pastoral eclogues called *Idea, the Shepherd's Garland*. This work is not to be confused, however, with Drayton's fine sonnet sequence of a later period. In 1605 or 1606 Drayton brought out a collection of old and new work, *Poems Lyric and Pastoral*, which contained "The Ballad of Agincourt," a celebration of Henry V's great victory, and "Ode to the Virginian Voyage," a patriotic poem commemorating Raleigh's conquests in the New World. This latter is among the first to present America as the new Garden of Eden ("Earth's only paradise"):

> Where nature hath in store
> Fowl, venison, and fish,

> And the fruitful soil—
> Without your toil,
> Three harvests more,
> All greater than you wish.

Among Drayton's other odes are two often anthologized because they are among the most graceful, felicitous verses in the language. "To His Coy Love"—a canzonet, as Drayton calls it, but meant to be sung, like his other odes—calls back the poet's heart from a half love, starved for pleasure "amidst an ocean of delight." Rejecting many of the lady's physical charms, he pleads:

> Come nice thing, let thy heart alone,
> I cannot live without thee.

About this same time Drayton published a number of historical verses titled *Mortimeriados* (republished as *The Baron's Wars* in 1603), a criticism of civil strife in which he presented the disturbed career of Edward II. He produced a more interesting work of poetic history in *England's Heroical Epistles*, an imaginary exchange of the love letters supposedly written by twelve English lovers such as James and Mary Suffolk, Edward IV and Jane Shore, Henry II and the fair Rosamond. Along with *Endimion and Phoebe*, verses in imitation of Marlowe, and a miscellany of conventional verses such as his *Fig for Momus*, Drayton during this period seems to have given more time to dramatic productions and social life than to the diligence in writing which characterizes his later life.

After Queen Elizabeth died, Drayton failed to enjoy the favor of King James. The first benefit posterity gained from this lack of acceptance was an excellent satire, *The Owl* (1604), that wise bird so hated by the crows and kites who made up the new court. With a return to his scriptural preoccupations, he published in that same year *Moses in a Map of His Miracles*. While not an original genius, Drayton displayed in this work a spirit of courtliness and an expert use of conventional themes: a lament over a loved one, a comparison of youth and age, a clearly patriotic celebration of the great Elizabeth, a lament for the dead Sidney, a praise of Idea (Anne), a song of deceased though venerated worthies of England.

The next year saw the publication of a sequence made up of fifty-one sonnets, four of which are still remembered and read. Here, in *Idea's Mirror*, the platonic conception is lost in what is clearly passionate love. Drayton, often thought of as a lesser Daniel and as the great imitator, struck out on his own here, rivaling the early Shakespeare and the later Cavalier poets. The sonnet form, here three iambic pentameter quatrains and a final couplet, reaches a maturity of style, especially in the poems starting with the line "To nothing fitter can I thee compare," continuing through "When first I ended, then I first began," to a climax of despair in "You're not alone when you are still alone," and then to the gravely beautiful conclusion:

Since there's no help, come, let us kiss
and part;
Nay, I have done, you get no more of
me;
And I am glad, yea, glad with all my
heart
That thus so cleanly I myself can free.

"To His Rival" is thought to be autobiographical in that it reflects a page's aspiration to marry into the nobility. In this poem Drayton gives the victorious lover saucy advice and warning.

Though out of favor now, the long poem was the mark of distinction in renaissance England. Unfortunately for Drayton, he planned his greatest work as a cartographer might by mapping out seas, lakes, streams, hills, islands, forests, towns—a complete poetic excursion from offshore islands through the southern districts to the Tweed River. In "Poly-Olbion" he intended to go right on north through Scotland and to add at least another 10,000 couplets to the 15,000 extant. Some critics have praised his use of Alexandrines for this literary excursion, saying that the ambling meter of twelve-syllable lines fits the pleasant landscapes viewed leisurely. Others feel that the meter, unnatural in our language, is dreary and boring. Certainly, all the couplets are not poetry or even good verse; but certainly some of the descriptive passages are beautiful. For this great work of thirty books a learned scribe, Selden, wrote notes nearly as voluminous and in some ways more interesting, especially those concerning the legendary and antiquarian sections. For Drayton included history and folklore as well as topography in the poem.

Drayton, by his own admission, was disappointed in the reception of what he hoped was an account of the Elizabethan discovering his own England, a panegyric of lofty dimensions which was also scholarly and profound. He was most successful in evoking the fairy glens, the legendary figures of saints and warriors. His pastoral scenes with shepherds still offer in verse the peace and tranquility of a life no longer possible in the bustling seventeenth century. He starts with an argument or prelude to each book or song which can be read as a gloss or summary, as this passage illustrates:

The sprightly Muse her wing displays,
And the French islands first surveys;
Bears up with Neptune, and in glory
Transcends proud Cornwall's promon-
tory. . . .

The really interesting thing, as the argument suggests and the first book reveals, is the intermingling of place and legend; for example, the river where Arthur's blood "By Mordred's murderous hand was mingled with her flood." Add to this material the lovely prospect, the homely cottage, the toiling peasant, and Old England lives on.

Two other works, inferior in length but superior in all other ways, need be mentioned: *Nimphidia* and *The Muses' Elizium*, the first a miniature epic of fairyland and the latter an ironic self-portrait of the poet in a pagan paradise. Like Shakespeare and Chaucer, Drayton combines the lusty and the magical, farm and fay, in "The Court of Faery," as the subtitle of *Nimphidia* reads, where the reader encounters Oberon the duped, Queen Mab, mischievous, teasing Puck, and Pigwiggen, the fairy knight.

A kind of epilogue to the life of the friend of Shakespeare, Spenser, and Ben Jonson is the brilliant work, *The Muses' Elizium*. Though the idea is classical, the earthly paradise presented is English: the rills, the flowers, the seasons (apart from the fact there is no winter), and especially the pastimes. Divided into Nimphalls, or books, which correspond to the epic struggles between the Eliziums and the Felicians, the last embattled satyr takes refuge in the imaginary, Elizium, though his heart is still in a world no longer felicitous. Here we may see in ironic portraiture the disappointed, embattled old poet writing in praise of earlier and happier times.

THE POETRY OF EMILY DICKINSON

Type of work: Poetry
Author: Emily Dickinson (1830-1886)
Principal published works: Poems, 1890; *Poems: Second Series,* 1891; *Poems: Third Series,*
1896; *The Single Hound,* 1914; *Further Poems,* 1929; *Unpublished Poems,* 1936; *Bolts
of Melody: New Poems,* 1945; *The Poems of Emily Dickinson,* 1955

The life and literary career of Emily Dickinson were filled with irony. In deciding that some of the poems she sent him were not strong enough for publication, the essayist and critic Thomas Wentworth Higginson is said to have remarked that they were "too delicate." This judgment is only one of the many strange blunders made in connection with a woman who has finally been accorded the rank of a major poet.

Proper evaluation of a contemporary writer is an uncertain business in any era, but literary criticism in Emily Dickinson's time produced some especially ironic judgments. Of those who saw her poems during her lifetime, only Helen Hunt Jackson seems to have appreciated their real worth; Emily herself (and Emerson, who was astute enough as a critic to recognize the genius of Walt Whitman) thought Mrs. Jackson to be one of the great poets of her time, but she is now remembered almost solely for her championing of Emily. "Creative editing" is another irony that has plagued the work of the inspired recluse of Amherst. Only six of her poems appeared in print before her death; the mutilation of these by zealous editors who wanted to "correct" her vagaries of rhyme, meter, and punctuation was a factor in her decision not to seek publication but to take her chances with fame after death. Well-meaning editing continued to haunt her work long after she died and only recently, in *The Poems of Emily Dickinson,* edited by Thomas H. Johnson and published in three volumes in 1955, has the world been allowed to read her lyrics as she wrote and punctuated them.

The bare facts of the life of Emily Dickinson were so simple that they would seem to permit no garbling, no misinterpretation, but even here what might be called "creative tampering" has also been at work. Legend says she fell madly in love with the Reverend Charles Wadsworth and he with her. Supposedly he was willing to give up family and career for Emily, to renounce everything for love; but, true to her Puritan background, she refused him. Now biographers are certain that no such double renunciation ever took place, that while she was greatly influenced by her feelings for Wadsworth and addressed to him many of her finest poems, their acquaintance was largely restricted to letters and he was probably never aware of her deep attachment.

Out of these tangles that have long surrounded her life and career, the reader is now able to judge and enjoy the work of one of America's most original and remarkable poets. Using the Bible as her chief source of inspiration and the rhythms of the hymn books as a metrical starting point, Emily Dickinson developed with care a technique that produced poems breath-taking in construction; they are full of the magic of a child who balances blocks on top of one another, performing feats impossible for a shaky adult hand. Almost as daring as the rhythms are her experiments in all the variations on part rhymes. With the help of Whitman, Emily Dickinson pushed open the door through which the "modern" poets have rushed to find new ways of expressing themselves. Here is an example of her metrics and musical effect:

Success is counted sweetest
By those who ne'er succeed.
To comprehend a nectar
Requires sorest need.

THE POETRY OF EMILY DICKINSON. Excerpts reprinted from POEMS BY EMILY DICKINSON by permission of the publishers, Little, Brown & Co. All rights reserved.

Not one of all the purple Host
Who took the Flag today
Can tell the definition
So clear of Victory

As he defeated—dying—
On whose forbidden ear
The distant strains of triumph
Burst agonized and clear!

Poems in this characteristic style were what brought forth Higginson's pronouncement—"too delicate." The judgment now seems particularly obtuse, for the very delicacy he objected to is one of the poet's chief charms; and sometimes that delicacy conceals the strength of iron:

The Soul selects her own Society—
Then—shuts the Door—
To her divine Majority—
Present no more—
Unmoved—she notes the Chariots—
pausing—
At her low Gate—
Unmoved—an Emperor be kneeling
Upon her Mat—

I've known her—from an ample nation—
Choose One—
Then—close the Valves of her attention—
Like Stone—

The spirit of Emily Dickinson's poems has been compared with that of the great metaphysicals, John Donne and William Blake; she is indeed like them in her ability to expand the little particularities of her everyday existence into ideas that are timeless and universal. For Emily Dickinson, who as her life slipped by confined herself almost entirely to her home and its grounds, these particularities were birds, flies, frogs, sunrises and sunsets, cups, saucers, doors, even a snake, that "narrow Fellow in the Grass" whom she never met "without a tighter breathing and Zero at the Bone." Broadening these simple subjects, the poet expresses her feelings about God, death, and immortality.

Her relationship with God is an interesting one, for even in her childhood she could not force herself to be orthodox. As a schoolgirl she had great difficulty in professing herself to be a Christian. The harsh God of the Old Testament—the God who created man in His own image, restricted him with all sorts of "thou-shall-nots," and then destroyed the image with death—had little appeal for Emily. In her poems her God is a very personal one, to be treated like a friend, praised for his good deeds and chided for his faults. Pompous piety has no place in any of her religious poems and when her feelings of intimacy lead her to address the Deity as "Papa above!" we are charmed rather than shocked by poetry that lets us become a part of a delightful woman to whom the trivialities of existence and the untouchable verities are of equal importance.

Like most poets, Emily Dickinson was intrigued by death; characteristically, she made it seem just another event in human experience. In one of her best-known poems, death is the driver of a carriage which picks her up, slowly takes her past a school where children are playing during recess, past fields, past the setting sun, until finally

We paused before a House that seemed
A Swelling of the Ground—
The Roof was scarcely visible—
The Cornice—in the Ground—

Since then—'tis Centuries—and yet
Feels shorter than the Day
I first surmised the Horses Heads
Were toward Eternity—

But death is not something the poet takes lightly. The loss of those she loved—particularly her father and Dr. Wadsworth—were blows from which she reeled; to one whose circle of acquaintanceship was so constricted each death assumed such great importance that it inspired a flood of little elegies in which the poet records both her grief and her love.

"Time," "eternity," and "immortality" are words that are insistently repeated in these poems. Always a skeptic, she once asked the question, "Is immortality true?" and like a proper metaphysician she lets her mind play with the two possible answers. In one of her last poems she seems to say that a person's identity can never be blotted out; the poem concludes with this stanza:

To die is not to go—
On Doom's consummate Chart
No Territory new is staked—
Remain thou as thou art.

Many readers of Emily Dickinson feel that she is a poet whom one may like or not like, that those who judge her a major poet have developed a sort of gourmet's taste in literature, preferring the delicate and dainty to the robust and wholesome. There are indeed times when her poetry is quaint to the point of being cranky, when her eccentricities, compressions, and indirections lead to incomprehensibility; but if the reader will give her a second or third chance he, like others before him, will find that her best poetry provides the essence of great literature—contact with a powerful, original, fascinating mind.

THE POETRY OF FRENEAU

Type of work: Poetry
Author: Philip Freneau (1752-1832)
Principal published works: A Poem on the Rising Glory of America, 1772 (with H. H. Brackenridge); The American Village, 1772; General Gage's Confession, 1775; The British Prison Ship, 1781; The Poems of Philip Freneau, 1786; Poems Written Between the Years 1786 and 1794, 1795; Poems Written and Published during the Revolutionary War, 1809; A Collection of Poems . . . Written Between the Year 1797 and the Present Time, 1815

The fact that Freneau's collected poetic works, at least in a definitive edition, were not published until over a hundred years after he had stirred the American conscience heightens the irony of the title of the best biography of the poet, *That Rascal Freneau: A Study in Literary Failure* (1941). The phrase comes from George Washington, who more than anyone had occasion to be grateful to Freneau, not only for the several laudatory poems addressed to him but also for lifting soldier morale during the nadir of the Revolution. Freneau's political poetry served the same purpose as Paine's incendiary essays, and was perhaps more effective.

These facts alone would make Freneau interesting historically, but his poetry of nature, of American life and culture, add an important dimension to his memory. Most literary historians and critics consider Freneau our first outstanding poet, a liberal in form as well as content. He dared to introduce native themes and idioms into poetry at a time when other writers remained slavishly Anglophile. While a student at Princeton he wrote a poem in collaboration with Hugh Henry Brackenridge, "A Poem on the Rising Glory of America," a cue to later cleverly designed propagandist pieces, written first in praise of British imperialism and then revised to express sharp denunciation of British usurpation. Significantly, the account that the poem was received at commencement, 1771, "with great applause," mentions only Brackenridge's name. In blank verse and dramatic dialogue, the work traces the history of America as the story of freedom-seeking men, establishing on this

Eden-like continent, prophetically, a haven for all the oppressed:

And when a train of rolling years are past,
(So sung the exiled seer in Patmos isle)
A new Jerusalem, sent down from heaven,
Shall grace our happy earth,—perhaps this land,

. . . . . .

and such America at last shall have
When ages yet to come, have run their round,
and future years of bliss alone remain.

From this patriotic writing Freneau turned to the often-quoted "The American Village," a poem in praise of this land in contrast to "The Deserted Village" of a decadent England. Though written in heroic couplets, the sentiments expressed, the names, and the idiom are American.

To yonder village then will I descend,
There spend my days, and there my ev'-nings spend;
Sweet haunt of peace whose mud' wall'd sides delight,
The rural mind beyond the city bright.

Perhaps the neglect of his early poems caused him to retreat to a more romantic life in the West Indies. Some memorable verse came out of this period in the 1770's, notably "The House of Night," a poem worthy of Poe with its vivid description of death attended by weird phantasms and graveyard symbols:

Around his bed, by the dull flam-beaux' glare,
I saw pale phantoms—Rage to madness vext,

2956

Wan, wasting grief, and ever musing
care,
Distressful pain, and poverty perplext.

Several times Freneau was captured by the British while going to and fro among his island paradises. Finally he was so incensed over the ruthless war on the sea and the sad disposition of prisoners that he wrote in 1781 his most powerful early work of condemnation, "The British Prison Ship," which contains a notable picture of horror on the high seas:

The various horrors of these hulks to
tell,
These Prison Ships where pain and
horror dwell,
Where death in tenfold vengeance
holds his reign,
And injur'd ghosts, yet unaveng'd,
complain;
This be my talk—ungenerous Britons,
you
Conspire to murder those you can't
subdue.

Though these were not Freneau's first satiric thrusts, his earlier diatribes had not the stuff of conviction. But the war on the sea he had suffered at first hand and he wrote about it from personal knowledge.

From that time on, Freneau followed closely the progress, or lack of it, of the Revolution, writing stirring patriotic pieces to boost morale, scourging lines to incense the colonials against their oppressors, rollicking ballads and celebrations of American victory or British defeat. He edited and editorialized during the latter days of the war, his poems being a special feature of various journals with which he was associated. For this work he was credited by Jefferson with saving the Constitution from the Monarchists and the Federalists. Attacked by critics and forgotten by his countrymen, he abandoned poetry and spent the years immediately following the war as a captain of coastal vessels. A collection of his early poetry and essays was published in 1786. He was aroused to cele-

brate the French Revolution to some memorable lines written in 1793, on Bastille Day:

The chiefs that bow to Capet's reign,
In mourning, now, their weeds display;
But we, that scorn a monarch's chain,
Combine to celebrate the DAY
Of Freedom's birth that put the seal,
And laid in dust the proud Bastille.

This partisan feeling eventually gave rise to the *Probationary Odes by Jonathan Pindar, Esq.*, some of the most mature of Freneau's satires against the decay of liberal, democratic sentiments. At the same time he wrote masterful, idiomatic prose under the pseudonym of Robert Slender. These together brought the wrath of the pompous against him, a prelude to the journalistic battle of the *United States Gazette* vs. the *National Gazette*, Hamilton vs. Freneau. From this affair came the abuse from which Freneau never recovered during his lifetime.

Freneau was first a poet, then a politician and patriot, as these very late lines in "The Brook in the Valley" reveal:

The world has wrangled half an age,
And we again in war engage,
While this sweet, sequestr'd rill
Murmurs through the valley still. . . .

But, with all your quiet flow,
Do you not some quarrels know!
Lately, angry, how you ran!
All at war—and much like man.

Of his work, the poems remembered and anthologized today are his unpretentious, indigenous nature lyrics such as "The Wild Honey Suckle" ("Fair flower, that dost so comely grow") or "On a Honey Bee" ("Thou, born to sip the lake or spring"). Also, his celebration of the first Americans deserves mention, especially "The Indian Burying Ground":

In spite of all the learned have said,
I still my old opinion keep;
The posture that we give the dead
Points out the soul's eternal sleep.

Recently, Freneau's verse has been reclaimed from neglect, very much as his reputation has been cleared of calumnious attacks by his contemporaries. Near his former home at Mount Pleasant, New Jersey, stands a monument inscribed:

Heaven lifts its everlasting portals high
And bids the pure in heart behold their
  God.

THE POETRY OF FROST

Type of work: Poetry
Author: Robert Frost (1874-1963)
Principal published works: A Boy's Will, 1913; *North of Boston,* 1914; *Mountain Interval,* 1916; *New Hampshire: A Poem with Notes and Grace Notes,* 1923; *West-Running Brook,* 1928; *A Further Range,* 1936; *A Witness Tree,* 1942; *A Masque of Reason,* 1945; *Steeple Bush,* 1947; *A Masque of Mercy,* 1947; *How Not to Be King,* 1951

They would not find me changed from
  him they knew—
Only more sure of all I thought was
  true.

Far in the pillared dark
Thrush music went—
Almost like a call to come in
To the dark and lament.

In a sense this early prediction by Robert Frost is an accurate description of the course of his writing career: Frost's poetry has not changed; it has simply grown stronger. The dominant characteristics of his work—his impeccable ear for the rhythms of speech; his realistic handling of nature that transcends the ordinary "love" we ascribe to poets of the outdoors; his revelation of human character by means of dramatic events; his warm philosophy that combines a whimsical poet with a dirt farmer whose feet are not only planted on the ground but in it—all these qualities were apparent (at least to some readers) early in his career. And they are still there, handled with greater precision, displaying more depth. As an example of this strengthening process, this growth of sapling into tree, look first at the little poem, "The Pasture," the last stanza of which invites the reader into Frost's *A Boy's Will:*

I'm going out to fetch the little calf
That's standing by the mother. It's so
  young,
It totters when she licks it with her
  tongue.
I sha'n't be gone long.—You come too.

The Frost charm is evident in these lines, but there is also a somewhat juvenile, Rilevesque quality. When one compares "The Pasture" with "Come In," a much later and firmer treatment of the same general theme, the superior diction is immediately apparent in such magnificent lines as these:

But equally apparent is a greater depth of psychological complexity, a stronger suggestion of the "death wish" that John Ciardi discusses in his controversial analysis of "Stopping by Woods on a Snowy Evening," the more famous lyric to which "Come In" is certainly a superb companion piece.

Frost has not changed, only grown surer; but there has been an amazing change, down through the years, in the attitude taken toward his poems. First, his fellow Americans could not see this most American of writers as a poet at all; it was necessary for him to go to England to be hailed for his talent. Secondly, when the English had pointed him out to us, we catalogued him as another cold New England poet who saw everything in black and white. This astonishing judgment becomes superegregious when we consider that *A Boy's Will* contains a poem of such warm understanding as "The Tuft of Flowers" and that *North of Boston,* his second volume, includes "The Death of the Hired Man," "Home Burial," and "The Fear," three dramatic poems that are intensely emotional. After Frost's reputation finally became established, the critics forced him into a third stage of his career: he was recognized as a major poet, but one not very interesting to talk or write about because his poetry was thought too simple and because Frost held aloof from the free-verse poets whose efforts, he felt, lacked discipline. Now, at last, Frost has en-

THE POETRY OF ROBERT FROST. Excerpts reprinted from COMPLETE POEMS OF ROBERT FROST by permission of the publishers, Henry Holt & Co., Inc. Copyright, 1930, 1949, by Henry Holt & Co., Inc.

tered a fourth period in which his great talents are fully recognized, and he is regarded as a poet of far more depth and subsurface complexity than anyone had previously realized. Two of Frost's poems that are provocative enough to satisfy the most eager analyst are "Directive," with its Grail imagery, and "The Subverted Flower," with its tantalizing psychological horror.

But Frost will always be a poet more loved than analyzed. He expresses himself in such an attractive way that his readers identify themselves with the poet; they would like to be Frost. The descriptive lines one finds in "After Apple Picking," for example, have a perfection that seems the only, the inevitable, way of describing the dream that the poet feels coming on. Many other poems by Frost contain this same perfection of word choice. "Two Tramps in Mud Time" is so meticulously written (and yet so effortless, with its touches of the famous Frost wit) that the reader feels surrounded by April weather; and he clearly sees those two hulking tramps who stand around idly, waiting for the poet to hire them to chop his wood.

If Frost had limited his poetry to descriptive and philosophical lyrics, he would still rank as a major poet; fortunately, his poems are also full of people, characters who are understandable and vividly real. In "The Death of the Hired Man" four people come alive: Mary, the sympathetic wife; Warren, the practical, somewhat cynical husband; Harold Wilson, the boy "who studied Latin like the violin because he liked it"; and Silas, the harmlessly wastrel hired man who had come "home" to die. Other people are scattered like old friends throughout the poems: Magoon, the timid professor, and Lafe, the burly bill collector, in "A Hundred Collars"; the casual witch in "The Witch of Coös"; the newlyweds who philosophize so well in "West-Running Brook"; the old farmer in "The Mountain" who lives at the foot of a mountain he refuses to climb simply because he sees no practical reason for doing so; and

that other dour farmer in "Brown's Descent" who takes a hilarious ride down a mountain on a slick crust of snow.

There are others equally memorable, but perhaps the outstanding character in all the poems is Frost himself. Everything he writes is warmed by his own personality, and he emerges from his volumes as a great and charming man who feels deeply but who never breaks the restraining tether of good taste. Emotional but never overly sentimental, he is dramatic but never melodramatic, conservative but not reactionary, sometimes pessimistic but never defeated, humorous without being flippant.

Trying to sum up the beguiling effect of Frost's outlook on life is difficult, for his writing personality is many-sided. Certainly he strikes the reader as a man who looks at life in a way that is both poetic and practical. The concluding lines of "Birches" beautifully illustrate this remarkable blend. In the poem the speaker has expressed a desire "to get away from earth awhile" and then come back for a new start:

> I'd like to go by climbing a birch tree,
> And climb black branches up a snow-white trunk
> *Toward* heaven, till the tree could bear no more,
> But dipped its top and set me down again.
> That would be good both going and coming back.
> One could do worse than be a swinger of birches.

Frost's wise outlook is not always concerned with only the broad generalities of life; sometimes he becomes specific about the events of our times, as in "To a Thinker," which gives advice to a President, and in "U. S. 1946 King's X," which is a mordant piece of irony:

> Having invented a new Holocaust,
> And been the first with it to win a war,
> How they make haste to cry with fingers crossed,
> King's X—no fairs to use it any more!

A poet must be more than a dramatist,

an analyst of human emotion, a humorist, and a philosopher: he must above all be a poet. Frost meets this difficult test. He chooses to write in the rhythms of human speech, and by sounding as natural as a man talking to his neighbor in simple language he has produced some of America's greatest poetry. His approach seems casual and disarming, rather like that of a champion athlete who breaks records without straining, who never tries too hard. To claim perfection for anyone—athlete or poet—is absurd. Frost has his defects. At times he is like a kindly teacher whose whimsicality is so sly as to be irritating, whose wisdom sometimes descends to mere crankiness. But Frost has written magnificent poetry—simple, sure, strong. Listen to this beautiful (but not often quoted) lyric called "Moon Compasses":

I stole forth dimly in the dripping pause
Between two downpours to see what
    there was.
And a masked moon had spread down
    compass rays
To a cone mountain in the midnight
    haze,
As if the final estimate were hers,
And as it measured in her calipers,
The mountain stood exalted in its place.
So love will take between the hands a
    face.

THE POETRY OF GRAY

Type of work: Poetry
Author: Thomas Gray (1716-1771)
Principal published works: Elegy in a Country Churchyard, 1751; *Six Poems by Mr.
T. Gray,* 1753; *Odes by Mr. Gray,* 1757; *Pindaric Odes,* 1758; *Poems by Mr. Gray,* 1768

Although the poem now titled "Elegy Written in a Country Churchyard" is justly the most famous of Thomas Gray's poems, anyone reading through the whole of his work will decide that he is not a poet of only one tone or one mode of sensibility. True, Gray could strike and maintain admirably a specific mood, such as that of gentle melancholy and regret that informs the "Elegy." This, however, was only one of his effects. The poetry of his great contemporary, Samuel Johnson, is sustained in one mode from beginning to end—abstract, moralistic, improving—but not so Gray's.

Although Gray's poetry was expressive of his time and displayed often enough the neo-classic qualities admired by eighteenth-century critics and readers, its small body displays a wide variety of interest that must be recorded in any report of a poet who withdrew as a boy from the playing fields of Eton (he was not one of the "idle progeny" who knew how to "chase the rolling circle's speed,/Or urge the flying ball") and spent a quiet adult life as a fellow-commoner at Cambridge. He did, in his twenties, take an extended Grand Tour with his friend Horace Walpole, and to the end of his life he varied the quietude of his life at Cambridge with frequent journeys. But Gray, in his travels, showed the qualities of the observer, the tourist. Capable of wide ranges of curiosity and considerable imaginative response to what he saw, he was willing to be entertained and diverted by sights and experiences that Samuel Johnson would simply have dismissed as foreign and barbarous. Gray also resembled other men of his time, even his friend Walpole of Strawberry Hill fame; he was willing to be amused, but the one price he would not pay for his amusement was his self-possession.

This reserve is what gives Gray's poe-

try the kind of unity it has. He attempts many things, and the variety of his poetry gives him minor importance as a forerunner of the Romantic Movement, both in the subjects he sometimes chose and in the simple language he sometimes employed. But those who want to claim Gray for the eighteenth century and neo-classicism have no trouble in doing so. Even Gray's best work, poems like "Ode on a Distant Prospect of Eton College," "Hymn to Adversity," and the "Elegy" abound in the elevated, figurative diction and the excessive personification popular in his time. In some of his verse fish hardly swim, and the poet himself is overshadowed by a thick penumbra of such literary abstractions as Adversity, Melancholy, and others. Often there cluster in the same poem so many of these that the effect becomes clotted and obscure. Consider these lines from "Ode on the Pleasure Arising from Vicissitude":

Smiles on past Misfortune's brow
  Soft Reflection's hand can trace;
And o'er the cheek of Sorrow throw
  A melancholy grace;
While Hope prolongs our happier
  hour. . . .

Succeeding verses present "rosy Pleasure," "a kindred Grief," "Misery," "Bliss," and a line which announces: "Humble Quiet builds her cell."

These tendencies are the marks of some of Gray's greatest poems, lines which have gained the immortality of proverb. The lines of the "Eton" ode ring with many a remembered, self-possessed phrase, such as ". . . where ignorance is bliss,/'Tis folly to be wise." Similarly, a moving and notable sadness, admirably kept within bounds, throws out phrase after phrase in the "Elegy" and enriches our common speech: "The paths of glory lead but to the grave"; "Full many a flower is born to blush un-unseen,/And waste its sweetness on the desert air"; "Some mute inglorious Milton here may rest. . . ." Truly noble is Gray's contemplation of the burial mounds, the rude inscriptions on the stones, the truncated careers, and the unanswerable silence of the modest graveyard at Stoke Poges. For the inglorious Miltons a tear is shed. This shedding of tears may, it is true, anticipate future Romantic glorification of the emotions; but the measured shedding keeps Gray the child of his century. Significantly, most of Gray's poems were written for sympathetic friends and were published only when pirated versions, as with the "Elegy," were about to appear.

The fact of Gray's self-control—the fact that he possessed a considerable range of feeling and powers of taste but was not possessed by them—is testified to by several items. He was a master of the going eighteenth-century style and could, for example, compose restrained and sincere epitaphs ("Epitaph on Mrs. Clerke," "Epitaph on Sir William Williams"). At the same time, with brilliant if trivial results, he could compose his "Ode on the Death of a Favorite Cat." He could be really dull, as in his "Alliance of Education and Government"; yet this sober earnestness did not inhibit his "Satire on the Heads of Houses," in which he ridicules the university masters to whom he was speaking soberly in his "Alliance."

Similarly, Gray had enough taste and curiosity to initiate the use of "Barbarian" materials in "The Fatal Sisters," "The Bard"—called a "Pindaric ode"—and "The Triumphs of Owen." True to the tone of his sources, he speaks in accents quite different from those of neo-classic convention; screams, mantic possession, and direct language sustain many passages in these pastiches from the Norse and other languages. But the Cambridge resident was no more possessed by savagery than he was by the refined sensibility expressed in the "Elegy" or the "Eton" ode. He moved from sincere epitaphs to a lament for a cat; he moved, at least once, from his recreation of bardic song to "A Long Story," in which much of the general machinery of Romantic narrative is burlesqued in advance.

As Gray indicated in "The Progress of Poesy," he believed that he lived in an age of twilight; the great luminaries of Greek, Roman, and English poetry had long since set ("Oh! Lyre divine, what daring Spirit/Wakes thee now?"). He shows us, however, that a conscientious connoisseur can find his way through twilight—perhaps toward a new dawn—and throughout follow a memorable course.

THE POETRY OF HOPKINS

Type of work: Poetry
Author: Gerard Manley Hopkins (1844-1889)
Principal published works: Poems of Gerard Manley Hopkins, Now First Published, with Notes by Robert Bridges, 1918; Complete Poems, 1947

Twenty-nine years elapsed from the time the poet Robert Bridges first published his edition of Gerard Manley Hopkins' Poems to publication of the definitive collection edited by the great Hopkins scholar, W. H. Gardner. Within that time Hopkins had been firmly established as an important if not a major British poet, not of his age but of the present. Undoubtedly, many of the conflicts over his life and work will have been resolved by the hundredth anniversary of the year Bridges first presented a small number of Hopkins' poems in important anthologies (1893).

Certain it is that the interest when this brilliant genius was in vogue, during the decade after 1918, has changed to something more deeply critical and scholarly. The letters, notebooks, and essays as well as the complete poems—no one now believes the best of the poet's work was destroyed—are now available to all, and hardly a year passes without the appearance of a volume of criticism or biography of the extremely paradoxical G. M. Hopkins.

Of utmost importance in understanding the very powerful poetry of this often misunderstood poet is his eclecticism, his wide knowledge and deep insights. While it is true that the preponderance of criticism has dwelt on Hopkins' innovations in rhythm-rhyme and imagery ("instress" and "inscape" summarize the two main facets), his whole poetic output indicates that he followed in the great European poetic tradition from Homer to Matthew Arnold. Hopkins' greatest poems are unique in powerful rhythmic effect, equal to or surpassing that of any other poet of like output; historically speaking, his poems prove that the genius of our

language lies in stress-rhythms (often "sprung") of our oldest traditional poetry, at least as important as syllabic meters in effect. His poetic diction, his use of common idiom as well as ingenious coinages, is without exact parallel. His ear for language was so acute, though highly individual, that he helped restore poetry as an oral-aural art, a fact the late Dylan Thomas so brilliantly demonstrated.

The lack of bulk, the slender volume of three hundred pages encompassing less than two hundred poems or fragments, makes arbitrary the distinction of whether Hopkins was a major poet. Certainly he is a classic in a very special sense. His central vision was deeply Christian, Jesuit, even mystical, often ecstatic though intellectually controlled. One of his greatest poems, "The Wreck of the Deutschland," was inspired as much by the "happy memory of five Franciscan Nuns" as their tragic death in 1875 by drowning. By his own account, the thirty-one-year-old theologian, deeply affected by the newspaper account of these nuns, exiled by the Falk Laws, who drowned in the Thames on a ship carrying them from Germany to America, responded to his rector's suggestion that a commemorative poem should be written of this. Hopkins was eager to try a new rhythm which had been haunting his ear, as he puts it. In spite of Robert Bridges' disapproval, he kept the rhythmic "oddnesses" because the technique was irrevocably bound to the sentiment he wanted to express, the sprung rhythm or "expressional rhythm . . . a vital fusion of the internal rhythm of thought-and-emotion and the external rhythm of sounds," as Gardner describes this phenomenon. As a threnody the poem is

THE POETRY OF GERARD MANLEY HOPKINS. Excerpts reprinted from POEMS OF GERARD MANLEY HOPKINS, third edition edited by W. H. Gardner, by permission of the publishers, Oxford University Press, Inc. Copyright, 1948, by Oxford University Press, Inc.

unique. An invocation to God to master rebellious feelings, a narrative of the tragic event, an elegy of one nun's heroism, a meditation on God's beneficence, a plea for intercession—all these and other arguments within the poem demanded a flexibility and felicity of form. The result is one of the great poems in English or any language. Stanza thirty-two, a poem of praise to a merciful God, will illustrate these subtleties:

> I admire thee, master of the tides,
> Of the Yore-flood, of the year's fall;
> The recurb and the recovery of the gulf's sides,
> The girth of it and the wharf of it and the wall;
> Stanching, quenching ocean of a motionable mind;
> Ground of being, and granite of it: past all
> Grasp God, throned behind
> Death with a sovereignty that heeds but hides, bodes but abides.

While no one definition of "inscape" or "instress" will suffice, this stanza contains both: the former is seeing of the internal and fundamental, significant form or nature of, say, the ocean in motion; and the latter would include the access to God's grace and a celebration of this, though the rhythmic expression is also implied.

Perhaps the searching eye and the recording ear are best illustrated in Hopkins' most famous lyric, "Pied Beauty." Here the poet as painter and musician is displayed, showing his deep concern for bringing to bear in a poem all the senses:

> Glory be to God for dappled things—
> For skies of couple-colour as a brinded cow;
> For rose-moles all in stipple upon trout that swim;
> Fresh-firecoal chestnut-falls; finches' wings;
> Landscape plotted and pieced-fold, fallow, and plough;
> And áll trádes, their gear and tackle and trim.

> All things counter, original, spare, strange;
> Whatever is fickle, freckled (who knows how?)
> With swift, slow; sweet, sour; adazzle, dim;
> He fathers-forth whose beauty is past change:
> Praise him.

Here are rhythmic contrasts, dramatic juxtapositions, unique word manipulations, a compelling meter as dappled and iridescent as the things described.

Another facet of Hopkins' talent, one of his most pronounced achievements, was his variation on the sonnet form, a revolt against the stilted structures and concepts of Victorian poesy. This is not to say he wrote loosely or without thought; quite the contrary is true, for his critical writings reveal the depth of his study and experimentation. Ascetic by habit and temperament, he elevated the form to a new lyricism by breaking with or modifying many old systems and establishing his own.

"The Starlight Night," a well-known sonnet not too revolutionary, illustrates the nervous counterpointed rhythms, the startling pauses, the jarring sound clashes, the harmonic word fusion among many other interesting poetic, semantic, and linguistic devices:

> Look at the stars! look, look up at the skies!
> O look at all the fire-folk sitting in the air!
> The bright boroughs, the circle-citadels there!
> Down in dim woods the diamond delves! the elves'-eyes!
> The grey lawns cold where gold, where quickgold lies!
> Wind-beat whitebeam! airy abeles set on a flare!
> Flake-doves sent floating forth at a farmyard scare!—
> Ah well! it is all a purchase, all is a prize.

> Buy then! bid then!—What?—Prayer, patience, alms, vows.
> Look, look: a May-mess, like on orchard boughs!

Look! March-bloom, like on mealed-
  with-yellow sallows!
These are indeed the barn; withindoors
  house
The shocks. This piece-bright paling
  shuts the spouse
Christ home, Christ and his mother
  and all his hallows.

This sonnet also illustrates Hopkins'
childlike joy in fairy lore, his deep love
of nature, and a metaphysical rapture
over God's munificence, a simple joy born
of a deep religion. In the *Deutschland*
poem Hopkins is critical of man's questioning of God's ways, but his later poems
show this questioning in his own lack of
balance—a conflicting of personal desires,
private impulses, and his theology. This
unrest is perhaps best expressed in the
priest-poet's sonnet "Peace" (1879):

When will you ever, Peace, wild wood-
  dove, shy wings shut,
Your round me roaming end, and under
  be my boughs?
When, when, Peace, will you, Peace?
  I'll not play hypocrite
To own my heart: I yield you do come
  sometimes; but

That piecemeal peace is poor peace.
  What pure peace allows
Alarms of wars, the daunting wars, the
  death of it?

O surely, reaving Peace, my Lord should
  leave in lieu
Some good! And so he does leave
  Patience exquisite,
That plumes to Peace thereafter. And
  when Peace here does house
He comes with work to do, he does not
  come to coo,
  He comes to brood and sit.

Here he seems to have found some measure of this peace through virtuous acts,
selfless serving of an often thankless mankind.

As most critics point out, Hopkins
combined in his interesting person a
depth of humanity with a height of mystical insight, with a whole spectrum of
emotions and attitudes infused. Most of
the contradictions in his nature, the ambiguities within his poetry, can be resolved by a thorough reading not only of
his poems, but of his letters, diaries, and
essays.

THE POETRY OF HORACE

Type of work: Poetry
Author: Horace (Quintus Horatius Flaccus, 65-8 B.C.)
Principal transcribed works: Satires, 35, 30 B.C.; *Epodes,* 30 B.C.; *Odes,* 23-13 B.C.; *Carmen Seculare,* 17 B.C.

Born two years before the Emperor Augustus, Horace, the son of a freed slave, was sent to Rome for the education he could not get in Venusia, Italy. In 44 B.C. he went to Athens for further study. There he met Brutus, after the assassination of Julius Caesar, and was appointed an officer in the republican army routed at Philippi in 42 B.C. Back in Rome, disillusioned, with his possessions confiscated and his father dead, he began verse writing. Vergil, attracted by his poetry, presented the country boy to Augustus' cultured minister, Maecenas.

Horace had the good taste to destroy his early angry poetry. His first published poems were his *Satires* in 35 B.C., followed by his *Epodes.* Then, still more mellow, he published three books of *Odes* in 23 B.C. During the last years of his life, Horace wrote his *Epistles.* In one ode, III, xvii, having heard of Maecenas' illness, he wrote: "If any untimely stroke snatches you away, you the half of my life . . . that day shall bring the end of us both." His wish was granted. He died in 8 B.C., only a few weeks after his protector, and their ashes were buried on the Esquiline hillside.

The early poetry of Horace betrays lack of self-confidence, as in his references to his "pedestrian Muse." But the publication of his *Odes* gave him assurance, and after the death of Vergil, in 19 B.C., he was commissioned by the emperor to compose and read an ode for the imperial secular games. Later Augustus demanded odes to celebrate the military victories of his stepsons, Drusus and Tiberius.

In his poetry, especially in his *Satires,* Horace re-creates his era with tolerance and good humor. He attacks the vanity of human desires, yet stresses the need to enjoy the pleasures of the world. While professing the epicurean philosophy, he generally practiced stoicism. Though praising the pleasures of wine, his health was too delicate to let him drink deeply. And his poems to women were just as conventional. For only one woman, Cinara, did he show real feeling. His affection was reserved for the men he knew; and his sincerity and ability to project himself beyond the lines of his poems have won him innumerable friends through the centuries.

The poetic satire was the invention of the Roman Lucilius, "untouched by the Greeks," as Horace declared, with its name derived from a dish composed of a variety of ingredients. Horace composed eighteen satires, in two volumes, but he made them more a friendly conversation than the bitter lampooning of his predecessor.

Book I, containing ten satires presented in no chronological order, was completed between his introduction to Maecenas in 38 B.C. and their appearance three years later. Number I, appropriately addressed to his patron, deals with Horace's favorite theme, the folly of the discontented man who wants something he does not have: "Oh, happy trader!" cries the soldier, while the trader, in his ship belabored by the south winds, envies the soldier. The poet follows this craving to its most unreasonable form, the hoarding of money, though he does not advocate being a spendthrift. His council is that a man should so live that he can leave his life, as he leaves a banquet table, contented.

In Satire IV, Horace explains why he uses this form: his father trained him for a good life by pointing out as bad examples those who lived it evilly. Besides, the form allows him "smilingly, to tell the truth." Satire V, describing a journey made with his protector, contains the poet's reply to those who charged

2967

he was cultivating Maecenas for personal profit, a subject taken up again in Satire IX. His first contacts with the wealthy statesman are described in the following poem, which take a side glance at the vice of aspiring to a higher position than one merits.

The eight satires of Book Two, which appeared five years later, are longer and generally in dialogue form. In one, the Lawyer Trebatius Testa clears the poet of the charge of being too bitter in his first volume. Paradoxes serve as themes for two others: All except the wise are mad, and all but the wise are slaves. Three express Horace's delight in plain living and his disgust at the vapid conversations overheard at formal banquets. He ends with an outburst against a woman he calls Canidia, who also figures in his later writings.

The earliest form of Horace's lyric poetry is his collection of epodes, as the grammarians called them. Horace named them "Iambi," a meter of alternating long and short lines designed by Archilochus for invectives. In these poems he expresses his pet dislikes, sometimes humorously, as in Number III, where he inveighs against the garlic in the food served at Maecenas' table. At other times he really hated the object of his verse, as in Number IV, written about a freedman who proudly strutted along the Via Sacra, or in the poem which expresses his hope that the ship will be wrecked when the poet Maevias goes on a sea voyage. In two epodes, V and XVII, he comes back to Canidia, first accusing her of being a witch who uses her spells on men, and then, when he apologizes, portraying her as threatening to use her vile charms against him.

Several others have the form, but not the substance, of an epode, as in Number I, written when Maecenas was departing for the battle of Actium and begging his patron not to endanger himself. Best known of all is probably the "Beatus ille," classified as an epode because of its surprise satirical ending:

How happy is his low degree,
How rich in humble poverty is he
Who leads a quiet country life
Discharged of busyness and void of strife.

After an enumeration of the joys of life in the country, the poem is revealed as the idle words of the usurer Alphius:

He called his money in,
But the prevailing love of pelf
Soon split him on the former shelf.
He put it out again.

To lovers of poetry, Horace probably makes his greatest appeal through his *Odes,* the artistic work of a mature writer. Composed after Actium, these poems were written between 23 and 13 B.C. The ideas are commonplace—the uncertainties of life, the joys of friendship—but they endure because they express sentiments that appeal to all readers. Number III, for instance, contains the much-quoted line, "Sweet and fitting it is to die for the fatherland." Poets good and bad ever since have enjoyed translating these poems into their own idiom.

In his *Odes,* Horace used a variety of meters to suit his subjects. The earliest are the gayest; the later odes, reflecting his own failing health and the deaths of friends, reveal an artist of subtle elegance and an effective arrangement of words. Even his pensive reflections conceal subtle humor.

The culminating form of Horace's genius was his *Epistles.* "You were the inspiration of my earliest Muse, Maecenas, and must be of my latest," he says, beginning this form. One, Number IX, is a fine example of a letter of introduction, presenting Septimus to the future Emperor Tiberius. The others, however, are letters only in form, being more in the nature of informal moral essays. "Modernism is wisdom" is the theme of the first; but instead of angrily attacking vice, the aging but kindlier poet gently rebukes folly. At the end he sets himself up as critic of the poets and poetic movements of his age. Surprisingly, Horace devotes little time to Lucretius and Catullus, the greatest of his predecessors. Carelessness marred the verses of both; perhaps the fault which he considered the gravest of all blinded him to their many virtues.

Having completed twenty-two epistles, Horace wrote: "You have played and eaten and drunk enough. It is time for you to depart the scene." He died, at the age of fifty-seven, one of the most genial and attractive of poets who have written undying verse.

THE POETRY OF LANIER

Type of work: Poetry
Author: Sidney Lanier (1842-1881)
Principal published works: Poems, 1877; Poems of Sidney Lanier, 1884

The poetic fame of Sidney Lanier, after Poe the most important nineteenth-century poet of the Southern United States, rests upon a small body of poetry found in the posthumous volume, *Poems of Sidney Lanier,* which contains the verse Lanier included in his *Poems,* along with a number of pieces which had received only magazine publication before the poet's death in 1881, plus a group of unrevised early poems that his wife felt were worthy of publication. Of approximately one hundred titles in the posthumous volume, only fifteen or twenty are known today except to students especially interested in Lanier. Most of the critical discussions of Lanier's poetic significance cite primarily these some fifteen or twenty poems in illustrating both his merits and his defects.

Lanier was a poet of both theory and practice. His theory of technique was influenced by his great love for music. Precociously musical, he was in manhood a brilliant flutist who played with symphony orchestras in Dallas and Baltimore. His moralistic theory of poetic content was possibly influenced by his early training in a devoutly Christian family as well as by his own fundamentally religious nature, which shows itself, in some of his nature poems, as a passionate love for God's plants and creatures approaching that of St. Francis of Assisi.

Lanier's theory of prosody is expounded principally in *The Science of English Verse* (1880), which develops in extensive detail and with copious illustration the thesis that the same laws govern both versification and music. Three brief quotations will illustrate this thesis:

. . . when we hear verse, we *hear* a set of relations between sounds; when we silently read verse, we *see* that which brings to us a set of relations between sounds; when we imagine verse, we *imagine* a set of relations between sounds.

When those exact co-ordinations which the ear perceives as rhythm, tune, and tone-color are suggested to the ear by a series of *musical sounds,* the result is . . . MUSIC.

When those exact co-ordinations which the ear perceives as rhythm, tune, and tone-color, are suggested to the ear by a series of *spoken words,* the result is . . . VERSE.

. . . there is absolutely no difference between the sound-relations used in music and those used in verse.

Lanier's application of his prosodic theory may be studied in many of his poems, but it may be easily seen in such poems as "The Symphony," "The Marshes of Glynn," and "Song of the Chattahoochee."

In "The Symphony," Lanier attempted the difficult task of composing a poem somewhat as a musician would. Such instruments as violins, flute, clarinet, horn, and hautboy (oboe) are personified and used to develop the theme of Love, the enemy of Trade (materialism), which pervades the poem. Nowhere is Lanier's belief in the essential identity of sound-relations in music and in verse better illustrated than in the four lines which introduce the horn passage in the poem:

There thrust the bold straightforward horn
To battle for that lady lorn.
With hearthsome voice of mellow scorn,
Like any knight in knighthood's morn.

It has been objected that Lanier tried the impossible in "The Symphony" and that his achievement, though notable, is successful only in part. Perhaps his theory is better illustrated in "Sunrise" and "The Marshes of Glynn." In "Sunrise," one easily catches the sibilance of the forest:

Ye lispers, whisperers, singers in storms,
Ye consciences murmuring faiths under
   forms,
Ye ministers meet for each passion that
   grieves,
Friendly, sisterly, sweetheart leaves.

In "The Marshes of Glynn" the sounds and even the silence of the great marshes near Brunswick, Georgia, may be heard and felt by the reader. A passage near the close of the poem describes in this fashion the coming of the high tide of evening:

The creeks overflow: a thousand rivu-
   lets run
'Twixt the roots of the sod; the blades
   of the marsh-grass stir;
Passeth a hurrying sound of wings that
   westward whirr;
Passeth, and all is still; and the currents
   cease to run;
And the sea and the marsh are one.

In these lines the sounds of the moving waters and grasses and of the whirring wings are followed by a silence that is palpable.

Because of Lanier's repeated use of onomatopoeia in his verse he has often been compared with Poe; but Lanier's theory of poetic content is quite different. Poe, in "The Philosophy of Composition," concedes that "passion, or even truth, may . . . be introduced, and even profitably introduced, into a poem"; but, he asserts, "Beauty is the sole legitimate province of the poem." In another essay, "The Poetic Principle," Poe attacks what he calls "the heresy of *The Didactic*." "Every poem, it is said, should inculcate a moral," he reminds us; "and by this moral is the poetical merit of the work to be adjudged." But, he continues,

would we but permit ourselves to look into our own souls, we should immediately there discover that under the sun there neither exists nor *can* exist any work more thoroughly dignified—

more supremely noble than this very poem—this poem *per se*—this poem which is a poem and nothing more— this poem written solely for the poem's sake.

Lanier loved art as much as Poe did, but Lanier was on the side of the moralists. In the series of lectures posthumously published as *The English Novel and the Principle of Its Development* (1883), he leaves no doubt as to his position when he states that

We may say that he who has not yet perceived how artistic beauty and moral beauty are convergent lines which run back into a common ideal origin, and who therefore is not afire with moral beauty just as with artistic beauty—that he, in short, who has not come to that stage of quiet and eternal frenzy in which the beauty of holiness and the holiness of beauty mean one thing, burn as one fire, shine as one light within him; he is not yet the great artist.

Although Lanier wrote occasional poems such as his verse narrative "The Revenge of Hamish," in which the moral element is not a major one, most of his poetry is charged with moral purpose or shines with "the beauty of holiness." "The Symphony" bitterly indicts the cruel, greedy practices of Trade and sings the gospel of brotherly love. In "The Marshes of Glynn," he writes:

As the marsh-hen secretly builds on the
   watery sod,
Behold I will build me a nest on the
   greatness of God.

Even a dialect poem like "Thar's More in the Man than Thar Is in the Land" contains a moral lesson, as the title itself suggests. Occasionally his moral earnestness dims Lanier's artistic sight, however, as in "Song of the Chattahoochee," in which the river is made to say:

. . . I am fain for to water the plain.
Downward the voices of Duty call—.

This is a flagrant example of what John Ruskin called the "pathetic fallacy." People may act with moral purpose; when the Chattahoochee River flows downward, however, it is not because it knows that

The dry fields burn, and the mills are to turn,
And a myriad flowers mortally yearn,

but because, as Lanier himself very well knew, the law of gravity is a part of the earthly scheme of things.

Though Lanier is not primarily a regional poet, many of his lines sing eloquently of his Southern origin. He is in love with the beautiful Marshes of Glynn, with their "moss-bearded live-oaks." He mourns that "Bright drops of tune, from oceans infinite/Of Melody" were ended when a pet mockingbird "died of a cat, May, 1878." He grieves in "Corn" that the rich soil of his native state is being washed away because of the greed of cotton farmers who lay the surface bare and then leave their erosion-ruined areas and head for Texas to repeat their folly. In "A Florida Sunday," he holds "in my being" rich-scented orange trees, pea green parrakeets, "pranked woodpeckers that ne'er gossip out," palmettos, pines, and mangroves. In such poems Lanier is as clearly a Southern poet as Robert Frost is a New England one when he describes his New Hampshire countryside.

A fault that many readers have found with Lanier is that, as a poet, he too often lets his heart overflow and his whole being "quiver with the passionate thrill"; at times a noble emotion may descend into sentimentality and at others the poet's feeling may blur the expression of "the great thought." The lush music of Lanier's lines may also create the lulling mental effect that one finds in Swinburne. Part of Lanier's trouble seems to be that he is striving too hard to attain the right combination of "rhythm, tune, and tone-color." He sometimes forces his comparisons so that they become too-obvious poetic conceits, as in "Marsh Song—at Sunset," with its metaphors drawn from Shakespeare's *Tempest*. Some of his sentences, such as the thirty-six-line one which opens "The Marshes of Glynn," lack clarity because of their great length and intricate structure.

In spite of the undisciplined emotionalism, hazy thought, and strained effects of his lesser poems, Lanier seems well assured of a permanent place in American literature. The melody of his best lines; the love of God, man, and nature found in poems like "The Marshes of Glynn" and "The Symphony"; the simple beauty of "A Ballad of Trees and the Master"; and the stoic acceptance of "The Stirrup-Cup," in which the consumptive poet says uncomplainingly to Death, "Hand me the cup whene'er thou wilt" —for these Lanier will continue to be loved.

THE POETRY OF LEWIS

Type of work: Poetry
Author: Cecil Day Lewis (1904-   )
Principal published works: Beechen Vigil and Other Poems, 1925; *Country Comet,* 1928;
Transitional Poem, 1929; *From Feathers to Iron,* 1931; *The Magnetic Mountain,* 1933;
A Time to Dance and Other Poems, 1935; *Overtures to Death,* 1938; *Poems in Wartime,*
1940; *Word Over All,* 1943; *Short is the Time: Poems, 1936-1943,* 1943; *Poems, 1943-
1947,* 1948; *An Italian Visit,* 1953; *Pegasus and Other Poems,* 1957

Cecil Day Lewis began writing poetry at Oxford along with his literary friends, W. H. Auden, Stephen Spender, and Louis MacNeice, but his early work shows little resemblance to that of his contemporaries. His first well-known work, *Transitional Poem,* was a long, Whitmanesque, searching work containing different styles and verse forms and filled with classical allusions. Although a few of its sections satirized contemporary life, it was generally diffuse and had little in common with the early sharp, ironic Auden or the early lyric MacNeice. It was followed by another long poem, *From Feathers to Iron.* More carefully controlled and more somber in tone, this work displayed a shrewd observation of contemporary English life. In it, Day Lewis criticized the flat, industrial suburb and contrasted the hardness of the iron life of most men in modern society. The poet also praised the natural process of birth, pitting the idea of creation and the child against the overwhelming industrialism of the age. He felt that there was, however, some limited amount of space left for the natural and spiritual. In this early poem several characteristics of Day Lewis' work are evident: his contemporary references and language and the loose, conversational quality of his style.

Day Lewis' poetry became more like that of his contemporaries, at least in theme, with his next long poem, *The Magnetic Mountain.* Here he attacks the complacent person who ignores social issues, the fool who does not see them, and the escapist who purposely avoids them.

The poem satirizes the old English, public-school tradition, the tradition which assumes that invariable guides for conduct exist, formulas for meeting every problem of society. Day Lewis pleads for all who would reform society, who would fashion a world based on the heart of man, to join him in his journey to the "Magnetic Mountain." The mountain symbolizes both the heart or faith of man and the enduring power or iron in his character, for iron is a magnetic and compelling substance. In his attack on the English colonizing and commercial past, Day Lewis calls for social action, for a "communal sense" in order that man may realize his full potentiality. His stinging reproach to the gray, gritty present and his great faith in the possibility of a new social order, as well as the qualities revealed in his earlier writing, are in evidence throughout this work. In this rhetorical declaration of faith, Day Lewis' writing is loose and allusive, with none of the hard, cryptic quality of Auden's work. Yet the looseness of Day Lewis' structure is frequently, as in the above passage, balanced by unexpected, musical alliteration.

Day Lewis' faith in the new social order began to wane in his next volume, *A Time to Dance and Other Poems,* a volume including a number of shorter lyrics. Although his allegiances were still just as strong to the new social order, he began to demonstrate an awareness of some of the difficulties of bringing about a reformation. He claimed, however, that he still wrote his poems in order to keep his faith and courage. The following vol-

THE POETRY OF CECIL DAY LEWIS. Excerpts reprinted from AN ITALIAN VISIT by permission of the publishers, Harper & Brothers. Copyright, 1953, by Harper & Brothers.

ume, *Overtures to Death*, demonstrates an even keener realization that man was not likely to become perfect within a generation or so by joining in a communal assault on the "Magnetic Mountain." The verse in this book is crisper, less shrill, and less rhetorical, conveying a deeper insight into man and the issues that face him. Although Day Lewis still attacks the complacent and those who love tradition for the simple reason that it is tradition, he realizes that he, too, may be bound to some sterile tradition, some impossible notion of human conduct. He develops this theme in one of his best short poems, "Regency Houses." The vague influence of Yeats in this poem has given it a terseness and power not always present in Day Lewis' work. At the same time the introspective quality, the realization of his own limitations, has given the poem a depth not apparent in his earlier calls to social action.

Day Lewis, alert to the dangers of Nazism, had attacked the complacent people who refused to acknowledge that war was imminent. During the war, however, his poetry became less social, less political, more personal. He began to write autobiographical poems dealing with childhood memories and concerns. He also wrote a number of poems on the theme of love, presenting both its pleasures and its difficulties. The range of the subjects he treated widened greatly: the life of the simple countryman, the impact of the war, places, poems in praise of literary figures such as Thomas Hardy and Walter de la Mare, the pleasures of Christmas. His thoughtful and introspective side continued, but his subjects grew more personal, more concerned with direct experience, and less dominated by the intensity of a single vision for mankind's salvation. In this shift of interest to more personal and direct concerns, Day Lewis mirrored the changing trend of a whole generation of English writers and intellectuals. Day Lewis still used satire, as he does in his most recent volume, *Pegasus and Other Poems*, but it was, and

has continued to be, a far more gentle and understanding kind of satire.

In 1953, Day Lewis published *An Italian Visit*, a long versified account of a journey to Italy. This is a thoughtful, descriptive work, full of powerful and often startling images. The style is conversational, like the easy flow of imaginative language and rich contemplation from an urbane and cultured gentleman. It is perhaps this kind of loose, ruminative writing that best suits Day Lewis' talent, for he has never been, save in rare moments, a poet of great intensity or linguistic magic. The poem, in its descriptions of Rome, Florence, and numerous smaller towns, also displays a deep appreciation of both art and tradition. Day Lewis is, for the contemporary reader, far more convincing as the guardian of tradition and culture than he was as the voice crying out for a new order. His conversational ease, along with his skill in fashioning images, is evident in the following passage which can also serve as his final comment on his pseudoprophetic role in the 1930's:

> We who 'flowered' in the Thirties
> Were an odd lot; sceptical yet suscep-
> tible,
> Dour though enthusiastic, horizon-
> addicts
> And future-fans, terribly apt to ask
> what
> Our all-very-fine sensations were in aid
> of.
> We did not, you will remember, come
> to coo.
> Still, there is hope for us. Rome has
> absorbed
> Other barbarians: yes, and there's no-
> body quite so
> Sensuously rich and reckless as the re-
> formed
> Puritan . . .

Day Lewis has become the intelligent gentleman of letters, able, with both richness and humor, to see his past convictions in perspective. Never a poetic innovator, he has been overshadowed, in critical accounts of his generation, by his more brilliant contemporaries. But he has produced a great variety of thoughtful and introspective verse, and he has written with honesty and intelligence on a wide range of subjects. In his maturity he has found the kind of verse and the kind of subject, as well as the gentle and ruminative tone, that he is making definitely his. Poems like the *An Italian Visit* and "Moods of Love" in his most recent volume are admirably readable and demonstrate the poetic attractions of a witty, cultured gentleman reporting on his travels, his observations of people, his feelings about himself. Cecil Day Lewis, though not a great poet, is an honest and attractive one.

THE POETRY OF LINDSAY

Type of work: Poetry
Author: Vachel Lindsay (1879-1931)
Principal published works: General William Booth Enters into Heaven, 1913; *The Congo and Other Poems*, 1914; *The Chinese Nightingale and Other Poems*, 1917; *The Golden Whales of California and Other Rhymes in the American Language*, 1920; *Going-to-the-Sun*, 1923; *Going-to-the-Stars*, 1926; *The Candle in the Cabin*, 1926; *Johnny Appleseed and Other Poems*, 1928; *Every Soul Is a Circus*, 1929

No complete collection of Vachel Lindsay's poetry has ever been published, nor does it seem likely that this would be a profitable venture for publisher, reader, or scholar. The vogue for this poet died out even before his death; the excellent collections of selected poetry and anthologies contain all that is likely to survive; and a consensus among scholars has already been established—Lindsay was a vital minor poet whose interesting experiments and some fifty poems will be remembered.

Setting aside his earliest poems, including the famous "Rhymes to be Traded for Bread," and his late ones, excluding "Johnny Appleseed," the critical reader will find a corpus of poetry which, if no longer startling, is at least substantial. These first collections sometimes include sketches which do not illuminate and poems without substance; they were a part of the poet's years when he considered himself a traveling mystic, an artist-writer with a rather vague creed based loosely on Swedenborgian philosophy. His later years before his suicide were clouded over by a despondency which the poems reflect.

In January, 1913, *Poetry: A Magazine of Verse* published "General William Booth Enters into Heaven," published in book form later that year along with other poems by the same author. The immediate—and lasting—popularity of this poem is justified, perhaps more so than that of the familiarly anthologized "The Congo." With cues for instruments and singing, the writer's very real tribute to the religious leader is a studied cacophony which ends in deep reverence:

And when Booth halted by the curb for
prayer
He saw his Master thro' the flag-filled
air.
Christ came gently with a robe and
crown
For Booth the soldier, while the throng
knelt down.
He saw King Jesus. They were face to
face,
And he knelt a-weeping in that holy
place.
Are you washed in the blood of the
Lamb?

Here is Lindsay's métier, the rhythmic portrayal of almost legendary persons: Lincoln, Bryan, Chapman, Altgeld, Sullivan, Jackson, and Alexander Campbell, the founder of his religious sect, among others. In these poems he created a new kind of poetic tribute, as unlike the usual versifying obituary as his own life was from those he celebrated.

Less successful, though even more popular on chautauqua and college platforms where he appeared for so many years in so many cities, are the "travel" poems, the sweeping Whitmanesque vistas of the Santa Fé Trail, the Congo, the Great Plains. Here, too, his poetry has its strongly personal and syncopated quality, a stress here and a manipulation there, which stamps it with a form no longer usable because, perhaps, he himself overused it. "The Congo" begins:

Fat black bucks in a wine-barrel room,
Barrel-house kings, with feet unstable,
Sagged and reeled and pounded on the
table,
Pounded on the table,
Beat an empty barrel with the handle of
a broom,

THE POETRY OF VACHEL LINDSAY. Excerpts reprinted from SELECTED POEMS OF VACHEL LINDSAY by permission of the publishers, The Macmillan Co. Copyright, 1936, by The Macmillan Co.

Hard as they were able,
Boom, boom, BOOM,
With a silk umbrella and the handle of
  a broom,
Boomlay, boomlay, boomlay, BOOM.

This is the four-stress line, with a kind of added syncopation which one critic has called "star-spangled jazz." Poems of this type are most effective when read aloud in keeping with the instructions Lindsay supplied in a marginal gloss.

A third category, and in some ways the most successful because the poems seem so artless, is that of "children's" poetry— the kind which is enchanting to all, the large child reading and the small one listening. "The Chinese Nightingale," although sullied by adult overtones, is the best known of this group with its chiming, clanging pigeon-Chinese symbols:

He lit a joss stick long and black.
Then the proud gray joss in the corner
  stirred;
On his wrist appeared a gray small bird,
And this was the song of the gray small
  bird:
"Where is the princess, loved forever,
Who made Chang first of the kings of
  men?"

A group of poems on all kinds of mice still delights youngsters when they are reprinted in children's anthologies. These little poems are more of a delight than those which Lindsay thought would charm children.

On the other hand, his exploitation of sounds always pleases, as in "The Kallyope Yell":

Music of the mob am I,
Circus day's tremendous cry:—
I am the Kallyope, Kallyope, Kallyope!
Hoot toot, hoot toot, hoot toot, hoot toot,
Willy willy willy wah HOO!
Sizz, fizz . . .

or the second part of "The Santa Fé Trail":

Listen to the iron-horns, ripping, rack-
  ing.
Listen to the quack-horns, slack and
  clacking.
Way down the road, trilling like a toad,
Here comes the dice-horn, here comes
  the vice-horn,
Here comes the snarl-horn, brawl-horn,
  lewd-horn,
Followed by the prude-horn, bleak and
  squeaking:—
(Some of them from Kansas, some of
  them from Kansas.)

The first echoes calliope dissonances, the latter, the klaxon racket.

From his last volume, Every Soul Is a Circus, comes what Lindsay thought was a tribute to P. T. Barnum, but which was really, as the opening lines reveal, an apology for his own works:

My brothers of the poet-trade,
Leave your ivory towers, and stand
On the porch, and watch this ardent
  band
And praise, with me,
This Masquerade.
From a cloud by the dark Art Institute
That old Barnum comes,
Followed by serene Greek Gods,
And the lake-breeze hums.

The Art Institute is the place where Lindsay started his career; like Barnum, he ended in the tent. Both brought thrilling moments, Barnum his Lind, Lindsay his Salvation Army hero-leader. A note from the poet suggests this poem is to read "with bardic and troubadour chanting," and Lindsay's postlude might well grace his epitaph:

So, come, let us be bold with our songs,
  brothers,
Come, let us be bold with our songs.

THE POETRY OF LOVELACE

Type of work: Poetry
Author: Richard Lovelace (1618-1658)
Principal published works: Lucasta, 1649; Posthume Poems, 1659

To most readers, Richard Lovelace is remembered for two lines each of two songs. He caught for all those spirits who have suffered in prison, who have thought or composed thoughts in gaols, the perfect expression of the free will in

> Stone Walls doe not a Prison make,
> Nor I'ron bars a Cage;

and he expressed his own high standards as a gentleman, soldier, scholar, and poet in lines which he wrote when going off to war:

> I could not love thee (Deare) so much,
> Lov'd I not Honour more.

A Royalist by birth and politics, the poet lost a modest fortune upholding his own high standards: he suffered imprisonment twice, ironically, and his entire life he spent surrounded by war's tragedies. He lost his father and a brother in battle, and he and his remaining brothers fought valorously for England (he attained the rank of colonel). His poetry, of limited popularity, was virtuous and modest in extreme and, as critics hasten to point out, the most moral written by the Cavalier poets. His most famous series, *Lucasta* (from *lux casta*, light of virtue), is his testimonial.

No conclusive evidence has yet come to light concerning the Lucasta of Lovelace's first volume, though it is now certain that this idealized figure was not Lucy Sacheverell. The woman to whom he addressed most of his early poems may have been a Lucas, however; hence the play on words.

Lovelace wrote in the age of the "conceit," that witty and often barbed line popularized by John Donne, but he must always rank in second place in its use. His two famous songs, written also in an age of words set to music, surpass those of his betters, but on moral grounds: "To Althea, from Prison," dem-onstrates Lovelace's indomitable spirit and "To Lucasta, Going to the Warres," his incorruptible soul. Lovelace was an amateur poet, a man of action whose education made of him a man of parts; and he is often compared to Sir Philip Sidney, "A Scholar, Souldier, Lover, and a Saint," as one epitaph verse reads.

The diversified poetry within *Lucasta* indicates that Lovelace followed in that great tradition of the Renaissance gentleman. His varied activities and tastes led sometimes to the exercise of a talent thinly spread, to poor taste, but especially to haste—Lovelace's besetting sin. His first volume lacked care, proofreading (even at a time of variable spellings, indifferent typography, and fanciful punctuation), not to mention chronological arranging, collating of stanzas, and other matters so necessary to a really professional work. One wonders, then, why Lovelace was a favorite poet of an age when better poets went begging for readers. As a contemporary and professional said of him, "He writes very well for a gentleman."

Only twenty-seven copies of the 1649 *Lucasta*, available in the seventeenth century for a few pence, are now known to be extant. The portrait included makes one wonder at the extravagant praise of Lovelace's looks, but not of his poetry, which is courtly, exuberant, at times pleasingly fanciful, though often ama-teurish in tone and style. This slender book of some sixty poems is dedicated to Lady Anne Lovelace, wife of his cousin John, though not to be thought of as Lucasta. A group of commendatory poems follows the dedication, by his brothers Francis and Dudley, the latter, ten years later, the compiler of Lovelace's posthu-mous poems. The most interesting poem in this commendatory group is by the author's friend and fellow poet, Andrew Marvell, who suggests the verses will please the ladies more than the critics, those "Word-peckers, Paper-rats, Book-scorpions."

The poems proper begin with two songs, both dedicated to ideal or Platonic love and both related to going overseas and fighting. Of the sixty, about a third were set to music and may still be found in books of "Ayres." Most of the poems conform to the seventeenth-century pattern of odes written on memorable days or for sad occasions, pastorals, sonnets, satires, and elegies. An interesting example of the latter is one of the poet's earliest poems, written when he was twenty and addressed to Princess Katherine "borne, christened, buried in one day." The interesting contrasts of birth and death, swaddling and winding clothes, joy and sorrow, with the overtones of pomp and circumstance befitting her royal-innocent lineage make of this poem a study in contrasts.

In addition to these varied types of poems, Lovelace wrote at least one acted play, a comedy called "The Scholars," the prologue and epilogue appearing in his first collection. Another play, "The Soldier," was a tragedy never acted because of the closing of the theaters in 1642. During the period of the Protectorate songs by Lovelace were probably sung in the so-called masques, thinly disguised plays produced privately for an aristocratic audience.

Lovelace prepared his second book, *Posthume Poems,* before his death, though it remained for his brother to bring out the volume. It is dedicated to Sir John Lovelace, an indication this time of his patronage. The first poem, "To Lucasta: Her Reserved Looks," epitomizes the gay-sad theme so prevalent among the Cavaliers, even at death:

Lucasta, frown and let me die,
  But smile and see I live;
The sad indifference of your Eye
  Both kills, and doth reprieve.
You hide our fate within its screen,
  We feel our judgment ere we hear:
So in one Picture I have seen
  An Angel here, the Divel there.

The poems in this volume show a mature writer, even a practiced one, and the salutary effect of careful editing by Dudley Lovelace assisted by Eldred Revett, makes this edition a more appealing one for the modern reader. Although the volume does not contain as many songs, the same types of poems appear, forty-four in all, with a series of translations from Latin and French appended. There is also a group of nature verses on "The Ant," "The Grasshopper," "The Falcon," "The Spider," "The Snail," and others.

Thought by the critics to be devoid of playful talent, Lovelace disputes the charge effectively in the poem "A Black patch on Lucasta's Face," a sonnet in which a bee "Mistook her glorious Face for Paradise," and the plaster placed on the sting serves as "the sweet little Bees large Monument."

It may be significant that Lovelace's longest poems, in the first volume a pastoral titled "Amarantha" and in the second a satire, "On Sanazar's Being Honoured with Six Hundred Duckets by the Clarissimi of Venice," display the courtier as a gallant and then as a cynic. In the later poem Lovelace sees woman as something less than perfect, but so much gentler is this knight than the other Cavalier poets that he would almost fit Chaucer's famous description of knightly grace.

From the sentiments expressed in a group of elegies in which the poet's friends lament his death, the character of Lovelace was exemplary. Such expressions were a literary convention, of course, but so much of what is said rings true of his life that a backward glance reveals in epitome a man of his age. His brother, revealing something of a family talent, wrote the concluding lines to Richard Lovelace's literary epitaph, lines in which the tragedy of premature death—"Snatcht the bright Jewell from the Case"—is softened by bright memory:

And now, transform'd, he doth arise
A Constellation in the Skies,
Teaching the blinded World the way,

Through Night, to startle into Day: hand
And shipwrackt shades, with steady   He steers unto th' Elizian Land.

THE POETRY OF MALLARMÉ

Type of work: Poetry
Author: Stéphane Mallarmé (1842-1898)
Principal published works: L'Après-midi d'un Faune, 1876 (*The Afternoon of a Faun*);
Poésies, 1887; *Vers et Prose,* 1893; *Poésies complètes,* 1899

Because of the highly individual qualities of his writing and in spite of his tremendous impact on modern poetry, Stéphane Mallarmé has never been a popular figure known to the general reader. It is difficult, however, to overestimate his importance as an innovator and as an influence on other poets.

Certainly the most striking characteristic of Mallarmé's poems is their obscurity. The reader meets in them a subjective formation of imagery and a warping of the normal patterns of syntax and grammar that has puzzled, at times even infuriated, students of French poetry for more than a century. This obscurity is no accident, and it plays an important part in the history of poetry. At the end of the Romantic period of French poetry (which paralleled that of English poetry), the figure of Charles Baudelaire loomed large, with his theory and practice of *correspondances* between things concrete and things human and emotional.

Of the followers of Baudelaire, Mallarmé assuredly holds first place as the leading exponent of the Symbolist school. It might be said that to understand Mallarmé, in itself a difficult task, is to understand Symbolism. Rimbaud and Verlaine are not so profound, although their personal lives reflected the rebellion that is often thought an important part of the movement. Mallarmé was a rebel only in his verse; outwardly he led a quiet, decorous life at home and in the classroom.

In a sense, Symbolism is to the regular run of poetry what Surrealism is to representational painting; and there seems little doubt that the early Impressionists in painting may well have had some of Mallarmé's theories in mind, even if only subconsciously. To Mallarmé, a symbol represented a feeling or sensation that cannot be logically explained or clearly expressed. Often, for him, the symbol was a very personal abstraction that remained unexplained even in the poem which it inspired.

This concept of the use of symbols was defended persistently by Mallarmé, who, like Baudelaire, was a *poète-critique.* Unfortunately, many of Mallarmé's critical dicta are as abstruse as his verse. Difficult as the reading of this verse is, however, the concept and the examples of it in the work are intriguing; and those who have been willing to put forth the great amount of effort needed usually declare themselves highly rewarded by their grasp of these poems. For the person who reads only English, or to whom French is a less familiar second language, the difficulty is compounded. Perhaps more so than for any other poet, the English-speaking reader is dependent upon the translator for his interpretation of one of Mallarmé's poems; such a reader will surely be perplexed to observe the important differences in translations of the same poem by different scholars.

In spite of these difficulties there is about Mallarmé's verses a strange, haunting beauty that has captured the fancy of many great minds, from Gide's to Joyce's and T. S. Eliot's. Eliot suggests an important fact that must be known in order to understand Mallarmé's poetry. The poems of Eliot are also difficult for the general reader to understand, but usually for a different reason from Mallarmé's obscurity. Whereas Eliot relies frequently on little-known allusions to convey his poetic meaning, Mallarmé used a very personal poetic diction and a chain of thought that puzzles the reader.

Like Browning, Mallarmé thought that poetry need not be simple and direct and that the reader should be willing to exert himself to discover the poet's meaning. For Mallarmé, however, the word "meaning" must be thought of in a very broad sense, for to say that his poems have "a meaning" may not be quite accurate. Often, all that Mallarmé wished to convey was a state of mind or an emotional mood, and certainly no poet ever worked harder at perfecting a poetic style designed for this purpose.

The basis of Mallarmé's poetic credo is fundamental, coming close to the essential nature of reality itself. To him the reality of an object was not in the object, or even in the poet's mind as he observes the object. True reality, he believed, lies in the poet's observation, his perception of the object; thus the poet must express the impression that he finds in a sort of reverie inspired by contemplation of the object within a twilight zone of awareness. Simply to describe the object is far from the poet's intention. Often the object will be transformed during a poem into one of its qualities, that one which strikes the poet as the true reality. In a well-known short poem, "Brise Marine" ("Sea Breeze"), the sheet of blank paper under the lamp has whiteness as its salient quality, a whiteness that protects the paper and which symbolizes the poetic sterility of the poet.

This obsession with sterility—and Mallarmé's poetic thinking was virtually a series of obsessions—which possessed the poet for a long time in his youth, represents another part of his basic outlook. The poet must find first of all the spirit of nothingness ("le Néant") that pervades and underlies the visible universe. Then the poet must re-create the universe from his own mind. In this framework of thought, Mallarmé concentrated on the movement of his mind, not on the data it possessed.

With such a theory of poetry in his mind, it was easy for the poet to use the "black rock" in the opening line of "Tombeau" ("Tomb"), a very difficult poem written at the grave of Verlaine, to symbolize a black cloud, and the cloud to represent the cloud of somber religious ideas and the notions of sin which shade the earth. This symbolism appears to the penetrating reader, however, only after long consideration of the opening stanza of the poem.

As Mallarmé lost his fear of poetic sterility and began to achieve in his mind the grasp of the spiritual nothingness that was to him a prerequisite to worthy creativity, his verse became more and more obscure, so that his later work remains a mystery to almost all readers, even to some of the most diligent poets and scholars. Throughout his work, however, run more or less regular currents of thought, or obsessions. His preoccupation with absence, silence, and death is part of his central poetic philosophy, as his interest in music reflects his conviction that music and poetry are much akin in their expression of truth. *L'Après-midi d'un Faune* demonstrates and expresses this conviction; the poem, appropriately, was the inspiration for Debussy's famous tone poem.

Side by side in Mallarmé's work the reader finds two other, very dissimilar "obsessions": religious belief—essentially a tragic subject for Mallarmé, as in "Toast Funèbre" ("A Funeral Toast")— and an erotic preoccupation with nudity which is found in *L'Après-midi d'un Faune* and in many other poems.

Mallarmé's later poems evidence not only the profound convolutions of his very personal poetic thinking but also some experimentation with the form of the poem on the printed page. One of his last works, "Un Coup de Dés Jamais N'Abolira Le Hasard" ("A Throw of the Dice Will Never Abolish Chance"), will remind an American reader of the interesting arrangements of the poems of E. E. Cummings. In this poem as in his other work, Mallarmé had the same overall purpose: to express, not clearly but none the less accurately, an impression of reality.

It may be said in Mallarmé's favor that he was, in his way, one of the most sincere of all poets. He was, in fact, so critical of his work and so demanding in his standards that his total poetic output can be contained in one regular-sized volume. Further, Mallarmé's verses have a fluidity about them that the reader at first senses only vaguely. As the poet was preoccupied with the movement of his mind, so the lines of his poems achieve a kind of movement: words flow into words; meanings blend and change; images fade and reappear with new evocations of significance.

Although the Symbolist movement as such can be said to have died with an immediate follower of Mallarmé, Paul Valéry, its influence, particularly in the English-speaking world, is still strong today. The modern poet, trying to impose the discipline of order on his fragmented world, works partly in the shadow of this French writer wholeheartedly devoted to a poetic ideal.

THE POETRY OF MARVELL

Type of work: Poetry
Author: Andrew Marvell (1621-1678)
Principal published works: Miscellaneous Poems, 1681; Poems on Affairs of State, 1689; An Horatian Ode upon Cromwell's Return from Ireland, 1776

Andrew Marvell, influenced by the work of Ben Jonson and John Donne, was the last major poet with their qualities and habits of mind. All his great poems are metaphysical; that is, they present feeling intellectually and synthesize thought and passion. Marvell is always aware of the multiplicity and the unity of the universe and the tension he maintains between them constitutes the peculiar poise and balance of his verse. This metaphysical reconciliation of seeming opposites appears in the imagery of the poems, which with characteristic hyberbole combine many areas of ideas and experience.

"An Horatian Ode upon Cromwell's Return from Ireland," generally acknowledged to be the finest poem of its kind in the language, exemplifies both his political feeling and the balance of thought in his verse. It is probably the last English poem in which the divine right of kings and a totally different type of rule could be presented simultaneously. Marvell celebrates Cromwell's phenomenal rise to power "from his private gardens" to

> . . . cast the Kingdoms old
> Into another mould.

The king's weakness rendered him helpless against the strength of Cromwell, and Marvell records the nobility of Charles I, who "adorned" the "tragic Scaffold." The transition from the account of the king's death to the time of Cromwell's rule are terse and effective:

> This was that memorable hour,
> Which first assured the forc'd Power.

Although he praises the efficiency and energy of Cromwell and acknowledges that he gave the government of the country to Parliament, Marvell sees also the necessity to continue fighting (after Ireland, Scotland remains to be subdued), and he

concludes with a muted warning:

> The same Arts that did gain
> A Pow'r, must it maintain.

The equipoise of the "Ode" is maintained through its combination of praise, reticence, and admonition: the recognition of the justice of Cromwell and of the tradition of kingship. Desire for the good of his country outweighs the poet's feelings about specific acts. He both disliked the execution of the king and declared that Cromwell's ability would be beneficial to England. This sustained tension between forces gives the "Ode" its power.

Marvell's reputation rests on a very few poems. Some of the loveliest of these are the poems in which he employs nature images. One of his outstanding characteristics is his use of a simple theme to develop a deeply serious idea. Wit and brilliant imagery enhance the seriousness of his thought, so that an apparently slight subject will thus carry religious and philosophic implications and express the complex sensibility which is so much a part of the metaphysical poetic tradition. In "The Bermudas," Marvell celebrates the joyous exile of a group of nonconformists who left England in the days of Anglican Bishop Laud. Those islands, "far kinder than our own," sheltered and welcomed them and they were able freely to practice their religion. The poem glows with joy and pleasure at God's grace manifested in the tropical luxuriance of the exiles' environment:

> He hangs in shades the Orange bright,
> Like golden Lamps in a green Night.

These images parallel their spiritual freedom.

Religious significance is implicit in "The Nymph Complaining for the Death of her Faun." The huntsmen cannot cleanse themselves of guilt, even though

2984

ᴜne nymph forgives them; the faun's whiteness and purity are matchless. The tone of gentle grief is perfectly maintained, however, and the precision of the images exactly conveys heartfelt emotion:

So weeps the wounded Balsome: so
The holy Frankincense doth flow.
The brotherless Heliades
Melt in such Amber Tears as these.

The most complex of the poems that draw their imagery from nature is "The Garden." Here Marvell's wit and resilience of mind are almost dazzlingly apparent. Coleridge has described the poetic imagination as a "more than usual state of emotion with a more than usual order." This statement could well describe the impact of "The Garden." The pleasure of recognition symbolized by "the palm, the oak bays," with reference to the slight shade these individual leaves cast, is contrasted with the shade given by flowers and trees. Quiet and innocence are not to be found among men:

Society is all but rude
To this delicious solitude.

No lovely woman is "As am'rous as this lovely green." The tree on which a mistress' name is carved is far more beautiful than she. The hyperbole of these assertions contains its own irony; the passionate insistence with which they are made obliquely denies some of their validity. The fourth stanza describes classical lovers who confirm the thesis that the garden contains all delights:

Apollo hunted Daphne so
Only that she might Laurel grow.

In the sensual delights of the garden, sexual pleasure is no longer sublimated but is provided by the fruit itself:

The nectarine, and curious Peach,
Into my hands themselves do reach.

Along with this sexual identification, the image of Eden and the fall of man is present in the image of "ripe *apples*" and the line, "*Insnar'd* with flowers, I fall on

grass."

The sixth verse contains the climax of the poem. Here the tension and poise are most marked. The sensual pleasure has led to intellectual joy, and "the Mind, from pleasure less./Withdraws into its happiness." In the mind are images of all material things and from these it creates transcendent worlds of its own until the quintessence of nature is perceived:

Annihilating all that's made
To a green Thought in a green Shade.

The remaining three stanzas are more relaxed, yet they carry the weight of, and are reinforced by, the previous argument. The poet's soul glides into the trees where "like a Bird, it sits and sings." It will stay there until it is ready to ascend. Meanwhile, it "Waves in its Plumes the various Light." Eden, the poet says, was like this, but the joy of solitude was "beyond a Mortal's share."

Two paradises t'were in one
To dwell in Paradise alone.

The last stanza returns to a man-made garden, where a sundial of herbs and flowers measures the "sweet and wholesome houres." The "skilled Gard'ner" is, of course, God as well as a human craftsman.

The levels of thought and feeling in this complex poem are so carefully wrought together that they could not exist alone. The ideas complement, balance, and reveal one another. The withdrawal of the mind to contemplation of paradise and its wry conclusion that such solitude is impossible are inextricable if their full force is to be appreciated. From the original conceit that all ambition can be satisfied by the delights of a garden, the themes are, through the allusive imagery, totally interdependent.

Marvell's two great love poems, "The Definition of Love" and "To his Coy Mistress," are passionate and urbane, intense and witty, violent and civilized. The reconciliation of opposites is the theme of the definition: it is the metaphysical proposition that in perfect love separation is essential. The validity of this proposition relies on the jealousy of fate. The poet's love was "begotten by despair/Upon impossibility." The decrees of Fate

Us as the distant Poles have plac'd,
(Though love's whole world on us doth wheel)
Not by themselves to be embraced.

The conceit, that heaven would have to fall

And, us to join, the world should all
Be cramped into a Planisphere

before the lovers could be together, emphasizes the inevitability of separation:

Therefore the love which doth us bind,
But fate so enviously debars,
Is the conjunction of the mind,
And opposition of the stars.

The punning conceit in these lines exemplifies the wit and logic of Marvell's verse.

The crowd of images, change of mood, and development of emotional tension combined with a subtle variation of rhythm and pace render "To His Coy Mistress" Marvell's greatest poetical achievement. His theme is the traditional one of "Gather Ye Rosebuds." The opening theme is that if there were time enough the lover would woo endlessly:

My vegetable love should grow
Vaster than Empires and more slow.

An urbane note is sounded in the lines:

For, lady, you deserve this state,
Nor would I love at lower rate.

Then comes the surprising reversal:

But at my back I always hear
Times wingéd chariot hurrying near,
And yonder all before us lye,
Deserts of vast eternity.

The lines ring with passionate desperation and the awful vision of the unknown. The next image is one of destruction in the grave, where the lady's beauty shall no longer exist and honor and lust alike will turn to dust and ashes. From this vision of death the poet turns to an evocation of the lady's present beauty. He adapts the theory that souls shine through the flesh of people of exceptional purity to a reason for consummating their love:

And while thy willing Soul transpires
At every pore with instant fires,
Now let us sport us while we may.

The ardor of the saint has become the heat of physical passion. The conceit of conquering time is developed in images of strength—they will "devour"—time, and will combine their powers "into one Ball" to force their pleasures "Through the iron gates of life":

Thus, though we cannot make our sun
Stand still, yet we will .make him run.

The power of this love is conveyed in the witty and determined assault on unconquerable time.

These poems, with the addition of the "Dialogue between The Resolved Soul and Created Pleasure" and "Clorinda and Damon," are those on which Marvell's reputation depends. His poetic ability was seemingly lost after the Restoration, and he wrote, in verse, only political satires. The flowering of his sensibility prior to this period is an outstanding example of that fusion of wit, passion, and intellect which had its roots in Latin culture and its last complete expression in the poetry of Andrew Marvell.

THE POETRY OF RONSARD

Type of work: Poetry
Author: Pierre de Ronsard (1524-1585)
Principal published works: Odes, Books I-IV, 1550; Book V, 1552; *Amours de Cassandre,* 1552; *Hymns,* 1555; *Elégies, mascarades et bergeries,* 1565; *La Françiade,* 1572

Pierre de Ronsard was in his own time, and to a less degree in later times as well, the "prince of poets." This was not merely an impression generally held. It was Ronsard's own conviction, and he did not hesitate to admonish a coy mistress by reminding her that her kindness to him was as nothing to his generosity in fixing her name in the midst of immortal lines. But the arrogance can, though infrequently, coincide with just estimate; Ronsard, the kings of France whom he served, and those enemies, Mary Stuart and Elizabeth of England, were at one in their estimate of his verses.

Some poets speak at variance with the conditions of their lives and their own time. Ronsard, however final and universal his accent, always speaks to us of his own era and the circumstances of his life. Great and moving as his poems are, they speak of Renaissance spirit as well as of humanity pure and simple.

The Renaissance, in France as elsewhere, was a time when several tendencies, not necessarily compatible, merged with each other. It was a time when nationalism was taking the place of the feudal loyalties that had once held society loosely together. At the center of Ronsard's political consciousness are the king and his court: from the king flow the favors, including ecclesiastical benefices, which allow a poet to live, and the king's court, the nobility that dine, talk, and dance there day after day, constitutes the audience for whom the poet writes. Ronsard addressed not a general public but a particular one in that it was small and self-conscious in its tastes. It expected a poet to be learned as well as moving, and it accepted and understood references to events known only to the privileged.

Related to this rarefied centrality is the growing patriotism that led Ronsard's friend Du Bellay, also a member of the literary group called the Pléiade to which Ronsard belonged, to write *La défense et illustration de la langue Française* (1549), in which the tendency of the learned to write Latin verse is censured and, perhaps inconsistently, the importance of classical studies to any French-writing poet is underlined. The result was that Ronsard's use of his mother tongue reflected literary conventions as old as Homer, Sappho, Theocritus, and Horace. Nymphs haunt Ronsard's home forest of Gastine; local fountains, like that of Ballerie, have all the grace and romantic significance of the ancient Arethusa; and the real charms of Ronsard's various mistresses—Cassandre, Marie, Astrée, Hélène —receive additions from what Catullus, many centuries before, wrote about his Lesbia.

Like numerous other Renaissance persons, Ronsard was a full-blooded man as well as a literary person. He did not, for example, escape the serious political turmoil of the century which divided Catholic France against Protestant France and, of course, one part of the court against another. Though he could mingle Christian and Greek views of deity in the same poem, Ronsard died enjoying the full rites of the Church, and he earlier lived perceptive of the superior advantages, to a cultured man, of the rich traditions of the Catholic Church as opposed to the stern moralism, the "Hebraism" of many of the "sectaries." Because of his adherence to the Catholic faith, Protestant writers attacked the poet, not for his advocacy of pleasant and amorous pursuit alone, but for darker sins which had once been a part of the pagan world.

The pattern of Ronsard's personal career but intensifies the lines drawn in his world. He was wellborn and demandingly educated; he served at court; he went twice to Scotland and once to England and Germany. Suffering from early deafness, he subsided into the role of court poet; he received the tonsure in order to enjoy ecclesiastical benefices; and the rest of his long life was an alternation between the court and his three country estates. His background provided Ronsard with two of his main themes: the peril and hypocrisy of courts and the charm and natural beauty of a life that is rural and retired. (This contention between city and country finds reflection in the essays of Ronsard's great contemporary, Montaigne.) A poem like "Institution pour l'Adolescence du Roy très-crestien Charles IXᵉ de ce Nom" is a stern, moving record of Ronsard's estimates of the moral perils that threaten a king, and "A la Forest de Gastine" is an account of Ronsard's country pleasures which mingles classical memories with vivid recollections of the real forest, greensward, and flowers.

Testimony to a rich, energetic life that was both patriotic and passionate echoes through Ronsard's poetry; friendship and piety, playful wit and sober reflection mingle in such collections as Odes, Hymns, Bocage Royale, and Elégies. His one real poetic disaster is the Françiade, an epic written at royal command, beginning with the tale of Troy and ending with the history of the Merovingian kings of early France.

No summary of Ronsard's poetic creation can omit the many sonnets which he wrote to his mistresses—some kind, some cruel. Here, too, recollections of Petrarch's Laura shape the diction of many a passionate declaration. But Ronsard, unlike many Elizabethan sonneteers in the last decades of the century, was always in pursuit of a flesh and blood woman rather than the "Idea" of Drayton. Passion was the occasion for extended poetic exercises, but the exercises were never, with Ronsard, an adequate substitute for passion gratified. Two of his mistresses, one early, one late, were cruel—Cassandre Salviati, who disappointed the young Ronsard by marrying; and Hélène de Surgères, who during several years never submitted to Ronsard's passion, dressed in black, and was painfully faithful to the shade of a dead sweetheart and the rites of amorous Platonism. It is to these two women rather than to more indulgent mistresses that his greatest sonnets are addressed. In one Ronsard declares to his servant that he wishes to shut himself up and read the Iliad of Homer in three days, unless a message comes from Cassandre. In another the name Hélène suggests to aging Ronsard some moving parallels with Homer's heroine; he adds, hopefully, that he believes his Hélène may also turn out to be a Penelope, a comfort as well as a torment. Or, anticipating Shakespearian accents ("Shall I compare thee to a summer's day . . .") Ronsard writes of Hélène's chill perfection: "Shall I compare your beauties to the moon. . . ."

Ronsard's abundance, his revival of certain parts of the medieval French vocabulary, his personal note—all these were censured by Malherbe, the tastemaker of the next century. Ronsard was also too direct for the oversubtle précieuses, the finicking, "learned" women of the Hôtel de Rambouillet. These seventeenth-century women, ironically, had a good deal in common with Ronsard's Hélène. But an eclipse of several centuries is now over, and Ronsard's poetic fame has now revived.

THE POETRY OF SPENDER

Type of work: Poetry
Author: Stephen Spender (1909-   )
Principal published works: Nine Entertainments, 1928; *Twenty Poems,* 1930; *Poems,* 1933;
Poems, 1934; *Vienna,* 1935; *The Still Centre,* 1939; *Ruins and Visions,* 1942; *Poems
of Dedication,* 1947; *Returning to Vienna,* 1947; *The Edge of Being,* 1949; *Collected
Poems, 1928-1953,* 1955

Stephen Spender explains in a brief introduction to his *Collected Poems* that the volume does not contain his entire poetic output over a period of twenty-five years, but rather a selection of those poems which he wished to gather together from earlier volumes with an aim "to retrieve as many past mistakes, and to make as many improvements, as possible, without 'cheating.'" He admits that he has altered a few readings here and there in the interest of clarity or aesthetics, but adds that he has retained, in the interest of honesty and truth, certain passages in which he now recognizes youthful imperfections and a few poems which reflect views he no longer holds. As printed, the poems have been grouped to represent roughly his development as a poet, as well as his interest in contemporary history—chiefly the Spanish Civil War and World War II—and in such eternal themes as love and separation. He views his book as "a weeded, though not a tidied up or altered garden."

The volume gives an opportunity for a studied reappraisal of one of a group of English poets who first achieved fame between the two world wars. The members of the Oxford Group, as they have sometimes been called, included W. H. Auden, Christopher Isherwood, Cecil Day Lewis, and Louis MacNeice. Spender dedicates three of his groups of poems to the first three of these poets. Though Spender has written elsewhere of the "teacher-to-pupil" relationship between Auden and himself at Oxford, his later development as a poet has been largely an independent one.

This is not to say, however, that he has followed poetic paths never traveled

before. Some of his critics have compared him to Shelley, for the young Spender was also a rebel against the society of his time; and in both poets criticism of their own eras is combined with a vision of a future, better time. Both saw themselves somewhat as prophets of their respective ages. Shelley addressed the West Wind:

Be through my lips to unawakened
earth

The trumpet of a prophecy! O, Wind,
If Winter comes, can Spring be far
behind?

More than a century later Spender exhorted, in "Exiles from Their Land, History Their Domicile":

Speak with your tongues,
O angels, fire your guns
•   •   •   •   •   •   •   •
And let my words appear
A heaven-printed world!

Though some similarities of attitude and theme are to be found in poems of Shelley and Spender, their poetic techniques are as different as the times in which they lived. Spender is as romantically emotional as Shelley: he believes in the unmistakable love of man for his fellow man; he often opposes the darkness of man's life with the bright sun which brings light and warmth into it. But Spender's poems echo twentieth-century phrasing, though some lines might be described as Shelleyan, as in the beautiful lyric which begins, "I think continually of those who were truly great."

At times Spender reminds one of T. S. Eliot (and Auden too), as in

THE POETRY OF STEPHEN SPENDER. Excerpts reprinted from COLLECTED POEMS, 1928–1953, by permission of the publishers, Random House, Inc. Copyright, 1934, by The Modern Library, Inc. Copyright, 1930, 1942, 1947, 1949, 1952, 1955, by Stephen Spender.

"The Uncreating Chaos":

Shall I never reach
The fields guarded by stones
Rare in the stone mountains
Where the scytheless wind
Flushes the swayed grasses. . . .

Spender himself has said, however, that he was more influenced by Wilfred Owen than by Eliot. Like Owen, Spender often employs subtle combinations of sound effects, as in the lines quoted above: "Where the scytheless wind/Flushes the swayed grasses." Owen's poetry was principally inspired by World War I, which brought early death to the poet whose pity had been stirred by the suffering and dying which he had witnessed. Spender seems to have been influenced not only by Owen's bitterness against the bloody injustices of the world, but also by what he himself had learned of war during his months in Spain and later in the Battle of Britain and even more directly, perhaps, by the content of certain of Owen's war poems. Compare, for example, Spender's "Two Armies," which describes enemy forces resting at night only a few yards apart,

When the machines are stilled, a common suffering
Whitens the air with breath and makes both one
As though these enemies slept in each other's arms,

with Owen's "Strange Meeting," an unfinished poem in which a soldier dreams he meets in Hell the enemy whom he killed and discovers in that "strange friend" the same hope and pity and compassion that was in his own heart.

In a critical essay on Auden which Spender published several years ago in the *Atlantic Monthly* (July, 1953), he pointed out that the essential direction of Auden's poetry has been toward a definition of Love. The reader of the *Collected Poems* discovers that, like his slightly older friend and mentor, Spender has written a series of variations on the same theme. In the early poems the love seems

often like Whitman's "manly love of comrades," even to the point of suggesting Whitmanesque ambiguities, as in the poem which begins "How strangely this sun reminds me of my love" or another which addresses directly an unnamed "Abrupt and charming mover." One is reminded of Whitman again in the hortatory "Oh young men, oh young comrades," in which the theme of loving comradeship is combined with the call to desert the dusty past, to leave the "great houses where the ghosts are prisoned," and to make a new and better world:

Oh comrades, step beautifully from the solid wall
advance to rebuild and sleep with friend on hill
advance to rebel and remember what you have
no ghost ever had, immured in his hall.

In other lyrics, as in the lovely sonnet "Daybreak," which describes a couple waking at dawn, first the man, then the woman, one finds both tenderness and the passionate intensity that suffuses so much of the poetry of D. H. Lawrence. But the mixture of desire and revulsion which unpleasantly mars so many of Lawrence's love poems is not in Spender. In Lawrence's "Lightning," for example, a lightning flash reveals to a lover the fear in the face of the woman he is preparing to kiss, and his passion is followed by hatred of both the woman and himself. Contrast with this Spender's "Ice," in which a woman comes "in from the snowing air" and is greeted by a kiss:

Then my lips ran to her with fire
From the chimney corner of the room,
Where I had waited in my chair.
I kissed their heat against her skin
And watched the red make the white bloom. . . .

The love of man and woman shows no hectic flush in Spender; the colors are those of radiant health.

Another aspect of love is revealed in

Spender's numerous poems about children. Several are about his daughter, but the group titled "Elegy for Margaret" are to or about the niece who died after a long, wasting illness on Christmas Day, 1945. Here, though there are morbid lines which describe the progress of the disease, the whole elegy is filled with pity and sorrow for both the child and her parents; and the final poem, in which he attempts to console his "Dearest and nearest brother," is as moving as anything that Spender has written.

Many of the poems for which Spender is best known were published in his widely reviewed *Poems* (1933). In the *Collected Poems* these are reprinted in a group under the title "Preludes." Here one finds such familiar poems as "The Express" and "The Landscape near an Aerodrome," both of which illustrate Spender's early interest in enlarging the language of modern poetry through the use of terms drawn from science, machinery, and industry. The first opens:

> After the first powerful, plain manifesto
> The black statement of pistons, without more fuss
> But gliding like a queen, she leaves the station.

The blending of the names of mechanical objects with language more usual in poetry is so skillfully achieved that the train becomes a mighty poem in motion. "The Express" is perhaps the finest train poem since Walt Whitman's portrait of a very different train in "To a Locomotive in Winter."

"The Landscape near an Aerodrome" contains poetic beauty like that in "The Express," but it is weakened by the attempt to combine arresting description with social commentary. The poem begins with the picture of a gliding air liner and then contrasts the quiet descent of the great machine with the scenes of squalor and misery which become clearer to the passengers as they approach the aerodrome. It ends with a sudden, trenchant last line that not only surprises the reader but seems totally uncalled-for by the preceding descriptive lines:

> Then, as they land, they hear the tolling bell
> Reaching across the landscape of hysteria,
> To where, louder than all those batteries
> And charcoaled towers against the dying sky,
> Religion stands, the Church blocking the sun.

Several of the "Preludes" and two or three poems in the next group, "A Heaven-Printed World," belong to the literature of protest of the 1930's and reflect Spender's leftwing politics which he later forswore. These poems, as Spender has said, "did not please the politicians." Notable are "The Funeral," "The Pylons," and "An Elementary School Classroom in a Slum." The last is full of the pity which is deep in Spender's poems, political or otherwise.

The introspective poems in the group called "Explorations" are as a whole less impressive than those in the other groups. Rather hazy and inchoate, these "explorations," when compared with Spender's other poems, lead one to conclude that he is a sensitive but not a cerebral poet.

It has been said that Spender is a humorless poet. He does usually take himself seriously, often too much so; but the gracefully witty conceit in one of his later poems called "Word" refutes the charge against him:

> The word bites like a fish.
> Shall I throw it back free
> Arrowing to that sea
> Where thoughts lash tail and fin?
> Or shall I pull it in
> To rhyme upon a dish?

THE POETRY OF STEFAN GEORGE

Type of work: Poetry
Author: Stefan George (1868-1933)
Principal published works: Hymnen, 1890 (*Hymns*); *Pilgerfahrten,* 1891 (*Pilgrimages*); *Algabal,* 1892 (*Heliogabalus*); *Die Bücher der Hirten und Preisgedichte; der Sagen und Sänge; und der hängenden Garten,* 1895 (*The Book of Eclogues and Eulogies; Legends and Lays; and The Hanging Gardens*); *Das Jahr der Seele,* 1897 (*The Year of the Soul*); *Der Teppich des Lebens und die Lieder von Traum und Tod,* 1899 (*The Tapestry of Life and Songs of Dream and of Death*); *Maximin,* 1906; *Der siebente Ring,* 1907 (*The Seventh Ring*); *Der Stern des Bundes,* 1914 (*Star of the Covenant*); *Das Neue Reich,* 1928 (*Kingdom Come*)

Stefan George was probably the strongest defender of the "art for art's sake" thesis ever to appear in Germany, and his exclusiveness led him to write his first poems in an invented language, a "lingua romana" similar to Spanish. For many years he printed his books privately and not before 1899 were they offered to the public. He disregarded the German rule of grammar which calls for capitalization of all nouns; the resulting loss in reading speed was a most desired effect for the author because he wanted his readers to note that words in themselves were artistic instruments which would evoke as many—or more—emotions as the colors of a painter's palette.

In 1890 George published his first series of poems, *Hymns.* The title of the first poem, "Initiation," indicates how conscious he was of his radical literary departure and of its limited appeal to an audience used to continuous outpour of modern naturalism. Nevertheless the signal was given:

The river calls! Defiant reeds unfurl
Their slender banners to the languid
  breeze
And check the coaxing ripples as they
  swirl
To mossy shores in tender galaxies.

The theme is repeated in "Invitation":
"Let us leave pavements and grime!"
How dear your offer sounded!
"Far, where more light and elate
Thought and breath seem to chime,
We shall enjoy the flower
And resurrection fete."

Not expecting the applause of many—the poems were still published privately —the author treasured his small circle of friends. Most of his works carry dedications; that of his next work, *Pilgrimages,* was written for the Austrian poet, Hugo von Hofmannsthal (the friendship never matured):

Then I journeyed forth
And became a stranger,
And I sought for some one
To share my mournfulness,
And there was no one.

Hymns and *Pilgrimages* reveal the conflict between the author's poetic ideals and the baseness of everyday life. He used for his next work earlier historical periods and the Orient as times and places for escape from the unpleasant realities of the present. Thus *Algabal,* written in Paris in 1892, is his own interpretation of a Roman emperor who moves in a world of time-removed serenity and passionate feelings:

The hall of yellow glitter and of sun!
On level dome among the stairs it
  reigns,
And from the fiery crater flashes run:
Topazes interfused with amber grains.

His sense of remoteness, however, never excluded his knowledge of the "mystical body of Christ" inherited from his Catholic childhood in a small town in the German Rhineland:

. . . For I, the one, comprise the multitude . . .

THE POETRY OF STEFAN GEORGE. Excerpts reprinted from THE WORKS OF STEFAN GEORGE by permission of the publishers, The University of North Carolina Press. Translated by Olga Marx and Ernst Morwitz. Copyright, 1949, by The University of North Carolina Press.

The Book of Eclogues and Eulogies; Legends and Lays; and The Hanging Gardens indicates a turn toward tranquility; the wanderer once in desperate search for beauty finds it in his own back yard:

> Struck with amazement, as though we were entering a region
> Frost-bound when last we had seen it, yet now full of flowers,
> We, who felt old and sorrowful, gazed at each other,
> And our reflections were fused in the river below us.

Thus the world of knighthood described in *The Book of Legends and Lays* contains much of this recognition of beauty around him:

> What a morning, what a day!
> Breath of sun on brook and tree
> Tunes your ear more swiftly to
> Melting promise, melting plea
> Which I shyly hid away.

The Year of the Soul, probably George's best-known book, indicates that the author no longer needed to search for remote backgrounds; an old park is sufficient for the description of images symbolizing the principles of nature and love. Beginning with autumn, the seasons of the year are portrayed, with the exception of the much used and abused season of spring. The poet invites an unseen friend:

> Come to the park they say is dead, and you
> Will see the glint of smiling shores beyond,
> Pure clouds with rifts of unexpected blue
> Diffuse a light on patterned path and pond.

In *The Year of the Soul* the lonely prophet speaks again:

> . . . The word of seers is not for common sharing. . . .

In 1900 George published *The Tapestry of Life and Songs of Dream and of Death*. Each part contains twenty-four poems. In the prelude he recollects his

struggles up to the present:

> When pale with zeal, I searched for hidden store . . .

and almost regrets that his stormy period has ended:

> Give me the solemn breath that never failed,
> Give me the fire again that makes us young,
> On which the wings of childhood rose among
> The fumes our earliest offerings exhaled.

The Tapestry of Life, a poet's picture book, gave the author ample opportunity to employ his impressionistic power of words:

> When days are done with memory-laden shadows
> In half-forgotten beauty's faded frame,
> Waves of white lambs draw slowly through the meadows
> From the broad clearing to the darkened stream.

It is not surprising that the author became also well-known for his translations of Mallarmé, Baudelaire, and Rimbaud. *Songs of Dream and of Death* is dedicated to persons or occasions in the poet's life; the sequence ends with a forceful description of everlasting conflict:

> All this whirls, tears and pounds, flames and flies,
> Until late in the night-vaulted skies
> They are joined to a bright jewelled beam:
> Fame and glow, pain and bliss, death and dream.

When George published *The Seventh Ring* in 1907, a decisive factor had entered his life. The partial fulfillment of his poetic vision was his encounter with a young man whom he called Maximin. To George, this youth was the embodiment of a dream and temporarily—Maximin died very young—an end to loneliness. The poet described the appearance of Maximin: ". . . softened by the mobility and vague sadness that centuries of Christian civilization have wrought in the faces of the people . . . youth in that unbroken fulness and purity that can still move mountains. . . ." When Maximin died George considered his death in the light of his mystical evaluation of the youth. He regrets his loss:

The forest shivers.
In vain it clothed itself in leaves of spring,
The field your foot made consecrate is numb
And cold without the sun you bring.
The fragile blades on hilly pastures quiver,
For now you never come.

His death was almost a religious event:

You also were elect, so do not mourn
For all the days which unfulfilment sheathed.
Praise to your city where a god was born,
Praise to your time in which a god has breathed!

George's next work, *Star of the Covenant*, a book of a thousand verses, again deals in its "Introit" with the significance of Maximin. Some of the poems are not rhymed, but a strong rhythmic flow is present at all times:

You took away the pain of inner schism,
You, who were fusion made incarnate, bringing
The two extremes together: light and frenzy!

The poet pleads again for a spiritual life and complains that Germans do not listen to their prophets, as in the case of Nietzsche, who, according to George, delivered his message

. . . With such insistence that his throat was cracked.
And you? The shrewd or dull, the false or true,
You acted as if nothing had occurred.

The book ends with a chorus expressing a firm reminder that the power to lead a spiritual life is available to man:

God has locked us in filiation,
God has swept us with his blaze,
God has lit us with elation,
God has steeped us in his grace.

In 1928 George published his last volume, *Kingdom Come*. In this collection he remembered once again the rich literary inheritance of Goethe and Hölderlin. The book also contains a poetic prophecy about war, written during World War I, which seems to anticipate the horrors of future world wars:

You shall not cheer. No rise will mark the end,
But only downfalls, many and inglorious.
Monsters of lead and iron, tubes and rods
Escape their maker's hand and rage unruly.

In "Secret Germany," George abhors again the present regime and asks for sincere understanding of the values which will remain part of the true German tradition:

Only what consecrate earth
Cradles in sheltering sleep
Long in the innermost grooves,
Far from acquisitive hands,
Marvels this day cannot grasp
Are rife with the fate of tomorrow.

Until his death in 1933 George abstained for unknown reasons from writing any more poetry.

George appealed to few, but his admirers recognized in him the high priest of German literature, a writer who appeared at a time when the ideals of Goethe were still venerated, but when poetic expression was already in danger of being suffocated by excessive romanticism and sentimentality. Under the leadership of the author a "George Circle" was founded and the idea of transforming life to mystical heights by way of art and not by scientific positivism was promoted by its members, who adhered to strict moral principles. George made the German language an instrument of art and as a poet he was best qualified to carry Germany's classical tradition into the twentieth century. After refusing to become identified with Hitlerian Germany's literary trends, George died in self-imposed exile in Switzerland in 1933. His inventiveness with the German language makes all translation efforts a most difficult undertaking, but *The Works of Stefan George* (1949), translated by Olga Marx and Ernst Morwitz, succeeds in conveying much of George's intensity of feeling into English.

THE POETRY OF THEOCRITUS

Type of work: Poetry
Author: Theocritus (305?-c. 250 B.C.)
Principal published works: The Bucolics; the Epics

Theocritus is the originator of pastoral poetry, that form which displays to us the labors, the songs and loves, and the sufferings of more or less simple shepherds. In Western literature it is a poetic tradition that is as deathless as it is—or has become—conventional. When Marie Antoinette and her court played at the simple life in the village near Le Petit Trianon, they were reviving modes of sensibility to which the Hellenistic poet first gave expression. Indeed, it would be possible to say that no society can produce pastoral poetry until it has become keenly aware that it is non-pastoral in actuality, old and sophisticated and worldly.

Although Theocritus composed forms of poetry that fit other classifications, he is best remembered for his idealization in verse of the simple, rustic life of the Sicilian shepherds. In his idyls he tells us of herdsmen and their loves; he writes of country singing contests on a mountain hillside, for which the prize is a new set of pipes; he surrounds the occasions his poems celebrate with pastoral grace and occasional rural crudity. Among the best of his pastoral poems is the elegy *Thyrsis*, a lament for Daphnis, traditional hero of shepherds.

It is highly likely that Theocritus' audiences included very few real country people. The bare facts of his life suggest that his ambition led him to courts and not to the country hillsides or gatherings of his verse. He was probably born in Syracuse in Sicily, and some of his poems were written in Alexandria, at the Egyptian court of Ptolemy Philadelphus: fulsome poems of praise to this ruler as well as to Hiero II of Syracuse suggest that Theocritus knew how to finger courtly instruments as well as oaten pipes. His tales of shepherds—their bucolic existence, simple fare, unsophisticated hopes in love,

and rude sports and games—were never destined for country ears at all. Rather might a ruler like Ptolemy Philadelphus, after he had had his considerable fill of praise from the poet, command a song about Daphnis or Theugenus, drawn from Theocritus' recollections of his native Sicilian countryside.

Theocritus' poetry, in short, is one of the chief representatives of the Alexandrian period of Greek poetry. This was a time generally regarded as an era when the direct, authentic utterances of poets like Homer, Hesiod, and Sappho had given away to more self-conscious garlands of verses woven self-consciously and with as much variety as possible, a time when the idyl, the epigram, and the mime were the style. It was a time, too, when verses were first written and then polished and a poet like Theocritus was as aware of the art of poetry as he was of what themes he was expressing.

It is significant that Theocritus often falls back on the traditional stories of the Greek-speaking peoples. He tells us of Cyclops in love with the sea-nymph Galatea—but Cyclops is no longer Homer's monster but a not entirely unattractive swain "sighing like a furnace" for a cold maiden. Or Theocritus takes incidents in the life of Hercules and uses the ancient web of the heroic tale as an occasion for elegant embroidery. We are less struck by the tale of Hercules strangling serpents that attack him in his cradle than we are by the deftness with which the poet elaborates the old brief tale; the gradual approach of the serpents is very gradual indeed, the confusion of the parents is very pretty, and the final triumph of the muscular infant is a foregone conclusion.

Theocritus is perhaps most brilliant and most himself in two fairly long poems that are far from the sloping fields of

Sicily and which reflect the rather fetid, cynical, and jaded life of a city like Alexandria. "Love Magic," or the "Spell," tells of a young woman, Simaetha, and her servant working an incantation to bring back a vigorous young lover who has only recently gone elsewhere. The mixture of sick desire and sicker hatred in the girl's song is remote from the simple lays of shepherds and herdsmen.

Less morbid and certainly wonderfully charming and revealing of busy street life of a Hellenistic city, is "The Women at the Festival of Adonis." In this mime, a brief dramatic sketch not unlike some of the more extended efforts of Menander, two women, Gorgon and Praxinoa, chatter with each other and re-create a world for us. They meet, they plan an outing, comment on each other's costumes, and arrange for their households to be cared for in their absence. Then they go out and walk through the hot, jostling streets; out of their mouths tumble phrases that allow us to see the city streets and their abundant distractions as clearly as if we were there. Then the women, never los-ing breath or dropping a syllable, come to the palace of Ptolemy, where a famous young woman will sing the lament for Adonis, the slain god. The two women attend the religious rites.

All this should indicate that Theocritus had a considerable range. But his country poems, now elegant, now crude in their language, but always fresh and vigorous, have left a greater mark on the literature of the Western world. Vergil's celebration of the simple life (so far from luxury and the cynicism of Augustan Rome) have for twenty centuries implored readers to go back to a Sabine farm; and Vergil took his cue from Theocritus. From Vergil, if not from Theocritus, many poets have learned to hope for escape from courts and cities. Spenser, Milton, Keats, Tennyson, Arnold are on the long list of English poets who have used the pastoral convention of Theocritus for their special purposes, often weaving into the plaintive rural song of pipe and voice political and religious themes that no shepherd—or even Theocritus for that matter—ever dreamed of.

THE POETRY OF YEATS

Type of work: Poetry
Author: William Butler Yeats (1865-1939)
Principal published works: Mosada: A Dramatic Poem, 1886; *The Wanderings of Oisin,*
1889; *Poems,* 1895; *The Wind Among the Reeds,* 1899; *In the Seven Woods,* 1903;
The Green Helmet and Other Poems, 1910; *Responsibilities,* 1914; *The Wild Swans at
Coole,* 1917; *Michael Robartes and the Dancer,* 1920; *Later Poems,* 1922; *The Cat and
the Moon and Certain Poems,* 1924; *The Tower,* 1928; *The Winding Stair,* 1933;
Collected Poems, 1933; *The King of the Great Clock Tower,* 1934; *A Full Moon in
March,* 1935; *New Poems,* 1938; *Last Poems and Plays,* 1940; *Collected Poems,* 1949

The conflict that the antimonies between dream and action caused in the mind of William Butler Yeats could not be resolved in the verse tradition of the Pre-Raphaelites. This was the poetry, together with that of Shelley and Keats and the plays of Shakespeare, with which he was most familiar. It was also the tradition to which he was closest in time. As he did not have a background of coherent culture on which to base his poetry, nor a personally satisfying faith, Yeats throughout his life had to create his own systems of thought—create, in fact, the convention in which he was to write.

In the introduction to *A Vision,* he said: "I wished for a system of thought that would leave my imagination free to create as it chose and yet make all it created, or could create, part of the one history, and that the soul's." His search for reality in belief and feeling was aided by his knowledge that the Romantic poets expressed faith in the power of the imagination. This knowledge also strengthened his conviction that the problems of human existence would never be solved by science and that answers would have to come from quite different disciplines: therefore, both his philosophy and his actions were of paramount importance to him in the writing of poetry.

Yeats spent many years in the study of the occult: spiritualism, magic, mysticism, and theosophy. His feelings for Ireland and for the Pre-Raphaelites led him, early in his life, to the study and use of ancient Irish myths. His hopes of independence for Ireland and his periodic identification with Irish nationalism, also a part of the fabric of his verse, were influenced by his passion for Maud Gonne and his friendship with his patron, Lady Gregory. He believed the system expounded in *A Vision* was revealed to him by his wife's power as a medium. Thus for Yeats, as for all poets, the pattern of his relationships, interests, beliefs, and loyalties was the material of his poetry. However, great poetry is always the expression of one man's personality in such a way that it is generally or universally meaningful. Magic, nationalism, and myth partly formed Yeats's complex personality, and his prose writings in these areas are undoubtedly esoteric. Although it was through these studies that Yeats was able to write· as he did, it is not through them that the reader appreciates his poetry. All Yeats's poetry can be enjoyed and understood when carefully read, without reference to any of his prose. Yeats, in fact, took care to make his work understandable, and one of the most interesting aspects in the study of his poetry is his lifelong preoccupation with clarity, simplicity, and exactness.

This clarity was the goal toward which he worked throughout his career. For Yeats, symbol was the means by which the natural and the supernatural could be fused and the antimonies be resolved. Writing in many *personae,* he worked toward this unified expression of reality, with the result that the continuous development of his powers and his ultimate

THE POETRY OF WILLIAM BUTLER YEATS. Excerpts reprinted from COLLECTED POEMS by permission of the publishers, The Macmillan Co. Copyright, 1903, 1906, 1907, 1912, 1916, 1918, 1919, 1924, 1928, 1931, 1933, 1934, 1935, 1940, 1944, 1945, 1946, 1950, by The Macmillan Co. Copyright, 1940, by George Yeats.

success are both rare and exciting achievements. Yeats's dedication to his art was such that to the end of his life his conscious goals were always in advance of the poems he had completed.

Yeats was a lyric poet, but his belief in and practice of "active virtue"—that is, following a discipline that one has forged oneself—makes his verse essentially dramatic. His first volumes of poetry express the sensibility of the Pre-Raphaelites; the lyrics are slight and the emotion, incompletely realized, often expresses his indecision between the life of dream and that of action. Twilight and longing predominate in these poems.

In his fourth volume, *In the Seven Woods*, published in 1903, Yeats began to find his true voice. Emotion is particularized and he has started to speak with authority. His technique is more sure and his tone more varied. In "Adam's Curse," in which the poet discusses the labor of writing poetry with a woman whom he loves, he uses common words and speech idioms which firmly link the poem to reality:

Better go down upon your marrow-bones
And scrub a kitchen pavement or break
stones
Like an old pauper, in all kinds of
weather;
For to articulate sweet sounds together
Is to work harder than all these.

In his verse plays of this period Yeats was beginning deliberately to eschew abstraction and to introduce more direct and bold speech into his work. His 1910 volume, *The Green Helmet and Other Poems*, shows this technique in his lyric verse, which is becoming more dramatic and assertive. In "No Second Troy" the use of Greek myth approximates a reconciliation between dream and reality.

The 1914 volume, *Responsibilities*, shows an increase in force. Here Yeats uses other voices, or *personae*, of beggars, fools, and hermits to present his ideas. At that time he was encouraged further in his progress toward exactness of expression and the use of only the most mean-

ingful images by his contact with Ezra Pound, who insisted that Yeats remove all abstractions from his verse. He appears to have learned quickly and well from the younger poet, and in subsequent poems he is able to integrate completely his theories of history and personality, and his feelings of despair for Ireland. He also learned to pare his images so that they are totally relevant to his emotion:

Things fall apart, the centre cannot
hold;
Mere anarchy is loosed upon the world,
The blood-dimmed tide is loosed, and
everywhere
The ceremony of innocence is drowned.

The Tower, published in 1928, contains several of Yeats's finest poems. The most brilliant and complex of these is "Sailing to Byzantium." The dazzling civilization of Byzantium which had successfully withstood the power of Rome as Yeats would probably have liked Ireland to withstand that of England, became for him the symbol of eternal art and of the fusion of the creator with the work of art. The reconciliation of youth and age, passion and intellect, is effected by the symbolic representation of the wisdom of the inspired soul in a supernatural form. In this poem, natural birds sing of the cycle of human life and the created birds of Byzantium, of the cycle of history. The glory of the old and of the young is here presented with a single steady vision, and the conflict between them has been resolved:

This is no country for old men. The
young
In one another's arms, birds in the trees
—Those dying generations—at their
song,
The salmon-falls, the mackerel-crowded
seas,
Fish, flesh, or fowl, commend all summer long
Whatever is begotten, born, and dies.
He continues:
An aged man is but a paltry thing,
A tattered coat upon a stick, unless
Soul clap its hands and sing, and louder
sing. . . .

The poet has sailed to Byzantium that he may thus sing. His soul after death will not take "bodily form from any natural thing" but will be one of the singing birds of metal and enamel that the goldsmiths make to amuse the Emperor,

Or set upon a golden bough to sing
To lords and ladies of Byzantium
Of what is past, or passing, or to come.

Another unified vision of life which is not dependent upon the supernatural is communicated in the poem "Among School Children." The mastery of technique which gives "Sailing to Byzantium" its *tour de force* brilliance, enables Yeats in this poem to communicate the feeling of peace after storm. The poet visits a convent school where the children see him as an old man, and as the children stare in mild curiosity, he is reminded of the "Ledaean body" of a woman he had loved, and this vision causes him to feel so joined in sympathy with her that he can visualize her as she must have been as a child:

For even daughters of the swan share
Something of every paddler's heritage.

The vision of the childhood of the woman who caused him much pain leads him to the thought that women would not think motherhood worth while if they could see their progeny at sixty. His suggestion that mothers as well as nuns worship images returns the poem to the convent school setting. In the last stanza of the poem Yeats, by a unifying image of continuity and completeness, reconciles the opposing forces of age and youth at the level of reality.

The poems written in the three years before Yeats's death at seventy-four show no diminution of power. He was still intent on his search for unity and reality

of expression. In "The Circus Animals' Desertion," he reviews his poetic output and says that until he was an old man the machinery of his poetry was still in evidence:

My circus animals were still on show,
Those stilted boys, that gilded chariot.

He lists his old themes: the Irish myths, his lost love, and his preoccupation with the theater, and he tells how he dramatized his love in his plays. He faces his own delight in dreams which he feared would inhibit him from reality: "This dream itself had all my thought and love." He speaks of the *personae* in which he wrote and of the characters of Irish history:

Players and painted stage took all my love
And not those things they were the emblems of.

The reversal and resolution of these ideas comes in the last verse where he evaluates the use of images in his poetry, by questioning their origin and finding that they indeed had their bases in reality. Thus his adolescent faith in the imagination had been justified and he could join the ranks of those whom he admired and who had fused the subjective and objective self into a meaningful whole: "The antithetical self comes to those who are no longer deceived, whose passion is reality."

The philosophy that Yeats so carefully constructed was the basis for a personal vision of life, which by unswerving dedication to craftsmanship and constantly renewed emotional and intellectual vitality he presented in his poetry in all its varied facets, and with always increasing significance.

POINT COUNTER POINT

Type of work: Novel
Author: Aldous Huxley (1894- 1963)
Type of plot: Social criticism
Time of plot: 1920's
Locale: England
First published: 1928

Principal characters:

PHILIP QUARLES, a novelist
ELINOR, Philip's wife
SIDNEY QUARLES, Philip's father
RACHEL, Philip's mother
JOHN BIDLAKE, Elinor's father
MRS. BIDLAKE, her mother
LITTLE PHILIP, Philip's and Elinor's son
BURLAP, editor of Literary World
BEATRICE GILRAY, his mistress
SPANDRELL, a cynic
EVERARD WEBLEY, a disciple of force
WALTER BIDLAKE, Elinor's brother
MARJORIE CARLING, Walter's mistress
LUCY TANTAMOUNT, Walter's infatuation

Critique:

Point Counter Point contains a novel within a novel. Within the framework of the outer novel, Huxley places a novelist who observes the activities of his own world of fictional characters and then plots a novel that is constructed exactly as Huxley has written Point Counter Point. From one set of individuals to another the focus of the novel moves, balancing each life against its counterpoint. The lives of these people repeat the same patterns in different forms, while Philip Quarles plots a novel based on their lives. It is apparent that Quarles is Huxley himself plotting Point Counter Point. Huxley would have us believe that the theme of this novel is one of variations on a single theme, the struggle of natural sexual desire and escapism against the bond of marriage.

The Story:

John Bidlake was an artist with an artist's temperament. He had been married three times. The first marriage had ended in bitter resentment. The second marriage had been idyllic for him, but Isabelle had died two years later, leaving her husband with a void that he had tried to erase by pretending that he had never known a woman named Isabelle. His third marriage had lasted, although John had not lived with his wife for many years. He merely maintained a home where he went whenever he became ill enough to need his wife's nursing skill.

The children of his third marriage, Walter and Elinor, had not been too successful in their own experiments with marriage as a social institution. Walter had been living with a married woman named Marjorie Carling for a year and a half, and he was growing tired of her. Worse than his moral ties to Marjorie was the fact that she tenaciously tried to possess him, rejecting his proposal that they live together as close friends, each going his own free direction with whomever he pleased. Now Marjorie was going to have a baby, and her whining jealousy toward his latest infatuation, Lucy Tantamount, was pricking Walter's conscience. It annoyed him immensely

POINT COUNTER POINT by Aldous Huxley. By permission of the author and the publishers, Harper & Brothers. Copyright, 1928, by Doubleday, Doran & Co., Inc.

that he was making Marjorie unhappy by going to a party at Tantamount House without her.

Elinor and Philip Quarles were traveling abroad, having left little Philip behind under the care of a governess and his grandmother, Mrs. Bidlake. Philip was a novelist. As he traveled through life, he jotted down in his notebook incidents and thoughts that might make rich material for his next novel. His mind was turned inward, introspective, and his self-centered interests gave him little time for emotional experience. Elinor, wishing that he could love her as much as she loved him, resigned herself to the unhappy dilemma of being loved as much as Philip could possibly love any woman.

Denis Burlap, editor of the *Literary World*, flattered himself with the just conceit that although his magazine was not a financial success, it as least contributed to the intellectual life of his time. When Walter, who was one of his chief contributors, asked for more pay, Burlap hedged until Walter felt ashamed of his demands. Burlap was attracted to Beatrice Gilray, a pathetic figure who had feared the very touch of a man ever since she had been attacked by her uncle while riding in a taxicab. Burlap hoped eventually to seduce Beatrice. Meanwhile they were living together.

Another significant member of this set was Spandrell, an indolent son of a doting mother who supported him. There was also Everard Webley, a friend of Elinor and an active political figure.

Philip's parents still lived together. Sidney Quarles pretended that he was writing a long history, but he had not progressed far beyond the purchase of office equipment. Rachel Quarles, assuming the burden of managing their affairs, endured with patience Sidney's whims and mild flirtations. Now it was someone in London, for Sidney made frequent trips to the British Museum to gather material for his history. The girl

in London with whom Sidney had been having an affair appeared one day at his country house and in loud and furious language informed her paramour that she was going to have a baby. When Mrs. Quarles appeared, Sidney quietly left the room. The girl threatened Rachel and then returned to London. Later the affair was settled quietly.

Marjorie appealed to Walter's pity enough to cause him some degree of anguish because of his association with Lucy Tantamount. Lucy herself was not much interested in Walter. Becoming tired of London, she went to Paris.

Elinor and Philip returned from abroad to find little Philip faring well under the care of his governess and his grandmother. John Bidlake, having learned that he was dying of cancer, had returned to his wife's home. He had become a cantankerous patient and treated little Philip with alternate kindness and harshness.

With Lucy in Paris, Philip had persuaded Walter to take Marjorie to the Quarles home in the country, in the hope that some sort of reconciliation would come about from this association. Rachel Quarles began to like Marjorie, and the pregnant woman found herself gaining cheer under this new affection. Shortly after she and Walter had come to the Quarles estate, Walter received a letter from Lucy in Paris, telling him that she had found a new lover who had seduced her in a shabby Parisian studio. With her newly-acquired content, Marjorie felt sympathetic toward Walter, who was crestfallen at the cruel rejection he had received from Lucy.

Everard Webley had long been in love with Elinor. Sometimes she wondered whether Philip would care if she went to another man, and she decided that it would be Philip's own fault if she turned to Everard. She felt that a breach was forming between herself and Philip, but she could not seem to gain enough attention or concern from him to make him realize what was happening.

She arranged a rendezvous with Everard.

Behind the scenes of love-making and unfaithfulness lurked the political enmity of Spandrell and Everard. Perhaps it was the lack of a useful purpose in his life that allowed Spandrell's plan to grow in his mind. Elinor Quarles was home alone awaiting Everard's call when Spandrell and a telegram arrived simultaneously. The telegram urged Elinor to come to her father's home, for little Philip was ill. Elinor asked Spandrell to wait and tell Everard that she could not keep her appointment with him. Spandrell agreed. When Everard arrived at Elinor's home, Spandrell attacked him and killed him. Spandrell lugged the dead body into an automobile and drove it away. Later that evening he met Philip and told him his son was ill.

Philip arrived at the Bidlake estate the next day in time to hear the doctor say that young Philip had meningitis.

For days Elinor stayed by the child's side, waiting for the crisis to pass. One night the sick boy opened his eyes and told his parents that he was hungry. They were overjoyed at his apparent recovery, but later that night he died suddenly. As they had done in the past, Elinor and Philip escaped their unpleasant world by going abroad.

For a long while the Webley murder baffled the police. Spandrell, haunted by his own conscience, sent the police a note which stated that Everard's murderer would be found at a certain address at a certain hour. On their arrival, the police found Spandrell dead with a letter of confession in his hands.

Burlap was the only happy man among these sensualists and intellectuals. One night he and Beatrice pretended they were children and splashed merrily taking their bath together. Happiness was like misery in the modern world, it seemed—lustful, dull, selfish.

POLYEUCTE

Type of work: Drama
Author: Pierre Corneille (1606-1684)
Type of plot: Religious tragedy
Time of plot: Third century
Locale: Mélitène, the capital of Armenia
First presented: c. 1643

Principal characters:
FÉLIX, Roman governor of Armenia
PAULINE, his daughter
POLYEUCTE, his son-in-law, an Armenian nobleman
NÉARQUE, Polyeucte's friend
STRATONICE, Pauline's friend
ALBIN, Félix' friend
SÉVÈRE, a Roman warrior, in love with Pauline

Critique:

Polyeucte, although a favorite of the general public in Corneille's time, was not considered his best play, that distinction being reserved for *The Cid* (1636). Modern criticism, however, has reversed this judgment. Despite its somewhat improbable plot, climaxed by miraculous conversions, the play holds for today's public particular religious interest, since it deals with the working of divine grace in the human soul. It is, however, the strong delineation of the main characters that has won for this work its present universal acclaim.

The Story:

Pauline, daughter of Félix, the Roman governor in Mélitène, had been married fourteen days to Polyeucte, an Armenian nobleman. Terrified by dreams which seemed to portend her husband's death, she vainly sought to delay his departure on a secret mission, the nature of which was known only to his friend Néarque. She related her fears to her friend Stratonice and told her of her earlier love for Sévère, a Roman of high birth whom her father would not allow her to marry because of Sévère's lack of fortune. When the Emperor Décie had appointed Félix governor of Armenia, she had accompanied him and dutifully married an Armenian nobleman of her father's selec-

tion. Meanwhile, they had heard that Sévère had met a hero's death while aiding the emperor in battle against the Persians. According to the report, the young Roman's body had never been found.

Now Pauline had dreamed that Sévère was not dead, but threatened her husband's life; that a band of impious Christians had thrown Polyeucte at the feet of Sévère, and that she, Pauline, crying out for aid from her father, had seen him raise a dagger to pierce Polyeucte's breast.

Her fears were further stirred when her father approached and said that Sévère was alive and was at that moment entering the city. It seemed that the King of Persia, struck by his gallantry, had reclaimed the body from the battlefield in order to gain the Roman honorable burial. But miraculously life had been restored to Sévère and the Persians had sent him to Rome in exchange for royal prisoners. Thereafter his greater deeds in war had bound him closer to the emperor, who had sent him to Armenia to proclaim the good news of his victories and to make sacrifices of thanksgiving to the gods.

Because his love for Pauline had really brought Sévère to Armenia, that Roman, informed by his servant that Pauline was

POLYEUCTE by Pierre Corneille, from CHIEF PLAYS OF CORNEILLE. Translated by Lacy Lockert. By permission of the publishers, Princeton University Press. Copyright, 1952, 1957, by Princeton University Press.

wedded, decided that life was not worth living and that he would rather die in battle. But first he would see Pauline. When they met, she told him that if hers alone had been the choice she would, despite his poverty, have chosen him; but that now she was married she would remain loyal to the husband whom she had learned to love. They bade each other farewell, he ready to die in battle, she to pray for him in secret.

Polyeucte returned from his mission, on which he had been secretly baptized a Christian. Ordered by a messenger from Félix to attend the sacrifices in the temple, he and Néarque planned to defy the idolatry of the worshipers there. Pauline told him of Sévère's visit but added that she had obtained his promise not to see her again.

Stratonice, a witness at the temple sacrifices, hurried to Pauline with the news that Polyeucte had become a Christian, a traitor to the Roman gods; he had mocked the sacred mysteries and, with Néarque, had declared that their god alone was the almighty king of earth and heaven. This defilement, Félix declared, would cost Néarque his life, but he hoped Polyeucte might come to his senses and recant after witnessing the punishment and death of his friend.

When Albin, the friend of Félix, brought news that Néarque was dead, he added that Polyeucte had witnessed his execution undismayed. Pauline, reminding her father that Polyeucte was his choice and that in marrying him she had but fulfilled her filial duty, begged him to spare his life. But Félix, fearing the thunderbolts of his gods and Sévère as well, refused to listen when Albin urged that Polyeucte's sentence be left to the emperor. Besides, he was tempted by the thought that Polyeucte's death would allow Sévère to wed his daughter and thus he would gain for himself a far more powerful protector than he now had. Meanwhile, Pauline visited Polyeucte in jail with the plea that if he must worship his chosen god he should do so silently and secretly, and thus give Félix

grounds for mercy. To her importunings Polyeucte replied that he was done with mortal ties, that he loved her, but loved his God more.

Polyeucte called for Sévère and told him that even as his wedding had parted the true love of Sévère and Pauline, so now by dying he hoped to bring them happily together. He hoped also that they would die Christians. Declaring himself ready for death, he was marched off by his guards.

Sévère was amazed at this example of magnanimity, but his hopes were shattered when Pauline told him she could never marry him, that it would stain her honor to wed anyone who, even innocently, had brought Polyeucte to his sad fate. She begged him, however, to try to save her husband from the death her father had ordered. He consented, if for no other reason than to prove to Pauline that he could equal her in nobility and thus be worthy of her. Félix, although he regarded this intervention on behalf of a rival as a trick to expose him to the full strength of the emperor's wrath, made one last effort to sway his son-in-law. He told Polyeucte that only on Sévère's account had he publicly taken his rigid stand and that he himself would adopt Christianity if Polyeucte would only pretend to follow the old gods until after Sévère had left the city. But Polyeucte saw through this wile and refused. Angered, Félix said he would avenge his gods and himself. When Pauline entered, Polyeucte commanded her to wed Sévère or die with him a Christian.

Again Pauline pleaded for Polyeucte's life, and again Félix was moved to make another attempt to persuade Polyeucte to abjure his new faith, but to no avail. Bidding farewell to Pauline, Polyeucte was marched out to death by Félix' order. Pauline rushed out after him, lamenting that she too would die if he were to die. Félix ordered Albin to deter her but issued his order too late; Pauline had seen her husband executed. Seeing him die, she felt that his death had unsealed her own eyes, acting as a divine visitation of grace. She declared herself a Christian, ready for death.

Sévère upbraided Félix for Polyeucte's death and threatened retaliation. Félix, suddenly yielding to a strange feeling that overcame him, declared that his son-in-law's death had made him a Christian. This sudden conversion struck Sévère as miraculous. He ordered Félix to retain his position of authority, and promised to use all his persuasion to urge Emperor Décie to revoke his cruel commands and to let all worship the gods of their choice without fear of punishment.

POOR PEOPLE

Type of work: Novel
Author: Fyodor Mikhailovich Dostoevski (1821-1881)
Type of plot: Impressionistic realism
Time of plot: First half of nineteenth century
Locale: St. Petersburg, Russia
First published: 1846

Principal characters:
MAKAR DIEVUSHKIN, a destitute government clerk
BARBARA DOBROSELOVA, his friend
POKROVSKI, a young tutor
THE ELDER POKROVSKI, the tutor's father
BWIKOV, a wealthy landowner

Critique:

Poor People, Dostoevski's first published work, appeared serially in 1846 in a literary periodical, Recueil de Saint Petersbourg. In this work, Dostoevski established a theme, the miseries of Russia's downtrodden masses, from which he never wandered far during his literary career. In Poor People, however, one can detect a sly humor that never appeared again in his work. Indeed, the already somewhat morbid and sick artist could hardly have seen anything but black despair in life after his sojourn in Siberia, where he was sent in 1849 for revolutionary political activities. Dostoevski's ruthless and unexpected manipulation of his characters' motives and personalities is foreshadowed in Makar's farewell letter to Barbara, in which Dostoevski has Makar admit that he had not been entirely sincere in his friendship with her.

The Story:

Makar Dievushkin, an impoverished government clerk, lived in an alcove in a rooming-house kitchen. Even though his accommodations were unpleasant, he consoled himself that he could see from his window the windows of Barbara Dobroselova, an unhappy young woman whom he supported in her shabby rooms across the street. Makar and Barbara corresponded; occasionally they walked together when Barbara felt well. Makar, poor but honorable, maintained the gravest dignity in his relationship and in his correspondence with Barbara. In their

poverty and loneliness, each had warm sympathy and understanding for the other.

Among the boarders was a public relations man of literary pretentions, whose style Makar greatly admired. He was also interested in a former government clerk, Goshkov, and his family of four. Goshkov had lost his job through a legal suit; he was deeply in debt to the homely, shrewish landlady.

Across the street, Barbara's cousin Sasha appeared for the purpose of resolving a difference which had long existed between the cousins. Sasha questioned Barbara's acceptance of Makar's bounty.

Meanwhile Makar sent gifts to Barbara and became poorer with each passing day. He pawned his uniform and, in his poverty, became the butt of jokes. Barbara, protesting somewhat weakly his sacrifices for her, sent him, in return, her life's story, which she had written.

Barbara was the daughter of the steward of a prince in the province of Tula. Her family moved to St. Petersburg when she was twelve. She did not like the city and she detested the boarding school she attended. When Barbara was fourteen, her father died, debt-ridden. Her mother was consumptive. Creditors took all their possessions, and Barbara and her mother moved to the house of a distant relative, Anna Thedorovna, whose source of income was a mystery to them. There Barbara, with her cousin Sasha, an orphan, was tutored by a sick young

3007

student, Pokrovski, who was intelligent but irritable. The young girls teased Pokrovski remorselessly. Barbara, however, soon regretted her behavior and vowed to redeem herself in his eyes.

Pokrovski was visited from time to time by his father, a wizened, obsequious little man who worshiped his son. Because the old man was inquisitive and talkative, Pokrovski had limited the number of his visits to two a week. Old Pokrovski would do anything for his son.

Barbara outgrew the tutoring, but she still had not redeemed herself with Pokrovski. Bent upon wide reading, she sneaked into his room and accidentally upset his bookshelf. Pokrovski entered, and while the pair were replacing the books they realized that they were in love.

As Pokrovski's birthday approached, Barbara joined forces with the elder Pokrovski to buy the young tutor the works of Pushkin; they would give the set to him together. At the birthday party Barbara magnanimously let the doting old father give the books to his son. Pokrovski died soon afterward. Grief apparently weakened the old man's mind. He took his son's books and, following the funeral procession on foot, dropped a pathetic trail of books in the mud of the streets leading to the cemetery. Barbara had stopped writing her life story at the point where her mother was dying of tuberculosis.

The friendship between Makar and Barbara continued. Barbara became concerned with Makar's indulgences, which he could not afford, in her behalf; she urged him to get himself a decent uniform.

At the rooming house Makar, utterly destitute, felt deep pity for Goshkov in his poverty. He sent Barbara a volume of the writings of the public relations man; Barbara declared the book was trash. When the possibility of her becoming a governess in a wealthy household presented itself to Barbara, Makar, in spite of his own poverty, proudly told her that he could continue to care for her.

Hearing that Barbara had been insulted by an importunate suitor, Makar got drunk and was brought home by the police. In desperation he borrowed money everywhere, even from Barbara. His penury seemed to affect his mind. Meanwhile the friendship between the two had become the source of laughter to the other boarders. Makar even suspected the public relations man of maliciously gossiping in civil service circles about his having been brought home by the police. He feared for his reputation, all that he had left. Barbara invited him to come live with her and her cook, Thedora; she urged him to stop borrowing and to stop copying the public relations man's style in his letters.

A lecherous old man, sent by Anna Thedorovna, called on Barbara. After Barbara and Thedora got rid of him, Barbara, in alarm, told Makar that she would have to move immediately. Lack of money, however, prevented her removal. Because he could offer no security, Makar was refused a loan by a rich usurer. Everything went wrong; Makar's position at the rooming house became impossible. Barbara burned her hand and could not sew for a living. She sent Makar money, which he spent on drink. But even in his abject condition Makar gave coins to Goshkov that he might feed his family.

Makar made a mistake in his official work and was ordered before his superior, who was so affected at the sight of Makar's wretched person that he gave the poor clerk one hundred roubles and took his hand. These gestures saved Makar physically and morally. He regained his self-respect and faced life with a new vigor. All went well at the office and at the rooming house.

Bwikov, a wealthy landowner who had once courted Barbara and had deserted her in her misfortune, came to St. Petersburg and offered her money, which she refused.

Goshkov, meanwhile, was officially absolved of guilt in a case involving misappropriation of funds and was awarded substantial damages. Moved deeply by his freedom and solvency, the man broke in mind and body and died of shock.

Bwikov returned to Barbara and offered marriage to atone for his desertion. He planned to take her to his country estate for her health. After much debate Barbara and Makar agreed that she must marry Bwikov. Makar could not help remarking, however, that Bwikov would probably be happier married to a certain merchant's daughter in Moscow.

Barbara, preparing excitedly for a magnificent wedding, employed Makar to run countless petty errands for her. Makar planned to move into Barbara's rooms and to retain Thedora as his cook. It saddened him to think of Barbara's leaving him, of her going to the steppes to become the lady of a great estate. In a last letter he implored her to stay but admitted that his passionate turns of phrase were to some extent only a literary exercise.

POOR WHITE

Type of work: Novel
Author: Sherwood Anderson (1876-1941)
Type of plot: Psychological realism
Time of plot: 1880-1900
Locale: Missouri and Ohio
First published: 1920

Principal characters:

HUGH McVEY, an inventor and manufacturer
SARAH SHEPARD, his foster mother
STEVE HUNTER, his partner
TOM BUTTERWORTH, his father-in-law
CLARA BUTTERWORTH, his wife

Critique:

Poor White is a significant novel, an early study of pioneer rural America invaded by industrialism. It is also the story of one man's rise from decadent, poor white folk to a life of creation and self-realization. Anderson graphically described, not only the growth of America, but also the conflicts and frustrations between man and the machine, a conflict that is today one of the major problems in our culture.

The Story:

As a young boy in Missouri, Hugh McVey was incredibly lazy. Hour after hour he would lie on the grass by the river doing absolutely nothing. Not having gone to school, he was ignorant and his manners were rude.

When the railroad came to town, Hugh got work sweeping the platform and doing odd jobs. His boss, Henry Shepard, took an interest in him, and bought him clothes. Soon Hugh went to live with Henry and his wife Sarah. Sarah, who was from New England, always preserved her memory of quiet Eastern villages and large industrial cities. Determined to educate Hugh, she lavished on him the discipline and affection she would have given her own child.

The situation was difficult, at first, for both of them. But Sarah Shepard was a determined woman. She taught Hugh to read, to write, to wonder about the world beyond the little town. She in-

stilled within him the belief that his family had been of no account, so that he grew to have a repulsion toward the poor white farmers and workers. Always she held out before him the promise of the East, the progress and growth of that region. Gradually, Hugh began to win his fight against natural indolence and to adjust himself to his new way of life. When the Shepards left town, Hugh was appointed station agent for the railroad.

He kept the job for a year. During that time the dream of Eastern cities grew more and more vivid for Hugh. He gave up his job and traveled east, working wherever he could. Always lonely, always apart from people, he felt an impenetrable wall between him and the rest of the world. He kept on, through Illinois, Indiana, Ohio.

Hugh was twenty-three when he settled down in Ohio. By accident, he got the job of a telegraph operator, just a mile from the town of Bidwell. There he lived alone, a familiar and puzzling figure to the people of the town. The rumor began to spread that he was an inventor working on a new device. Others suggested that he was looking over the town for a possible factory site. But Hugh was doing neither as yet. Then during his walks around the farmlands, he became fascinated by the motions of the farmers planting their seeds and their crops. Slowly there grew in his mind

POOR WHITE by Sherwood Anderson. By permission of Mrs. Sherwood Anderson and her agent Harold Ober. Copyright, 1920, by B. W. Huebsch Inc. Renewed, 1948, by Eleanor C. Anderson.

an idea for a crop-setting machine that would save the labor of the farmers and their families.

Steve Hunter, who had just come back from school in Buffalo, was another dreamer. He dreamed of being a manufacturer, the wealthiest in Bidwell. He succeeded in convincing the town's important people that Hugh was his man, and that he was working on an invention that would make them both rich. He persuaded them to invest in a new company which would build a factory and promote Hugh's invention. Steve went to see Hugh, who had progressed so that the blueprint for a plant-setting machine was complete. The two young men came to an agreement.

The town idiot, who had skill in woodworking, made models of the machine, and the machine itself was finally constructed in an old building carefully guarded from the curious. When the machine was not successful, Hugh invented another, his mind more and more preoccupied with the planning of devices and machines. A factory was then built and many workers were hired. With the factory, Bidwell's industrialization began.

What was happening in Bidwell was the same growth of industrialism that was changing the entire structure of the nation. It was a period of transition. Bidwell, being a small town, felt the effects of the new development keenly. Workers became part of the community, in which there had been only farmers and merchants.

Joe Wainsworth, the harness-maker, had invested his life-savings in Hugh's invention, and he had lost them. An independent man, a craftsman, he came to resent the factory, the very idea of the machine. People came into his shop less often. They were buying machine-made harness. Joe became a broken man. His employee, Jim Gibson, a spiritual bully, really ran the business, and Joe submitted meekly.

Meanwhile, Clara Butterworth came back to Bidwell after three years at the university in Columbus. She too was lonely, unhappy. When she returned, she saw that the old Bidwell was gone, that her father, Tom Butterworth, was wealthier than before, that the growth of the town was due primarily to one person, Hugh McVey. A week after she met Hugh, he walked up to the farm and asked her to marry him. They eloped and were married that night.

For four years they lived together in a strange, strained relationship. During those four years Joe Wainsworth's fury against Steve Hunter, against the new age of industry which had taken his savings, increased. One day he heard Jim Gibson brag about his hold over his employer. That night Joe Wainsworth killed Jim Gibson. As he fled from the scene, he met Steve Hunter and shot him.

Clara, Hugh, and Tom Butterworth were returning from a drive in the family's first automobile when they learned what had happened. Two men had captured Joe, and when they tried to put him into the automobile to take him back to town, Joe jumped toward Hugh and sank his fingers into his neck. It was Clara who broke his grip upon her husband. Somehow the incident brought Hugh and Clara closer together.

Hugh's career as an inventor no longer satisfied him. Joe Wainsworth's attack had unnerved him, made him doubt the worth of his work. It did not matter so much if someone in Iowa had invented a machine exactly like his, and he did not intend to dispute the rights of the Iowan. Clara was bearing his child, an individual who would struggle just as he had. Clara told him of the child one night as they stood listening to the noises of the farm and the snoring of the hired hand. As they walked into the house side by side, the factory whistles blew in the night. Hugh hardly heard them. The dark Midwestern nights, men and women, the land itself —the full, deep life current would go on in spite of factories and machines.

PORGY

Type of work: Novel
Author: DuBose Heyward (1885-1940)
Type of plot: Regional romance
Time of plot: Early twentieth century
Locale: Charleston, South Carolina
First published: 1925

Principal characters:
PORGY, a crippled Negro beggar
CROWN, a stevedore
BESS, his woman

Critique:

Porgy tells of Negroes living in a society dominated by whites, and the Negroes are presented as being elemental, emotional, amoral, and occasionally violent. Heyward develops in the reader a sympathy not only for the crippled Porgy, whose goatcart excites so much amusement among the whites, but also for Bess, who comes to live with him. Bess honestly tries to be true to Porgy, but she knows the weakness of her will and flesh when the brutal Crown touches her or when she has had liquor or dope. The story was dramatized in 1927 by Heyward and his wife Dorothy. The novel was also the basis for the opera Porgy and Bess (1935), for which Heyward wrote the book and, with Ira Gershwin, the lyrics.

The Story:

Porgy, a crippled Negro beggar, lived in a brick tenement called Catfish Row, once a fine old Southern mansion in Charleston, South Carolina. Different from the eager, voluble beggars of his race, Porgy sat silent day by day, acknowledging only by lifting his eyes the coins dropped in his cup. No one knew how old he was, and his large, powerful hands were in strange contrast to his frail body. His single vice was gambling. In a gambling session one evening in April he witnessed the brutal murder of Robbins by Crown, a stevedore who thought he had been cheated.

In May Porgy made his first trip by homemade goatcart through the city streets, to the mocking amusement of the white folks. The goatcart gave Porgy a new freedom. He no longer had to stay at one stand all day; but he could roam at will and take in more money than before.

In June Crown's woman, Bess, came to live with Porgy, and the cripple became a new man. He seemed less an impassive observer of life and he developed a tender affection for children. Bess left off her evil ways and became in truth Porgy's woman.

On the day of the grand parade and picnic of "The Sons and Daughters of Repent Ye Saith the Lord," Crown came upon Bess cutting palmetto leaves for the picnic on Kittiwar Island. He took her to his hut. At the end of the day he let her return to Porgy with the promise that in the fall, when cotton shipments would provide stevedoring work in Savannah, she would again be Crown's Bess.

In September, while the "Mosquito Fleet" was at the fishing banks, the hurricane flag was up over the custom house. Jake's wife, Clara, shuddered with fear for her husband whom she had warned not to go out that day in his boat, the Seagull. After an ominous calm the hurricane struck the city. The water of the bay, driven by the shrieking wind, rose above the sea wall, crossed the street, and invaded the ground floor of Catfish Row. Forty frightened Negroes huddled in the great second-story ballroom of the old mansion. During a lull in the storm Clara saw the

PORGY by DuBose Heyward. By permission of Mrs. DuBose Heyward, the Trustee of the estate of DuBose Heyward, and the publishers, Doubleday & Co., Inc. Copyright, 1925, by Doubleday & Co., Inc.

wreck of her husband's boat near the wharf. Leaving her baby with Bess, Clara went out into the flood. A few minutes later she was overwhelmed during a sudden return of the storm's great fury. Bess and Porgy kept Clara's baby.

In October drays loaded with heavy bales of cotton came rumbling down the street. In Catfish Row there was excitement and happiness, for stevedoring jobs and· money would be plentiful again. But the coming of the cotton seemed to Porgy to portend disaster. He asked Bess whether she was his woman or Crown's. His, she answered, unless Crown put his hot hands on her again as he did that day of the picnic. She could not answer for herself if that happened again. Porgy assured her he would not let Crown take her away from him. When Crown broke into their room one midnight not long afterward, Porgy stabbed him. Next day the body was found in the river nearby. The police got nowhere in their questioning of the occupants of Catfish Row, and there was a kind of communal sigh of relief when the officers left without having made any arrests. But when one of the buzzards that had fed upon Crown's body lighted on the parapet above Porgy's room, the frightened little cripple felt that doom was in store for him. The next day Porgy, having been asked to identify Crown's body at the morgue, fled in terror in his goatcart, hotly pursued by a patrol wagon full of officers. Passersby laughed uproariously at the ridiculously one-sided race. Porgy was caught at the edge of town, but by the time he had been brought downtown he was no longer needed since another Negro had identified the body. Crown was declared to have come to his death at the hands of a person or persons unknown. Porgy was jailed for five days for contempt of court.

When he returned from jail and found Serena Robbins holding Jake's and Clara's orphan baby, Porgy suspected the worst. From a neighbor he learned that some stevedores had gotten Bess drunk and taken her off to Savannah. Porgy knew she would never return. Serena had adopted the baby. Porgy had for one brief summer known the joys that come to other people. Now he was just a pitiful old man sitting sadly in a goatcart with the morning sunlight shining upon him.

THE PORTRAIT OF A LADY

Type of work: Novel
Author: Henry James (1843-1916)
Type of plot: Psychological realism
Time of plot: About 1875
Locale: England, France, Italy
First published: 1881

Principal characters:
ISABEL ARCHER, an American heiress
GILBERT OSMOND, her husband
RALPH TOUCHETT, her cousin
MADAME MERLE, her friend and Osmond's former mistress
PANSY OSMOND, Osmond's daughter
LORD WARBURTON, Isabel's English suitor
CASPAR GOODWOOD, Isabel's American suitor
HENRIETTA STACKPOLE, American newspaper correspondent, Isabel's friend

Critique:

With the exception of the English Lord Warburton, *The Portrait of a Lady* contains a gallery of Americans who work out their destinies against a European background. The influence of European culture is seen most closely as it affects the heroine, high-minded Isabel Archer. By means of careful penetration into her mental processes, the steps which lead to her marriage with the dilettante, Gilbert Osmond, are delineated, as well as the consequent problems which arise from this marriage. The novel is an excellent example of the Jamesian method of refracting life through an individual temperament.

The Story:

Isabel Archer, upon the death of her father, had been visited by her aunt, Mrs. Touchett. She proved so attractive to the older woman that Mrs. Touchett decided to give her the advantage of more cosmopolitan experience, and Isabel was quickly carried off to Europe so she might see something of the world of culture and fashion.

On the day the women arrived at the Touchett home in England, Isabel's sickly young cousin, Ralph Touchett, and his father were taking tea in the garden with their friend, Lord Warburton. When Isabel appeared, Warburton had been confessing to the two men his boredom and his distaste for his routine existence. The young nobleman was much taken

with the American girl's grace and lively manner.

Isabel had barely settled at Gardencourt, her aunt's home, before she received a letter from an American friend, Henrietta Stackpole, a newspaper woman who was writing a series of articles on the sights of Europe. At Ralph's invitation, Henrietta went to Gardencourt to spend some time with Isabel and to obtain material for her writing.

Soon after Henrietta's arrival, Isabel heard from another American friend. Caspar Goodwood, a would-be suitor, had followed her abroad. Learning her whereabouts from Henrietta, he wrote to ask if he might see her. Isabel was much irked by his aggressiveness, and she decided not to answer his letter.

On the day she received the letter from Goodwood, Lord Warburton proposed to her. Not wishing to seem indifferent to the honor of his proposal, she asked for time to consider it. At last she decided she could not marry the young Englishman, for she wished to see considerably more of the world before she married. She was afraid that marriage to Warburton, although he was a model of kindness and thoughtfulness, would prove stifling.

Because Isabel had not seen London on her journey with Mrs. Touchett and since it was on Henrietta Stackpole's itinerary, the two young women, accompanied by Ralph Touchett, went to the capital. Henrietta quickly made the acquaintance of a Mr. Bantling, who undertook to squire her around. When Caspar Goodwood visited Isabel at her hotel, she again refused him, though his persistence made her agree that if he still wished to ask for her hand he might visit her again after two years had passed. While the party was in London a telegram came from Gardencourt. Old Mr. Touchett was seriously ill of the gout, and his wife was much alarmed. Isabel and Ralph left on the afternoon train. Henrietta remained under the escort of her new friend.

During the time Mr. Touchett lay dying and his family was preoccupied, Isabel was forced to amuse herself with a new companion. Madame Merle, an old friend of Mrs. Touchett, had come to Gardencourt to spend a few days. She and Isabel, thrown together a great deal, exchanged many confidences. Isabel admired the older woman for her ability to amuse herself, for her skill at needlework, at painting, at the piano, and for her ability to accommodate herself to any social situation. On the other hand, Madame Merle spoke enviously of Isabel's youth and intelligence, lamenting the life which had left her, at middle age, a widow with no children and no visible success in life.

When her uncle died, he left Isabel, at her cousin's instigation, one-half of his fortune. Ralph, greatly impressed with his young kinswoman's brilliance, had persuaded his father that she should be given an opportunity to fly as far and as high as she might. For himself, he knew he could not live long because of his pulmonary illness, and his legacy was enough to let him live in comfort.

As quickly as she could, Mrs. Touchett sold her London house and took Isabel to Paris with her. Ralph went south for the winter to preserve what was left of his health. In Paris the new heiress was introduced to many of her aunt's friends among American expatriates, but she was not impressed. She thought their indolent lives worthy only of contempt. Meanwhile Henrietta and Mr. Bantling had arrived in Paris, and Isabel spent much

time with them and Edward Rosier. She had known Rosier when both were children and she was traveling abroad with her father. Rosier was another dilettante, living on the income from his inheritance. He explained to Isabel that he could not return to his own country because there was no occupation there worthy of a gentleman.

In February Mrs. Touchett and her niece went to the Palazzo Crescentini, the Touchett house in Florence. They stopped on the way to see Ralph, who was staying in San Remo. In Florence they were joined once more by Madame Merle.

Unknown to Isabel or her aunt, Madame Merle also visited her friend, Gilbert Osmond, another American who lived in voluntary exile outside Florence with his art collection and his young, convent-bred daughter, Pansy. Madame Merle told Osmond of Isabel's arrival in Florence saying that as the heir to a fortune, Isabel would be a valuable addition to Osmond's collection.

The heiress who had rejected two worthy suitors did not refuse the third. She was quickly captivated by the charm of the sheltered life Gilbert Osmond had created for himself. Her friends were against the match. Henrietta Stackpole, who was inclined to favor Caspar Goodwood, was convinced that Osmond was interested only in Isabel's money, as was Isabel's aunt. Mrs. Touchett had requested Madame Merle, the good friend of both parties, to discover the state of their affections; she was convinced that Madame Merle could have prevented the match. Ralph Touchett was disappointed that his cousin should have fallen to the ground from her flight so quickly. Caspar Goodwood, learning of Isabel's intended marriage when he revisited her after the passage of the two years agreed upon, could not persuade her to reconsider her step. Isabel was indignant when he commented on the fact that she did not even know her intended husband's antecedents.

After her marriage to Gilbert Osmond,

Isabel and her husband established their home in Rome, in a setting completely expressive of Osmond's tastes. Before three years had passed, Isabel began to realize that her friends had not been completely wrong in their objections to her marriage. Osmond's exquisite taste had made their home one of the most popular in Rome, but his ceaseless effort to press his wife into a mold, to make her a reflection of his own ideas, had not made their marriage one of the happiest.

He had succeeded in destroying a romance between Pansy and Edward Rosier, who had visited the girl's stepmother and found the daughter attractive. He had not succeeded, however, in contracting the match he desired between Pansy and Lord Warburton. Warburton had found Pansy as pleasing as Isabel had once been, but he had dropped his suit when he saw that the girl's affections lay with Rosier.

Ralph Touchett, his health growing steadily worse, gave up his wanderings on the continent and returned to Gardencourt to die. When Isabel received a telegram from his mother telling her that Ralph would like to see her before his death, she felt it her duty to go to Gardencourt at once. Osmond reacted to her wish as if it were a personal insult. He expected that, as his wife, Isabel would want to remain at his side, and that she would not disobey any wish of his. He also made it plain that he disliked Ralph.

In a state of turmoil after her conversation with her husband, Isabel met the Countess Gemini, Osmond's sister.

The countess, visiting the Osmonds, had seen how matters lay between her brother and Isabel. An honest soul, she had felt more sympathy for her sister-in-law than for her brother. To comfort Isabel, she told her the story of Gilbert's past. After his first wife had died, he and Madame Merle had an affair that lasted six or seven years. During that time Madame Merle, a widow, had borne him a child, Pansy. Changing his residence, Osmond had been able to pretend to his new circle of friends that the original Mrs. Osmond had died in giving birth to the child.

With this news fresh in her mind, and still determined to go to England, Isabel stopped to say goodbye to Pansy, who was staying in a convent where her father had sent her to recuperate from her affair with Rosier. There, too, she met Madame Merle. Madame Merle, with her keen perception, had no difficulty realizing that Isabel knew her secret. When she remarked that Isabel would never need to see her again, that she would go to America, Isabel was certain Madame Merle would also find in America much to her own advantage.

Isabel was in time to see her cousin before his death. She stayed on briefly at Gardencourt after the funeral, long enough to bid goodbye to Lord Warburton, who had come to offer condolences to her aunt, and to reject a third offer from Caspar Goodwood, who knew of her husband's treatment. When she left to start her journey back to Italy, Isabel knew what she must do. Her first duty was not to herself, but to put her house in order.

A PORTRAIT OF THE ARTIST AS A YOUNG MAN

Type of work: Novel
Author: James Joyce (1882-1941)
Type of plot: Psychological realism
Time of plot: 1882-1903
Locale: Ireland
First published: 1916

Principal characters:
STEPHEN DEDALUS, an Irish student
SIMON DEDALUS, his father
EMMA, his friend

Critique:

In telling the story of his own youth under a thin disguise of fiction, Joyce has written one of the most compelling and forceful of recent autobiographies. He tried to show the beginnings of his artistic compulsion, and the events that led him to think and to act as he did. Highly descriptive, the book moves from incident to incident in an unhurried way, sketching in all the important moments and thoughts of Joyce's youth as he remembered them. This novel is a forerunner of Joyce's more significant and experimental *Ulysses.*

The Story:

When Stephen Dedalus went to school for the first time, his last name soon got him into trouble. It sounded too Latin, and the boys teased him about it. Seeing that he was sensitive and shy, the other boys began to bully him. School was filled with unfortunate incidents for Stephen. He was happy when he became sick and was put in the infirmary away from the other boys. Once, when he was there just before the Christmas holidays, he worried about dying and death. As he lay on the bed thinking, he heard the news of Parnell's death. The death of the great Irish leader was the first date he remembered—October 6, 1891.

At home during the vacation he learned more of Parnell. His father, Simon Dedalus, worshiped the dead man's memory and defended him on every count. Stephen's aunt, Dante Rior-

dan, despised Parnell as a heretic and a rabble-rouser. The fierce arguments that they got into every day burned themselves into Stephen's memory. He worshiped his father, and his father said that Parnell had tried to free Ireland, to rid it of the priests who were ruining the country. Dante insisted that just the opposite was true. A violent defender of the priests, she leveled every kind of abuse against Simon and his ideas. The disagreement between them became a problem which, in due time, Stephen would have to solve for himself.

Returning to school after the holidays, Stephen got in trouble with Father Dolan, one of the administrators of the church school he attended. Because he had broken his glasses, Stephen could not study until a new pair arrived. Father Dolan saw that Stephen was not working, and thinking that his excuse about the glasses was false he gave the boy a beating. The rest of the boys for once were on Stephen's side, and they urged him to complain to the head of the school. With fear and trembling, Stephen went to the head and presented his case. The head understood, and promised to speak to Father Dolan about the matter. When Stephen told the boys about his conversation, they hoisted him in their arms like a victorious fighter, and called him a hero.

Afterward life was much easier for Stephen. Only one unfortunate incident marked the term. In a spirit of fun,

A PORTRAIT OF THE ARTIST AS A YOUNG MAN by James Joyce. By permission of the publishers, The Viking Press, Inc. Copyright, 1916, by B. W. Huebsch. Renewed, 1944, by Nora Joyce.

one of his professors announced in class that Stephen had expressed heresy in one of his essays. Stephen quickly changed the offending phrase and hoped that the mistake would be forgotten. After class, however, several of the boys accused him not only of being a heretic but also of liking Byron, whom 'they considered an immoral man and therefore no good as a poet. In replying to their charges, Stephen had his first real encounter with the problems of art and morality. They were to follow him throughout his life.

On a trip to Cork with his father, Stephen was forced to listen to the often-told tales of his father's youth. They visited the places his father had loved as a boy. Each night Stephen was forced to cover up his father's drunkenness and sentimental outbursts. The trip was an education in everything Stephen disliked.

At the end of the school year Stephen won several prizes. He bought presents for everyone, started to do over his room, and began an ill-fated loan service. As long as the money lasted, life was wonderful. Then one night, when his money was almost gone, he was enticed into a house by a woman wearing a long pink gown. At sixteen he learned what love was.

Not until the school held a retreat in honor of Saint Francis Xavier did Stephen realize how deeply conscious he was of the sins he had committed with women. The sermons of the priests about heaven and hell, especially about hell, ate into his mind. At night his dreams were of nothing but the eternal torture which he felt he must endure after death. He could not bear to make confession in school. At last he went into the city, to a church where he was unknown. There he opened his unhappy mind and heart to an understanding and wise old priest, who advised him and comforted his soul. After the confession Stephen promised to sin no more, and he felt sure that he would keep his promise.

For a time Stephen's life followed a model course. He studied Aquinas and Aristotle and won acclaim from his teachers. One day the director of the school called Stephen into his office and, after a long conversation, asked him if he had ever thought of joining the order of the Jesuits. Stephen was deeply flattered. Priesthood became his life's goal.

When Stephen entered the university, however, a change came over his thinking. He began to doubt, and the longer he studied, the more confused and doubtful he became.

His problems drew him closer to two of his fellow students, Davin and Lynch and farther away from Emma, a girl for whom he had felt affection since childhood. With Davin and Lynch he discussed his ideas about beauty and the working of the mind. Because he would not sign a petition for world peace, Stephen won the enmity of many of the fellows. They called him anti-social and egotistic. Finally neither the peace movement, the Irish Revival, nor the Church itself could claim his support.

Davin was the first to question Stephen about his ideas. When he suggested to Stephen that in everything Ireland should come first, Stephen answered that to him Ireland was an old sow that ate her own children.

One day Stephen met Emma at a carnival, and she asked him why he had stopped coming to see her. He answered that he had been born to be a monk. When Emma said that she thought him a heretic instead of a monk, his last link with Ireland seemed to be broken. At least he was not afraid to be alone. If he wanted to find beauty, and to understand beauty, he had to leave Ireland, where there was nothing in which he believed. The prayers of his friends asking that he return to the faith went unanswered. Stephen got together his things, packed, and left Ireland, intending never to return. He did intend, some day, to write a book that would make clear his views on Ireland and the Irish.

THE POSSESSED

Type of work: Novel
Author: Fyodor Mikhailovich Dostoevski (1821-1881)
Type of plot: Psychological realism
Time of plot: Mid-nineteenth century
Locale: Russia
First published: 1867

Principal characters:
STEPAN VERHOVENSKY, a provincial patriot and mild progressive
PYOTR, his nihilist son
VARVARA STAVROGIN, a provincial lady and employer of Stepan
NIKOLAY, her son, a victim of materialism
MARYA, his idiot wife
SHATOV, the independent son of one of Varvara's serfs

Critique:

The Possessed is Dostoevski's answer to Turgenev's treatment of Russian nihilism in *Fathers and Sons.* By means of a large number of characters representing all classes of Russian society, Dostoevski shows how an idle interest in nihilism brought on robbery, arson, and murder in one Russian community. The plot is exceedingly complex, but this very complexity tends to emphasize a similar quality in nineteenth-century Russian life, which convulsed violently when it concerned itself with denial of an ordering principle in the universe.

The Story:

Stepan Verhovensky, a self-styled progressive patriot and erstwhile university lecturer, was footloose in a provincial Russian town until Varvara Stavrogin hired him to tutor her only son, Nikolay. Although Stepan's radicalism, which was largely a pose, shocked Varvara, the two became friends. When Varvara's husband died, Stepan even looked forward to marrying the widow. They went together to St. Petersburg, where they moved daringly in radical circles. After attempting without success to start a literary journal, they left St. Petersburg, Varvara returning to the province and Stepan, in an attempt to assert his independence, going to Berlin. After four months in Germany, Stepan, realizing that he was Varvara's thrall emotionally

and financially, returned to the province in order to be near her.

Stepan became the leader of a small group that met to discuss progressive ideas. Among the group were Shatov, the independent son of one of Varvara's serfs, a liberal named Virginsky, and Liputin, a man who made everyone's business his business.

Nikolay Stavrogin, whom Stepan had introduced to progressivism, went on to school in St. Petersburg and from there into the army as an officer. He resigned his commission, however, returned to St. Petersburg, and went to live in the slums. When he returned home, at Varvara's request, he proceeded to insult the members of Stepan's group. He bit the ear of the provincial governor during an interview with that dignitary. Obviously mentally unbalanced, Nikolay was committed to bed. Three months later, apparently recovered, he apologized for his actions and again left the province.

Months later Varvara was invited to visit a childhood friend in Switzerland, where Nikolay was paying court to her friend's daughter, Lizaveta. Before the party returned to Russia, however, Lizaveta and Nikolay broke their engagement because of Nikolay's interest in Dasha, Varvara's servant woman. In Switzerland, Nikolay and Stepan's son, Pyotr, met and found themselves in sympathy on political matters.

THE POSSESSED by Fyodor Mikhailovich Dostoevski. Published by The Modern Library, Inc.

In the province, meanwhile, there was a new governor, one von Lembke. Stepan, lost without Varvara, visibly deteriorated during her absence. Varvara arranged with Dasha, who was twenty, to marry Stepan, who was fifty-three. Dasha, who was the sister of Shatov, submitted quietly to her mistress' wishes. Stepan reluctantly consented to the marriage, but he balked when he discovered from a member of his group that he was being used to cover up Nikolay's relations with the girl.

New arrivals in the province were Captain Lebyadkin and his idiot, crippled sister, Marya. One day Marya attracted the attention of Varvara in front of the cathedral, and Varvara took the cripple home with her. Nikolay, she learned, had known the Lebyadkins in St. Petersburg. Pyotr assured Varvara, who was suspicious, that Nikolay and Marya Lebyadkin were not married.

By his personal charm and a representation of himself as a mysterious revolutionary agent returned from exile, Pyotr began to dominate Stepan's liberal friends and became, for his own scheming purposes, the protégé of Yulia, the governor's wife. Nikolay at first followed Pyotr in his political activities, but he turned against the revolutionary movement and warned Shatov that Pyotr's group was plotting to kill Shatov because of information he possessed. Nikolay confessed to Shatov that on a bet he had married Marya Lebyadkin in St. Petersburg.

As a result of a duel between Nikolay and a local aristocrat who hated him, a duel in which Nikolay emerged victorious without killing his opponent, Nikolay became a local hero. He continued intimate with Dasha, Lizaveta having announced her engagement to another man. Pyotr, meanwhile, sowed seeds of dissension among all classes in the town; he disclosed von Lembke's possession of a collection of radical manifestoes; he caused a break between his father and Varvara, and he secretly incited the working people to rebel against their masters.

Yulia led the leaders of the town in preparations for a grand fête. Pyotr saw in the fête the opportunity to bring chaos into an otherwise orderly community. He brought about friction between von Lembke, who was an inept governor, and Yulia, who actually governed the province through her salon.

At a meeting of the revolutionary group, despair and confusion prevailed until Pyotr welded it together with mysterious talk of orders from higher revolutionary leaders. He talked of many other such groups engaged in like activities. Shatov, who attended the meeting, denounced Pyotr as a spy and a scoundrel and walked out. Pyotr disclosed to Nikolay his nihilistic beliefs and proposed that Nikolay be brought forward as the Pretender when the revolution had been accomplished.

Blum, von Lembke's secretary, raided Stepan's quarters and confiscated all of Stepan's private papers, among them some political manifestoes. Stepan went to the governor to demand his rights under the law and witnessed in front of the governor's mansion the lashing of dissident workers who had been quietly demonstrating for redress of their grievances. Von Lembke appeased Stepan by saying that the raid on his room was a mistake.

The fête was doomed beforehand. Many agitators without tickets were admitted. Liputin read a comic and seditious poem. Karmazinov, a great novelist, made a fool of himself by recalling the follies of his youth. Stepan insulted the agitators by championing the higher culture. When an unidentified agitator arose to speak, the afternoon session of the fête became a bedlam, so that it was doubtful whether the ball would take place that night. Abetted by Pyotr, Nikolay and Lizaveta eloped in the afternoon to the country house of Varvara.

The ball was not canceled, but few of the landowners of the town or countryside appeared. Drunkenness and brawling soon reduced the ball to a rout which came to a sorry end when fire was discovered raging through some houses along the river. Captain Lebyadkin, Marya, and their servant were discovered murdered in their house, which remained unburned in the path of the fire. When Pyotr informed Nikolay of the murders, Nikolay confessed that he had known of the possibility that violence would take place, but that he had done nothing to prevent it. Horrified, Lizaveta went to see the murdered pair; she was beaten to death by the enraged townspeople because of her connections with Nikolay. Nikolay left town quickly and quietly.

When the revolutionary group met again, all mistrusted one another. Pyotr explained to them that Fedka, an ex-convict, had murdered the Lebyadkins for robbery, but he failed to mention that Nikolay had all but paid Fedka to commit the crime. He warned the group against Shatov and said that a fanatic named Kirillov had agreed to cover up the proposed murder of Shatov. After Fedka denounced Pyotr as an atheistic scoundrel, Fedka was found dead on a road outside the town.

At the same time, Marie, Shatov's wife, returned to the town. The couple had been separated for three years; Marie was ill and pregnant. When she began her labor, Shatov procured Virginsky's wife as midwife. The couple were reconciled after Marie gave birth to a baby boy, for the child served to regenerate Shatov and make him happy once more.

Shatov left his wife and baby alone in order to keep an appointment with the revolutionary group, an appointment made for the purpose of separating himself from the plotters. Attacked and shot by Pyotr, his body was weighted with stones and thrown into a pond. After the murder Pyotr went to Kirillov to get Kirillov's promised confession for the murder of Shatov. Kirillov, who was Shatov's neighbor and who had seen Shatov's happiness at the return of his wife, at first refused to sign, but Pyotr finally prevailed upon him to put his name to the false confession. Kirillov, morally bound to end his life, shot himself. Pyotr left the province.

Stepan, meanwhile, left the town to seek a new life. He wandered for a time among peasants and at last became dangerously ill. Varvara went to him, and the two friends were reconciled before the old scholar died. Varvara disowned her son. Marie and the baby died of exposure and neglect when Shatov failed to return home. One of the radical group broke down and confessed to the violence that had been committed in the town at the instigation of the completely unmoral Pyotr. Liputin escaped to St. Petersburg, where he was apprehended in a drunken stupor in a brothel.

Nikolay wrote to Dasha, the servant, suggesting that the two of them go to Switzerland and begin a new life. Before Dasha could pack her things, however, Nikolay returned home secretly and hanged himself in his room.

THE POT OF GOLD

Type of work: Drama
Author: Titus Maccius Plautus (c. 254-184 B.C.)
Type of plot: Comedy
Time of plot: Second century B.C.
Locale: Athens
First presented: c. 195 B.C.

Principal characters:
EUCLIO, a miser
MEGADORUS, Euclio's rich neighbor, who wished to marry Euclio's daughter
EUNOMIA, Megadorus' sister
LYCONIDES, Eunomia's son, in love with Euclio's daughter
STAPHYLA, a slave belonging to Euclio

Critique:

Although the miser is unusual in Roman comedy, Plautus was not the first dramatist to use such a character, and he had as his models the older Greek dramatists who had made use of various kinds of misers in their plays. Menander, for instance, wrote three or possibly four plays which might have been Plautus' source or inspiration for his *The Pot of Gold.* Dating the Plautine play is difficult. Internal evidence indicates that the violation of Euclio's daughter occurred in August and that the play was produced for the Megalensian games, which were first held in 194 B.C. Like most Plautine comedies, this play had considerable influence on European drama. In the seventeenth century, versions by Ben Jonson, Molière, Thomas Shadwell, and Hooft appeared. Fielding's *The Miser,* written in the eighteenth century, also was based in part on this Plautine comedy.

The Story:

The grandfather of Euclio, an Athenian miser, had entrusted a pot of gold to his household deity after burying the pot within the hearth. The god, angered in turn at the grandfather, the father, and Euclio himself, had kept the secret of the treasure from all, until finally the daughter of Euclio had endeared herself to the god. In an effort to help the girl, the deity then showed Euclio where the gold was hidden, so that the miser, by using the money as a dower, might marry his daughter to Lyconides, the young man who had seduced her.

Euclio, miserly and distrustful by nature, was thrown into a feverish excitement by the discovery of the gold. He feared that someone would learn of its existence and either steal or gull it from him. After carefully hiding the gold in his house once more, he was afraid that even his old female slave, Staphyla, might learn of its whereabouts. Staphyla, in her turn, was worried by her master's strange behavior and by the fact that her young mistress was pregnant.

Meanwhile Megadorus, a wealthy neighbor and uncle of Lyconides, planned to marry Euclio's daughter, and he enlisted the aid of his sister Eunomia in his suit. Megadorus said that he was so pleased with the girl's character that he would marry her, contrary to the Athenian custom, without a dowry.

Seeing Euclio in the street, Megadorus went out to ask the old miser for his daughter's hand. Euclio, distrustful because of his new-found gold, thought Megadorus was actually plotting to take the gold from him. But Megadorus assured him that all he wanted was to marry the girl, with or without a dowry; even offered to pay the expenses of the wedding. Upon these terms Euclio agreed to marry his daughter to Megadorus. After Megadorus left, however, Euclio could not convince himself that the prospective bridegroom was not after the pot of gold.

Euclio informed Staphyla of the proposed marriage, which was to take place the same day. Staphyla, knowing that when Euclio's daughter was married she could not conceal her pregnancy, immediately began to wory about her mistress. Staphyla had little time to worry, however, for very shortly a caterer, bringing cooks, entertainers, and food, arrived at Euclio's house to prepare the wedding feast. The caterer had been hired by Megadorus, as he had promised.

Returning from the market place with some incense and flowers to place on the altar of his household god, Euclio was horrified to see all the strangers bustling about his house, for he immediately thought they were seeking his pot of gold and would steal it from him. Euclio first drove all the caterer's people from the house in a fury and then removed his pot of gold from its hiding place. After he had removed it from the house he told them to return to their work.

Euclio decided to take the gold and hide it in the nearby temple of Faith. On the way he met Megadorus, who asked Euclio to join him in drinking a bottle or two of wine. Euclio refused, suspecting that Megadorus wanted to get him drunk and then steal the pot of gold. Going on to the temple of Faith, Euclio hid the money. Although he did not know it, a slave belonging to Lyconides, the young man who had violated Euclio's daughter, observed where the money was placed. The slave took the money from its hiding place, but Euclio, rushing back to see if it was still safe, prevented the theft.

In an effort to find a safe hiding place for his gold, Euclio took it to the grove of Silvanus. The slave, anxious to please his master and repay Euclio for a beating, watched where Euclio hid the gold in the grove.

In the meantime, Lyconides, having learned of Megadorus' plans to marry Euclio's daughter, went to Eunomia, his mother, and told her that he himself wanted to marry the girl. Pressed by Eunomia for his reasons, Lyconides revealed that he had violated the girl while he

was drunk and wished to make amends by marrying her. Even as they spoke, the excitement in Euclio's house among the women told Eunomia and Lyconides that the baby had been born to Euclio's daughter. Eunomia then agreed to help her son marry the girl.

Lyconides went to Euclio to tell of his guilt in violating the miser's daughter. He found Euclio greatly upset, for the miser had just discovered the theft of his gold from Silvanus' grove. Lyconides believed that Euclio was angry with him because he had fathered the daughter's child. Euclio, on the other hand, thought that the crime to which Lyconides was confessing was the theft of the gold. Finally the young man convinced Euclio that he had not stolen the miser's gold. He then told Euclio about his violation of the girl and the birth of the child Megadorus, in the meantime, had renounced the girl. Euclio, who had looked forward to the marriage of his daughter and the rich Megadorus, felt that he was utterly betrayed by the world.

After Euclio and Lyconides parted, the slave appeared and told Lyconides about the pot of gold he had stolen. Lyconides insisted that the slave bring the gold to him. After a lengthy argument the slave reluctantly obeyed; he hated to think that the gold would be returned to miserly Euclio.

When the slave brought the gold to Lyconides, the young man went to the house of Euclio and returned the treasure. The miser, glad to have the pot of gold once more in his hands, was so happy that he readily agreed to a marriage between his daughter and Lyconides, in spite of the fact that Lyconides had violated the girl and caused her to bear a child out of wedlock.

Strangely enough, after the wedding Euclio had a change of heart and gave the entire pot of gold to the newly wedded couple.

POWER

Type of work: Novel
Author: Lion Feuchtwanger (1884-   )
Type of plot: Historical novel
Time of plot: Mid-eighteenth century
Locale: Germany
First published: 1925

Principal characters:

JOSEF Süss OPPENHEIMER, a court favorite
RABBI GABRIEL, his uncle
NAEMI, his daughter
KARL ALEXANDER, the Duke
MARIE AUGUSTE, the Duchess
WEISSENSEE, a politician
MAGDALEN SIBYLLE, his daughter

Critique:

What is a Jew? What causes a Jew, in the midst of disdain, antipathy, and persecution, to remain a Jew? Feuchtwanger deals with this problem through his fictional minister, Josef Süss Oppenheimer, the half-Christian Jew who chose to remain a Jew until his death. Subtly, Feuchtwanger shows us the metamorphosis of a rank materialist. At first Süss chose to remain a Jew because he wanted to be the greatest Jew in Germany. As a Christian he could never be at the top. At the end, he chose Judaism because he found inspiration in its teachings. The outer Süss was no more than a moneymonger, but the inner man was sensitive and human.

The Story:

All of Prussia rejoiced, and European courts lost their best topic of scandal when Duke Eberhard Ludwig broke with the countess who had been his mistress and returned to his wife to beget another heir to the throne. The countess had been his mistress for thirty years, bleeding the country with her extravagant demands for wealth and jewels. Ludwig was too vain, however, to remain her lover when she grew fat and middle-aged.

The countess sent for Isaac Landauer, the wealthy international banker who was her financial agent. Unable to advise her as to the means by which she could keep her hold on the duke, he offered to liquidate her possessions and send them to another province. But the countess, who had a strong belief in black magic, insisted that Landauer must bring to her the Wandering Jew to help cast a spell on Ludwig.

Landauer went to his young friend, Joseph Süss Oppenheimer, and offered half of what his dealings with the countess would bring him, if the young man would aid Landauer in the countess' scheme. The so-called Wandering Jew was an uncle of Süss, Rabbi Gabriel, whose melancholy demeanor and mystic ways had caused people to think that he was the legendary Wandering Jew. Süss considered the offer. It was tempting, but for some unknown reason the young man was half afraid of his uncle, whose presence always instilled in his nephew a feeling of inferiority. Furthermore, Rabbi Gabriel was rearing motherless, fourteen-year-old Naemi, the daughter whom Süss wished to conceal from the rest of the world. But at last he sent for Rabbi Gabriel.

Penniless Prince Karl Alexander came to Wildbad in hopes of gaining the grant of a substantial income from the duke. Süss, discovering the poverty of the prince, made himself the financial adviser of that destitute nobleman. Al-

POWER by Lion Feuchtwanger. Translated by Willa and Edwin Muir. By permission of the publishers, The Viking Press, Inc. Copyright, 1926, by The Viking Press, Inc.

though Landauer warned him that Karl Alexander was a poor risk, Süss continued his association with the prince merely because he hoped to ingratiate himself with the nobility. Half in gratitude, half in jest, the prince granted Süss admission to his levees.

On his arrival in Wildbad, Rabbi Gabriel told Süss that he intended to bring Naemi to his nephew. But Landauer no longer needed Gabriel to help carry out the countess' scheme, and the rabbi returned to his home. The countess had been banished from the duchy, taking with her the money procured by Landauer.

Süss became the favorite of Prince Karl Alexander. To Wildbad also came Prince Anselm Franz von Thurn and Taxis and his daughter, Princess Marie Auguste. Their mission was to urge Prince Karl Alexander to marry the princess and turn Catholic. Angry because the duke had refused to give him a pension, the prince consented.

Duke Eberhard Ludwig died suddenly, and Karl Alexander, now a Catholic, inherited the duchy. Süss became a court favorite, appointed by the new duchess to be keeper of her privy purse. Although Jews were forbidden to live in the duchy, the people had to acknowledge that the duke should be allowed his private court Jew.

Rabbi Gabriel had bought a little white house where he lived with Naemi and a servant. For three days, while the uncle was away, Süss went to Hirsau to visit his daughter. Then he returned to his duke. Since Karl Alexander's succession Süss had slyly directed him in measures which were resulting in a complete control of Swabia by the duke himself. The Constitution and the Parliament were powerless. Great noblemen had been ruined. Although his income was enormous, Süss himself refrained from holding any office. Süss had picked one former cabinet member, Weissensee, as President of the Ecclesiastical Council. One night he gave a party to which Weissensee brought his daughter, Magdalen Sibylle. Süss, noting the duke's attentiveness toward the girl, enticed her into his bedroom, where the duke followed. After that evening, the duke sent gifts to Magdalen Sibylle, his declared mistress, and Weissensee was promoted to a high office. Hating Süss, Weissensee secretly hoped to bring the favorite into disfavor at court. Learning that Süss had a daughter, he planned to place the Jew in the same position that Süss had placed him on the night Karl Alexander had taken Magdalen Sibylle.

The murder of a child revived the old legend that Jews sacrificed a Christian child at the Passover feast, and a Jew, Reb Jeckeskel Seligmann, was arrested for the crime. Pressure was put on Süss to use his power to save the innocent man, but he refused because of the danger to his position at court. Then Rabbi Gabriel sent word to Süss that Naemi had heard rumors of his wickedness. At last Süss decided that he would help the arrested man. In rescuing Seligmann, he felt anew his power as the court Jew. Soon afterward, at the request of Rabbi Gabriel, he went to visit his mother. From her he learned that his real father had been a great Christian marshal in the German army. Confused, Süss finally decided that he was a Jew and would remain so.

Convinced at last that Süss was a swindler, the duke threatened to dismiss and dishonor him. But when Süss offered his own fortune in exchange for proof of any financial trickery, the duke changed his mind and roared his anger at the enemies of Süss. Realizing that the favorite now had more power than ever, Weissensee continued to plot his revenge. Arranging for the duke to spend some time at his home in Hirsau while Rabbi Gabriel was not at home, Weissensee took the duke to Süss' daughter. With visions of a heavenly rescue, the quiet, lonely child climbed to the roof of the house to escape from her attacker. She fell from the roof to her death.

Outwardly Süss professed forgiveness

toward the duke, but he pocketed more and more funds from the ducal treasury. His personality altered. Instead of ingratiating himself at court, he criticized and ridiculed his acquaintances. Filling the duke's head with dreams of conquest, Süss inveigled him into leading a new military coup. At the same time he planned the duke's destruction. While Karl Alexander lay dying at the scene of his defeat, Süss rained over his head a torrent of pent-up abuse. His enemies ordered his arrest.

For many months the case against Süss dragged on. Finally he was put into a stinking, rat-infested hole, where every day the authorities plied him for a confession, but he remained stubbornly alive and sane. Sentenced to hang, he assailed the court with icy, cutting words. He could have freed himself by declaring his Christian birth. He kept silent.

On the day of the hanging Süss died with the name "Adonai," the Hebrew name for God, on his lips, and the word was echoed by all the Jews who had gathered to watch him die.

THE POWER AND THE GLORY

Type of work: Novel
Author: Graham Greene (1904-   )
Type of plot: Psychological realism
Time of plot: The 1930's
Locale: Mexico
First published: 1940

Principal characters:
FATHER MONTEZ, a fugitive priest
MARCÍA, the mother of his child
FATHER JOSÉ, a renegade priest
A LIEUTENANT OF POLICE
A POOR MESTIZO

Critique:

This novel reflects the author's interest in Mexico and his experience as a resident of that country. It is not surprising that he should write a sympathetic novel about the persecution of priests in Mexico, since Greene himself is a convert and his serious novels are in keeping with Catholic idiom and doctrine. In this book he deals, as usual, with the psychology of the individual. *The Power and the Glory* was published in the United States in 1940 under the title *The Labyrinthine Ways*. It proved unpopular. A new edition, with the original title restored, has increased the body of readers familiar with the novel. In particular, Greene is a master of suspense.

The Story:

In a particular Mexican state the Church had been outlawed and the priests driven underground by the threat of being shot. After several months, word went out from the governor's office that there was still one priest, Father Montez, who was moving from village to village carrying on the work of the Church by administering the sacraments and saying masses. A young lieutenant of police, an ardent revolutionist and an anti-clerical, persuaded his chief to let him search for the priest who, as the authorities saw it, was guilty of treason.

Two photographs were pasted up together in the police station. One was the picture of an American bank robber who had killed several police officers in Texas; the other was that of the priest. No one noticed the irony, least of all the young lieutenant, who was far more interested in arresting the clergyman. While the officer was receiving permission to make a search for Father Montez, the priest was already in the village, having come there in order to get aboard a boat that would take him to the city of Vera Cruz and safety.

Before Father Montez could board the boat word came to him that an Indian woman was dying several miles inland. True to his calling, the priest mounted a mule and set out to administer the last rites to the dying woman, even though he realized that he might not find another ship to carry him to safety. There was one other priest in the vicinity, Father José. But Father José had been cowardly enough to renounce the Church, even to the point of taking a wife, a shrewish old woman. The authorities paid no attention to him at all, for they felt, and rightly so, that the priest who had renounced his vows was a detriment and a shame to the Church.

After completing his mission, Father Montez came back to the coast, where he spent the night in a banana warehouse. The English manager on the plantation allowed him to hide there.

THE POWER AND THE GLORY by Graham Greene. By permission of the publishers, The Viking Press, Inc. Copyright, 1940, by Graham Greene.

The following day, hoping to find refuge from the police and from the revolutionary party of Red Shirts, he set out on muleback for the interior. As he traveled, he thought of his own past and of himself as a poor example of the priesthood. For Father Montez was a whiskey priest, a cleric who would do almost anything for a drink of spirits. In addition, he had in a moment of weakness fathered a child by a woman in an inland village. Thinking himself a weak man and a poor priest, he was still determined to carry on the work of the Church as long as he could, not because he wanted to be a martyr but because he knew nothing else to do.

After twelve hours of travel he reached the village where his one-time mistress and his child lived. The woman took him in overnight, and the following morning he said a mass for the villagers. Before he could escape the police entered the village. Marcía claimed him as her husband, and his child, a little grown girl of seven, named him as her father. In that manner, because of his earlier sins, he escaped. Meanwhile the police had decided on a new tactic in uncovering the fugitive. As they passed through each village they took a hostage. When a certain length of time had passed without the apprehension of Father Montez, a hostage was shot. In that manner the lieutenant of police in charge of the hunt hoped to persuade the people to betray their priest.

After the police had left the village without discovering him, Father Montez mounted his mule and went on his way. He traveled northward in an effort to escape the police and, if possible, to make his way temporarily into another state.

Some hours after leaving the village, Father Montez met with a mestizo who fell in with him. Before long the halfbreed discovered that Father Montez was the priest for whom the police were searching. He promised that he, a good Catholic, would not betray the secret, but Father Montez was afraid that the promised reward of seven hundred pesos would be too much of a temptation for the poor man.

When they reached a town, however, it was Father Montez' own weakness which put him into the hands of the police. He had to have some liquor, the sale of which was against the law. He managed to buy some illegally, but his possession of the contraband was discovered by one of the revolutionary Red Shirts, who raised a cry after him. Tracked down by a posse, the priest was caught and placed in jail. Fortunately, he was not recognized by the police, but since he had no money he was kept in jail to work out the fine.

The lieutenant of police who was searching feverishly for him unexpectedly did Father Montez a good turn. Seeing the ragged old man working about the jail, the lieutenant stopped to talk with him. The priest claimed to be a vagrant who had no home of his own. The lieutenant, feeling sorry for the old fellow, released him and gave him a present of five pesos. Leaving town, Father Montez started out across the country to find a place of temporary safety. After traveling for some time, he met an Indian woman who could speak only a few words of Spanish. She managed to make him understand that something was wrong with her child. He went with her and found that the baby had been shot; his immediate guess was that the American bandit had done the deed.

After performing rites over the child, Father Montez continued his flight. He eventually made his way into the next state, where he was given sanctuary by a German plantation owner. After resting a few days, he planned to go to a city and there present his problems to his bishop. Before he could leave, however, he was found by the mestizo, who said that the American bandit, a Catholic, was dying and needed the priest. Father Montez answered the call, even though he was sure he was being led into a trap. The bandit was really dying, but he lay in the state from which Father Montez had just escaped. With him was a party of police, waiting for the priest's appearance in order to arrest him.

Immediately after the bandit's death the police closed in and Father Montez was captured. Taken back to the capital of the state and tried for treason, he was found guilty and sentenced to be shot. The lieutenant of police, who felt sorry in a way for the old priest, tried to persuade the renegade Father José to hear Father Montez' last confession, but Father José, who feared the authorities, refused. Father Montez was led out and shot without the benefit of the Church's grace. Yet the lieutenant of police had not succeeded in removing the Church's influence; in the evening of the day on which Father Montez died another priest made his way, in secret, into the town where the execution had taken place.

THE POWER OF DARKNESS

Type of work: Drama
Author: Count Leo Tolstoy (1828-1910)
Type of plot: Domestic tragedy
Time of plot: Nineteenth century
Locale: Russia
First presented: 1886

Principal characters:
NIKÍTA AKÍMITCH TCHILÍKIN, a laborer
ANÍSYA, his mistress
PETER IGNÁTITCH, Anísya's husband, a well-to-do peasant
MATRYÓNA, Nikíta's mother
AKÍM, Nikíta's father
AKOULÍNA, Peter's daughter by his first marriage
MARÍNA, an orphan girl

Critique:

This play on a theme of sin and redemption is embodied in the traditional Russian conflict of father against son, of the natural against the artificial life. Nikíta finds himself led into adultery and murder almost unknowingly, the implication being that evil is a state into which anyone can fall unless he is diligently wary of it. The plot may seem unexciting because of the didactic way in which Tolstoy deals with the evils of idleness, greed, and luxury, but his ability to depict the triumph of spiritual humility over materialistic arrogance must still be admired.

The Story:

Peter Ignátitch, a well-to-do peasant, was forty-two years old and sickly. His second wife, Anísya, was only thirty-two. She still felt young and had started an affair with Nikíta, their hired man. Peter, who considered Nikíta a loafer, had thought of dismissing him. As he was explaining his intention to his wife they learned that Nikíta was talking about getting married and leaving their farm. Anísya complained to Peter that Nikíta's departure would leave her with more work than she could handle.

When Anísya and Nikíta were alone, he told her that in spite of his marriage plans he would always come back to her. Anísya threatened to do violence to herself if Nikíta went away, adding that when her husband died Nikíta could marry her and become master of the farm. Nikíta declared, however, that he was satisfied with his lot. Then Matryóna, Nikíta's mother, came in and said that Nikíta's marriage was his father's plan, not her own, and that he need not worry about it. She then asked Nikíta to leave the room.

Left alone with Matryóna, Anísya confessed her love for Nikíta. Matryóna, who said that she had known of their affair all along, gave Anísya some poison and advised her to bury her husband before spring; she suggested also that Nikíta would make a good master on the farm. Concerning the marriage, she explained that Nikíta had had an affair with Marína, an orphan girl, and that when Akím, his father, learned about it he had insisted that Nikíta marry her. Matryóna had suggested that they talk the matter over with Peter, who was Nikíta's master. Having explained the situation, Matryóna again urged Anísya to use the poison on Peter, who was near death anyway.

At that point Peter and Akím came in, discussing Nikíta's proposed marriage.

THE POWER OF DARKNESS by Count Leo Tolstoy, from THE PLAYS OF LEO TOLSTOY. Translated by Louise and Aylmer Maude. By permission of the publishers, Amen House. Copyright, 1910, by Constable & Co. Copyright, 1923, by Oxford University Press, Inc. Renewed. All rights reserved.

Peter seemed to approve of the match until Matryóna told him that Marína was promiscuous and so had no claim on Nikíta. To determine the truth of this charge, Peter sent for Nikíta, who falsely swore that there had been nothing between him and Marína. As a result, the marriage was called off. Nikíta was then visited by Marína, who pleaded her love and said that she had always been faithful to him. Nikíta sent her away, saying that he was no longer interested in her.

Six months later Anísya and Matryóna were worried because Peter was about to die but had not told anyone where his money pouch was hidden. Anísya also told Matryóna that she had put the poison into Peter's tea. As they stood talking in the courtyard, Peter appeared on the porch of his house, saw Nikíta, who was happening by, and asked his forgiveness, a formal request made by the dying. Nikíta was temporarily struck with remorse. Matryóna, who then helped Peter back into the house, discovered that the money pouch was hanging by a cord around the sick man's neck. Anísya went into the house and came out again with the money pouch, which she gave to Nikíta. She then returned to the house, only to reappear a short time later, wailing a formal lament for Peter, who had just died.

Nine months after Peter's death, Nikíta, who had married Anísya and become the master of the farm, grew tired of his wife and began an affair with Akoulína, Peter's daughter by his first marriage. Anísya was afraid to say anything for fear that her murder of Peter would be discovered.

In the following autumn, Matryóna arranged a marriage for Akoulína, who had become pregnant by Nikíta. Matryóna told the father of the suitor that Akoulína herself could not be seen because she was sickly; at that moment, in fact, Akoulína was delivering her child in the barn. Nikíta could not decide what to do about the child, but Anísya gave him a spade and told him to dig a hole in the cellar.

Nikíta balked at the suggestion, feeling that he was not to blame for all his troubles. Anísya, happy that she could force Nikíta into sharing her own guilt, told him that he was already guilty because he knew that she had poisoned Peter and because he had accepted Peter's money pouch. At last Nikíta went to the cellar and dug the hole.

When Anísya brought the baby to him, covered with rags, Nikíta was horrified to discover that the infant was still alive. Anísya and Matryóna pushed Nikíta into the cellar, where he murdered the baby. After he had completed the deed he reappeared in a frenzy, threatening to kill his mother and claiming that he could still hear the baby whimpering. He then went off to forget his troubles in drink.

Some time after that Akoulína's wedding feast was held at Nikíta's farm. Nikíta saw Marína, who had been able to marry respectably and who was now a wedding guest. Alone and troubled, he told Marína that his only happiness had been with her. Distraught, Marína left Nikíta to himself. Then Matryóna and Anísya came to tell him that the bridal pair awaited his formal blessing. Feeling that it would be impossible to give his blessing, Nikíta thought of committing suicide until Mítritch, a drunken ex-soldier, appeared and began to talk of his experiences, concluding with the thought that a person should never be afraid of anyone. With this thought in mind, Nikíta decided to join the wedding feast.

When Nikíta appeared before the guests he was holding Akím by the hand. Suddenly, instead of blessing the bridal pair, he fell on his knees before his father. Proclaiming that he was guilty and wished to make his confession, he begged forgiveness of Marína, whom he had misused, and of Akoulína, saying that he had poisoned Peter. Although Akoulína said that she knew who had poisoned her father, a police officer, who happened to be a guest at the wedding, wanted to arrest Nikíta immediately. Akím prevented him by saying that his son must attend to God's business first. Nikíta then confessed that he had seduced Akoulína and murdered her child. Finally, turning again to his father, Nikíta asked for his forgiveness. Akím told him that God would forgive him and show him mercy. Nikíta was then bound and led away.

PRAGMATISM

Type of work: Philosophical essays
Author: William James (1842-1910)
First published: 1907

No more illuminating or entertaining account of pragmatism has ever been written than James's *Pragmatism: A New Name for Some Old Ways of Thinking.* But this is more than a popular exposition prepared for the academic audiences of Lowell Institute and Columbia University during the winter of 1906-1907: it is historic philosophy in the making. Although James was profoundly influenced by Charles Sanders Peirce, who invented the basic statement and name of pragmatism, he was an independent thinker with a distinctive creative direction of his own.

Peirce's essay, "How to Make Our Ideas Clear," introduced the pragmatic notion that ideas are clarified by considering what we would expect in the way of experience if we were to act in a certain manner. The whole of our conception of the "sensible effects" of an object is the whole of our conception of the objects, according to Peirce. This essay, clear, radical, entertaining, appeared in the *Popular Science Monthly* in January, 1878. But professional philosophers were not interested in theory advanced by a mathematician, particularly when the theory went against the prevailing idealism of American philosophers. It was not until James revived the idea in 1898 with a talk on "Philosophical Conceptions and Practical Results" that the pragmatic philosophy began to stir up controversy. With the lectures on meaning and truth which were published under the titles *Pragmatism* and *The Meaning of Truth,* the former in 1907 and the latter in 1909, James brought pragmatism into the forefront of American thought.

In his first lecture on "The Present Dilemma in Philosophy," James distinguished between the "tender-minded" and the "tough-minded" in temperament,

the former inclining toward a philosophy that is rational, religious, dogmatic, idealistic, and optimistic, and the latter, the tough-minded, inclining toward a philosophy that is empirical, irreligious, skeptical, materialistic, and pessimistic. He then went on to state his conviction that philosophy can satisfy both temperaments by becoming pragmatic.

His lecture on the pragmatic method begins with one of the most entertaining anecdotes in philosophical discourse. James describes a discussion by a group of philosophers on this question: Does a man go around a squirrel that is on a tree trunk if the squirrel keeps moving on the tree so that the trunk is always between himself and the man? Some of the philosophers claimed that the man did not go around the squirrel, while others claimed that he did. James settled the matter by saying, "Which party is right depends on what you *practically mean* by 'going round' the squirrel." It could be said that the man goes around the squirrel since he passes from the north of the squirrel to the east, south, and west of the squirrel. On the other hand, the man could be said not to go around the squirrel since he is never able to get on the various sides of the squirrel—on the right of him, then behind him, and so forth. "Make the distinction," James said, "and there is no occasion for any further dispute."

James then applied the method to a number of perennial philosophical problems, but only after a careful exposition of the meaning of pragmatism. He described the pragmatic method as a way of interpreting ideas by discovering their practical consequences—that is, the difference the idea's truth would make in our experience. He asks, "What difference would it practically make to anyone if this notion rather than that notion were true?" and he replies, "If no practical difference whatever can be traced, then the alternatives mean practically the same thing, and all dispute is idle."

In his lecture James argued that the pragmatic method was not new: Socrates, Aristotle, Locke, Berkeley, and Hume had used it. But what was new was the explicit formulation of the method and a new faith in its power. Pragmatism is to be understood, however, not as a set of grand theories but as a method which turns attention away from first principles and absolutes and directs it to facts, consequences, and results in our experience.

A bare declaration would hardly have been enough to make pragmatism famous. James devoted a considerable part of his lectures to brief examples of the application of the pragmatic method. He cited with approval Berkeley's analysis of matter as made up of sensations. Sensations, he said, "are the cash-value of the term. The difference matter makes to us by truly being is that we then get such sensations. . . ." Similarly, Locke applied the pragmatic method, James claimed, when he discovered that unless by "spirit" we mean consciousness, we mean nothing by the term.

Is materialism or theism true? Is the universe simply matter acting and interacting, or is God involved? James considers this problem pragmatically and reaches a curious result. As far as the past is concerned, he says, it makes no difference. If rival theories are meant to explain what is the case and if it makes no difference in our experience which theory is true, then the theories do not differ in meaning. If one considers the difference now and in the future, however, the case is different: "Materialism means simply the denial that the moral order is eternal . . . spiritualism means the affirmation of an eternal moral order and the letting loose of hope."

To this kind of analysis some critics have answered with the charge that James is one of the "tender-minded" philosophers he spoke harshly of in his earlier lectures. But throughout the course of this series of lectures and in subse-

quent books James continued to use pragmatism as a way of combining the tough and tender temperaments. He extended the use of the term "difference" so that the meaning of an idea or term was no longer to be understood merely in terms of sense experiences, as Peirce had urged, but also in terms of passionate differences, of effects upon human hopes and fears. The essays in *Pragmatism* show this liberalizing tendency hard at work.

The temperate tone of James's suggestions concerning the religious hypothesis is clear in one of his later lectures in the book, "Pragmatism and Religion," in which he writes that "Pragmatism has to postpone dogmatic answer, for we do not yet know certainly which type of religion is going to work best in the long run." He states again that the tough-minded can be satisfied with "the hurly-burly of the sensible facts of nature," and that the tender-minded can take up a monistic form of religion; but for those who mix temperaments, as James does, a religious synthesis that is moralistic and pluralistic, allowing for human development and creativity in various directions, is to be preferred.

Pragmatism is important not only as a clear statement of the pragmatic method and as an illustration of its application to certain central problems, but also as an exposition, although introductory, of James's pragmatic theory of truth. His ideas were developed more fully two years later in *The Meaning of Truth*.

Beginning with the common notion that truth is a property of ideas that agree with reality, James proceeded to ask what was meant by the term "agreement." He decided that the conception of truth as a static relation between an idea and reality was in error, that pragmatic analysis shows that true ideas are those which can eventually be verified, and that an idea is said to be verified when it leads us usefully to an anticipated conclusion. Since verification is a process, it becomes appropriate to say that truth "happens to" an idea, and that an idea "*becomes* true, is *made* true by events." A revealing summary statement is this: " 'The true,' to put it very briefly, is only the expedient in the way of our thinking, just as 'the right' is only the expedient in the way of our behaving."

The ambiguity of James's account, an ambiguity which he did not succeed in removing, allows extremes of interpretation. On the one hand, a reader might take the tender-minded route, something in the manner of James himself, and argue that all kinds of beliefs about God, freedom, and immortality are true in so far as they lead a man usefully in the course of his life. On the other hand, a tough-minded reader might be inclined to agree with James that an idea is true if the expectations in terms of which the idea makes sense are expectations that would be met, if one acted—but he might reject James's suggestions that this means that a great many ideas which would ordinarily be regarded as doubtful "become true" when they satisfy the emotional needs of a believer.

One difficulty with which James was forced to deal because of his theory of truth resulted, it might be argued, not from his idea of truth as the "workableness" of an idea, but from his inadequate analyses of the meanings of certain terms such as "God," "freedom" and "design." James maintained that, pragmatically speaking, these terms all meant the same thing, viz., the presence of "promise" in the world. If this were so, then it would be plausible to suppose that if the idea that the world is promising works out, the idea is true. But if James's analysis is mistaken, if "God" means more than the possibility of things working out for the better, James's claim that beliefs about God are true if they work loses its plausibility.

Whatever its philosophic faults, *Pragmatism* is saved by its philosophic virtues. For the general reader it offers the rare experience of confronting first-rate ideas by way of a clear and entertaining, even informal, style.

THE PRAIRIE

Type of work: Novel
Author: James Fenimore Cooper (1789-1851)
Type of plot: Historical romance
Time of plot: 1804
Locale: Western Plains of the United States
First published: 1827

Principal characters:
NATTY BUMPPO, an old frontiersman
ISHMAEL BUSH, a desperado
ESTHER BUSH, his wife
ELLEN WADE, Esther's niece
ABIRAM WHITE, Esther's brother
DR. BATTIUS, a naturalist
PAUL HOVER, Ellen's lover
CAPTAIN MIDDLETON, of the United States Army
INEZ, Middleton's wife
HARD-HEART, a Pawnee chief

Critique:

This novel, the fifth and last volume of Cooper's familiar Leatherstocking series, closes the career of his famous frontiersman and scout, Natty Bumppo The plot is full of incident, but it depends too much on coincidence to seem realistic to many modern readers. The character portrayal is not vivid; the women, especially, seem dull and unreal. Much of the action is slowed down by the stilted dialogue. Yet, in spite of these defects, *The Prairie* catches much of the spirit of the old West.

The Story:

Shortly after the time of the Louisiana Purchase the family of Ishmael Bush traveled westward from the Mississippi River. Ishmael was accompanied by his wife, Esther, and their sons and daughters. Also in the caravan were Ellen Wade, a niece of Esther; Abiram White, Esther's brother; and Dr. Battius, a physician and naturalist. As this company searched for a camping place one evening, they met an aged trapper, Natty Bumppo, and his dog. The trapper directed them to a nearby stream.

After night had fallen, Bumppo discovered Ellen in a secret meeting with her lover, Paul Hover, a wandering bee hunter. The three were captured by a band of Sioux. While the Indian raiders stole all the horses and cattle from Ishmael's party, the captives made their escape. Unable to proceed across the prairie, the emigrant family occupied a naturally fortified hilltop shown to them by Bumppo.

A week later, Paul, Bumppo, and Dr. Battius were gathered at Bumppo's camping ground. They were soon joined by a stranger, who introduced himself as Captain Middleton of the United States Army. Bumppo was delighted to find that Middleton was the grandson of an old friend whom he had known in the days of the French and Indian wars. The young officer had come to find his wife, Inez, who had been kidnaped by Abiram White shortly after her marriage. She was now a captive in Ishmael's camp. Paul, Bumppo, and Dr. Battius agreed to help Middleton rescue her.

On the same day Ishmael and his sons left their camp to hunt buffalo. That evening they returned with meat, but Asa, the oldest son, did not return with the rest of the hunters. In the morning the entire family set out to search for him. At last his dead body was found in a thicket; he had been shot in the back with one of Bumppo's bullets. His family buried him and returned to camp. There they found that both Ellen and Inez were gone.

3036

The girls, who had been rescued by Middleton and his friends, were rapidly making their escape across the prairie, when their progress was interrupted by a meeting with a Pawnee warrier, Hard-Heart. After the Indian had galloped away on his horse, the travelers found themselves in the path of a stampeding herd of buffalo. The group was saved from being trampled to death at the last moment by the braying of Dr. Battius' donkey, for at the strange sound the buffalo turned aside. However, Middleton's party was soon captured by a band of Sioux pursuing the buffalo herd. They were the same Indians who had captured Bumppo, Paul, and Ellen once before. At the same time Ishmael and his sons approached on foot in search of the two girls. The Indians remounted and gave horses to their captives so that all could ride to Ishmael's camp while he and his sons were away. During the Indian raid on the camp, Bumppo helped his friends escape on horseback.

They rode as far as possible before making camp for the night. But in the morning they found that the Sioux had followed them and had set fire to the prairie in order to drive them into the open. Bumppo rescued the party by burning off the nearby prairie before the larger fire reached it. As they started off, they met the lone Hard-Heart again. From him they learned that the Sioux and Ishmael's family had joined forces in order to search for them. Since Hard-Heart and the little band had a common enemy in the Sioux, he agreed to take them to his Pawnee village for protection.

In order to evade their pursuers, the fugitives crossed a nearby river. As they reached the far bank the Sioux appeared on the opposite shore. That night the fugitives remained free, but snow fell and made it impossible for them to escape without being tracked. They were captured and taken to the Sioux village.

Hard-Heart, Paul, and Middleton were bound by their savage captors. Out of respect for his age, Bumppo was allowed to roam freely, but he declined to leave his friends. The women were placed in the lodge of the Sioux chief.

Using Bumppo as an interpreter, the Sioux chief asked Inez to be his wife. At the same time Ishmael asked the chief to hand over to him Inez, Ellen, and Bumppo, as had been previously agreed. When the chief refused, Ishmael departed angrily.

The Indians then gathered in council to decide the fate of Hard-Heart, and many wished to torture him to death. But an old warrier stepped forward and declared that he wished to make the Pawnee his adopted son. Hard-Heart, however, refused to become a member of the Sioux tribe. The Sioux began their torture, but in the midst of it Hard-Heart escaped and joined a war party of his own Pawnees, who arrived on the scene at that moment.

Leaving their women to guard the prisoners, the Sioux prepared to fight. The braves of the two tribes gathered on the opposite banks of a river, neither side daring to make the first move. Then Hard-Heart challenged the Sioux chief to single combat.

Meanwhile, Bumppo helped the rest of the captives to escape. Shortly afterward they fell once more into the hands of Ishmael.

Hard-Heart was victorious in the single-handed combat, and his warriors put the Sioux to flight in the battle which followed.

The next morning Ishmael held a court of justice in order to deal with his captives. He realized his mistake in carrying Inez away from her husband and allowed the couple their freedom. He gave Ellen her choice of remaining with his family or going with Paul. She chose to go with her lover. Ishmael allowed Dr. Battius his freedom because he did not think the scientist worth bothering about. Then Bumppo came up for judgment.

Ishmael still believed that Bumppo had shot his son, Asa. Bumppo, however, revealed that it was really Abiram who had done the cowardly deed. Abiram confessed his crime and then fainted. Ishmael was reluctant to pronounce judgment on his brother-in-law, but he felt it his duty to do so. That evening he gave Abiram the choice of starving to death or hanging himself. Late that night Ishmael and Esther returned to find that Abiram had hanged himself. They buried him and continued on their way back to the frontier settlements.

Middleton, Paul, and the girls invited Bumppo to return to the settlements with them, where they would make comfortable his last days. He refused, giving as his reason his desire to die away from civilization. He chose to remain in the Pawnee village with Hard-Heart.

A year later, when Middleton's duties as an army officer brought him near the Pawnee village, he determined to pay Bumppo a visit. Arriving at the camp, Middleton found the old trapper near death. It was late afternoon. Bumppo revived enough to greet his old friend. At sundown, however, he seemed to be breathing his last. As the sun sank beneath the horizon, he made one last tremendous effort. He rose to his feet and, as if answering a roll call, he uttered a loud and firm "Here" — then fell back dead into the arms of his friends.

THE PRAISE OF FOLLY

Type of work: Essay
Author: Desiderius Erasmus (1466?-1536)
First published: 1511

Although written some four hundred and fifty years ago, *The Praise of Folly* is still an effective analytic examination of man's abilities and vanities. It not only gives the modern reader an idea of the struggle of the early humanists in their effort to rid the world of the conventions and forms of the Middle Ages, but it also gives him some insight into those problems of living with which we are still faced today.

Erasmus himself never thought very highly of this work which, even though written quickly and as something of a jest, is the one for which he is best remembered. He wrote it in about seven days in 1509 while he was recovering from an illness at the home of his English friend, Sir Thomas More. And it was not until two years after its writing that he had the book secretly printed in France. However, the fact that there were at least seven editions within a few months proves its immediate success and popularity.

Because of this work and several others Erasmus became one of the most popular men of letters of his time, and, consequently, he became one of the most influential. He was of prime importance in the spread of humanism throughout the northern part of Europe and was instrumental in many aspects of both the Reformation and the later phase of the Renaissance. Everything he did was to aid man in tearing away the veils of foolish traditions and customs and to help him find the road back to the true God and to his true self.

The form itself is an immediate indication of the type of work that the book is to be. Written as a parody of a classical oration, the essay sets Folly as the orator. Her subject is society and she quickly becomes a many-sided symbol which stands for all that is natural in man, for all his misdirected effort, and for all of his attempts to get the wrong things out of life. She discusses the problem of man's wisdom and tells how it can be united with man's action to gain success in a world of folly; she is concerned with the way in which reason and simple Christian advice can be presented to mankind; she wonders what the Christian humanist can do for himself and the world. Parody, irony, and satire are used throughout the essay to show man what he does and what he should do. And no one is spared. Neither king nor prince, pope nor priest, aristocrat nor working man escapes the indignation which Erasmus feels toward society.

At the beginning of her oration Folly declares that she is giving a eulogy of herself, and she justifies the impertinence by saying that she knows herself better than anyone else and that no one else will do it for her. Her father, she says, is Plutus, the real father of all men and gods, and she was born out of his passion for Youth. Significantly, her birth took place in the Fortunate Isles, and she lists among her followers Drunkenness, Ignorance, Self-love, Flattery, Forgetfulness, Laziness, Pleasure, Madness, Sensuality, Intemperance, and Sound Sleep—all of whom help her to gain control of all things.

It is Folly, for instance, who leads man to marriage and the conception of life, thus prolonging this life that is so foolish. It is Pleasure, one of her followers, who makes life bearable at all. It is Forgetfulness who makes youth such a carefree time, and who restores this same characteristic to old age, thereby bringing about a second childhood. By throwing off care and avoiding wisdom, we are told, one can achieve perpetual youth.

Folly goes on to say that she is the source of all that is pleasurable in life.

Man will never be completely divorced from Folly because he is ruled more by passion than by reason, and the two most important aspects of passion are anger and lust. One of the chief sources of man's pleasure, of course, is women, who are even more subject to folly than men. Men's coarser looks are a result of the infection of wisdom.

Friendship also derives from Folly because it makes us ignore the faults and defects of other people. Marriage itself is held together with compromise, infatuation, and duplicity. Without Folly man could not get along with others; he would soon begin to hate himself and everything would seem sordid and loathsome.

Folly praises herself under the guise of Prudence because she allows man to have first-hand experience with the world. She frees us from the shame and fear which cloud our minds and inhibit our actions, thus preventing any real experience. Because of Prudence we go along with the crowd, which is Folly. Indeed, it is Folly who has caused all the great achievements of mankind, wisdom and learning are no great help. Everything that man does is motivated by self-love, vainglory, flattery, or other followers.

To lead such a life of folly, error, and ignorance is to be human; it is to express one's true nature. All other forms of life are content with limitations but man is vainly ambitious. The most ignorant men are the happiest and some of the most deluded men are those who delight in telling lies. As an example, we are asked to consider the priests—those who propose to gain happiness by relying on magic charms and prayers, saints and particular rites. One cannot find happiness, we are told, without Folly, since all our emotions belong to Folly, and happiness depends on expressing our human nature which is full of Folly.

One of the most foolish of men, therefore, is that person who tries to deny his true nature and find happiness through the Christian religion. Folly proves that this religion has more to do with her own nature than with wisdom by showing that children, women, old people and fools take more delight in it than anyone else. It is they who are always nearest the altars. In the way that Christianity is most often taught and practiced, man must deny his true nature by disdaining life and preferring death. He must overlook injuries, avoid pleasure, and feast on hunger, vigils, tears, and labors. He must give up and scorn all physical pleasures, or at least he must take them more lightly than he does spiritual pleasures.

Folly is at her most serious when she tells us that this is the most foolish way, and the only sure way, to true happiness. Only by forgetting our bodies and everything physical can we approach this goal. We must give ourselves up completely to the spiritual aspects of life in order to achieve it. Only a very few men are able to accomplish this task completely enough while in this world, in order to approach an experience which she tells us is very close to madness. This madness, in turn, is similar to the heavenly joys that one will experience after death when the spirit has completely left the body.

PRECIOUS BANE

Type of work: Novel
Author: Mary Webb (1881-1927)
Type of plot: Regional romance
Time of plot: Mid-nineteenth century
Locale: England
First published: 1924

> Principal characters:
> PRUDENCE SARN, a harelipped girl
> GIDEON, her brother
> WIZARD BEGUILDY, an evil neighbor
> JANCIS BEGUILDY, his daughter
> KESTER WOODSEAVES, the weaver

Critique:

Just as Prudence Sarn seemed to view the past events of her life through a veil, so she tells her story. The story is not autobiographical, but into it Mrs. Webb put many experiences of her own youth. In this novel man seems to be controlled by forces of nature. The Bane, the poison that was in Gideon Sarn, moved him even to murder, for powers outside him drove him beyond his will. But when nature was satisfied, the Bane was exorcised; and peace came to the Sarns.

The Story:

The country people said there had been something queer about the Sarn family ever since old Timothy Sarn was struck by forked lightning. The lightning seemed to have gone into Timothy and into all the Sarns. In Prue's father the lightning took the form of a raving temper, and in Prue's brother Gideon the lightning was the more frightening because it was quiet but deadly. Dogs and horses turned away from Gideon's gray eyes. Prue understood her brother better than most, but even she was frightened when Gideon offered to be the sin-eater at their father's funeral. For a sin-eater took the sins of the dead person and sold his soul for a price. Gideon's price was the farm which would have been his mother's. Mrs. Sarn feared to accept the terms, for a sin-eater's

destiny was dreadful; but she feared more to let her husband go to his grave with all his sins, and so she gave Gideon the farm.

On the night after the funeral, Gideon told Prue his plans. They were going to become rich, own a house in town, and have fine clothes and beautiful furniture. Gideon promised Prue that for her help he would give her fifty pounds to get her harelip cured. He warned her, however, that he would work her as he would an animal. Because Prue had hated her harelip for many years, she consented to his terms. They signed an agreement and took an oath on the Bible that Gideon would be the master and Prue his servant.

Prue was also to learn to read and write and do sums so that she could keep the farm accounts. Her teacher would be Wizard Beguildy, a neighbor who was preached against in church because he earned his living by working spells and charms. Wizard was the father of Jancis Beguildy, a childhood friend of Prue and Gideon.

During the next four years Prue and Gideon slaved long hours in the field. Prue grew thinner and thinner and their mother became quite feeble. She was compelled to watch the pigs, for Gideon would let no one be idle. The farm prospered.

One part of Gideon's plan did not

PRECIOUS BANE by Mary Webb. By permission of the publishers, E. P. Dutton & Co., Inc. Copyright, 1926, by E. P. Dutton & Co., Inc.

work out, however, as he had arranged. In love with Jancis Beguildy, he decided that he would make his fortune and then marry her. Jancis did not want to wait that long, but Gideon would not change his mind.

Gideon and Jancis were handfasted and Jancis had a love-spinning, even though her father swore that she could never marry Gideon. At the love-spinning Prue first saw Kester Woodseaves, the weaver. When Kester came into the room, it seemed to Prue that a beautiful mist surrounded her. Then she turned sadly away. Gideon had told her often enough that no man would love a girl with a harelip.

A few days after the spinning Jancis went to tell Gideon that her father threatened either to sell her to a rich squire for his pleasure or to hire her out for three years as a dairymaid. Her only salvation was immediate marriage to Gideon. But Gideon told her that he had not made enough money, that she must be bound over for three years. Even Jancis' tears would not move him. Jancis was sent to work for Mr. and Mrs. Grimble.

After several months Jancis ran away from the Grimble farm. Because Gideon had a good crop of grain coming up, he promised to marry her after the harvest. Wizard Beguildy still swore that there would be no wedding, and Prue was afraid.

One day, as Prue was walking through the fields, Kester met her. When she tried to hide her face, Kester took her by the shoulders and looked straight into her eyes. He did not laugh, but talked to Prue as a man talks to a woman who is beautiful and attractive. His words were almost more than Prue could bear.

Never had there been such a harvest. Gideon's crop was piled in high ricks, and all the neighbor folks who had helped with the harvest came to the house to dance and feast. As soon as the grain buyer came to buy the crop, Jancis and Gideon would be married. But Gideon, unable to wait until their wedding, went to Jancis' home to be with her. Mrs. Beguildy tricked her husband into leaving so that the lovers could be together. Wizard Beguildy, arriving home early, found Jancis and Gideon in bed together, and the two men quarreled. Prue was more frightened than ever.

Prue had reason for her premonition of danger, for that night Wizard set the ricks on fire and everything burned except the house and the barn. Gideon was like a madman. When Jancis tried to comfort him, he said she was cursed by her father's blood, and he drove her away. He tried to get to Wizard to kill him, but Prue prevented this deed by having Wizard arrested. Gideon cursed the Beguildy family, even Jancis. Jancis swooned and lay for days in a trance. She and her mother were put off their farm, for no landowner would have the family of an arsonist on his land.

Gideon began to rebuild his dream, but Jancis was no longer a part of it. He worked himself and Prue and their mother almost to death. When the mother became too weak to work, Gideon put poison into her tea, for he would feed no one who could not earn her way. Prue knew that her brother's mind was deranged after the fire, but she had not known that he would kill for money.

Jancis returned with Gideon's baby. When Gideon drove her out of the house, Jancis took her baby to the pond and drowned herself and her child. Gideon began to see visions. He told Prue often that he had seen Jancis or his mother, and sometimes he heard Jancis singing. He talked queerly about the past, about his love for Jancis. He no longer wanted the money that had been his whole life. One day he rowed out on the pond and threw himself into the water and drowned. Prue was left alone.

Her vow to Gideon ended, Prue decided to leave the farm. When she rounded up the livestock and went into the village to sell them, the people called her a witch and blamed all the trouble on her harelip. They said that the forked lightning was in her worse than in all the other Sarns, and they put her in the ducking chair and ducked her in the pond until she was senseless. When she awakened, Kester was beside her, to lift her upon his horse and take her away to be his wife. Prue knew then that the forked lightning was not in her; the curse of the Sarns had been lifted.

PREJUDICES: Six Series

Type of work: Essays on social and literary themes
Author: H. L. Mencken (1880-1956)
First published: 1919-1927

During the fantastic decade of the 1920's, few literary events were so eagerly awaited as the appearance of a new volume of Mencken's *Prejudices*, so that one might enjoy the spectacle of the Sage of Baltimore as he pulled yet another popular idol down from its moss-covered pedestal and gloated over the fragments. This iconoclasm was accomplished with so much gusto and with such vigorous and picturesque language as to enchant a whole generation that had grown weary of the solemnity of much American writing. And the decade badly needed an iconoclast, for it must be remembered that what is now thought of as "the jazz age" was also the era of the Ku Klux Klan and the Anti-Saloon League, of Babbittry and Boosterism.

The essays in these volumes can be divided into two categories: literary criticism and criticism of the American scene as it appeared at that time. Literary criticism Mencken defined as a "catalytic process," with the critic serving as the catalyst. Actually, as a critic Mencken derived mainly from James Huneker, whom he enormously admired and had known personally. Huneker had been familiar with Continental writers, then not too well known in America; his criticism was essentially impressionistic, often written in breezy, epigrammatic language. Mencken carried certain of these characteristics much further; indeed, his verbal acrobatics became his hallmark. It was a racy, pungent style, very effective for the "debunking" then so popular and deliberately calculated to drive conservative readers into frenzies. His chief target, at which he never grew tired of heaving bricks, was the Puritan tradition in American literature with its consequent timidity, stuffiness, and narrowmindedness. As he saw it, the Puritan was afraid of aesthetic emotion and thus could neither create nor enjoy art. This

fear had inhibited American literature, he claimed, and had made American criticism equally timid and conventional. Further, criticism had fallen into the hands of the professors, and there was nothing—not even a prohibition agent—that Mencken detested so much as the average American university professor. Hence, such men as Paul Elmer More, Irving Babbitt, Stuart P. Sherman, and William Lyon Phelps had scorn poured over them for years.

It is ironic that the critical writings of some of these men have withstood the passage of time more successfully than have those of Mencken. For though less a geographical provincial than they, he was more provincial in time and was interested mainly in the contemporary. Of the older native writers, he really admired only Poe, Twain, and Whitman—the nonconformists. Even among the moderns his preferences were curiously limited. He had great regard for Conrad and Dreiser, but he overlooked much of the talent that was budding during the 1920's. That he should have overpraised some of his contemporaries, Cabell, for example, should not be held against him; few critics are sufficiently detached to escape this fault. Dreiser was an important writer but not the "colossal phenomenon" that Mencken called him. But his greatest failure as a critic was his blindness to poetry. In the Third Series of *Prejudices* he included an essay, "The Poet and His Art," a study so full of false assumptions, logical fallacies, and plain misstatements of fact that it is a gruesome relic for a critic to have left behind him. And his remarks on Dante stagger belief: Dante's theology was unacceptable to Mencken; therefore, Dante could not *really* have believed it, and *The Divine Comedy* was, he said, a satire on the whole Christian doctrine of heaven and hell. Surely no gem that Mencken garnered from the Bible Belt could equal this statement in absurdity. The essays dealing with the national scene were written in the same slashing manner and naturally infuriated far more readers, since Mencken attacked men, institutions, and ideas more familiar to them. Obviously, many of these pieces have little significance now, for they dealt with situations peculiar to that decade. But some of them are still valid: "The Sahara of the Bozart" (Second Series) is in some ways almost as true of the South today as it was in 1920; his comments on the farmer ("The Husbandman," Fourth Series) are even more appropriate. And his dissections of such eminent figures as Theodore Roosevelt and Thorstein Veblen are still funny.

Of Americans in general, Mencken had a low opinion, considering them a mongrel people incapable of high spiritual aspiration. His opinion of democracy was equally low. It was, he felt, merely a scheme to hearten the have-nots in their unending battle with the haves. The inferiority of Americans Mencken attributed to the lack of a genuine aristocracy and to Puritanism. Without an aristocracy, there could be no real leadership in America, and the vacuum would inevitably be filled by politicians, whom he detested. Nor did he have any faith in reform or reformers.

As for Puritanism, Mencken believed that it had always been the dominant force in our history and had left Americans the narrow-minded victims of religious bigotry. The predominance during the 1920's of the more extreme forms of Fundamentalism gave some support to his argument. But in his attacks on religion he made the mistake of throwing the baby out with the bath water; since he was himself a complete skeptic, he simply could not conceive of such a creature as a sincere and yet intelligent Christian. The terms were to him incompatible; quite genuinely, he could see no difference between Billy Sunday and Archbishop Temple.

Mencken's enemies were always urging him, in anguished tones, to leave this country if he found it so distasteful. His reply was that nowhere else could so much entertainment be had so cheaply. According to his calculations, it cost him personally only eighty cents a year to maintain Harding in the White House. Where could a better show be found for the money?

In spite of his exaggerations, crudities, and often bad taste, Mencken performed a valuable service. America always needs a gadfly, and his cynical wit provided the sting at just the right moment. Unfortunately, he has had no successor.

THE PRELUDE

Type of work: Poem
Author: William Wordsworth (1770-1850)
First published: 1850

Planned as the introductory portion of a long autobiographical and philosophical poem that was never finished, *The Prelude, or, Growth of a Poet's Mind,* was not published until shortly after Wordsworth's death in 1850. The projected, long poem, *The Recluse,* was to present a comprehensive development of the poet's views on man, society, and nature, but of the projected three parts, only the second, *The Excursion* (1814) was ever completed and published.

The Prelude was to provide the autobiographical introduction to *The Recluse,* tracing the development of the poet and his mind to the point where he was ready to formulate his beliefs and philosophy. Written between 1799 and 1805 and addressed to Coleridge as the important "Friend," the poem is a long and ambitious work, an attempt in blank verse to trace the history and development of the poet's feelings, ideas, and convictions.

Since Wordsworth so strongly advocated the use of poetry for individual emotions and insights, it is appropriate that we should have such a thorough description of the development of his mind. In addition, *The Prelude* contains some fine passages that illustrate the clarity and force of Wordsworth's use of language to convey both a precise description and a sense of the meaning of nature. Although the poem suffers from long prosaic stretches, it also contains much of the sense of the calm beauty and power of nature which distinguishes Wordsworth's verse.

The poem begins with an account of the poet's childhood in the English Lake Country, and Wordsworth, with many digressions addressed to nature and its power, wisdom, and infusing spirit, tells of the influence of nature on his solitary childhood. Some of the sense of awe and pleasure that he found in nature, as well as some of his clearest and most pene-

trating use of diction, is evident in the following passage. Young Wordsworth has found a boat in a cave, unchained the boat, and rowed out into the center of a lake. He continues:

> . . . lustily
> I dipped my oars into the silent lake,
> And, as I rose upon the stroke, my boat
> Went heaving through the water like a swan;
> When, from behind that craggy steep till then
> The horizon's bound, a huge peak,
> .black and huge,
> As if with voluntary power instinct
> Upreared its head. I struck and struck again,
> And growing still in stature the grim shape
> Towered up between me and the stars, and still,
> For so it seemed, with purpose of its own
> And measured motion like a living thing,
> Strode after me.

The image of the peak is invested with such simplicity and power that it is transformed into a kind of force holding terror and beauty for the guilty boy who has stolen a ride in a boat.

In describing his early years, the poet speaks of his youthful love of freedom and liberty. He found this sense of freedom in his rambles through the woods and on mountain paths where he did not feel fettered by the claims of society and school work. But, he reassures the reader, he was docile and obedient externally, keeping his rebellion and sense of freedom as a matter of the spirit. This mixture of the calm and docile exterior with the independent and rebellious interior seems part of the origin of Wordsworth's ability to control highly individualistic thought in calm, dignified, unostentatious verse forms and diction. It is not that, in *The Prelude,* Wordsworth uses the speech of common man. His speech is often abstract, speculative, pervaded with a sense of the mystery and meaning of nature. Rather, Wordsworth's diction, at its best, has a dignity and calm control, a lack of pretense, through which the force of his inner meaning gently radiates.

Wordsworth continues his journey through Cambridge, telling of experiences there, discussing the fact that he neither was nor cared to be a scholar. He still, despite his studies, concentrates inwardly on the spirit of things, the power of nature and the impetus nature gives to his feelings. At this point, Wordsworth begins to speculate on the differences between reason and emotion or passion, to equate the reason with the scholars and the emotion with his own apprehension of the world of nature:

But all the meditations of mankind,
Yea, all the adamantine holds of truth
By reason built, or passion, which itself
Is highest reason in a soul sublime;

Throughout the poem, Wordsworth makes the distinction between reason and passion, attributing an ultimate sterility to the quality of reason, while glorifying the element of passion or imagination.

Wordsworth tells next of his journey to the Alps after leaving Cambridge. The mountains there reminded him of the mountains familiar in his childhood, and he felt again, even more keenly, the majesty and awe of the scenery reflected in his spirit. He begins, more strongly, to feel his kinship with nature. In perhaps the dullest section of the poem, he describes his life among the crowds and industries of London, along with his tours of the historical monuments, after his return from Europe. Dissatisfied with life in London, he then went to France during the early stages of the French Revolution. In this section he expresses his feeling that he had not cared for man sufficiently, that, in his devotion to nature, he has neglected his feeling for his fellow creatures. Recalling his early love for freedom and liberty and adding his

new conviction of the importance of political liberty for man, Wordsworth became strongly attracted to the cause of the French Revolution, feeling, as he said in *The Prelude*, that he was tied emotionally and spiritually to the popular struggle against the monarchy. But the bloodiness of the revolution, popular ingratitude and popular refusal to acknowledge the heroes who championed its cause with greatest fervor and sincerity, soon disillusioned Wordsworth. Beginning to feel that blood had poisoned the cause of liberty, he returned to England.

Wordsworth relates how, disillusioned and alone, he sought to bring meaning back into his life. The penultimate section of *The Prelude* is titled "Imagination and Taste, How Impaired and Restored." At that period of his life he turned back to nature, finding there not solace alone but a sense of law and order that was lacking in man. He began to realize the difference in scale between nature and man, the range and effect of nature in comparison to the tiny ineffectuality of man. His sections of resolution frequently include passages like the following interpolation in the midst of a narrative section:

O Soul of Nature! that, by laws divine
Sustained and governed, still dost overflow
With an impassioned life, what feeble ones
Walk on this earth!

In his view, nature provides not only awe and spiritual impetus for man, but also order, rules of conduct, and the means of man's molding his behavior on this planet. In the final sections of the poem, Wordsworth uses nature as the authority for his new morality and assumes a much more overtly moral tone. He didactically advocates the importance of faith, of obedience, of not relying on man's unaided reason in human affairs. What was, in the earlier sections, the praise of emotion and freedom in opposition to rational restraint becomes the praise of the restraint of faith and spirit in opposition to rational license. This change is illustrative of the change in Wordsworth's whole career from the poet advocating the simple joy and freedom of nature to the sage defending abstract and conventional truths. His attitude is demonstrated in the following passage from the conclusion of the poem:

> . . . but, the dawn beginning now
> To re-appear, 'twas proved that not in vain
> I had been taught to reverence a Power
> That is the visible quality and shape
> And image of right reason; that matures
> Her processes by steadfast laws; gives birth
> To no impatient or fallacious hopes,
> No heat of passion or excessive zeal,
> No vain conceits; provokes to no quick turns
> Of self-applauding intellect; but trains
> To meekness, and exalts by humble faith.

As *The Prelude* shows Wordsworth's changing attitudes toward nature and man, both relating and illustrating the changes and development in his mind, so the poem also shows the different characteristics of Wordsworth's diction and poetic power. No other single poem has so much of his clear reverence for nature expressed with greater power and simplicity along with so much of his moralizing expressed with repetitive flatness. *The Prelude* is truly an autobiographical poem, a monument to the career, the changing ideas, and the changing use of poetry of and by William Wordsworth.

PRIDE AND PREJUDICE

Type of work: Novel
Author: Jane Austen (1775-1817)
Type of plot: Comedy of manners
Time of plot: Early nineteenth century
Locale: Rural England
First published: 1813

>Principal characters:
>MR. BENNET, father of five daughters
>MRS. BENNET, his wife
>ELIZABETH BENNET, her father's favorite
>JANE BENNET, the family beauty
>MARY,
>CATHERINE (KITTY), and
>LYDIA BENNET, younger sisters
>MR. BINGLEY, an eligible bachelor
>CAROLINE BINGLEY, his sister
>MR. DARCY, a proud gentleman, Bingley's friend
>MR. COLLINS, a conceited bore
>LADY CATHERINE DE BOURGH, Collins' arrogant patroness

Critique:

Elizabeth Bennet, one of the most delightful heroines of all time, would be enough to make *Pride and Prejudice* outstanding among English novels. In addition, the book has a beautifully symmetrical plot in which the action rises and falls as inevitably as does an ocean wave. Many of the other characters besides Elizabeth are superbly drawn. Jane Austen's delicate but telling satire of the English country gentlefolk of her day—and indeed of her neighborhood—remains a delightful commentary upon the little foibles of human nature.

The Story:

The chief business of Mrs. Bennet's life was to find suitable husbands for her five daughters. Consequently she heard with elation that Netherfield Park, one of the great houses of the neighborhood, had been let to a London gentleman named Mr. Bingley. Gossip such as Mrs. Bennet loved reported him a rich and altogether eligible young bachelor. Mr. Bennet heard the news with his usual dry calmness, suggesting in his mild way that perhaps Bingley was not moving into the county for the single purpose of marrying one of the Bennet daughters.

Mr. Bingley's first public appearance in the neighborhood was at a ball. With him were his two sisters, the husband of the older, and Mr. Darcy, Bingley's friend. Bingley was an immediate success in local society, and he and Jane, the oldest Bennet daughter, a pretty girl of sweet and gentle disposition, were attracted to each other at once. His friend, Darcy, however, created a bad impression, seeming cold and extremely proud. In particular, he insulted Elizabeth Bennet, a girl of spirit and intelligence and her father's favorite. He refused to dance with her when she was sitting down for lack of a partner, and he said in her hearing that he was in no mood to prefer young ladies slighted by other men. On future occasions, however, he began to admire Elizabeth in spite of himself. At a later ball she had the satisfaction of refusing him a dance.

Jane's romance with Bingley flourished quietly, aided by family calls, dinners, and balls. His sisters pretended great fondness for Jane, who believed them completely sincere. The more critical and discerning Elizabeth suspected them of hypocrisy, and quite rightly, for they made great fun of Jane's relations, especially her vulgar, garrulous mother and her two ill-bred officer-mad younger sis-

3049

ters. Miss Caroline Bingley, who was eager to marry Darcy and shrewdly aware of his growing admiration for Elizabeth, was especially loud in her ridicule of the Bennet family. Elizabeth herself became Caroline's particular target when she walked three muddy miles to visit Jane, who was sick with a cold at Netherfield Park after a ride through the rain to accept an invitation from the Bingley sisters. Until Jane was able to be moved home, Elizabeth stayed to nurse her. During her visit Elizabeth received enough attention from Darcy to make Caroline Bingley long sincerely for Jane's recovery. Nor were her fears ill-founded. Darcy admitted to himself that he would be in some danger from the charm of Elizabeth, if it were not for her inferior family connections.

Elizabeth now acquired a new admirer in the person of Mr. Collins, a ridiculously pompous clergyman and a distant cousin of the Bennets, who would some day inherit Mr. Bennet's property because that gentleman had no male heir. Mr. Collins' patroness, Lady Catherine de Bourgh, had urged him to marry, and he, always obsequiously obedient to her wishes, hastened to comply. Thinking to alleviate the hardship caused the Bennet sisters by the entail which gave their father's property to him, Mr. Collins first proposed to Elizabeth. Much to her mother's displeasure and her father's joy she firmly and promptly rejected him. He almost immediately transferred his affections to Elizabeth's best friend, Charlotte Lucas, who, twenty-seven and somewhat homely, accepted at once his offer of marriage.

During Mr. Collins' visit, the younger Bennet sisters, Kitty and Lydia, on one of their many walks to Meryton, met a fascinating new officer, Mr. Wickham, stationed with the regiment there. Outwardly charming, he became a favorite among the ladies, even with Elizabeth. She was willing to believe the story that he had been cheated out of an inheritance left him by his godfather, Darcy's father. Her suspicions of Darcy's arrogant and grasping nature deepened when Wickham did not come to a ball given by the Bingleys, a dance at which Darcy was present.

Soon after the ball, the entire Bingley party suddenly left Netherfield Park. They departed with no intention of returning, as Caroline wrote Jane in a short farewell note which hinted that Bingley might soon become engaged to Darcy's sister. Jane accepted this news at face value and believed that her friend Caroline was telling her gently that her brother loved elsewhere, and that she must cease to hope. Elizabeth, however, was sure of a plot by Darcy and Bingley's sisters to separate him and Jane. She persuaded Jane that Bingley did love her and that he would return to Hertfordshire before the winter was over. Jane almost believed her until she received a letter from Caroline assuring her that they were all settled in London for the winter. Even after Jane told her this news, Elizabeth remained convinced of Bingley's affection for her sister, and deplored the lack of resolution which made him putty in the hands of his designing friend.

About that time Mrs. Bennet's sister, Mrs. Gardiner, an amiable and intelligent woman with a great deal of affection for her two oldest nieces, arrived for a Christmas visit. She suggested to the Bennets that Jane return to London with her for a rest and change of scene and — so it was understood between Mrs. Gardiner and Elizabeth — to renew her acquaintance with Bingley. Elizabeth, not too hopeful for the success of the plan, pointed out that proud Darcy would never let his friend call on Jane in the unfashionable London street on which the Gardiners lived. Jane accepted the invitation, however, and she and Mrs. Gardiner set out for London.

The time drew near for the wedding of Elizabeth's friend, Charlotte Lucas, to the obnoxious Mr. Collins. Charlotte asked Elizabeth to visit her in Kent. In spite of her feeling that there could be little pleasure in such a visit, Elizabeth promised to do so. She felt that in taking

3050

such a husband Charlotte was marrying simply for the sake of an establishment, as was indeed the case. Since she herself could not sympathize with her friend's action, Elizabeth thought their days of real intimacy were over. As March approached, however, she found herself eager to see her friend, and she set out with pleasure on the journey with Charlotte's father and sister. On their way, the party stopped in London to see the Gardiners and Jane, Elizabeth found her sister well and outwardly happy, though she had not seen Bingley and his sisters had paid only one call. Elizabeth was sure Bingley had not been told of Jane's presence in London and blamed Darcy for keeping it from him.

Soon after arriving at the Collins' home, the whole party was honored, as Mr. Collins repeatedly assured them, by a dinner invitation from Lady Catherine de Bourgh, Darcy's aunt and Mr. Collins' patroness. Elizabeth found Lady Catherine a haughty, ill-mannered woman and her daughter thin, sickly, and shy. Lady Catherine was extremely fond of inquiring into the affairs of others and giving them unasked advice. Elizabeth turned off the meddling old woman's questions with cool indirectness, and saw from the effect that she was probably the first who had dared to do so.

Soon after Elizabeth's arrival, Darcy came to visit his aunt and cousin. He called frequently at the parsonage, and he and Elizabeth resumed their conversational fencing matches. His rather stilted attentions were suddenly climaxed by a proposal of marriage, but one couched in such proud and condescending terms that Elizabeth indignantly refused him. When he requested her reason for such an emphatic rejection, she mentioned his part in separating Bingley and Jane, and also his mistreatment of Wickham. Angry, he left abruptly, but the next day brought a letter answering her charges. He did not deny his part in separating Jane and Bingley, but he gave as his reasons the improprieties of Mrs. Bennet and her younger daughters, and

also his sincere belief that Jane did not love Bingley As for his alleged mistreatment of Wickham, he proved that he had in reality acted most generously toward the unprincipled Wickham, who had repaid his kindness by attempting to elope with Darcy's young sister. Elizabeth, at first incensed at the proud tones in which he wrote, was at length forced to acknowledge the justice of all he said, and her prejudice against him began to weaken. Without seeing him again, she returned home.

She found her younger sisters clamoring to go to Brighton, where the regiment formerly stationed at Meryton had been ordered. When an invitation came to Lydia from a young officer's wife, Lydia was allowed to accept it over Elizabeth's protests. Elizabeth herself was asked by the Gardiners to go with them on a tour which would take them into Derbyshire, Darcy's home county. She accepted, reasoning that she was not very likely to meet Darcy merely by going into the same county with him. While they were there, however, Mrs. Gardiner decided they should visit Pemberly, Darcy's home. Elizabeth made several excuses, but her aunt was insistent. Then, learning that the Darcy family was not at home, Elizabeth consented to go.

At Pemberly, an unexpected and most embarrassing meeting took place between Elizabeth and Darcy. He was more polite than Elizabeth had ever known him to be, and asked permission for his sister to call upon her. The call was duly paid and returned, but the pleasant intercourse between the Darcys and Elizabeth's party was suddenly cut short when a letter came from Jane telling Elizabeth that Lydia had run away with Wickham. Elizabeth told Darcy what had happened, and she and the Gardiners left for home at once. After several days the runaway couple was located and a marriage arranged between them. When Lydia came home as heedless as ever, she told Elizabeth that Darcy had attended her wedding. Elizabeth, suspecting the truth, learned from Mrs. Gardiner that it was indeed Darcy who brought about the marriage by giving Wickham money.

Soon after Lydia and Wickham left, Bingley came back to Netherfield Park, and with him came Darcy. Elizabeth, now more favorably inclined to him than ever before, hoped his coming meant that he still loved her, but he gave no sign. Bingley and Jane, on the other hand, were still obviously in love with each other, and became engaged, to the great satisfaction of Mrs. Bennet. Soon afterward Lady Catherine paid the Bennets an unexpected call. She had heard it rumored that Darcy was engaged to Elizabeth. Hoping to marry her own daughter to Darcy, she had charged down with characteristic bad manners to order Elizabeth not to accept his proposal. The spirited girl was not to be intimidated by the bullying Lady Catherine and coolly refused to promise not to marry Darcy. She was far from certain she would have another chance, but she had not long to wonder. Lady Catherine, unluckily for her own purpose, repeated to Darcy the substance of her conversation with Elizabeth, and he knew Elizabeth well enough to surmise that her feelings toward him had greatly changed. He returned to Netherfield Park, and he and Elizabeth became engaged. Pride had been humbled and prejudice dissolved.

THE PRINCE

Type of work: Philosophy of politics
Author: Niccolò Machiavelli (1469-1527)
Time: Fifteenth and sixteenth centuries
Locale: Principally Italy
First published: 1532

Principal personages:
  CESARE BORGIA, Duke of Valentinois and Romagna
  FRANCESCO SFORZA, Duke of Milan
  POPE ALEXANDER VI, Roderigo Borgia, father of Cesare and Lucrezia
    Borgia
  POPE JULIUS II
  CATERINA SFORZA, Countess of Forlì
  LOUIS XII, King of France

This is the book that gives meaning to the critical adjective "Machiavellian." It is an ingenious and fascinating study of the art of practical politics, composed by a man who never rose higher than the position of secretary to the Second Chancery in Florence. The success of his book is due partly to his wit and partly to his having known some of the most clever and powerful rogues of the Renaissance. His model for the "Prince" was Cesare Borgia, a man who used all means of conquest, including murder, to achieve and hold political position.

Machiavelli never pretended that his book was a guide to the virtuous. On the other hand, he did not set out to prescribe the way to wickedness. He meant his account to be a practical guide to political power, and through a combination of experience, logic, and imagination he constructed one of the most intriguing handbooks of Western civilization: a primer for princes.

In beginning a discussion concerned with the manners and attitudes of a prince—that is, a ruler of a state—Machiavelli writes:

> Since . . . it has been my intention to write something which may be of use to the understanding reader, it has seemed wiser to me to follow the real truth of the matter rather than what we imagine it to be. For imagination has created many principalities and republics that have never been seen or

known to have any real existence, for how we live is so different from how we ought to live that he who studies what ought to be done rather than what is done will learn the way to his downfall rather than to his preservation.

This passage makes it clear that Machiavelli intended to explain how successful politicians actually work rather than how they ought to work.

The Prince begins with a one paragraph chapter which illustrates Machiavelli's logical approach to the problem of advising prospective princes. He claims that all states are either republics or monarchies. Monarchies are either hereditary or new. New monarchies are either entirely new or acquired. Acquired states have either been dominated by a prince or been free; and they are acquired either by a prince's own arms or by those of others; and they fall to him either by fortune or because of his own character and ability.

Having outlined this inclusive logical bifurcation, Machiavelli first discusses the problems connected with governing a hereditary monarchy, and then goes on to discuss mixed monarchies.

In each case, as his argument develops, Machiavelli considers what the logical alternatives are, and what should be done in each case if the prince is to acquire and hold power. In writing of mixed monarchies, for example, having pointed out

3053

that acquired states are either culturally similar to the conquering state or not, he then considers each possibility. If the acquired state is culturally similar, it is no problem to keep it; but if the acquired state is different in its customs, laws, or language, then there is a problem to be solved. One solution might be to have the ruler go to the acquired territory and live there. As an example, Machiavelli refers to the presence of the Turkish ruler in Greece.

Another possibility for solving the problem which arises when an acquired territory differs culturally from the conquering state is the establishment of colonies. Colonies are inexpensive to acquire and maintain, he argues, because the land is acquired from a few landowners of the conquered territory and they are the only ones who complain. Such a plan is preferable to maintaining soldiers, for policing a new state is expensive and, in addition, offends the citizens being policed.

Thus, by the somewhat mechanical device of considering logical alternatives, Machiavelli uses his limited experience to build a guide to power. What he says, although refreshing in its direct approach to the hard facts of practical politics, is not entirely fanciful or naïve. Not only did Machiavelli, through his diplomatic missions, come to know intimately such leaders as Louis XII, Julius II, the Emperor Maximilian, and Cesare Borgia, but he also used his time to advantage, noting political tricks that actually worked and building up his store of psychological truths.

It is doubtful that any ruler or rebel ever succeeded simply because he followed Machiavelli to the letter, but it may well be that some political coups have been the result of inspiration from The Prince. (Indeed, shortly after Fidel Castro's overthrow of the Batista government in Cuba in 1959, a newspaper account reported that among the books on Castro's revolutionary reading list was Machiavelli's The Prince.)

What is inspiring for the politically ambitious in The Prince is not the substance but the attitude, not the prescription but the unabashed, calculating, and aggressive air with which the author analyzes the means to power.

For the reader without political ambition The Prince is a sometimes amusing and sometimes frightening reminder of the realities of political fortune. For example, Machiavelli writes that anyone who helps another to power is bound to fall himself because he has contributed to the success either by his cleverness or his power, and no prince can tolerate the existence of either in another person close to him. This is a lesson which would have been useful to some of the men close to the top in the U.S.S.R.

Machiavelli considers this question: Why did the kingdom of Darius, occupied by Alexander the Great, not rebel after Alexander's death? The answer is that monarchies are governed either by a prince and his staff or by a prince and a number of barons. A monarchy controlled by the prince through his representatives is very difficult to conquer, since the entire staff owes its existence to the prince and is, consequently, loyal. But once such a monarchy is captured, power is easily maintained. So it was in Alexander's case. But a nation like the France of Machiavelli's day is ruled by a king and barons. The barons are princes of a sort over their portions of the state, and they maintain control over their subjects. It is easy to conquer such a state because there are always unhappy barons willing to join a movement to overthrow the king. But once conquered, such a state is difficult to hold because the barons may regroup and overthrow the new prince.

Sometimes power is acquired through crime, Machiavelli admits, and he cites a violent example: the murder of Giovanni Fogliani of Fermo by his nephew Oliverotto. Machiavelli advises that the cruelty necessary to attain power be kept to a minimum and not be continued, for the purely practical reason that the prince will lose power otherwise. The best thing to do, says the author, is to commit one's acts of cruelty all at once, not over an extended period.

This cold practicality is echoed in such injunctions as those to the effect that if one cannot afford to be generous, accept with indifference the name of miser; it is safer to be feared than to be loved, if one must choose; a prince need not have a morally worth-while character, but he must *appear* to have it; if a prince's military support is good, he will always have good friends; to keep power one must be careful not to be hated by the people; it is always wiser for a prince to be a true friend or a true enemy than to be neutral; a prince should never listen to advice unless he asks for it; and it is better to be bold than cautious.

Machiavelli's prime examples are Francesco Sforza and Cesare Borgia, particularly the latter. The author writes that he is always able to find examples for his points by referring to the deeds of Borgia. Considering the value of using auxiliary arms, the military force of another state, Machiavelli refers to Borgia's unfortunate experience with auxiliaries in the capture of Romagna. Finding the auxiliaries untrustworthy, Borgia turned to mercenaries, but they were no better, so he finally used only his own troops. Machiavelli's conclusion in regard to auxiliary troops is that "If any one . . . wants to make sure of not winning he will avail himself of troops such as these."

After reviewing Cesare Borgia's rise to power (with the remark that "I could not suggest better precepts to a new prince than the examples of Cesare's actions"),

Machiavelli concludes that "I can find nothing with which to reproach him, rather it seems that I ought to point him out as an example . . . to all those who have risen to power by fortune or by the arms of others." This praise follows a description of such acts as Borgia's killing of as many of the hapless lords he had despoiled "as he could lay hands on."

Machiavelli praises the actions of other leaders, such as Francesco Sforza and Popes Alexander VI and Julius II, but only Cesare Borgia wins unqualified praise. Sforza, for example, is recognized as having become Duke of Milan "by the proper means and through his own ability," but later on he is criticized because of a castle he built when he should have been trying to win the good will of the people.

The Prince concludes with a plea to the Medici family to free Italy from the "barbarians" who ruled the republic of Florence and kept Italy in bondage. Machiavelli makes a plea for liberation, expresses his disappointment that Borgia is not available because of a turn of fortune, and closes with the capitalized cry that "THIS BARBARIAN OCCUPATION STINKS IN THE NOSTRILS OF ALL OF US."

Unfortunately for the author, his plea to the Medici family did him no good, and he died with the Republic still in power. Perhaps he himself was not bold enough; perhaps he was not cruel enough. In any case, he left behind a work to be used by any leader willing to be both.

THE PRINCE AND THE PAUPER

Type of work: Novel
Author: Mark Twain (Samuel L. Clemens, 1835-1910)
Type of plot: Social criticism
Time of plot: Sixteenth century
Locale: England
First published: 1882

Principal characters:
TOM CANTY, a London street beggar
JOHN CANTY, his father
EDWARD, Prince of Wales
MILES HENDON, a disinherited knight
HUGH HENDON, his brother
HUGO, a thief

Critique:

In many ways, The Prince and the Pauper is a companion piece to A Connecticut Yankee at King Arthur's Court. Both are historical satires; both deplore the lack of democracy and cleanliness of early England; both scrutinize the past from a viewpoint of modern morality. Lastly, both exhibit humor derived from ludicrous situations. In its compactness and relative brevity The Prince and the Pauper is in some ways superior to A Connecticut Yankee. But the denouement of the novel is disappointing. It is as if the fantasy got away from the author and overwhelmed him. The outstanding quality of this novel is the beloved simplicity of the prince himself, his unswerving tenacity to his royal training throughout all his difficulties, and his final act of clemency.

The Story:

On the same day, in London, Tom Canty and the Prince of Wales were born, the first unwanted and the second long awaited. While the prince, Edward Tudor, lay robed in silks, Tom Canty wallowed in the filth of Offal Court.

Tom's father forced him to beg during the day and he beat the boy at night; but Tom had private dreams of his own. Pretending that he was a prince, he gathered his ragtaggle court of street urchins around him. One day, hoping to see Prince Edward of England, he invaded the royal precincts, but when he tried to approach the prince he was cuffed by a guard and ordered away. Edward, witnessing the incident, protected Tom and took the young beggar into the palace. There, in the privacy of Edward's chamber, Tom confessed his longing to be a prince. When the two boys exchanged garments they discovered that they were identical in appearance. Unrecognized as the real prince and mistaken for the beggar boy, Edward was promptly thrown into the streets of London, where he wandered helplessly, mocked by people whom he approached with pleas that they pay homage to him as their rightful prince.

Meanwhile, in the palace, it was thought that the prince had gone mad because he could recall none of the royal matters which he was supposed to know. King Henry issued an edict that no one should discuss the royal lapse of memory, and the Princesses Mary and Elizabeth mercifully tried to aid their supposed brother, who by that time was too frightened to confess that he was Tom Canty, a beggar dressed in the prince's clothing.

King Henry VIII, sick in bed, had given the Great Seal of the kingdom to Prince Edward for safekeeping. When Henry demanded the return of his seal, Tom reported that he did not know where it was.

While the Prince of Wales, a homeless waif, wandered the streets under the

3056

crowd's mocking raillery, King Henry died. Edward was found by John Canty, Tom's father, and brought to Offal Court; but during the wild celebration of Tom's ascension to the throne Edward escaped from John Canty. Again tormented by skeptical crowds who laughed at his protests that he was now King of England, Edward was rescued by Miles Hendon, the disinherited son of a baronet. Thinking Edward was mad, Miles pitied the little waif and pretended to pay him the homage due to a monarch.

Miles had loved a girl named Edith, who was coveted by Miles' brother Hugh. By trickery, Hugh had gained his father's confidence and Miles was turned away from home. Edward declared that Miles had suffered unjustly and promised the adventurer any boon he might ask. Recalling the story of De Courcy, who, given a similar opportunity by King John, requested that he and all his descendants might be permitted to wear hats in the presence of the King of England, Miles wisely asked that he be permitted to sit down in Edward's presence, for the young king had been ordering Miles about like any other personal servant.

In the role of King of England, Tom was slowly learning to conduct himself royally. Regarded by his attendants as mad, he was able to display his lack of training, and his failure to recall events familiar to Edward, with no calamitous results. At the same time his gradual improvement offered hope that his derangement was only temporary.

John Canty lured Edward away from Miles' protection and took the boy to Southwark, there to join a pack of thieves. Still vainly declaring himself king, Edward was again the center of ridicule. One of the thieves, Hugo, undertook to teach Edward the tricks of his trade. Making his escape, Edward wandered to a farmhouse where a kind woman, pitying the poor, insane beggar boy who declared himself King of England, fed him. Edward wandered on to the hut of a hermit who accepted naïvely Edward's claim to royalty. In turn, the hermit revealed to Edward that he was an archangel; the hermit was really mad. While Edward slept, the hermit brooded over the wrongs done him by King Henry. Believing Edward really to be the king, and planning to murder him, the hermit managed to tie up the boy while he slept. John Canty and Hugo, following the trail of the escaped waif, rescued him and forced him to rejoin the band of rogues. Again he was compelled to aid Hugo in his dishonest trade. At last Miles found the boy and saved him.

Miles was on his way back to Hendon Hall to claim his heritage and Edith for a wife. Arriving at their destination, they learned that Miles' father was dead and Hugh, married to Edith, was master of Hendon Hall. Only five of the old servants were still living, and all of them, in addition to Hugh and Edith, pretended not to recognize Miles. Denounced as a pretender, Miles was sentenced to the stocks, where the abuse showered upon him by the mob so enraged Edward that he protested loudly. When the guards decided to whip the boy, Miles offered to bear the flogging instead. Grateful to his friend, Edward dubbed Miles an earl, but the imprisoned man sorrowed at the boy's display of insanity. Upon Miles' release from the stocks the two set out for London, where they arrived on the day before the coronation of King Edward VI.

In regal splendor, enjoying the adulation of his subjects, Tom Canty rode through the streets of London toward Westminster Abbey. There, just as the crown was about to be set on his head, a voice rang out demanding that the ceremony cease, and the real king, clothed in rags, stepped forth. As the guards moved to seize the troublemaker, Tom, recognizing Edward, ordered them to halt. The Lord Protector solved the mystery by asking the ragged king to locate the Great Seal that had been lost since King Henry's death. Edward, after much dramatic hesitation, managed to remember the exact location of the Seal. Tom admitted that he had innocently used it to crack nuts.

When Miles was brought before the rightful King Edward, he exercised his privilege of sitting in the king's presence. At first he had doubted that the waif was really the king, but when Edward ordered his outraged guards to permit that disrespectful act, Miles knew that his young friend had not been insane after all. Furthermore, Edward confirmed Miles' title of earl. Hugh was stripped of his titles and land. Later he died, whereupon Miles married Edith, whose earlier refusal to acknowledge his identity had been the result of Hugh's threat to kill his brother.

Tom returned to Offal Court with Edward's promise that he and his family would be honored for the rest of their lives. Edward righted many wrongs he had encountered during his adventures. John Canty, whom he wanted to hang, was never heard from again.

THE PRINCE OF HOMBURG

Type of work: Drama
Author: Heinrich von Kleist (1777-1811)
Type of plot: Historical tragedy
Time of plot: 1675
Locale: Prussia
First presented: 1821

Principal characters:
FREDERICK WILLIAM, Elector of Brandenburg
THE ELECTRESS
PRINCESS NATALIE OF ORANGE, niece of the elector
FIELD MARSHAL DÖRFLING
PRINCE FREDERICK ARTHUR OF HOMBURG
COLONEL KOTTWITZ, of the regiment of the Princess of Orange
COUNT HOHENZOLLERN, of the elector's suite

Critique:

Heinrich von Kleist led a short, turbulent life as a poet and died by his own hand at the age of thirty-four. Predestined by family tradition to spend a life of service to his own country, he entered the army at the age of fourteen. However, constant yearnings toward creativeness led him to secure a discharge. He then embarked on a course of study which included Kant's philosophy and the theories of Rousseau. He began to pour all of his creative powers, which were singular for a man in his mid-twenties, into a series of plays. One of these was the farcical *The Broken Jug,* the only light piece he was to compose. His early works met with little success, for he had a limited knowledge of the techniques of writing for the stage. He was essentially a romanticist. *The Prince of Homburg,* his last dramatic work, employs romantic poetic imagery, but its subject presupposes a vital, realistic framework. The play contains rich characterizations which convey the Prussian virtues of discipline and obedience. Its chief fault lies in the lack of stage techniques; it is episodic, lacking in action, and cluttered with a number of secondary characters.

The Story:

After three days of heading a cavalry charge in pursuit of the Swedes, Prince Frederick Arthur of Homburg had returned to Fehrbellin. Exhausted and battle weary, the prince fell into a dreamlike sleep, weaving a laurel wreath as he half dozed. The Elector Frederick William was informed by Count Hohenzollern of the prince's strange condition, and as the elector, the electress, and their niece, Princess Natalie, appeared in the garden where he slept, a strange thing occurred. The elector took the wreath from the prince, entwined it in his neckchain and gave it to Natalie. They backed away as the somnambulistic prince followed murmuring incoherently, and as they retreated inside, the prince snatched a glove from Natalie's hand.

When the prince awoke, he told Count Hohenzollern about the occurrence, which he thought had been a dream. Hohenzollern reproved him for his romantic fantasies and urged him to make ready for the coming battle with the Swedes.

The field marshal of Brandenburg was dictating the orders of battle to his officers; but the prince, who was to play an important role in the battle, was absorbed with his thoughts. Hoping to remember from whom he had got the glove, he wore it in his collar. The electress and Natalie were present, and plans were being formed to send them to a place of safety. As the field marshal reached the section of the orders which pertained to the prince, Natalie, prepar-

3059

ing to depart, suddenly realized that she had but one glove. The prince, who loved Natalie, quickly became aware that he held the missing glove. In order to be sure it was hers, he dropped it on the floor in front of him. Natalie claimed it, and the prince, in a fit of ecstasy, did not hear his battle orders clearly though his mission was to be a key one.

The battlefield of Fehrbellin resounded with cannon and the elector's forces were sure of victory. As the rout of the Swedes became apparent, the prince precipitously gave orders to advance. His colleagues made an effort to dissuade him from this impetuous action, insisting that he hear the order of battle again; he was definitely supposed to remain in his position until a given signal. However, when the arduous prince rebuked Kottwitz, an elderly colonel, for lack of fervency, Kottwitz, rather than appear unpatriotic, joined the prince in the advance.

The electress and Natalie had paused during their journey to safety at a house in a nearby village, where news reached them that the elector had died in battle; both he and his great white horse were reported killed during the bombardment. The prince sought out the women and took the opportunity to tell the distraught Natalie of his love for her, and to offer her his protection. The elector was her last relative; now that he was dead she had no one to turn to.

But the elector was not dead. He had changed horses with one of his officers, and the officer astride the white horse had been mistakenly identified as the elector. The same messenger who brought word that the elector was still alive had further news for rejoicing. The war was over for the time being, and the elector had returned to Berlin.

It became apparent to the elector that Prince Frederick was responsible for ignoring the battle order, and although terms for peace with the Swedes were being discussed, the strong military spirit of the elector prompted him to punish the prince for failing to follow orders. The prince was sentenced to die and placed in prison to await the day of his execution.

The prince, given permission to visit the electress, begged clemency through her. She was touched by his plea, as was Natalie, who threw herself at the feet of the elector to beg for the prince's life. In addition to Natalie's plea, the officers of the elector's army circulated a petition asking that the prince's life be spared. At last the elector agreed to pardon him.

Natalie took the letter of pardon from the elector to the prince's cell. But upon his reading the pardon, events took a different turn. In his letter the elector had specified that the prince's sword would be returned if the young man thought the elector had been unjust in his sentence. The prince then refused the pardon; his military training and nationalistic spirit prompted him to realize that the sentence was just.

The officers of the army visited the elector to plead on the prince's behalf. Count Hohenzollern made the strongest case. Had the elector not deceived the young prince by snatching the laurel wreath and entwining it with his neck-chain, the prince would not have felt an uncontrollable destiny forcing him into battle. Therefore, it was the elector's own fault that the prince's mind had been clouded by what he thought was a vision foretelling valorous deeds. The elector countered by blaming Count Hohenzollern himself for the whole affair, for he was the one who had led the elector to the sleeping prince.

When the prince appeared before the assembled officers and the elector, he was ready to die; nevertheless, he made such a strong plea to the elector that he was able to save himself. Meanwhile, peace with Gustaf Karl of Sweden had been effected by promising Natalie's hand to a Swedish nobleman. The prince begged the elector to revoke the agreement and to attack the Swedes instead. The elector, ordering his troops to resume battle, tore up the death warrant. Prince Frederick Arthur was hailed as the hero of the field of Fehrbellin.

THE PRINCESS OF CLÈVES

Type of work: Novel
Author: Madame Marie de Lafayette (1634-1693)
Type of plot: Sentimental romance
Time of plot: Sixteenth century
Locale: France
First published: 1678

Principal characters:

THE PRINCESS DE CLÈVES, née Chartres, a beautiful young noble-woman
THE PRINCE DE CLÈVES, her husband
THE DUKE DE NEMOURS, in love with the princess
THE VIDAME DE CHARTRES, uncle of the princess
THE QUEEN DAUPHINE, Mary, Queen of Scots, friend of the princess

Critique:

Because *The Princess of Clèves* is superior to any of the other romances written by Madame de Lafayette, some literary historians and critics have hesitated to credit her with the authorship of a book so simple in outline but elegant in detail. There seems no reason to doubt the authenticity of the work, however, if we remember that during its composition the novel was discussed and criticized by the brilliant men and women who attended the salon over which Madame de Lafayette presided. These included the Duke de Rochefoucauld, Madame de Sévigné, Huet, the royal tutor, Segrais, the poet, Cardinal de Retz, and many others. The writer undoubtedly profited by the suggestions and advice of her friends. Certainly, out of their personal memories of an earlier time, they aided in reconstructing the historical background and details of the book. More important, this early novel defined areas of experience which later writers have charted more completely. The careful analyses of emotion, the atmosphere of intrigue, the conflict between duty and desire, and the subjective portrayal of character, as presented here, have made the romance one of the landmarks of French literature. The influence of the book can be traced through two distinct literary trends: the psychological novel and the *roman à clef*, which presents real people and events under a thin fictional disguise.

The Story:

The court of Henri II of France was filled with many intrigues, as much of the heart as of anything else. The court itself was divided into several groups. One group was partial to the queen, who was at odds with Henri II because he chose to be guided in his personal life and in his government by Diane de Poitiers, the Duchess de Valentinois, who had been his father's mistress and was now a grandmother in her own right. A second group was that which surrounded the Duchess de Valentinois. A third group was that which had as its center Princess Mary, wife of the dauphin, the beautiful and brilliant young woman who was also Queen of Scotland.

Into this scene of rivalry came Madame de Chartres, with her very beautiful daughter, to be married to a nobleman with rank as high as possible; Madame de Chartres hoped even for a prince of the blood. Unfortunately for the mother's hopes, the intrigues of the court kept her from arranging a match so brilliant or advantageous. A marriage with either M. de Monpensier, the Chevalier de Guise, or the Prince de Clèves seemed the best that could be made, and there were obstacles to a marriage with either of those, as Mme. de Chartres discovered. Each of the groups at the court was afraid that such a marriage would upset the status of the powers as they stood. Finally the arrangements were made for a marriage to the Prince de Clèves.

3061

The gentleman was perturbed, however, by the attitude of his bride. He loved her greatly, and she seemed to love him dutifully but without the abandon he wished for. He tried to be satisfied when she told him that she would do her best to love him, but that she felt no real passion for him or any man. The marriage was celebrated in grand style, and a fine dinner party, attended by the king and queen, was given at the Louvre.

For many months no one at the court, where extramarital attachments were the rule rather than the exception, dared to say anything about the young wife. Thanks to her mother's solicitude and her own lack of passion where men were concerned, the Princess de Clèves kept a spotless reputation. Her mother, who soon was on her deathbed, knew from various conferences the princess had had with her—unusual conferences for a married woman to have with her mother, for in reality they were confessions—that the princess had no inclinations to stray from her marital vows.

One evening, however, there was a court ball given in honor of one of the king's daughters, whose marriage was impending. A late arrival at the ball was the Duke de Nemours, the handsomest, most gallant courtier in France. At his entrance the Princess de Clèves who had never seen the duke before, was ordered by the king to dance with him.

In spite of the fact that Queen Elizabeth of England had taken an interest in the Duke de Nemours and had expressed the wish that the young man would visit her court, he remained where he could be near the Princess de Clèves. Even the repeated requests of the French king, who saw in de Nemours a possible consort for Queen Elizabeth, could not remove the duke from her side. Meanwhile the Princess de Clèves did everything she could to conceal her love for the duke from everyone, even from her lover himself. She was determined to remain a faithful and dutiful wife.

One day, while the princess and the duke were in the apartments of the Queen Dauphine, the princess saw de Nemours steal a miniature portrait of herself. Although she had ample opportunity, the princess said nothing to stop him from taking her picture. Some time later the duke was injured by a horse in a tournament, and several people noted the look of distress on the face of the Princess de Clèves. The court was beginning to realize that love was blossoming between the two.

As soon as she realized what was happening in her heart, the Princess de Clèves went to her husband and asked him to take her away from Paris for a time. They went to an estate in the country. While they were there, the princess confessed to her husband that she was falling in love with someone. Admiring her candor, he promised to help her overcome the passion. Although she refused to name the man she loved, the Prince de Clèves guessed that it was one of three men, a trio which included the Duke de Nemours. But he had no proof.

Although neither knew it, while the princess was confessing her love, the Duke de Nemours was hiding so close to them that he could overhear what was said.

Months went by, and gradually, despite her efforts to keep away from him, the princess indicated to her husband that the Duke de Nemours was the man she loved. The prince was torn by jealousy, but his wife's confession and her obvious efforts to curb her love prevented him from taking any action in the matter. His only recourse was to accuse her at intervals of not being fair to him in loving another.

The strain becoming too much for the Princess de Clèves, she asked her husband's permission to retire to a country estate near Paris. He yielded graciously but sent one of his own retainers to make sure of her conduct while she was away. The retainer returned to report that twice, at night, the Duke de Nemours had entered the garden where the princess was; the retainer did not know, and so could not report, that his mistress had refused to see the man who loved her.

After the retainer had made his report, the prince fell ill of a fever. When the princess returned, she was unable to convince him that she had not been unfaithful, even though he wanted to believe her. Rather than stand in the way of her happiness, he languished and died.

Some months after her husband's death the Duke de Nemours prevailed upon the princess' uncle, the Vidame de Chartres, to intercede for him with the princess. The uncle did, even to arranging for an interview between the two. At that time the princess told the duke that, in spite of her love for him, she could never marry him. Soon afterward she entered a convent for a time. Later she retired to an estate some distance from Paris. Shortly after her arrival at the country estate she fell ill and died within a matter of days.

*

THE PRISONER OF ZENDA

Type of work: Novel
Author: Anthony Hope (Sir Anthony Hope Hawkins, 1863-1933)
Type of plot: Adventure romance
Time of plot: 1880's
Locale: "Ruritania"
First published: 1894

Principal characters:
RUDOLF RASSENDYLL, an English gentleman
LADY ROSE BURLESDON, his sister-in-law
RUDOLF, King of Ruritania
MICHAEL, DUKE OF STRELSAU, King Rudolf's half-brother
ANTOINETTE DE MAUBAN, in love with Michael
PRINCESS FLAVIA, betrothed to King Rudolf
FRITZ VON TARLENHEIM, a loyal subject of the king
COLONEL SAPT, another loyal subject

Critique:

Many novels have been written about the intrigues and plots of royalty, but few hold the reader's attention as does *The Prisoner of Zenda*. In its pages we meet kings and would-be kings, beautiful ladies, loyal subjects, and those who would sell out their leader for the promise of gold or power. There are thrills and excitement enough for all: murder, duels at midnight, trysts, daring rescues. If Anthony Hope's desire was to give his readers a few hours of pure enjoyment, and it seems to have been his sole purpose in writing this novel, he was successful. His success is confirmed by the fact that the story is almost as popular today as it was when first published.

The Story:

To his sister-in-law, Lady Rose Burlesdon, Rudolf Rassendyll was a great disappointment. In the first place, he was twenty-nine years old and had no useful occupation. Secondly, he bore such a striking resemblance to the Elphbergs, ruling house of Ruritania, that Rose thought him a constant reminder of an old scandal in which her husband's family had been involved. More than a hundred years before, a prince of the country of Ruritania had visited Eng-

land and had become involved with the wife of one of the Rassendyll men. There was a child, who had the red hair and the large straight nose of the Elphbergs. Since that unfortunate event, five or six descendants of the English lady and the Ruritanian prince had had the characteristic nose and red hair of their royal ancestor. Rose thought Rudolph's red hair and large nose a disgrace for that reason.

Rassendyll himself, however, had no concern over his resemblance to the Ruritanian royal family. A new king was to be crowned in that country within a few weeks, and he decided to travel to Ruritania for the coronation, in order to get a close view of his unclaimed relatives. Knowing that his brother and sister-in-law would try to prevent his journey, he told them that he was going to take a tour of the Tyrol. After he left England, his first stop was Paris, where he learned something more about affairs in the country he was to visit. The new king, also called Rudolf, had a half-brother, Michael, Duke of Strelsau. Michael would have liked to become king, and it was hinted that he would try to prevent the coronation of Rudolf. Rassendyll also learned that there was a beautiful lady, Antoinette

THE PRISONER OF ZENDA by Anthony Hope. By permission of the publishers, Henry Holt & Co., Inc. Copyright, 1898, by Henry Holt & Co., Inc. Renewed, 1921, by A. H. Hawkins.

de Mauban, who loved Michael and had his favor. She, too, was traveling to Ruritania for the coronation.

When he reached Ruritania and found the capital city crowded, Rassendyll took lodging in Zenda, a small town some fifty miles from the capital, and prepared to go by train for the coronation. Zenda was part of Michael's domain, his hunting lodge being only a few miles from the inn where Rassendyll stopped. Rassendyll learned also that King Rudolf was a guest at his half-brother's hunting lodge while waiting for the coronation. There were more rumors of a plot against the king and talk that Black Michael, as he was called, planned to seize the throne.

Rassendyll walked every day through the woods near the hunting lodge. One day he heard two men discussing how much he resembled the king. The men introduced themselves as Fritz von Tarlenheim and Colonel Sapt, faithful friends of King Rudolf. While they talked, the king himself appeared. The king had shaved his beard, but otherwise he and Rassendyll were identical. Pleased to meet his distant cousin, the king invited Rassendyll to the lodge. There the king drank so much that Fritz and Sapt could not wake him the next morning.

This was the day of the coronation, and as the king slept in his stupor Fritz and Sapt proposed a daring plan to Rassendyll. They knew that if the king did not appear for the coronation Black Michael would seize the throne. Their plan was to shave Rassendyll's beard and dress him in the king's clothes and have him crowned in the king's place. By the time the ceremonies were over, the king would have recovered, would take his rightful place, and no one would be the wiser. It was a dangerous gamble, for exposure would mean death, but Rassendyll agreed to the plot.

Fritz and Sapt locked the king in the wine cellar and left a servant to tell him of the plan when he awoke. Rassendyll, with Fritz and Sapt, proceeded to the palace. With the two men to help him, he carried off the deception, even convincing the Princess Flavia that he was the real king. His role with Flavia was the most difficult for Rassendyll, for he must be gracious and yet not commit the king too far.

The success of the conspirators was not to last. When they returned that night to the lodge, they found the servant murdered and the real king gone. Black Michael's men had worked well. Black Michael knew that the supposed king was an impostor, and Rassendyll, Fritz, and Sapt knew that Black Michael had the real king. But neither group dared call the other's hand. Rassendyll's only chance was to rescue the rightful king. Black Michael's hope was to kill both Rassendyll and the king and thus seize the throne and Princess Flavia for himself. Rassendyll was attacked and almost killed many times. Once he was saved by a warning from Antoinette de Mauban, for although she loved Michael she would not be a party to murder. Also, she did not want Michael to be successful, for his coup would mean his marriage to Flavia. Michael learned of her aid to Rassendyll and held her a semi-prisoner in the hunting lodge where he had hidden the king.

Playing the part of the king, Rassendyll was forced to spend much time with Flavia. He wanted to tell her his real identity, but Fritz and Sapt appealed to his honor and persuaded him that all would be ruined if Flavia learned that he was not the true king.

When they learned that King Rudolf was dying, Rassendyll, Fritz, and Sapt knew that they must take a daring chance to rescue him. They and part of the king's army attacked the lodge. Those not aware of the deception were told that Black Michael had imprisoned a friend of the king. There was a bloody battle both outside and inside the lodge. Black Michael was killed and King Rudolf wounded before the rescue was completed. When he knew that the king would live, Rassendyll realized that his part in the deception was over. The king sent for him and thanked him for his brave work in saving the throne. Princess Flavia also sent for him. She had been told the whole story, but her only concern was to learn whether Rassendyll had spoken for himself or the king when he had given her his love. He told her that he would always love only her and begged her to go away with him. But she was too honorable to leave her people and her king, and she remained in Ruritania, later to marry the king and rule with him.

Rassendyll left Ruritania and spent a few weeks in the Tyrol before returning to England. His sister-in-law, still trying to get him to lead a more useful life, arranged through a friend to get him a diplomatic post. When he learned the post would be in Ruritania, he declined it. Rassendyll resumed his former idle life, with one break in his monotonous routine. Each year Fritz and Rassendyll met in Dresden, and Fritz always brought with him a box containing a rose, a token from Flavia.

THE PRIVATE LIFE OF THE MASTER RACE

Type of work: Drama
Author: Bertolt Brecht (1898-1956)
Type of plot: Social chronicle
Time of plot: 1933-1938
Locale: Germany
Partial presentation: 1938; first published: 1944

Principal characters:
VARIOUS CITIZENS OF THE THIRD REICH

Critique:

The Private Life of the Master Race, an exposé of the Nazi regime, is composed of seventeen scenes or one-act plays taken from a longer work, The Fears and Miseries of the Third Reich. The scenes form a pageant of the first five years of Hitler's reign. In the usual sense these scenes do not make a play, for there are no characters who appear in more than one scene; the unity of the work is maintained only by the historical sequence and by a fragmentary narration. Brecht here aims at an epic drama, and he does achieve by documentary presentation a vivid sweep in time. He is highly regarded as a poet. The worth of the play lies in the poetry and in the cumulative details of a reign of terror under National Socialism.

The Story:

During the first years of the Nazi regime, techniques for suppressing opposition were rapidly perfected. One object of suppression was any radio capable of receiving broadcasts from Russia. The Nazis relied on the German distrust of Communism to aid in harsh enforcement of the law. Soon neighbors were betraying neighbors. Sets were confiscated and the owners beaten.

In Berlin, in 1933, a storm trooper came to visit his sweetheart who was a maid in a wealthy home. While she was feeding him in the kitchen, the cook's brother came in with a tube to repair the family radio. Since the brother, a common worker, did not give the Heil Hitler greeting plainly enough, the trooper put on a demonstration to show the Nazi power. He pretended to explain the current methods of exposure by staging a scene at the welfare office. He was the more anxious to scare the worker because he had drunk the Nazi's beer.

The trooper, ostensibly in mufti, pretended that he was in a welfare line discussing the things wrong in Germany. The worker answered him by imitating the common complaints heard from non-Nazis. Simulating camaraderie, the trooper clapped the worker on the shoulder. On arriving at the office, the man would be closely interrogated, for there was a chalk cross on his shoulder. The trooper had drawn the cross on his hand and transferred it to the worker's shoulder with a friendly pat. After that bit of dramatizing the worker left abruptly.

In the concentration camps the Socialists, the Communists, and the non-political liberals realized too late that they should have been united before Hitler came to power. Now they were impotent. In the factories there were broadcasts by happy workers who had been carefully coached in what they were to say. In private homes a member of the family would be returned in a zinc box; the official explanation was always that death had come from natural causes.

By 1935 even the scientists were afraid. Spied on by their Nazi employees, they were often handicapped in their laboratories by the prohibition against

THE PRIVATE LIFE OF THE MASTER RACE by Bertolt Brecht. Translated by Eric Russell Bentley. By permission of the publishers, New Directions. Copyright, 1944, by E. R. Bentley.

correspondence with foreign scientists. It was forbidden even to mention the name of Einstein, for he was a Jew.

In Frankfort a Jewish wife was packing. Her husband was a prominent physician and an Aryan. She had stood her racial stigma as long as she dared, but now their friends were beginning to cut them socially. Carefully tending to her wifely duties, she telephoned to friends, asking them to look after things in her absence. After she had finished calling, she prudently burned the notebook containing the telephone numbers. Then she began rehearsing the speech she would make to her husband.

She would be brave. She would go to Amsterdam for a few weeks until the persecution died down. Really, the only reason she was leaving was to relieve her husband from embarrassment. As she went through the carefully thought-out speech, her husband came in. At once she broke down. The husband pretended to believe that she would be gone only a short while, and when things were better he would come to Amsterdam for her. He would like a few days outside of Germany himself. Surely the Nazis could not for long shackle the intellectuals.

Even the judges were confused. They had come to the point where they gave decisions the way the party wanted them, but sometimes it was difficult to know just what the party desired. In Augsburg three storm troopers broke into a store run by a Jew and took some valuable jewelry after wounding the Jew. To the judge the case looked like a simple one; the Jew had offered great provocation, the storm troopers had acted rightly in defending the honor of the party. But after talking with the prosecutor the judge was not sure how he should decide.

There was race pollution mixed in the case. The Jewish store manager had a nineteen-year-old daughter about whom there had been rumors. The father also had an Aryan partner who had access to party headquarters. The owner of the building had changed his testimony. Per-haps the case was clear cut; the judge would decide against the storm troopers, for German justice was honorable even for Jews.

But the inspector in the case confused him again. He said the prosecutor was inducing the judge to give the wrong decision because he wanted the judge's post for himself. The harassed judge asked an older colleague for advice, but the other man could give him little help. With a heavy heart the judge prepared to go into his courtroom, where ribald storm troopers occupied every seat.

Perhaps one of the most effective devices of the regime was to teach the children in the youth organizations to inform on their parents.

In 1936 a man who had been released from a concentration camp came to call on a man and a wife with whom he had worked in the resistance movement. The couple were afraid to take him into their confidence again, for the pressure in the concentration camps was great. The meeting was an embarrassing one. The couple tried not to notice the released man's shrunken hand with the missing fingers, and he in turn pretended not to notice their lack of confidence in him.

As food became scarcer in the stores, the waiting lines were longer in the mornings. Butter was sacrificed to cannons and prices rose beyond the ability of the people to pay. The store owners themselves led a precarious existence, for they never knew when they would be arrested for infractions of rules. A butcher, who had been a Nazi before 1933, forced his son to join the storm troopers, but his loyalty did him little good. When he refused to put cardboard hams in his window, the Nazis began to persecute him. In despair the butcher hanged himself in his shop window over a card which announced to the world that he had voted for Hitler.

There were faint signs of resistance to the all-powerful regime. Farmers were supposed to hand over their grain to the government and buy feed at a fixed price.

Here and there, however, a farmer would take the precaution of having his wife and children stand guard. While they watched he would feed grain to his hungry pigs.

In Lübeck, in 1937, a fisherman lay dying. He had argued long hours with his storm trooper son over Hitler's evident determination to start a war. Now as the dying man talked with his pastor he dared to mention the life to come. The son left his father's bedside without speaking. The pastor had referred to the Sermon on the Mount; no good Nazi could be taken in by Jewish superstition.

In Hamburg, in 1938, just after the union with Austria, a small group discussed ways and means of getting out an opposition leaflet. Such a project was almost impossible. A woman in the group read a letter from an executed father to his small son, a letter in which the father declared that his hard fate would not have been in vain if his son remained true to the common people.

PRIVATE LIVES

Type of work: Drama
Author: Noel Coward (1899-   )
Type of plot: Comedy of manners
Time of plot: 1930
Locale: France
First presented: 1930

Principal characters:
SIBYL CHASE, a bride
ELYOT CHASE, her husband
AMANDA PRYNNE, Elyot's first wife
VICTOR PRYNNE, her husband

Critique:

One of the most popular of the plays of Noel Coward, Private Lives is sophisticated high comedy at its best, a story of misadventures created by an exchange of husbands and wives. Originally performed by Coward himself and the late Gertrude Lawrence, it won immediate success. There is little plot, but the brilliant dialogue and unconventionality of theme more than sustain the play and place it among the best brittle farces of the modern stage.

The Story:

Sibyl Chase loved being married. She was as much in love with the idea of being a bride as she was with her husband Elyot, perhaps more so. On her honeymoon night Sibyl went into raptures over Elyot, but she did not forget, or let him forget, that she knew he had loved his first wife Amanda madly. She was certain that their breakup had been Amanda's fault, that she had been a mean-tempered and probably a wanton woman. When Sibyl told him that she knew how to handle a husband, how to make him happy, Elyot feared that she meant she knew how to manage a husband. He was a trifle disturbed.

Unknown at first to the Chases, Amanda was honeymooning at the same hotel with her new husband, Victor Prynne. Victor had much the same ideas about marriage as Sibyl had. He would take care of Amanda, make her forget that dreadful brute to whom she had been married. The fact that Amanda never asked to be taken care of was unimportant. Victor would teach her to be a suitable wife.

When Amanda and Elyot saw each other again, each wanted to move out of the hotel before their respective mates knew about the presence of the other couple. But Sibyl and Victor were not accustomed to making abrupt changes without reason, and so they refused to leave. Thus Amanda and Elyot thought they were not responsible when they talked together again and found that they still loved each other passionately after five years of separation. Recalling their happy times together, each tried for a time to avoid the issue uppermost in their hearts and minds. At last Elyot broke the polite conversation by saying that he still loved Amanda. They fell into each other's arms.

Amanda tried for a time to make them consider Sibyl and Victor, but Elyot easily convinced her that those two would suffer more if they all lived a lie. After making their plans to go to Paris, Amanda left without telling her husband, Elyot without telling his wife.

Because they had fought so violently and so often in their married days, Amanda made Elyot promise that whenever they started to bicker they would use a password and each keep quiet for two minutes. In Amanda's flat in Paris

PRIVATE LIVES by Noel Coward, from PLAY PARADE by Noel Coward. By permission of the author's representative, Holtzmann & Holtzmann, New York, and of the publishers, Doubleday & Co., Inc. Copyright, 1930, by Noel Coward.

they were often forced into quick use of the magic password, for they were torn equally between love and hate. Amanda's conscience bothered her a little, but Elyot could easily soothe that nagging little voice with love, logic, or a flippant remark. Sorry that they had wasted five years of separation after their divorce, they agreed to marry each other again as soon as Sibyl and Victor would divorce them. Elyot was annoyed when he learned that Amanda had spent those five years in having little affairs with various men, but he saw no reason for her being annoyed at his own transgressions.

Their quarrels occurred over nonsensical things for the most part. At the root was often Amanda's concern for the moral questions involved in their past and present relationship. When Elyot brushed these aside with worldly and flippant comment, Amanda came back to him more passionately than before.

The last explosion occurred as a result of Amanda's mention of another man of whom Elyot had always been jealous. Without knowing quite how the quarrel got out of hand, they found themselves throwing things at each other and slapping each other viciously. The magic password failed to work during their quarrel. As each slammed into a different bedroom, neither was aware that Sibyl and Victor had come into the room at the height of the rumpus and settled themselves quietly on the sofa.

The next morning Sibyl and Victor had a very sensible discussion concerning the situation they had found the night before. Sibyl wept copiously, not so much from sorrow as from custom; it was the right thing for an injured wife to do. Each blamed the other's mate for the sordid scene in Amanda's apartment. When Amanda and Elyot joined them. they were very polite with each other and with Sibyl and Victor. At first the situation was like a cozy morning call for coffee. When Amanda and Elyot admitted that they were sorry, that it was all a mess and a mistake, Sibyl and Victor agreed that the culprits were not contrite enough. Elyot, in particular, seemed crass about the whole thing, particularly to Victor, who wanted to thrash him. But Elyot could see no use in heroics; he honestly admitted that his flippancy was only an attempt to cover real embarrassment.

At the beginning of the unpleasant scene Amanda and Elyot had refused to speak to each other, but as Sibyl and Victor continued to do the proper thing, mouthing little platitudes about morals and the sanctity of marriage, Elyot winked at Amanda. While the injured spouses made and reversed plans for divorces, the sinners paid less and less attention. At last Sibyl and Victor began to quarrel, each accusing the other of weakness in still loving such a wicked and worldly person as Amanda or Elyot. When Sibyl gave Victor a resounding slap, he in turn shook her soundly. In the midst of the quarrel Amanda and Elyot picked up their suitcases and tiptoed out the door together.

THE PRIVATE PAPERS OF HENRY RYECROFT

Type of work: Novel
Author: George Gissing (1857-1903)
Type of plot: Reflective romance
Time of plot: Late nineteenth century
Locale: England
First published: 1903

Principal character:
HENRY RYECROFT, a thoughtful man

Critique:

This work, sometimes called a novel, is a kind of biography of the reflections of a thoughtful, literate man. It is held together by the person of Henry Ryecroft, but there is little structure for the book as a whole. Rather, the episodes and sketches give Ryecroft's views on the widest variety of subjects from Xenophon to berries. The character of Ryecroft himself is revealed with scrupulous minuteness. Essentially a withdrawn humanist, he is gentle and remote but aware of his England.

The Story:

For many years Henry Ryecroft had toiled unceasingly at all kinds of writing. He did straight hack work, translating, and editing. At first he knew the bitterest of poverty, but at long intervals a book appeared under his name and at last he gained a somewhat less precarious livelihood. At rare intervals some modest affluence enabled him to take a short trip abroad. By the time he was fifty his health was failing; his wife had been dead for years, and his married daughter had a home of her own.

By a stroke of luck he inherited a legacy from an acquaintance, a sufficient income for his modest needs. He lost no time in leasing for twenty years a cottage in rural Devon and in bidding goodbye to his writing. In Devon he settled down contentedly with a quiet housekeeper. After his death his private papers, written during his few years in Devon, were arranged by a friend and published.

It was spring. For more than a week Ryecroft had done no writing. His house was perfect, with just enough room, a completely rustic setting, an interminable quiet. His housekeeper, who rarely spoke more than a word or two at a time, kept the house shining and cheerful. Ryecroft walked about the countryside in the pleasant weather. He was no botanist, but before long he knew the names of most of the common plants he saw.

One day he came upon a boy crying bitterly. The child had been given sixpence and sent to repay a debt, but he had lost the money and for hours he had been weeping in the wood. He did not fear his parents' wrath; rather, he was aware of how much a sixpence meant to them. Ryecroft gave him a sixpence. Not long before he could not have afforded such a sum.

Ryecroft remembered the many years when he was bound to the pavements of London. He lived in a mean room, ate irregularly, begrudged time away from his hack writing. The beds he slept in so soundly would now seem an abomination. He had been young in those days, but not for anything, not even for a regained youth, would he go through those lean years again.

Ryecroft had always purchased books, even when he was poor. Once he got a complete Gibbon at a bargain and carried it home in two trips. To look at booksellers' windows and at advertisements one might think that the English were literary or at least book lovers. But the

THE PRIVATE PAPERS OF HENRY RYECROFT by George Gissing. By permission of the publishers, E. P. Dutton & Co., Inc. From EVERYMAN'S LIBRARY, published 1927, by E. P. Dutton & Co., Inc. All rights reserved.

daily newspaper was a better measuring rod. It was devoted to horse racing, scandal, war, and threats of war; books got very little space.

In the summer Ryecroft sat reading one day in his garden. A chance breeze carried a perfume that reminded him of his boyhood. His wise father had seen to it that his family was seldom in crowds. In those days it was still possible to find spots along the English coast where crowds were unknown, and the Ryecrofts always spent tranquil vacations at the seaside. It always seemed that their keenest pleasure came on the trip home when the train stopped at their station.

At one period of his life Ryecroft, with little respect for the Sabbath, had reserved his best satire for the day of sanctified rest. Now Sunday had become the culmination of a quiet week; its deeper quiet made a perfect day. The housekeeper, doing only necessary work, went to church twice. Surely it did her good. Ryecroft arose later than usual and dressed in different clothes. While the housekeeper was gone, he looked into rooms he seldom saw during the week. In London Sunday had always meant cacophonous church bells. When he was a boy, Sunday had been the day he was permitted to look at expensive adult books.

One thing about contemporary England was the decline of taste in food. Faddists vaunted the delights of vegetarianism, but lentils were a poor foreign substitute for good, honest English meat. Ryecroft had even met a man who boasted of eating only apples for breakfast.

A friend, a successful author, came to visit for two days. The friend, working only two or three hours a day, made two thousand pounds a year. He and Ryecroft, poor scriveners together in London, had never dreamed that they both should know prosperous times. His friend's visit recalled London more sharply; the only things he really missed in the metropolis were concerts and picture galleries.

In autumn Ryecroft was busy learning to distinguish the hawkweeds. He had no notion of a scientific classification; common names were more fitting. At dusk, as he was walking past a farmhouse, he saw the doctor's rig at the gate. After he had passed by he turned back to see the chimney silhouetted in the sunset afterglow. The scene was irresistible; he hurried home to read *Tristram Shandy* again after twenty years. Such impulses came fairly often. One morning he awoke an hour early, in great impatience to read the correspondence of Goethe and Schiller.

The triumph of Darwinism and the spread of positivism had many consequences. Agnosticism was an early result, too reasonable to last. Oriental magic, Buddhism, hypnotism were all the rage for a while, as psychical phenomena and telepathy were now, but Ryecroft was equally indifferent to esoteric fads and to the discoveries of Marconi and Edison. Boasts about triumphs of human knowledge were childish. He agreed somewhat with Spinoza, who said that the free man thinks of death only rarely, although he was not free in Spinoza's sense. Thinking of death very often, he found the stoics a comfort.

During his first winter in Devon, Ryecroft tried to keep a wood fire. Now he had a comfortable coal grate. A storm recalled the days when he would gladly have tramped far in the wind and rain, but such an exploit would kill him now. His room seemed the most comfortable in all England. Comfortable also because he was able to spend money, he sent fifty pounds to an indigent friend and passed a pleasant hour thinking of his friend's delight at the windfall.

In those days it was the fashion to condemn the English kitchen. Cooks were called gross and unimaginative, but Ryecroft believed that English cooking was the best in the world. The beef tasted like beef, and the mutton was decidedly mutton. Rather than being a nation with one sauce, only England knew the virtues of meat gravy. However, English cooking had been better before the oven became the cook's friend and refuge; a spitted joint was incomparably better than a modern oven roast.

The strength of England probably came from two sources. First there had been Puritanism, which set moral standards. Also, the English read the Old Testament; they were the chosen people. Perhaps the last thirty years had seen the decline of conventional religion and the growth of materialism. The old prudishness, however, had given way to new strength.

THE PROFESSOR

Type of work: Novel
Author: Charlotte Brontë (1816-1855)
Type of plot: Psychological romance
Time of plot: Nineteenth century
Locale: Belgium and England
First published: 1857

Principal characters:
WILLIAM CRIMSWORTH, the narrator, a young teacher
EDWARD CRIMSWORTH, his brother
MR. HUNSDEN, a wealthy mill owner
M. PELET, master of a boys' school
MLLE. ZORAÏDE REUTER, mistress of a girls' school
MLLE. FRANCES EVANS HENRI, a student

Critique:

The Professor, Charlotte Brontë's first completed novel, was not published until after her death. Simplified in plot and free from the atmosphere of mysticism and mystery contained in *Villette*, *The Professor* reads like an early study for that later novel. The story of an English teacher who seeks fortune in Europe, the book presents a rather touching love story and deals with certain problems which seem to have disturbed the young author: Catholicism, marriage, continental culture. The brief picture of Hunsden suggests an embryonic Rochester, and the characterization of Zoraïde Reuter is quite well drawn. Much of the material in this novel was drawn from Charlotte Brontë's own experience; the location of the girls' school in Brussels, for example, is that of the institution attended by the Brontë sisters in 1842.

The Story:

Orphaned in infancy, William Crimsworth had been meagerly supported by his mother's brothers, Lord Tynedale and the Hon. John Seacombe. William's brother Edward, ten years his senior, had taken over his deceased father's mill and prospered.

Upon his graduation from Eton, William, refusing to accept further aid from the uncles who had treated his mother so coldly, asked his brother for employment. When he arrived at Bigben Close, where the mill was located, Edward censured his young brother for having submitted to Tynedale and Seacombe for so many years. Edward was harsh and cold in speech and act, and his pretty young wife, although inclined at first toward warmth, began to treat William in much the same way. Edward hired William as a clerk at ninety pounds a year and requested that the young man live away from Crimsworth Hall.

A grudging brother and a harsh master, Edward invited William to his house only once, along with some other mill workers, to attend a party. That evening William met Mr. Hunsden, a flippant, wealthy mill owner who, judging Edward a false brother and a tyrant, publicly denounced him. As a result Edward furiously dismissed William. Hearing of William's decision to go to the continent, Mr. Hunsden gave him a letter of introduction to a Mr. Brown in Brussels.

When William presented his letter, Mr. Brown suggested teaching as a possible career. Through his influence William became a teacher of English and Latin in the pension of M. Pelet. Next door to M. Pelet's day school was a seminary for girls headed by Mlle. Reuter. Shortly afterward Mlle. Reuter asked William to give lessons to her girls during part of each week.

Having met Madame Reuter, a gross and droll woman, William was surprised to find her daughter, Zoraïde Reuter, young and charming. Teaching young ladies, William discovered, was not the same as teaching young boys. Mademoiselles Eulalie, Hortense, and Caroline proved to be haughtily disdainful but at the same time coquettish. M. Pelet, taking deep interest in William's personal relationships at Mlle. Reuter's school, questioned him about his impressions of Mlle. Reuter and the three young coquettes of the classroom.

William admired Mlle. Reuter. When he made a weak attempt at flirtation, she did not discourage him. But one night he overheard M. Pelet and Mlle. Reuter talking in the park about their forthcoming marriage, which M. Pelet wished to hasten and she wished to delay. M. Pelet then accused her of encouraging William, who was obviously in love with her, and he described the affair as ludicrous, since she was ten years William's senior. Mlle. Reuter, laughing pleasantly at M. Pelet's disclosure, denied interest in William.

Although William knew M. Pelet to be insincere in his friendship, he did not reveal his knowledge. He did, however, attempt to overcome his attraction toward Mlle. Reuter. William sensed that she was trying to regain his favor when she appealed to him to treat kindly a new pupil, Mlle. Frances Henri, who was also a teacher at the seminary. William, not disposed to please Mlle. Reuter, harshly criticized Frances on her first appearance. Later he was surprised at the girl's fine accent in reading English, and his interest turned from Mlle. Reuter to Frances, who was an enigma to him. Once, taking time for private and encouraging discourse with his apt pupil, he found that the schoolmistress had been eavesdropping. William learned that the girl's mother had been English, that she had been reared by an aunt, and that she was trying to educate herself in the hope of teaching French in England, where her present profession as a teacher of sewing would not be a stigma upon her dignity if she were also a teacher of language.

William, watching Frances grow in poise and wit, made special efforts to encourage her, until Mlle. Reuter warned him that he gave Frances too much of his time. The directress seemed to hover over him constantly in an attempt to recapture his affections; but he found her deceitful, artful, cruel. After she abruptly dismissed Frances from the seminary, she innocently pleaded that she did not know the young woman's address.

Frances returned to the seminary to find William, but the directress kept them from meeting. Instead, William received a note of thanks from his pupil and twenty francs in payment for his teaching. William gave Mlle. Reuter notice that he intended to quit the seminary.

After a month's futile search for Frances he accidentally came upon her mourning over the grave of her father. When it began to rain, Frances took William to her rooms, where the pair drank tea and read from an English book. Frances was earning a living by lace mending. She could not seek another position as a teacher because she feared that Mlle. Reuter would not give her satisfactory references. Bitterly resenting Mlle. Reuter's treachery, William took his leave. He managed to return the twenty francs before he departed.

Drawn to William by his coolness, Mlle. Reuter had repulsed M. Pelet with hints that she favored the English schoolmaster. After William's resignation, perceiving that she had overplayed her hand, she returned her favor to M. Pelet. Smirking with victory, he informed William of his forthcoming marriage. William, deciding that the school would be intolerable with Mme. Pelet under the same roof, resigned his position.

Frances wrote that she had been employed by a Mrs. D. to teach in an English school in Brussels. Along with this communication came a letter from Hunsden announcing his arrival. Hunsden, after berating William for his failure to forge ahead, casually announced that Edward's mill had failed. He had sold Crimsworth Hall and abused his wife until she left him, but he had managed to renew

3076

his credit, start another business, and regain his wife. William's one concern over the matter was the whereabouts of his mother's portrait, which had hung in Crimsworth Hall. The next morning William received from Hunsden, as a gift, the missing portrait.

Within a few weeks William was fortunate enough to be appointed professor of English in a college in Brussels. Cheered by the promise of his new position, William went to Frances, whom he had not seen since the night he had met her in the cemetery, and asked her to marry him. She accepted on the condition that she retain her teaching post. Although William's income was large enough for both, she pleaded that she did not wish to marry him merely to be supported.

William and Frances were married. Within a few months Mrs. Crimsworth proposed that she elevate her position by starting a school, and William agreed to her plan.

When they had been married ten years, a period in which Frances' school flourished and a son had been born, the Crimsworths went to England to live. They settled near Hunsden, who during the years that followed became their close friend. Young Victor Crimsworth, reflecting in character many of the attributes of each parent, grew up in the atmosphere of a tranquil and loving home.

THE PROFESSOR'S HOUSE

Type of work: Novel
Author: Willa Cather (1876-1947)
Type of plot: Psychological realism
Time of plot: A few years after World War I
Locale: Hamilton, a Midwestern university town
First published: 1925

Principal characters:
GODFREY ST. PETER, a middle-aged teacher and historian
LILLIAN ST. PETER, his wife
ROSAMOND, and
KATHLEEN, their daughters
LOUIE MARCELLUS, Rosamond's husband
SCOTT McGREGOR, Kathleen's husband
TOM OUTLAND, a former student at Hamilton
AUGUSTA, a seamstress

Critique:

Although Willa Cather uses a minimum of lively incident in *The Professor's House*, the novel is intricate in both its character portrayal and its plot structure. Godfrey St. Peter is one of the author's most sensitive and sympathetic creations, and it is the mirror of his nostalgic but discerning mind which reflects the tensions of shifting relationships in the St. Peter family. The story does not move in straightforward fashion; flashbacks and indirect revelation of past events are used to throw light on a baffling and complicated personal problem. There is little surface drama in what happens to Godfrey St. Peter, but his inward struggle is unfolded with uncommon directness and illumination.

The Story:

The Oxford prize for history brought Professor Godfrey St. Peter not only a certain international reputation but also the sum of five thousand pounds. The five thousand pounds, in turn, built the St. Peter family a new house, into which the Professor had been frankly reluctant to move.

For half a lifetime the attic of the old house had been his favorite spot—it was there that he had done his best writing, with his daughters' dress forms for his only company—and it was in this workroom that Augusta, the family sewing-woman, found him when she came to transfer the dress forms to the new house. To her astonishment, the Professor declared quizzically that she could not have them; he intended to retain the old house in order to preserve his workroom intact, and everything must be left as it was.

Nevertheless, the new house made its own claims. That same evening found the Professor host at a small dinner party for a visiting Englishman. The Professor's daughters and their husbands were present, and during dinner the conversation turned to the new country house being built by Rosamond and Louie. Louie explained to the visitor why the name Outland had been selected for the estate. Tom Outland had been a brilliant scientific student at Hamilton, as well as The Professor's protégé. Before being killed in the war, he had been engaged to Rosamond. His will had left everything to her, including control of his revolutionary invention, the Outland vacuum. Later, Louie Marcellus himself had married Rosamond and successfully marketed Tom's invention. The new house, Louie concluded, would serve in some measure as a memorial to

THE PROFESSOR'S HOUSE by Willa Cather. By permission of the publishers, Alfred A. Knopf, Inc. Copyright, 1925, by Willa Cather.

Outland.

Louie's lack of reserve visibly irritated the McGregors, and the Professor himself maintained a cool silence. The next morning his wife took him to task for it. Lillian had been fiercely jealous of her husband's interest in Tom Outland. The Professor found himself reflecting that people who fall in love, and who go on being in love, always meet with something which suddenly or gradually makes a difference. Oddly enough, in the case of Lillian and her husband, it had seemed to be his pupil, Tom Outland.

More and more the Professor sought the refuge of his study in the old house, where he could insulate himself against increasing family strain. Even here, however, interruptions came. Once it was Rosamond, self-conscious about accepting all the benefits of the Outland invention. Her father refused to share her good fortune but suggested that she aid cancer-ridden Professor Crane, who had collaborated with Tom in his experiments. Rosamond stiffened immediately, for outside the family she recognized no obligations.

Soon there was more evidence that the family was drifting apart. Kathleen confessed to her father her violent reaction to Rosamond's arrogance. It became known that Louie, attempting to join the Arts and Letters Club, had been blackballed by his brother-in-law. The Professor was distressed by the rift between his daughters, both of whom he loved, although he had a special affection for Kathleen.

Louie Marcellus' real fondness for the St. Peters was demonstrated when the time came for the Professor to fill a lecture date in Chicago. He and Rosamond, paying all bills, took them to Chicago, installed them in a luxurious hotel suite, and tempted them with diversions. During a performance of *Mignon*, Lillian, softened by memories aroused by the opera, confirmed the Professor's impression that her resentment of Tom Outland had affected their marriage.

Louie's next plan was even more elaborate: he and Rosamond would take the Professor and Lillian to France for the summer. The Professor loved France, but he recognized the futility of trying to compromise his and Louie's ideas of a European vacation. He begged off, pleading the pressure of work, and eventually the others departed without him.

The Professor moved back into the old house and luxuriated in independence. He decided to edit for publication Tom Outland's youthful diary, and constantly he turned over in his mind the events in Tom's dramatic history.

Years before, Tom had appeared on the Professor's doorstep as a sunburned young man who was obviously unaccustomed to the ways of society. Tom wanted to go to college, although his only previous instruction had come from a priest in New Mexico. Interested and curious, the Professor saw to it that Tom had a chance to make up his deficiencies and enter the university. The St. Peter house became the boy's second home, and the little girls were endlessly fascinated by his tales of the Southwest. To them he confided that his parents had died during their wagon journey westward and that he had been adopted by a kindly worker on the Sante Fé Railroad.

Tom's diary was chiefly concerned with his strangest boyhood adventure. To regain his strength after an attack of pneumonia, he became a herd rider on the summer range. With him went his closest friend, Roddie Blake. On the range Tom and Roddie were challenged by the nearness of the mysterious Blue Mesa, hitherto unclimbed and unexplored. They saved their wages and made plans; when their job was finished, they set out to conquer Blue Mesa.

They made a striking discovery. In the remote canyons of the mesa were Indian rock villages, undisturbed for three hundred years and in a miraculous state of preservation. This gift of history stirred Tom to a strong decision. His find should be presented to his country; the relics must not be exploited for profit. With Roddie's consent he took six hundred dollars, boarded a train, and left for Washington. Weeks later he returned, worn out by red tape and indifference, only to learn that Roddie had finally weakened and sold the Indian treasures to a foreign scientist. In a climax of bitterness he quarreled with Roddie. A year later he walked into the Professor's garden.

Recalling Tom Outland had always brought the Professor a kind of second youth. Tom was the kind of person the Professor had started out to be—vigorous, unspoiled, ambitious. Marrying Lillian had brought happiness, none the less real for having now faded; but it had chained him, he felt, and diverted the true course of his life. Now, reviewing the past, the Professor suddenly felt tired and old. At the news that the travelers would soon return, he thought he could not again assume a family role that had become meaningless.

When Augusta came for the keys to re-open the new house, she found the Professor lying unconscious on the floor of his den. Its one window had blown shut, and the unvented gas stove had done the rest. Augusta sent for the doctor, and the Professor was revived. He found that his temporary release from consciousness had cleared his mind. He was not only ready to face his family, but he was ready to face himself and a problem that came too late for him to flee.

PROMETHEUS BOUND

Type of work: Drama
Author: Aeschylus (525-456 B.C.)
Type of plot: Classical tragedy
Time of plot: Remote antiquity
Locale: A barren cliff in Scythia
First presented: Date unknown

Principal characters:
PROMETHEUS, a Titan
HEPHAESTUS, his kinsman and the god of fire
KRATOS, Might
BIA, Force
OCEANUS, god of the sea
Io, daughter of Inachus, a river god
HERMES, the winged messenger of the gods

Critique:

Displaying perfectly the Aeschylean pattern, *Prometheus Bound* is a dramatic treatment of the legend of Prometheus, the Fire-Bearer. The spectacle of a demigod in conflict with his destiny, defiant in the face of severe punishment, makes for compelling drama. The mood is one of sharp irony and deep reflection, for the suffering of Prometheus is a symbol of man's inhumanity to man.

The Story:

Condemned by Zeus for giving fire to mere mortals, the Titan Prometheus was brought to a barren cliff in Scythia by Hephaestus, the god of fire, and two guards, Kratos and Bia. There he was to be bound to the jagged cliffs with bonds as strong as adamant. Kratos and Bia obeyed willingly the commands of Zeus, but Hephaestus experienced pangs of sorrow and was reluctant to bind his kinsman to the storm-beaten cliff in that waste region where no man came, where Prometheus would never hear the voice or see the form of a human being. He grieved that the Titan was doomed forever to be guardian of the desolate cliff. But he was powerless against the commands of Zeus, and so at last he chained Prometheus to the cliff by riveting his arms beyond release, thrusting a bitin wedge of adamant straight through his heart, and putting iron girths on both his sides with shackles around his legs. After

Hephaestus and Bia departed, Kratos remained to hurl one last taunt at Prometheus, asking him what possible aid mankind might now offer their benefactor. The gods who gave Prometheus his name, Forethinker, were foolish, Kratos pointed out, for Prometheus required a higher intelligence to do his thinking for him.

Alone and chained, Prometheus called upon the winds, the waters, mother earth, and the sun, to look on him and see how the gods tortured a god. Admitting that he must bear his lot as best he could because the power of fate was invincible, he was still defiant. He had committed no crime, he insisted; he had merely loved mankind. He remembered how the gods first conceived the plan to revolt against the rule of Kronos and seat Zeus on the throne. At first Prometheus did his best to bring about a reasonable peace between the ancient Titans and the gods. Failing, and to avoid further violence, he had ranged himself on the side of Zeus, who through the counsel of Prometheus overthrew Kronos. Once on the throne, Zeus parceled out to the lesser gods their share of power, but ignored mortal man with the ultimate plan in mind of destroying him completely and creating instead another race which would cringe and be servile to Zeus' every word. Among all the gods, only Prometheus objected to this heartless proposal, and it was Prometheus' courage, his act alone,

3081

which saved man from burial in the deepest black of Hades. It was he who taught blind hopes to spring within man's heart, and gave him the gift of fire. Understanding the significance of these deeds, he had sinned willingly.

Oceanus, brother of Prometheus, came to offer aid out of love and kinship, but he first offered Prometheus advice and preached humility in the face of Zeus' wrath. Prometheus remained proud, defiant, and refused his offer of help on the grounds that Oceanus himself would be punished were it discovered that he sympathized with a rebel. Convinced by Prometheus' argument, Oceanus took sorrowful leave of his brother.

Once more Prometheus recalled that man was a creature without language, ignorant of everything before Prometheus came and told him of the rising and setting of stars, of numbers, of letters, of the function of beasts of burden, of the utility of ships, of curing diseases, of happiness and lurking evil, of methods to bring wealth in iron, silver, copper, and gold out of the earth. In spite of his torment, he rejoiced that he had taught all arts to humankind.

Io, a young girl changed into a heifer and tormented by a stinging gadfly, came to the place where Prometheus was chained. Daughter of Inachus, a river god, she was beloved by Zeus. His wife, Hera, out of jealousy, had turned Io into a cow and set Argus, the hundred-eyed monster, to watch her. When Zeus had Argus put to death, Hera sent a gad fly to sting Io and drive her all over the earth. Prometheus prophesied her future wanderings to the end of the earth, predicting that the day would come when Zeus would restore her to human form and together they would conceive a son named Epaphus. Before Io left, Prometheus also named his own rescuer, Hercules, who with his bow and arrow would kill the eagle devouring his vital parts.

Hermes, messenger of Zeus, came to see Prometheus and threatened him with more awful terrors at the hands of angry Zeus. Prometheus, still defiant, belittled Hermes' position among the gods and called him a mere menial. Suddenly there was a turbulent rumbling of the earth, accompanied by lightning, thunder, and blasts of wind, as angry Zeus shattered the rock with a thunderbolt and hurled Prometheus into an abysmal dungeon within the earth. Such was the terrible fate of the Fire-Bearer who defied the gods.

PROMETHEUS UNBOUND

Type of work: Poem
Author: Percy Bysshe Shelley (1792-1822)
Type of plot: Lyric drama
Time of plot: Remote antiquity
Locale: Asia
First published: 1820

Principal characters:
PROMETHEUS, a Titan
EARTH, his mother
ASIA, his wife
JUPITER, king of the gods
DEMOGORGON, supreme power, ruling the gods
MERCURY, messenger of the gods
HERCULES, hero of virtue and strength
PANTHEA, and
IONE, the Oceanides

Critique:

This poem, called a lyric drama by the author, is more lyric than dramatic. The poem owes its form to Shelley's study of Greek drama, however, and the characters are drawn from Greek mythology. Through the combined mediums of drama and poetry Shelley expounds his idea that universal love is the one solution to mankind's ills. *Prometheus Unbound* is valuable as a key to Shelley's philosophy; it is also enjoyable as a work of art.

The Story:

Prometheus, the benefactor of mankind, was bound to a rocky cliff by order of Jupiter, who was jealous of the Titan's power. Three thousand years of torture Prometheus suffered there, while heat and cold and many torments afflicted him. An eagle continually ate at his heart. But Prometheus still defied the power of Jupiter.

At last Prometheus asked Panthea and Ione, the two Oceanides, to repeat to him the curse he had pronounced upon Jupiter when Jupiter had first begun to torture him. But neither Earth, his mother, nor the Oceanides would answer him. At last the Phantasm of Jupiter appeared and repeated the curse. When Prometheus heard the words, he repudiated them. Now that he had suffered tortures and found that his spirit remained

unconquered, he wished pain to no living thing. Earth and the Oceanides mourned that the curse had been withdrawn, for they thought Jupiter had at last conquered Prometheus' spirit.

Then Mercury approached with the Furies. Mercury told the captive that he would suffer even greater tortures if he did not reveal the secret which Prometheus alone knew — the future fate of Jupiter. Jupiter, afraid, wished to avert catastrophe by learning the secret, and Mercury promised that Prometheus would be released if he revealed it. But Prometheus refused. He admitted only that he knew Jupiter's reign would come to an end, that he would not be king of the gods for all eternity. Prometheus said that he was willing to suffer torture until Jupiter's reign ended. Although the Furies tried to frighten him by describing the pains they could inflict, they knew they had no power over his soul.

The Furies mocked Prometheus and mankind. They showed him visions of blood and despair on earth; they showed the Passion of Christ and men's disregard for His message of love. Fear and hypocrisy ruled; tyrants took the thrones of the world.

A group of spirits appeared and prophesied that Love would cure the ills of mankind. They prophesied also that Prometheus would be able to bring Love

3083

to earth and halt the reign of evil and grief.

When the spirits had gone, Prometheus acknowledged the power of Love, for his love for Asia, his wife, had enabled him to suffer pain without surrendering.

While Asia mourned alone in a lovely valley for her lost husband, Panthea appeared to tell of two dreams she had had. In one, she saw Prometheus released from bondage and all the world filled with sweetness. In the other dream she had received only a command to follow. Just then the echoes in the valley broke their silence. They called Asia and Panthea to follow them. The listeners obeyed.

Asia and Panthea followed the echoes to the realm of Demogorgon, the supreme power ruling the gods. They stopped on a pinnacle of rock, but spirits beckoned them down into Demogorgon's cave. There he told them that he would answer any question they put to him. When they asked who had made the living world, he replied that God had created it. Then they asked who had made pain and evil. Prometheus had given knowledge to mankind, but mankind had not eradicated evil with all the gifts of science. They asked whether Jupiter was the source of these ills, the evil master over man.

Demogorgon answered that nothing which served evil could be master, for only eternal Love ruled all. Asia asked when Prometheus would gain his freedom and bring Love into the world to conquer Jupiter. Demogorgon then showed his guests the passage of the Hours. A dreadful Hour passed, marking Jupiter's fall; the next hour was beautiful, marking Prometheus' release. Asia and Panthea accompanied this spirit of the Hour in her chariot and passed by Age, Manhood, Youth, Infancy, and Death into a new paradise.

Meanwhile, Jupiter, who had just married Thetis, celebrated his omnipotence over all but the soul of man. Then Demogorgon appeared and pronounced judgment on Jupiter. Jupiter cried for mercy, but his power was gone. He sank downward through darkness and ruin.

At the same time Hercules approached Prometheus. In the presence of Asia, Panthea, the Spirit of the Hour, and Earth, the captive was set free. Joyfully, Prometheus told Asia how they would spend the rest of their days together with Love. Then he sent the Spirit of the Hour to announce his release to all mankind. He kissed Earth, and Love infused all of her animal, vegetable, and mineral parts.

The Spirit of Earth came to the cave where Asia and Prometheus lived and told them of the transformation that had come over mankind. Anger, pride, insincerity, and all the other ills of man had passed away. The Spirit of the Hour reported other wonders that took place. Thrones were empty, and each man was king over himself, free from guilt or pain. But he was still subject to chance, death, and mutability, without which he would oversoar his destined place in the world.

Later in a vision Panthea and Ione saw how all the evil things of the world lay dead and decayed. Earth's happiness was boundless, and even the moon felt the beams of Love from Earth as snow melted on its bleak lunar mountains. Earth rejoiced that hate, fear, and pain had left mankind forever. Man was now master of his fate and of all the secrets of Earth.

THE PROMISED LAND

Type of work: Novel
Author: Henrik Pontoppidan (1857-1943)
Type of plot: Social criticism
Time of plot: Late nineteenth century
Locale: Denmark
First published: 1891-1895

Principal characters:
EMANUEL HANSTED, a clergyman and reformer
HANSINE, his wife
MISS TONNESEN, his former fiancée
DR. HASSING, a physician

Critique:

Pontoppidan's novel reflects the class distinctions and the division between town and country folk in nineteenth-century Denmark, at a time when the peasants were struggling for a greater voice in the affairs of that country. As in the case of so many European novels dealing with social problems, the characterization, the plot, and the happenings are secondary to the social meaning and the tone of the work. As a result, the characters are types rather than individuals, and in a plot subordinate to theme the happenings are not skillfully tied together. Quite obviously these items were relatively unimportant to the author; he was intent upon giving a picture of the struggle between the People's Party and the Conservatives, and the effects of that struggle on individuals. Sympathetic to the less-favored group, Pontoppidan, like so many problem novelists, told only one side of the story; one result is that his upper-class characters, like those of the American novelist Theodore Dreiser, are often overdrawn.

The Story:

Emanuel Hansted, son of a wealthy Copenhagen family, and a minister, had left his home city years before to take over a pastorate in the country. Somewhat of a reformer, he had become addicted to the socialism rife in Europe in the second half of the nineteenth century, and to prove his fellowship with the peasants whom he served he had married a peasant girl and undertaken to farm the land on which the rectory was situated.

As the years passed Hansted's wife, Hansine, presented him with three children; his land, however, repaid him only with debts. Although he tried experiment after experiment, Emanuel's fields did not produce enough to support his family. Stubbornly, Emanuel refused to acknowledge that he was no farmer; he even continued to refuse any payment from his parishioners and gave away the money he received for the benefit of the poor.

In spite of his sacrifices, despite his never-flagging efforts to share their lives, and his ties with them through marriage, the peasants did not accept him as one of themselves. The fact that he had come among them as an outlander was too strong for them to forget, even in the times of stress that came when the newly-formed People's Party of Denmark, representing chiefly the peasantry, was trying to control the government, in order to provide for the education of the masses and to improve the lot of the common people generally.

To the casual eye Emanuel might have seemed a peasant, for he had nothing to do with the few gentry who lived in the vicinity. He even distrusted the doctor, whom he had to call in occasionally to treat a member of his family. Indeed, Emanuel summoned Doctor Hassing only

THE PROMISED LAND by Henrik Pontoppidan. By permission of the publishers, J. M. Dent & Sons, Ltd. Copyright, 1896, by J. M. Dent & Sons, Ltd. Renewed.

when an emergency existed. As for his family, Emanuel had put his father and his sister entirely out of his mind; only his wife and children, who tied him to the peasantry, were acknowledged as kin.

One summer all of nature and mankind seemed determined to show that Emanuel was a misfit in the rural area he had adopted. His crops were even poorer than usual. He had borrowed the seed he put into the ground, and, after it was in, nature refused to send the weather he needed to produce successful yields in the fields. In Copenhagen the Conservative Party gained in strength and defeated the People's Party, first in small items, then in large. As the peasants lost their political power, the people of Emanuel's parish began to look upon him as one who belonged on the other side.

As if that were not enough, Emanuel's oldest child, a son, began to suffer from an ear inflammation that had gone untended for two years. At last, upon Hansine's insistence, Emanuel sent for Dr. Hassing. The physician could not believe that Emanuel had permitted the child's health to fall into such a dangerous state; Emanuel, on his part, could not understand that the child was really ill. Failing to follow the doctor's advice, he treated his son as if he were well and healthy. Because of his father's failure to face reality, the boy died.

Before long Emanuel and Hansine began to drift apart, for their son's death had erected a barrier between them that had been years in the making. Hansine felt that her husband really was unhappy, and she believed that he actually wanted to escape from the dismal, unappreciative rural parish.

Quite by chance, while out walking alone to prepare his Sunday sermon, Emanuel came upon Dr. Hassing and a small party of picnickers. Prevailed upon to join the group, he found among them Miss Tonnesen, his former fiancée from Cophenhagen. Emanuel walked back to Dr. Hassing's home with the picnickers and, because it was growing dark, remained for supper. The genteel conversation, the quiet wealth of the home, the very food on the table, the music after supper—all of these things reminded Emanuel of what he had lost when he had refused Miss Tonnesen's love, rejected the family warmth of his parents' home, and turned instead toward the simple, rude life of the peasants. In the days following he ridiculed the people with whom he had spent a few hours, but Hansine saw that he was merely trying to convince himself that he had chosen the right path in his life's work.

A few weeks later Miss Tonnesen, who had gone out into the rural area to prove to herself that her former suitor had sunk beneath her, visited the rectory. Her father had been the former rector of the parish; under his care the rectory had been a place of beauty, both within and without. His daughter, seeing it for the first time in many years, was amazed to see how Emanuel had let it fall into disrepair. Only a few of the rooms, equipped with the barest of essentials, were in use. The gardens and lawns were overgrown; even the outbuildings and fields had been years without proper care. Miss Tonneson could scarcely believe that the man she had loved could have permitted the grounds in his charge, and himself as well, to slip into the state in which she found them.

Miss Tonnesen's visit bothered Hansine. She saw in the other woman all that her husband had given up when he had married her instead of a woman from his own social class. Even Hansine's children asked if they could go to Copenhagen to visit the beautiful lady. Emanuel himself realized that Miss Tonnesen represented something he had lost, but could still regain. He became dissatisfied with the peasantry, and they quickly sensed his unrest. His farm workers left him when, angry because the rains ruined any chance he had of harvesting a crop of rye, he abused them for their laziness.

The climax came when the director of the district high school, a man who as head of the institution had done much for the peasants, died. Everyone in the region went to the funeral. After it was over a political meeting formed of its own accord. Emanuel, when asked to address the meeting, spoke out against the sloth and narrow prejudices of the peasants. As he spoke, murmurings arose; he finally had to stop speaking when the crowd began to shout insults and ridicule. As he slowly left the meeting, he could hear a new speaker declaring that the pastor should return to his own people.

He met Hansine at the edge of the crowd; slowly they started home. On the way back Hansine told Emanuel that he ought to return to Copenhagen and she to her former life. He sadly agreed. The children, it was decided, would go with their father. To Emanuel's delight, his father and sister wrote him to return as soon as possible. As a result, one morning he and his remaining two children climbed into a carriage and drove away, while Hansine turned to walk to her parents' cottage.

PROSERPINE AND CERES

Type of work: Classical myth
Source: Folk tradition
Type of plot: Allegory of fertility and death
Time of plot: Remote antiquity
Locale: Mediterranean region
First transcribed: Unknown

Principal characters:
CERES, goddess of fertility
PROSERPINE, her daughter
HADES, king of the underworld
VENUS, goddess of love
CUPID, her son
TRIPTOLEMUS, builder of a temple to Ceres
ARETHUSA, a fountain nymph
ALPHEUS, a river god
DIANA, goddess of the hunt
JUPITER, king of the gods
MERCURY, messenger of the gods

Critique:

Prominent in popularity among the legends created by the Greeks and the Romans is the story of Proserpine and Ceres. As a fable which identifies itself with the simplest explanation of the seasons, it has lived by being transferred in oral legend, in poetry, and in prose from generation to generation. Although the story has changed in certain details, its basic structure remains. Its hold upon the imagination of the Western world lies in its appeal as a record of man's search for a beautiful interpretation of grief.

The Story:

One of the Titans, Typhoeus, long imprisoned for his part in the rebellion against Jupiter, lay in agony beneath Mount Aetna on the island of Sicily in the Mediterranean Sea. When Typhoeus groaned and stirred, he shook the sea and the island of Sicily so much that the god of the underworld, Hades, became frightened lest his kingdom be revealed to the light of day.

Rising to the upper world to make entrance to his kingdom, Hades was discovered by Venus, who ordered her son Cupid to aim one of his love darts into the breast of Hades and so cause him to fall in love with Proserpine, daughter of Ceres, goddess of fertility.

Proserpine had gone with her companions to gather flowers by the banks of a stream in the beautiful vale of Enna. There Hades, stricken by Cupid's dart, saw Proserpine, seized her, and lashed his fiery horses to greater speed as he carried her away. In her fright the girl dropped her apron, full of flowers she had gathered. At the River Cyane, Hades struck the earth with his scepter, causing a passageway to appear through which he drove his chariot and took his captive to the underworld.

Ceres sought her daughter everywhere. At last, sad and tired, she sat down to rest. A peasant and his daughter found her in her disguise as an old woman, took pity on her, and urged her to go with them to their rude home. When they arrived at the house they found that their only son, Triptolemus, was dying. Ceres first gathered some poppies. Then, kissing the child, she restored it to health. The happy family bade her join them in their simple meal of honey, cream, apples, and curds. Ceres put some of the poppy juice in the boy's milk and that night when he was sleeping she placed the child in the fire. The mother, awakening, seized her child from the flames. Ceres assumed her proper form and told the parents that it had been her plan to make the boy immortal. Since the mother had hindered that plan, she would teach him the use of the plow.

Then the goddess mother continued her search for Proserpine until she returned to Sicily. There, at the very spot Hades had entered the underworld, she asked the river nymph if she had seen anything of her daughter. Fearful of being punished, the river nymph refused to tell what she had seen but gave to Ceres the belt of Proserpine, which the girl had lost in her struggles.

Ceres decided to take revenge upon the land, to deny it further gift of her favors so that herbage and grain would not grow. In an effort to save the land which Ceres was intent upon cursing, the fountain Arethusa told the following story to Ceres. Arethusa had been hunting in the forest, where she was formerly a woodland nymph. Finding a stream, she decided to bathe. As she sported in the water, the river god Alpheus began to call her. Frightened, the nymph ran, the god pursuing.

The goddess Diana, seeing her plight, changed Arethusa into a fountain which ran through the underworld and emerged in Sicily. While passing through the underworld, Arethusa saw Proserpine, now queen of the dead, sad at the separation from her mother but at the same time bearing the dignity and power of the bride of Hades.

Ceres immediately demanded help from Jupiter, ruler of the gods. The king of the gods said that Proserpine should be allowed to return to the valley of Enna from which she had been abducted only if in the underworld she had taken no food.

Mercury was sent to demand Proserpine for her mother. But Proserpine had eaten of a pomegranate. Because she had eaten only part of the fruit, a compromise was made. Half of the time she was to pass with her mother and the rest with Hades. Ceres, happy over the return of Proserpine during one half of each year, caused the earth to be fertile again during the time Proserpine lived with her.

Ceres remembered her promise to the peasant boy, Triptolemus. She taught him to plow and to plant seed, and he gathered with her all the valuable seeds of the earth. In gratitude the peasant's son built a temple to Ceres in Eleusis where priests administered rites called the Eleusinian mysteries. Those rites surpassed all other Greek religious celebrations because in the mysteries of nature, men saw symbolized the death of man and the promise of his revival in future life.

PURPLE DUST

Type of work: Drama
Author: Sean O'Casey (1884-
Type of plot: Satiric comedy
Time of plot: The present
Locale: Clune na Geera, Ireland
First presented: 1940

Principal characters:
CYRIL POGES, a pompous English businessman
O'KILLIGAIN, a foreman stonemason
BASIL STOKE, Poges' colleague
SOUHAUN, Poges' mistress
AVRIL, Stoke's mistress
THREE IRISH WORKMEN

Critique:

In *Purple Dust*, Sean O'Casey returned to certain stylistic aspects of his earlier plays: the mixture of moving poetry with extravagant comedy. However, though the occasional poetic passages of the Irish workmen concerning their noble past are indeed beautiful, the emphasis of the play is on the profoundly comic aspects of two stuffy Englishmen trying to adjust to the rigors of the bucolic life. O'Casey, as usual, is extolling the hardy Irish, and quite disapproves of men who cling to the past without partly looking to the future. When men venerate the past without a true sense of understanding and appreciation, as do Poges and Stoke, the result is especially disastrous.

The Story:

Three workmen were standing languidly in a large, gloomy room that obviously was once the living room of a ruined Elizabethan mansion. The three pondered on the wisdom of two English gentlemen, Cyril Poges and Basil Stoke, in coming to live in such a decaying old house. Though the fresh paint had brightened things up a bit, it covered, for the most part, rotting wood. The sudden appearance of the sixty-five-year-old Poges and the thirtyish, serious Basil followed by their mistresses, Souhaun and Avril, confirmed the workmen's suspi-cions that the owners were slightly awry in their thinking; the group danced in, boisterously singing of the joys of country living. The handsome foreman, O'Killigain, explained to the workmen that these were people who saw historical loveliness in decaying ruins, and who took foolish delight in any locale with a story behind it. With the reappearance of the pretty Avril, O'Killigain exerted his poetic Irish charm to entice her into a rendezvous later that night.

Poges, Basil, and Souhaun returned from a tramp in the fields. Poges and Basil talked excitedly about the glories of past history and its better times, much to the disgust of O'Killigain, who firmly believed that life in its present state was far more worth living. His philosophy was lost on the other two, who went about their comic business of hanging pictures and discovering new aspects of country living—new business for them, but common enjoyment for the hardy Irish workmen.

Although Poges wanted to forget the outside world and its ways, his reverie was constantly interrupted by prosaic oc-currences: arguments with Basil and the girls, altercations with his butler over men outside who wished to know if he desired roosters and hens, and interrup-tions by one of the workmen, who in-

PURPLE DUST by Sean O'Casey. By permission of the publishers, The Macmillan Co. Copyright, 1940, by Sean O'Casey.

formed him of an excellent buy in a cow. Poges raged that he would get in touch with the Department of Agriculture. At Poges' displeasure over the disconnected telephone, another workman lost his temper. Poges heard himself scorned as a man who thought that the glory of the world could be stuffed into a purse, a man who was patronizing toward the Irish, a mighty race a thousand years older than his own. Basil and Avril left for a horseback ride, in spite of warnings that Irish horses were true horses, instead of English animals. The predictions were accurate; a battered Basil appeared shortly afterward and announced that his horse indeed had become a wild animal, and that, when last seen, Avril was riding away quite naked with O'Killigain.

The next day brought a cold dawn. Though Poges and Basil had spent the night fully clothed, they had almost frozen to death in the old house, along with the rest of the household. Poges still tried to rationalize; the cold air would revitalize them and exhilarate them. Barney, the butler, and Cloyne, the maid, were none the less disgusted with the whole situation; they thought the place an unlighted dungeon. As Barney struggled to light a damp fire, Cloyne rushed back into the room to scream that there was a wild bull in the entrance hall. This announcement caused a great panic among the transplanted city dwellers. Basil reëntered with a gun, then ran for his life as Poges roared for help and Cloyne fainted. A workman saved them all by shooing out a harmless cow which had innocently wandered into the hallway.

Later Poges thought he had found a friend in the same workman, who reminisced with him over glorious days in the past. Once again Poges expressed his philosophy that all the greats had gone with their glory, their finery turned to purple dust, and that today's man was shallow by comparison. However, O'Killigain and another workman later transfixed Poges by their poetic visions of the glorious Irish past and the fight for independence. Although Poges was momentarily surprised to find that these country workers had such depth, his spirit of English nationalism soon reasserted itself.

Poges' calamities continued. His next misadventure was with an oversized, heavy garden roller. Though his friends warned him, Poges persisted in his efforts to operate the machine. The result was a wrecked wall, as Poges let the roller get away from him to roll into and through the side of the house. Following closely on this incident, a terrified Basil shot and killed the indolent cow which had earlier invaded the hallway.

An interview with the local canon lifted Poges' spirits when the churchman praised Poges for restoring a portion of the past to slow down the reckless speed of the present. As the workmen continued to bring in furniture, Souhaun, like Avril to O'Killigain, almost succumbed to one of the workmen and his poetic charm. The moving into the room of a gilded desk-bureau proved to be another disaster. The top was first scarred by a workman's boot; then the bureau and the entrance were both damaged as the piece of furniture was pushed and pried through the door.

Because the wind was rising and storm clouds were brewing ominously, the workmen were sent away, but not before O'Killigain and the workman had entreated Avril and Souhaun to accompany them. The beautiful picture of Irish life conjured quickly by the man left the girls quite unsettled, but Poges and Basil made great fun of the workmen's poetic proposals. As the day grew darker and the rain fell, Poges found still other troubles; the postmaster arrived to complain about Poges' midnight phone calls to him. Suddenly the sound of a galloping horse was heard over the howl of the wind.

Warned that the river was rising, the terrified group in the darkened room made plans to climb to the roof before the house was flooded. Souhaun was nowhere to be found; she was with the workman on the galloping horse. O'Killigain, who had said that he would come for Avril when the river rose, appeared as he had promised. Avril left, renouncing Basil as a gilded monkey. Basil ran for the roof and a defeated Poges followed slowly, longing, once more, for dear England.